Mutual Aid

for Beginners

1st Edition

J.R. Mortimer

**MERCURY
GUIDES**

MERCURY GUIDES

Produced in partnership with RevolutionTV, a collective of content creators.
For supplemental videos on mutual aid, go to: www.revolutionTV.org.
For inquiries, contact: info@revolutiontv.org.

Credits: Icons used in this book are provided by The Noun Project (www.thenounproject.com) and are used in accordance with their licensing agreements. Most photos used in this book are provided by Canva (www.canva.com) and Envato (www.elements.envato.com) and are used in accordance with their licensing agreements.

Special Photo Credits: p. 11: Woo-Giyeon, CC BY-SA 4.0 <https://creativecommons.org/licenses/by-sa/4.0>, via Wikimedia Commons; p. 26: Chicago Sun Times / Larry Graff, Public domain, via Wikimedia Commons; p. 27: Black Panther Party, American, 1966 - 1982, CC BY-SA 4.0 <https://creativecommons.org/licenses/by-sa/4.0>, via Wikimedia Commons; p. 29: Joe Mabel, CC BY-SA 3.0 <http://creativecommons.org/licenses/by-sa/3.0/>, via Wikimedia Commons; p. 39: Eden, Janine and Jim from New York City, CC BY 2.0 <https://creativecommons.org/licenses/by/2.0>, via Wikimedia Commons; p.49: Win Henderson, Public domain, via Wikimedia Commons; p. 50: USAID in Africa, Public domain, via Wikimedia Commons

Portions of this book were initially generated using ChatGPT, an AI language model. These sections have been extensively edited, fact-checked, and verified by the author to ensure accuracy and relevance. All content reflects the author's insights, experiences, and perspectives. The author welcomes information about errors or omissions at info@revolutiontv.org. Future editions will be updated.

Table of Contents

Introduction

Mutual aid comes in many forms. It might take the form of a refrigerator set up in a public space where people can give and take food freely as needed. Or it might be a disaster response network, where people mobilize after a hurricane to provide shelter and supplies to those affected. Or it might be workers creating a communal fund they can use to cover living expenses while they go on strike as they demand better pay. There is no singular image that encapsulates what mutual aid looks like because it adapts to the circumstances and resources available in any given community.

At its heart, mutual aid is about people taking care of people. It's not an abstract idea—it's the everyday ways we come together to meet each other's needs. Mutual aid extends to a wide range of grassroots efforts, such as ride-sharing networks, childcare co-ops, neighborhood clean-ups, among many others. These actions may seem disconnected on the surface, but they all share the same underlying concept: they are about communities addressing their own needs through cooperation and shared responsibility.

What makes mutual aid distinct is that it is not about acts of charity or isolated exchanges of goods and services. It rejects the transactional nature of traditional aid systems, where assistance is often conditional or comes with strings attached. Instead, mutual aid is rooted in solidarity, the idea that helping others strengthens the whole community and that we are all interconnected. The goal is not just to provide short-term relief but to build long-term systems of support that empower people to take care of each other and themselves. Mutual aid networks grow organically because they are built on relationships, trust, and a collective understanding that when one person benefits, the entire community does.

Indigenous peoples have understood this for literally thousands of years. Whether through hunting and gathering practices, communal farming, or collective child-rearing, Indigenous groups have long relied on cooperation and mutual support to thrive in challenging environments. These systems of mutual aid are often guided by cultural traditions and spiritual beliefs that emphasize the interconnectedness of people and nature, ensuring that no individual or family is left without the support they need.

Marginalized and working-class groups have also long understood the power of mutual aid, especially in the United States. In the early 20th century, an estimated 30 to 40 percent of the U.S. adult male population were members of a mutual aid society. These organizations provided healthcare, unemployment benefits, and funeral assistance, and they hosted cultural and social events to bring people together. These societies were vital in supporting poor and marginalized groups at a time when government welfare systems were nonexistent or inaccessible.

Today, membership in formal mutual aid societies has dramatically declined, largely due to the establishment of government programs like Social Security, Medicare, and unemployment insurance, which took on many of the roles mutual aid once filled. However, in recent years, there has been a resurgence of informal mutual aid networks, particularly in response to the COVID-19 pandemic. With widespread unemployment, food insecurity, and limited access to healthcare, grassroots efforts filled critical gaps, especially for those left out of government relief.

The ugly truth about living in the 21st century is that we face unprecedented challenges that threaten both our planet and our society. Climate change is accelerating, leading to extreme weather events, rising sea levels, and widespread environmental degradation. Corporate exploitation continues to deplete natural resources, pollute ecosystems, and exacerbate social inequalities, as profit-driven agendas prioritize short-term gains over long-term sustainability. Meanwhile, domestic terrorism and political instability are on the rise, fueled by divisive ideologies, economic insecurity, and systemic injustice. These interconnected crises demand urgent action, yet many of the institutions tasked with addressing them are slow to respond or complicit in maintaining the status quo, leaving communities to bear the brunt of these mounting dangers.

That is why now is the time to learn about mutual aid. It is a time-tested method that has allowed us to not only survive but also to flourish in the face of adversity. By embracing mutual aid, we tap into the collective strength and creativity of our communities, forming deep connections and a shared resilience. As we navigate the challenges of these times, mutual aid offers a hopeful path forward, showing us that through cooperation we can build a brighter future for us all.

Who This Book Is For

Mutual Aid for Beginners is designed for a diverse audience interested in understanding and participating in community-driven support networks. This includes people who are new to the concept of mutual aid, activists, community organizers, and anyone seeking practical ways to address local needs through collective action. The book aims to reach those who are curious about how mutual aid can enhance existing support systems, as well as those who are eager to get involved in grassroots efforts but may not know where to start.

This book is also intended to serve as a resource for educators and leaders looking to incorporate mutual aid principles into their work or to create a culture of solidarity and cooperation within their communities. By offering accessible explanations and actionable insights, *Mutual Aid for Beginners* seeks to inspire and empower readers to engage in projects that promote collective well-being.

How to Use This Book

This book is not intended to be read cover to cover (although, by all means feel free to do that). Instead, it is structured so that you can dive into the sections most relevant to your current needs and interests. Whether you're just starting out, looking for specific strategies, or seeking to deepen your understanding of mutual aid principles, you can navigate directly to the chapters that resonate with your situation. The detailed Table of Contents is your guide to finding the right spot.

How This Book Is Organized

The first three chapters establish a solid foundation for anyone new to mutual aid. *Ch.1: What is Mutual Aid?* introduces the concept and its historical context, while *Ch.2: The Principles of Mutual Aid* delves into the core values that drive mutual aid efforts. *Ch.3: Understanding Community Needs* provides guidance on how to conduct a community assessment.

We then transition into the operational aspects of running a mutual aid group. *Ch.4: Building Trust & Relationships* emphasizes the importance of making strong, supportive connections among members, and *Ch.5: Organizing a Mutual Aid Group* will take you through the process of starting a project from scratch or joining an existing group. *Ch.6: Legal & Ethical*

Considerations should answer any questions you have about organizational structures, policies/procedures, and legal compliance. *Ch. 7: Fundamentals of Resource Mobilization* dives into the best practices used in coordinating volunteers, running fundraisers, and figuring out the logistics involved with supplies and donations. *Ch.8: Communicating with the Public* applies branding strategies to mutual aid endeavors and outlines ways to organize outreach campaigns. *Ch.9: Education & Skill-sharing Programs* discusses how mutual aid groups can create a culture of continuous learning in their communities, and *Ch.10: Emergency Preparedness & Response* goes into how to establish a disaster relief network.

Chapters 11 to 13 are tailored for activists and those who are deeply involved in mutual aid. *Ch.11: Advocating for Systemic Change* provides an overview of societal issues and how mutual aid groups can get involved politically. *Ch.12: Interactions with Law Enforcement* goes into the very delicate relationship mutual aid groups have with the police and how to prioritize safety. *Ch.13: Mental Health & Well-being* addresses how mutual aid work can often have a negative effect on our mental and physical health and provides ways to remain resilient. The book concludes with *Ch.14: Future Trends in Mutual Aid*, which utilizes artificial intelligence to envision a world where mutual aid is widely practiced, providing guidance on how we get there.

Every chapter ends with an overview of its main topics, as well as 2 questions to facilitate discussions.

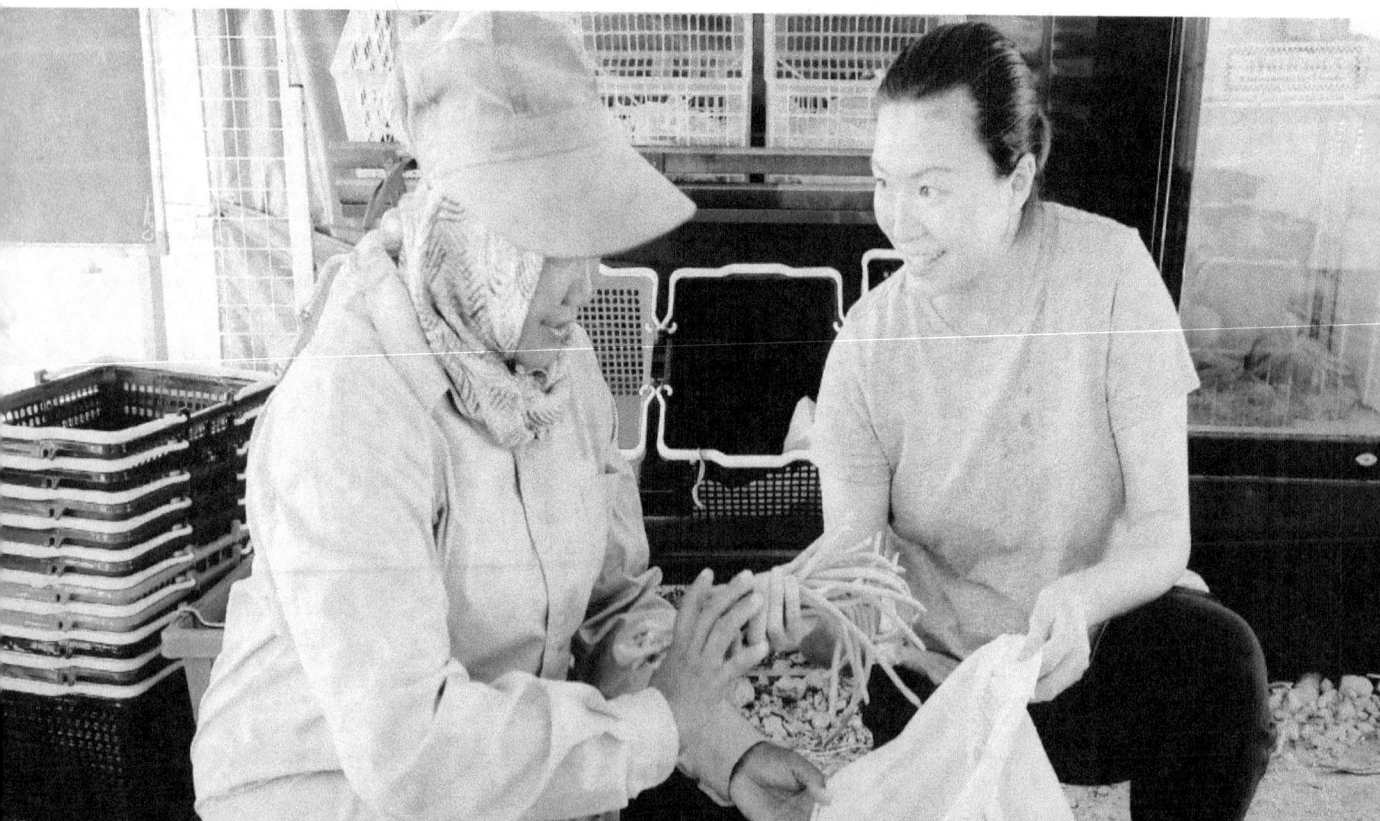

Chapter **1**

What Is Mutual Aid?

Imagine your neighborhood is hit by a sudden storm, leaving several families without power, food, or safe shelter. Instead of waiting for outside help, the community springs into action. Neighbors check on each other, sharing whatever resources they have—generators, extra blankets, meals, and a place to stay. Someone sets up a space for people to gather, while another organizes a list of who needs what. There's no hierarchy, no one directing the effort—just people coming together, pooling what they have to ensure everyone gets through the crisis.

This is mutual aid in action. It's not charity, where help comes from a distance, but a collective response born out of necessity and a deep sense of shared responsibility. Mutual aid is about recognizing that everyone has something to contribute, whether it's a skill, a resource, or simply the willingness to help. In this chapter, we'll explore what mutual aid truly means, how it has been a vital force in communities long before the term was widely recognized, and how it continues to empower people to take care of one other in the face of challenges, big and small.

Defining Mutual Aid

Mutual aid is a form of voluntary, reciprocal support where people help one another meet their basic needs, often in response to systemic failures or crises. This concept is rooted in the idea that communities are best equipped to address their own challenges through direct cooperation and collective action. When formal institutions—such as governments or non-profits—fall short in providing adequate support, mutual aid steps in to fill the gaps. It empowers people to take control of their own well-being by pooling resources, sharing skills, and building networks of care.

A powerful display of mutual aid occurred in the aftermath of Hurricane Katrina in 2005. Grassroots groups like the Common Ground Collective were formed, organizing volunteers to offer food, water, medical care, and rebuilding assistance to those affected in New Orleans. Neighbors and volunteers worked side-by-side to meet immediate needs, build homes, and restore a sense of community in the face of widespread devastation and institutional neglect.

While mutual aid often emerges in natural disasters, the practice isn't limited to these crisis situations. It can also be a constant, empowering way for communities to take care of each other and build resilience over time. Mutual aid might involve organizing a community pantry where neighbors can both donate and take food as needed. Or it might be a network for sharing childcare or transportation.

Here are some other examples of mutual aid that will be discussed later in this chapter:

Community Garden:

Community gardens are public spaces that allow members to grow their own food collectively and share resources, knowledge, and labor. The mutual aid aspect involves the shared responsibility of cultivating and harvesting, as well as the shared benefit of having fresh produce.

Community Fridge:

A community fridge is a refrigerator that is set up in a public space so that people can take what they need and contribute what they can. It is stocked by local residents, restaurants, and businesses who want to help ensure that no one in the community goes hungry.

Free Store:

A free store is a community-based initiative where people donate and acquire goods without any monetary exchange. By eliminating financial transactions, free stores emphasize the idea that all people should have access to essential items, regardless of how much money they have.

Time Bank:

Time banking is a system where people exchange services based on time rather than money. Participants offer their skills or services to others in the community and, in return, they can receive assistance from someone else. This model values each person's time equally and promotes a sense of interconnectedness.

Some forms of mutual aid might initially seem similar to charity, but the two are fundamentally different. While charity often operates as a one-way transaction where resources are given from the "haves" to the "have-nots," mutual aid is based on solidarity and reciprocity, where everyone involved supports and relies on each other. The differences between mutual aid and charity will be explored in greater detail below.

Mutual Aid Is Not Charity

In mutual aid work, you may hear the phrase "solidarity, not charity." This refers to people standing together as equals, rather than creating a relationship where one party gives and the other simply receives. This means that support is shared based on collective needs and strengths, rather than being dispensed from a position of power.

Mutual aid is about fostering relationships built on trust, empathy, and respect, where everyone contributes to and benefits from the collective well-being. This approach challenges traditional models of charity by focusing on empowerment and community resilience, rather than dependency or temporary relief. While some mutual aid groups may become formalized 501(c)(3) non-profits/charities to access funding and resources (as discussed in Chapter 6), many choose to remain informal so they can stay true to their grassroots principles and autonomy.

Let's tease out some of the key differences between the mutual aid and charity models:

Reciprocity vs. One-Way Assistance:

In mutual aid, there is a focus on reciprocity and two-way support. Communities come together to exchange resources, skills, and assistance, with the understanding that everyone has something to give and receive.

Charity, on the other hand, involves one-way assistance, where individuals or organizations provide resources to those in need without necessarily expecting support in return. The dynamic is unidirectional, with the giver providing assistance to the receiver.

●

Community Empowerment vs. Dependency:

Mutual aid empowers communities by fostering self-reliance, collaboration, and collective problem-solving. It encourages members to actively participate in addressing their own needs.

Conversely, charity can create a dependency dynamic, where recipients rely on external assistance without participating in decision-making or contributing to the solutions. This can perpetuate reliance on external sources for support.

Bottom-Up vs. Top-Down Approach:

Mutual aid is a bottom-up, grassroots approach initiated by community members themselves. It is driven by the needs and priorities identified within the community, allowing for more localized solutions.

Charity efforts are top-down, as they are often organized by external entities, such as non-profit organizations, corporations, or individuals. While charitable activities can address immediate needs, the decision-making and priorities are generally controlled by the organization or donors.

Long-Term Relationships vs. Temporary Assistance:

Mutual aid involves the development of long-term relationships and networks within a community. It goes beyond providing temporary relief by creating sustainable structures for ongoing support.

In contrast, charities may focus more on immediate relief and short-term solutions. While critical in emergencies, charity may not always address the underlying issues contributing to the need for assistance.

In the next subsections, we will delve into real-world examples of mutual aid, illustrating how these principles are applied in various contexts. By exploring specific cases, we'll gain a deeper understanding of how mutual aid operates in practice and its impact on communities.

Disaster Relief Networks

 A **disaster relief network** is a coordinated system of individuals and organizations that come together to provide immediate assistance during a large-scale crisis, such as a natural disaster. These networks are designed to quickly mobilize and deploy aid, offering everything from food, water, and shelter to medical care and emotional support. Unlike formal emergency management organizations—which operate within strict hierarchies and protocols—disaster relief networks can be more flexible and responsive, adapting to the specific needs of the communities they serve.

In a mutual aid context, disaster relief networks are not just about providing help; they are also about empowering communities to take care of one another in times of need. Mutual aid emphasizes collective action and shared responsibility, where members of a community support each other without the expectation of external help. This grassroots approach often fills the gaps left by government agencies or large non-profits, ensuring that aid reaches those who need it most.

When Superstorm Sandy struck New York City in 2012, it left behind a path of destruction that caused around $19 billion in damage, destroyed thousands of homes, and claimed the lives of at least 43 people. Amid the chaos, a group of friends who had come together during the 2011 Occupy Wall Street protests decided to take action. They recognized that many New Yorkers were in dire need of basic necessities like food, clothing, and medical supplies. Leveraging the organizing skills and community connections they had built during the Occupy movement, they formed "Occupy Sandy", a grassroots initiative that would grow to become one of the most effective relief efforts in the aftermath of the storm.

![Occupy Sandy banner reading "OCCUPY SANDY Mutual Aid Not Charity"]

Occupy Sandy was not a typical disaster relief organization. There were no appointed leaders, no bureaucratic structures, and no pre-existing plans to follow. Instead, it was a decentralized, people-powered response that relied on the collective efforts of volunteers. Over time, this initiative grew to include around 60,000 volunteers who spanned the five boroughs of New York City. These volunteers distributed supplies, helped rebuild homes, and connected those in need with vital resources. The group's approach was highly adaptive and responsive to the immediate needs of the affected communities, stepping in to help where the Red Cross and FEMA could not.

The effectiveness of Occupy Sandy can be attributed to the horizontal structure of the organization, where decisions were made collectively and everyone was encouraged to contribute in whatever way they could. Volunteers set up communication hubs across the city, cooked meals, distributed clothing, and provided essential tools like sump pumps and generators. These hubs—located in community centers, housing developments, and even on street corners—became lifelines for people struggling to recover from the disaster. The group also used technology to coordinate their efforts, setting up an online wedding registry to collect supplies and using social media to identify areas where help was needed.

One of the most significant aspects of Occupy Sandy's work was its ability to arrive on the scene before official relief organizations. Volunteers went door-to-door in hard-hit neighborhoods—like the Lower East Side, Red Hook, Coney Island, and Staten Island—checking on residents, refilling medical prescriptions, and mucking out flooded homes. They also worked closely with local organizations that had deep ties to their communities, ensuring that aid was distributed quickly and responsibly.

Community Pantries & Fridges

 A **community pantry** or **fridge** is a publicly accessible space where people can donate and take food and essential items, typically located in areas with high food insecurity. These initiatives are often set up by local volunteers or community groups and rely on the principle of "take what you need, leave what you can." Community fridges and pantries are usually stocked with fresh produce, non-perishable goods, and sometimes hygiene products—all contributed by neighbors, local businesses, or charitable organizations.

Community pantries and fridges are powerful examples of mutual aid. Rather than relying on top-down charity models, these initiatives empower communities to care for one another directly. They help to fill gaps in the formal social safety net by providing immediate, tangible support to those in need, especially in times of crisis or economic hardship. By fostering a culture of giving and mutual support, community fridges and pantries strengthen social bonds and create resilient networks that can respond to challenges.

One example is Fareground, a women-led mutual aid organization dedicated to addressing food insecurity and hunger in the Hudson Valley in New York. The group operates free marketplaces, community fridges, food pantries, and other programs to distribute fresh and prepared foods to those in need. Fareground emphasizes inclusivity, equity, and environmental responsibility, working with local farms and organizations to provide organic food whenever possible. Their mission is to eliminate hunger by bridging gaps within communities and addressing poverty through collaborative partnerships and sustainable practices.

Fareground's roots trace back to 2012 when residents of Beacon, NY grew concerned about food insecurity and decided to form a food justice initiative. Since then, the organization has implemented many programs, such as 'Pay What You Can' Pop Up Dinners and Tiny Food Pantries (TFPs), which are accessible 24/7 and stocked with non-perishable items, toiletries, and baby supplies.

The community supports these efforts through donations from local businesses and in-kind contributions. Fareground also responds to crises in the community, aiming to create a robust safety net of food security for all, driven by the dedication of volunteers and ongoing support from grant funding and local contributions.

Community Gardens

A **community garden** is a shared space where members collectively grow fruits, vegetables, herbs, and flowers. These gardens often occupy unused land in urban or suburban areas and provide a venue for residents to cultivate their own food, learn about sustainable practices, and engage in horticultural activities. Community gardens can vary in scale and structure, from small plots managed by individuals to larger gardens maintained by groups or organizations.

A community garden that practices mutual aid is centered on the collective well-being of all participants, with a focus on sharing resources, skills, and produce without any expectation of payment or personal gain. In such gardens, the emphasis is on equal access to food and community support, with members contributing to and benefiting from the garden based on their abilities and needs.

14

One example is the Kansas Mutual Aid Community Garden in Lawrence, KS. Established in 2004, the garden is dedicated to providing free, accessible food to the community, emphasizing that food is a basic right and not a commodity. The garden operates communally, with no individual plots, and it encourages participants to contribute to and share in the harvest equally. The garden hosts four work days each week, where people can collaborate, learn, and ensure the success of the crops.

It's important to note that not all community gardens practice mutual aid. In such gardens, operations are more individualistic, where participants have designated plots, and the produce is often kept for personal use or sold. These gardens may lack the same focus on collective responsibility and equity, and participation might be more dependent on individual resources or financial contributions.

Time Banks

A **time bank** is a system where people exchange services based on time rather than money. In a time bank, one hour of service is typically equal to one time credit, regardless of the type of service provided. Participants earn time credits by helping others, and they can then spend these credits to receive services from other members.

Time banks operate on the principle that everyone's time and skills are equally valuable, regardless of the task. This model challenges conventional economic norms by prioritizing human connections and community support over financial transactions. For example, a person might offer legal advice or tutoring in a time bank and receive assistance with household chores or transportation in return.

In the context of mutual aid, time banks enhance the collective capacity of communities to address their own needs and challenges. Mutual aid emphasizes reciprocal relationships and sharing resources to achieve common goals. Time banks operationalize these principles by creating a structured system where people can contribute to and benefit from a pool of communal resources.

Time banks can also play a significant role in addressing social and economic inequalities. By valuing diverse skills and creating a sense of community ownership, they offer a way for marginalized or economically disadvantaged people to participate fully and benefit from the collective resources of the group. This inclusivity can help mitigate some of the barriers faced by those who might otherwise be excluded.

Babysitting Co-ops

Babysitting co-ops are a prime example of mutual aid in action, where families within a community come together to share the responsibilities of childcare. In these co-ops, parents take turns watching each other's children, allowing everyone involved to benefit from free babysitting services. This system not only alleviates the financial burden associated with traditional childcare options, but also it builds trust and camaraderie among participating families.

To establish a babysitting co-op, a group of parents agrees to a set of guidelines and schedules for exchanging babysitting duties. Typically, these co-ops use a point system, or time bank, where parents earn points for every hour they spend babysitting another family's child and then use those points to "pay" for babysitting services from others. This ensures that the exchange of services is fair and balanced. The co-op may also set up a rotating schedule or an on-call system to accommodate the varying needs and availability of its members. Regular meetings are held to discuss any issues and make adjustments to the system.

One of the key benefits of babysitting co-ops is the trust and peace of mind they provide to parents. Knowing that their children are being cared for by other parents within their community, who they know and trust, can be much more reassuring than leaving them with a stranger. The children also benefit from socializing with their peers in a familiar and friendly environment. This community-based approach to childcare allows parents to build stronger relationships with their neighbors and ultimately create a support network that extends beyond just babysitting.

Communes

 **Communes** are intentional communities where people live together, share resources, and work to address collective needs. They embody the principles of mutual aid by prioritizing shared responsibility, cooperation, and support for one another. Resources like housing, food, and labor are pooled, with the idea that by sharing, the community can reduce individual burdens and ensure that everyone has what they need.

The process of forming a commune typically begins by gathering a core group of like-minded people who are committed to creating a collective living environment. This group works together to define the commune's purpose, structure, and guiding principles, such as how decisions will be made, how work will be divided, and how resources will be shared.

Once the vision is established, the next step is securing a location, which could involve purchasing land or renting property where communal living can take place. Legal and financial considerations come into play at this point, and the group may choose to form a legal entity, like a cooperative, to manage ownership and responsibilities. As the commune is officially established, ongoing discussions about roles, responsibilities, and conflict resolution help build a strong foundation for the community to thrive.

Skill-shares

 A **skill-share** is a community-driven event or platform where people come together to exchange knowledge without the expectation of payment. These exchanges can cover a wide range of topics, from practical skills like cooking, gardening, or carpentry to creative pursuits like art, music, or writing. Participants in a skill-share both teach and learn, creating an environment where everyone's expertise is valued and accessible. The format of a skill-share can vary—including workshops, one-on-one tutoring, or online tutorials—but the core principle is the free and open sharing of knowledge.

Skill-shares are closely aligned with the principles of mutual aid, as they encourage a culture of cooperation and collective empowerment. By sharing skills, participants help each other become more self-sufficient, reducing reliance on external systems and creating a sense of community interdependence. In a mutual aid context, skill-shares are not just about personal growth; they are about strengthening the entire community by ensuring valuable knowledge is distributed and accessible to all. In Chapter 9, we will discuss the logistics of hosting a skill-share in greater detail.

Free Stores

A **free store** is a community space where goods and services are freely given and taken without any form of monetary exchange. These stores operate on the idea that everyone should have access to basic necessities regardless of their financial situation. Items available in free stores usually include clothing, food, books, household goods, and other essentials. People are encouraged to take what they need and to donate items they no longer use, creating a cycle of sharing that reduces waste and develops a sense of interdependence.

Free stores embody the principles of mutual aid by promoting collective care and sharing resources. This model challenges the traditional consumer economy by prioritizing human need over profit, and it strengthens social bonds by encouraging people to actively participate in the well-being of their community. Through free stores, mutual aid ensures that everyone has access to the goods they need to thrive.

One example is the Pulaski County Free Store in Dublin, Virginia. In 2018, local resident Hazel Wines saw there wasn't a mutual aid network to help the people living in poverty in her community. That's when she decided to start one out of the back of her van, offering it as a space where people could drop off donations and pick up other items they needed. As support grew, Hazel and other volunteers moved the operation to a storage unit and eventually into an old school building that had been empty for years. Now they serve about 150 people on the first and third Sunday every month.

Strike Funds

A **strike fund** is a financial reserve created by labor unions or worker collectives to support employees during a strike. When workers decide to strike, they often lose their regular income, putting them at financial risk. A strike fund provides essential financial support, covering basic needs like rent, food, and utilities while the strike is ongoing. This safety net is crucial in allowing workers to maintain their stance during negotiations with employers, as it helps alleviate the economic pressure that might otherwise force them back to work prematurely.

Strike funds are typically built up over time through regular contributions from union members or community supporters. The fund is a collective resource, reflecting the principle that the struggle of one worker is the struggle of all. When workers know that they have financial backing, they can negotiate from a position of greater strength, making it more likely that they will secure fair wages, better working conditions, or other demands. This collective financial support is an expression of solidarity, as it demonstrates a shared commitment to achieving common goals.

In the context of mutual aid, strike funds are a powerful example of community-based support systems where people pool resources to help one another in times of need. Just as mutual aid networks provide resources and assistance to those facing hardships, strike funds ensure that workers are not left to fend for themselves during a labor dispute.

Strike funds strengthen the sense of solidarity among workers and their allies, reinforcing the idea that collective action can lead to meaningful change. By providing the financial means to sustain a strike, these funds help workers challenge exploitative practices and advocate for their rights without fear of financial ruin. In this way, strike funds are not just about survival during a strike; they are about empowering workers to demand justice and equality, aligning closely with the broader goals of mutual aid in promoting social and economic equity.

Now that we've explored some of the many real-life applications of mutual aid, it's important to understand how these practices have evolved over time. Mutual aid isn't a new concept. It has deep historical roots that stretch across cultures and eras. In the next section, we'll take a journey through the history of mutual aid, uncovering how communities have long relied on these networks of solidarity and support to survive and thrive. This context will help us appreciate how mutual aid has shaped, and continues to shape, the ways we care for one another today.

Historical Overview

The history of mutual aid is deeply intertwined with the story of human survival and resilience. Thousands of years ago, our ancestors formed close-knit groups who worked together to hunt, gather, and protect themselves from threats. This communal approach to life ensured that everyone's basic needs were met, and it was understood that the well-being of the individual was tied to the well-being of the group. Without these collective efforts, their survival would have likely been impossible.

As societies grew more complex, mutual aid continued to play a crucial role. In many cultures, cooperative practices like communal farming, collective child-rearing, and group protection were common. As a result, mutual aid became rooted in many beliefs and traditions. For example, in some African societies the concept of "Ubuntu" is a philosophical framework that emphasizes communal interdependence and mutual care. Ubuntu, often translated as "I am because we are," reflects the belief that a person's humanity is inextricably linked to the humanity of others.

In the late 19th and early 20th centuries, the concept of mutual aid was formalized in the scientific community, most notably by the Russian anarchist philosopher Peter Kropotkin. In his influential book *Mutual Aid: A Factor of Evolution* (1902), Kropotkin argued that cooperation and mutual support were just as important as competition in the evolution of species. Kropotkin's work highlighted how mutual aid has been a powerful force over millennia, shaping not only the natural world but also human societies.

During the same period, mutual aid organizations began to emerge, particularly among immigrant and working-class communities in the U.S. and Europe. These groups were often formed by people who were excluded from mainstream social services and economic opportunities. For example, Black Americans who were unable to access white-dominated institutions created their own mutual aid networks. One of the earliest organizations was the Free African Society, established in Philadelphia in 1787, which provided financial and social support to freed slaves. Similarly, immigrants from Italy, Ireland, and China established mutual aid societies to help newcomers with housing, employment, and healthcare.

Throughout the 20th century, mutual aid continued to be a vital strategy for marginalized groups, especially during times of social and economic upheaval. During the Great Depression, for instance, communities organized cooperatives, soup kitchens, and other mutual aid efforts to survive widespread unemployment and poverty. The Civil Rights Movement of the 1960s also saw the rise of mutual aid in the form of initiatives like the Black Panther Party's Free Breakfast for Children Program, which provided meals to thousands of children in need.

In recent years, mutual aid has experienced a resurgence, particularly in response to crises like natural disasters, economic inequality, and the COVID-19 pandemic. As traditional systems of support have faltered, communities have once again turned to mutual aid to fill the gaps–organizing to provide everything from food and medical supplies to legal assistance and emotional support.

The history of mutual aid is a testament to the power of collective action and community resilience. It shows that, across time and cultures, people have always found ways to come together and support one another, especially in times of need. As we move forward, understanding this can inspire us to continue building strong, supportive communities that prioritize the well-being of all of us. In the next pages, we will take a closer look at some of the specific examples of mutual aid throughout history.

South American Indigenous Practices

 In many Indigenous cultures, the concept of mutual aid is not just a response to crises but a way of life, embedded in social, economic, and spiritual practices. That has been the case for the Quechua and Aymara peoples of Peru, Bolivia, and Ecuador for many generations (see Incan ruins below). They believe in a foundational principle of reciprocity called "ayni," which operates on the idea that what someone gives now will eventually be returned, creating a cycle of balance and harmony within their community. This concept is not limited to material exchanges but extends to labor, resources, and even emotional support, reinforcing social cohesion and ensuring that no one is left behind.

A classic example of ayni in practice is in the agricultural work of the Andean highlands. When a family needs to plant or harvest their crops, they call upon their neighbors for help. In return, the family is expected to reciprocate by assisting those same neighbors when it is their turn to work their fields. This cooperative system, known as "minka" or "mita" in some regions, ensures that everyone has enough labor power to complete vital tasks, particularly in the challenging terrain of the Andes. The exchange is not always immediate, but the obligation to return the favor is honored.

Beyond agriculture, ayni has also played an important role in the construction of homes and community infrastructure. For example, when a new house needs to be built, the community comes together to provide the necessary labor, materials, and expertise. This collective effort ensures that everyone has shelter and that the community itself grows stronger through the bonds formed during these cooperative activities. In return, the family benefiting from the help will contribute to similar projects for others, perpetuating the cycle of mutual aid.

Medieval Guilds

A guild was a formal association of artisans, craftsmen, or merchants in medieval Europe (c. 1000 - 1400 CE), organized to protect and promote the economic interests of its members. Guilds regulated the practice of a specific trade or craft within a particular town or region, setting standards for quality and providing mutual support among members.

Guilds in medieval Europe were not only professional associations, but they were also social organizations that practiced mutual aid. For example, if a member fell ill or faced financial hardship, the guild would often provide monetary assistance or other resources to help them through tough times. Guilds also offered support to the families of deceased members, providing pensions or direct aid to widows and orphans.

This sense of collective responsibility extended to professional matters as well—if a member's workshop was damaged by fire or if their goods were lost at sea, other guild members would contribute to help them rebuild or recover their losses. Through these practices, guilds ensured that individual misfortunes did not lead to ruin and that all members were supported.

Guilds were also vital networks of mutual protection for their members. Recognizing the risks associated with their trades—whether from theft, piracy, or market competition—guilds collectively organized measures to safeguard their members' interests. For instance, merchant guilds often banded together to protect their trade routes, sometimes hiring armed escorts for caravans or ships to defend against bandits and pirates. In times of conflict, guilds could pool resources to fortify their towns or support local militias, ensuring the safety of both their members and their goods.

The Rise of Mutual Aid Societies

In the 19th and early 20th centuries, mutual aid societies rose to prominence among marginalized communities and working-class people in both the United States and Europe. These organizations emerged as grassroots responses to the harsh economic and social conditions faced by those who were often excluded from institutional support systems. For many immigrants, laborers, and minorities, mutual aid societies became essential lifelines, offering not just financial assistance but also a sense of community.

In the United States, mutual aid societies were particularly important among Black communities during and after the Reconstruction era. With limited access to government support and facing systemic discrimination, Black Americans organized their own networks of mutual aid to address needs like healthcare, burial services, and financial support during times of illness or unemployment. Organizations like the Free African Society, founded in 1787, laid the groundwork for later mutual aid efforts.

One example was the Société d'Économie et d'Assistance Mutuelle, a prominent Creole mutual aid society in New Orleans. Established in 1836, the organization served as a center for cultural and social life, helping to preserve and promote the rich Creole heritage amidst the challenges of a racially segregated country. The Société was known for its emphasis on self-reliance, education, and community solidarity, offering members not only financial help but also opportunities for networking, skill-building, and civic engagement.

During this time, fraternal organizations like the Freemasons, Odd Fellows, and Knights of Pythias also became popular and marked a significant expansion of mutual aid practices. These organizations provided members with a sense of belonging and social support while offering practical benefits, like sickness and funeral insurance, unemployment assistance, and financial aid. Fraternal organizations were guided by a principle of brotherhood, and they pooled resources from member contributions to create safety nets for those facing hardship.

Fraternal associations also organized social events, educational programs, and charitable activities, which reinforced community bonds and fostered a spirit of solidarity. Through their widespread networks and structured systems of aid, these groups played a crucial role in helping members navigate the uncertainties of life during a time when government welfare programs were minimal or nonexistent.

In Europe, the rise of mutual aid was closely tied to labor movements, particularly in rapidly industrializing cities. Workers, often facing dangerous working conditions, low wages, and little to no social safety net, formed "friendly" societies as a way to protect themselves and their families. These organizations, often associated with trade unions or specific industries, provided essential services such as sickness benefits, funeral expenses, and pensions. The guilds of the Middle Ages laid some of the groundwork for these practices, but the scale and necessity of mutual aid grew significantly with the advent of industrial capitalism.

There are fewer mutual aid societies today than in the 20th century largely due to the expansion of government social welfare programs and the rise of modern insurance systems. As governments began to implement social safety nets—such as Social Security, unemployment insurance, and public healthcare—the need for privately organized mutual aid societies diminished. As a result, many mutual aid organizations either disbanded, merged with other entities, or transformed into social clubs with a focus on community and cultural activities rather than mutual aid.

The Black Panthers

The Black Panther Party was founded in 1966 in response to systemic racism, police brutality, and socio-economic disparities affecting Black American communities in the United States. Fueled by the principles of self-defense, self-determination, and community empowerment, the party sought to address not only the symptoms but also the root causes of inequality. The Panthers recognized the importance of collective action and mutual support in challenging oppressive structures.

The Black Panthers faced intense scrutiny and opposition from the U.S. government, which viewed their activism and community programs as a threat to its control and dominance. The party was infiltrated by the FBI's COINTELPRO program, leading to internal conflicts and challenges. Police officers even raided school cafeterias while children ate breakfast and urinated on the food.

Despite these obstacles, the Black Panthers' legacy endures as a powerful example of mutual aid in action. By addressing immediate needs and challenging systemic injustices, the Panthers created a blueprint for collective action that transcended traditional models of charity. Their legacy serves as a testament to the transformative potential of mutual aid in empowering communities to challenge and change the structures that perpetuate inequality.

The Black Panthers implemented a range of successful community programs that exemplified the principles of mutual aid. Here are a few:

Free Breakfast Program:

One of the most well-known mutual aid initiatives launched by the Black Panthers was the Free Breakfast for Children Program. Recognizing that children cannot learn on an empty stomach, the Panthers initiated a nationwide effort to provide free, nutritious breakfasts to thousands of children before they went to school. This program not only addressed an immediate need but also highlighted the systemic failure to ensure basic sustenance for vulnerable communities.

Health Clinics:

The Black Panther Party established the People's Free Medical Centers (PFMCs) to provide accessible and community-driven healthcare. These clinics offered a range of services, including testing and lab work, immunizations, and treatment for common illnesses. By establishing health clinics, the Panthers aimed to combat systemic health disparities and provide a model for community-based healthcare delivery.

Seniors Against a Fearful Environment (SAFE):

Recognizing the unique challenges faced by elderly community members, the Black Panthers initiated the SAFE program. This initative focused on providing self-defense education and transportation to seniors who endured robberies and muggings. The SAFE program exemplified the Panthers' commitment to intergenerational solidarity and mutual aid across all segments of the community.

Sickle Cell Anemia Research:

The Black Panthers were pioneers in raising awareness about sickle cell anemia, a genetic disorder disproportionately affecting Black Americans. Through the Sickle Cell Anemia Research program, the Panthers set up testing centers and provided education about its prevalence.

Intercommunal Youth Institute:

The Black Panthers' Intercommunal Youth Institute sought to provide an alternative to public schools, where curriculums came from a largely white perspective and many Black students faced unfair treatment. The Institute's programs focused on teaching critical thinking skills through experiential learning.

Food Distribution:

The Black Panther Party recognized the impact of food insecurity on Black communities. In response, they initiated food distribution programs, providing groceries and fresh produce to those in need. This not only addressed immediate hunger but also underscored the Panthers' commitment to challenging systemic inequalities that perpetuated poverty and limited access to essential resources.

Housing Initiatives:

Recognizing the urgent need for affordable and safe housing within marginalized communities, the Black Panthers launched programs that aimed to confront discriminatory leasing practices and helped tenants take action when landlords neglected their properties. They demanded pest control, regular maintenance, repairs, and the ability to collectively negotiate for fair rent.

The AIDS Crisis

During the AIDS crisis of the 1980s and 1990s, the LGBTQ community mobilized to practice mutual aid in response to the lack of government support and widespread stigma. As HIV/AIDS began to spread, many found themselves ostracized by society and abandoned by their families. Grassroots organizations and informal networks emerged to fill the gap and provide essential care.

The concept of "buddy systems" became popular, where volunteers would pair up with those living with HIV/AIDS to offer emotional support, help with daily tasks, and ensure they had access to medical treatment. These relationships became a crucial part of the social fabric within the LGBTQ community, as people banded together to navigate the harsh realities of the epidemic. This grassroots caregiving was vital, especially in the early years of the crisis when the stigma surrounding the disease was intense.

The Chicken Soup Brigade in Seattle was another significant example of mutual aid during the AIDS crisis. Founded in 1983, the Chicken Soup Brigade began as a grassroots effort to provide nutritious meals—including homemade chicken soup—to people living with HIV/AIDS. The initiative was started by a group of volunteers who recognized the need for direct support as many people with AIDS were unable to care for themselves due to the debilitating effects of the disease.

COVID-19 Pandemic

During the COVID-19 pandemic beginning in 2020, mutual aid networks became a vital lifeline for many communities, stepping in to address urgent needs that traditional systems were slow or unable to meet. These grassroots initiatives were often formed by neighbors and local activists who recognized the immediate challenges posed by the pandemic, such as food insecurity, lack of access to essential supplies, and the isolation of vulnerable populations. They organized quickly, leveraging social media and community networks to mobilize volunteers and resources.

For example, groups like Mutual Aid NYC created detailed guides on how to apply for unemployment benefits or rent relief, while others organized online workshops to teach neighbors about staying safe during the pandemic. This rapid, decentralized information-sharing helped vulnerable communities access resources more quickly than formal institutions could manage.

Also in New York City, groups like West Brooklyn Waterfront Mutual Aid delivered groceries to seniors and immunocompromised residents who could not risk going out. As the economic impact of the pandemic deepened, these groups expanded their efforts and fundraised to provide free groceries to those who had lost their jobs or were otherwise financially struggling. By the fall of 2020, the West Brooklyn network was serving over 100 households regularly, illustrating how quickly and effectively these grassroots efforts scaled up to meet growing needs.

In Queens, the group Woodbine collaborated with the Hungry Monk—a local homeless outreach organization—to extend the reach and impact of their food pantries. Woodbine operated on Wednesdays and Fridays, while the Hungry Monk operated on Tuesdays, Thursdays, and Saturdays. This collaboration exemplified how mutual aid during the pandemic often involved creating and strengthening connections between various community groups and resources, ensuring that aid was comprehensive and sustained over time.

Mutual aid during the COVID-19 pandemic also extended to emotional and social support. As lockdowns led to widespread isolation, these networks provided a sense of community and solidarity. Volunteers checked in on isolated neighbors, organized virtual social events, and helped those struggling with mental health issues connect to support services. This holistic approach to mutual aid—addressing not just material needs but also the social and emotional well-being of community members—highlighted the adaptability and compassion at the heart of these efforts.

The history of mutual aid shows how communities have always come together to support one another, especially in times of crisis. But these efforts have been about more than just survival—they've been about resistance to oppressive systems. This historical legacy underscores how mutual aid has consistently been a means of addressing gaps left by larger, more powerful institutions.

Looking to the future, mutual aid remains a critical tool for addressing systemic issues, which we will discuss in Chapter 11. As we confront wealth inequality, racial injustice, and environmental crises, mutual aid can continue to provide both immediate relief and a vision for long-term transformation. Most certainly, the future of mutual aid will be about more than responding to urgent needs. It will also be about reshaping society to ensure that everyone has access to the resources and support we need to thrive.

Chapter Review

Mutual aid is the practice of communities coming together to support one another, particularly during times of crisis or need. Unlike charity, which often creates a power imbalance between a giver and a receiver, mutual aid is built on reciprocity and solidarity, emphasizing that everyone has something to contribute and that collective well-being is key to individual survival. A notable modern example is the mutual aid efforts during the COVID-19 pandemic, where neighbors delivered groceries and supplies, raised funds, and organized to meet the growing needs of their communities when government support systems fell short.

Throughout human history, mutual aid has been deeply embedded in different cultures. Indigenous societies, for example, have long practiced forms of collective resource management and care. Similarly, guilds in medieval Europe offered mutual protection and financial support to members, including assisting the widows and orphans of deceased workers.

Mutual aid has not only been a response to immediate crises but has also challenged the larger systems of power that perpetuate inequality and suffering. In the 20th century, movements like the Black Panther Party's community programs—offering free meals and health clinics—demonstrated how mutual aid could be a tool for both survival and resistance. As history has shown, mutual aid is not just a response to societal failure but a powerful means of creating new, more equitable social structures where communities take control of their collective well-being.

Discussion Questions

1 Reflecting on historical examples of mutual aid, what lessons can be applied to the current challenges facing your community? How can mutual aid efforts address long-term systemic issues rather than just providing temporary relief?

2 Thinking on your own experiences, consider moments when you have participated in mutual aid or witnessed acts of solidarity within your community. In what ways did people come together to support one another during times of need?

Chapter 2

The Principles of Mutual Aid

In this chapter, we will explore the key principles that underpin mutual aid and how they guide the actions of communities who practice it. We'll examine how solidarity creates a sense of shared responsibility, how reciprocity builds trust and long-term cooperation, and how self-determination empowers people to shape the direction of their collective efforts.

These principles not only strengthen community bonds, but they also provide a framework for creating more equitable, inclusive, and resilient systems of support. By understanding and embracing these core ideas, we can better appreciate the transformative potential of mutual aid in addressing both everyday needs and larger societal challenges.

Strength in Solidarity

Imagine you are part of a small community where a local factory suddenly cuts wages for its workers, leaving many families struggling to afford basic necessities. The workers, who have limited resources, decide to go on strike. As they face the threat of losing their jobs and are harassed by factory owners and local authorities, they turn to their neighbors for support. What would happen if other members of the community, instead of looking away, rallied around the workers and offered food, shelter, and financial help? How would this mutual aid impact the fight for fair wages? This scenario invites us to consider the power of **solidarity**—how standing together can change the course of events.

Solidarity is about uniting in pursuit of a common goal, often in response to shared challenges or oppression. It is grounded in the recognition that the struggles of one group are interconnected with those of another. Solidarity involves mutual support, empathy, and feeling responsible for another's well-being. Throughout history, it has been a key driver of social movements and change, allowing marginalized communities to pool their resources, amplify their voices, and challenge systems of injustice.

For example, during the labor movements of the 19th and 20th centuries, workers organized strikes and protests to demand fair wages, better working conditions, and the right to unionize. These acts of solidarity were not limited to individual factories or industries; instead, they often spread across regions and even countries. Workers recognized that their struggles were shared, and by uniting in common cause, they could challenge the power of employers and push for systemic change.

The Pullman Strike of 1894 was an impressive example of worker solidarity in U.S. history. After the Pullman Company cut wages without lowering rent in its company-owned town, workers near Chicago went on strike, demanding fair treatment. Their cause quickly gained nationwide support as the American Railway Union, led by Eugene V. Debs, called for a boycott of all trains using Pullman cars. This act of solidarity spread across the country, with more than 125,000 railway workers refusing to operate trains in support of the Pullman strikers. Despite the federal government intervening to break the strike, the widespread support for the workers demonstrated the power of collective action and the willingness of laborers across different regions to stand together against unjust corporate practices.

Another powerful example of solidarity was in the Civil Rights Movement during the Freedom Rides of 1961 (see photo). Black and white activists, organized by the Congress of Racial Equality (CORE), boarded buses together to challenge segregation in interstate travel across the South. In an era when Jim Crow laws enforced racial separation in public spaces, these Freedom Riders demonstrated immense courage and unity. They risked violence and arrest as they traveled through deeply segregated areas, encountering violent mobs and resistance from local authorities.

The Freedom Riders' act of solidarity transcended racial lines, as both Black and white participants stood together in defiance of unjust laws. When some were brutally beaten and jailed, others quickly joined the effort to continue the rides, refusing to be intimidated. Their collective action drew national attention, sparking federal intervention and eventually leading to the desegregation of interstate travel. This moment showed how solidarity among activists, regardless of race, could disrupt entrenched systems of oppression and bring about meaningful change.

But solidarity is not just demonstrated in social justice and labor movements. One contemporary example was during the height of the COVID-19 pandemic in 2020. Residents across New York City and in other places showed solidarity with frontline workers through a daily ritual of banging on pots and pans. At 7 p.m. each evening, residents would step onto their balconies, lean out of their windows, and gather on rooftops to make noise in support of doctors, nurses, delivery drivers, and other essential workers risking their lives. This act of collective appreciation became a powerful symbol of unity, as thousands of residents participated to express gratitude and remind frontline workers that their efforts were seen, valued, and supported. The noise echoed throughout the cities, reinforcing a sense of shared resilience during a time of immense hardship.

These examples highlight the strength that comes from uniting around a common cause. Solidarity is a foundational principle of mutual aid because it represents a shared commitment to supporting all members in a community. Solidarity means standing with others not out of pity, but with the understanding that our fates are interconnected. By helping others, we also help ourselves in creating a more resilient and equitable society.

From "Me" to "We"

Solidarity, in practice, fundamentally challenges the deeply ingrained **individualism** that defines modern capitalist societies. In an individualistic mindset, success and survival are seen as personal responsibilities with everyone expected to look out for themselves, often at the expense of others. This way of thinking encourages competition rather than cooperation, making it difficult to build collective movements for change.

Capitalism emphasizes personal responsibility for our lot in life, suggesting that those who succeed do so because of our own hard work and merit, while those who struggle are seen as failing to take advantage of the same opportunities. Personal wealth and achievements are celebrated, while poverty, unemployment, and hardship are attributed to individual shortcomings rather than the broader economic system. As a result, larger issues like inequality or lack of access to resources are overlooked in favor of an emphasis on personal effort. We are expected to "pull ourselves up by our bootstraps" rather than rely on communal aid or structural change.

When individualism is taken to an extreme, it can have significant impacts on society as a whole. Here are a few:

Social Fragmentation:

Excessive individualism can lead to social fragmentation, where people prioritize their own needs and interests over those of the community. This can weaken social bonds, erode trust, and diminish collective solidarity—making it harder for society to address common challenges.

Inequality & Social Stratification:

An emphasis on individualism can exacerbate inequality and social stratification by reinforcing disparities in wealth, opportunity, and access to resources. When people are solely responsible for their own success or failure, those who face systemic barriers or disadvantages may struggle to compete on an uneven playing field, perpetuating cycles of poverty and marginalization.

Erosion of Social Responsibility:

Individualism can undermine a sense of social responsibility, where people feel less accountable to the broader community and more inclined to prioritize their own interests at the expense of others. This can lead to a lack of empathy and civic engagement—hindering efforts to address collective issues such as poverty, inequality, and environmental degradation.

Loneliness & Isolation:

In highly individualistic societies, people may experience feelings of loneliness and isolation as they prioritize self-interests over interpersonal relationships within a broader community. This can have detrimental effects on mental health and well-being, contributing to higher rates of depression and anxiety.

Short-Term Thinking & Consumerism:

Individualism can foster a culture of short-term thinking and consumerism, where people prioritize immediate gratification and personal consumption over long-term sustainability and collective well-being. This contributes to environmental degradation, overconsumption of resources, and a lack of concern for future generations.

In contrast to individualism, solidarity operates on the understanding that our well-being is interconnected, and that addressing issues collectively can lead to more equitable and sustainable outcomes. Solidarity pushes us to reconsider the narrative that we can "go it alone" and instead encourages us to stand together. Shared struggles require shared solutions.

Consider a scenario where a group of workers In a factory faces unsafe working conditions. In an individualistic framework, each worker might feel they need to tolerate the conditions for fear of losing their job, believing that speaking up would result in personal consequences. However, if the workers engage in solidarity, they begin to recognize that their power lies in their collective voice. One worker, initially afraid to confront the issue alone, finds strength in knowing that others share the same concerns. Together, they organize, demand safer conditions, and offer mutual support. In this context, solidarity directly opposes individualistic thinking, as it demonstrates that by working collectively, the group can achieve what no one person could do alone.

This shift from "me" to "we" extends beyond workplace struggles and into broader societal issues. Whether it's combating climate change, advocating for housing rights, or providing healthcare to underserved communities, solidarity reminds us that our fates are intertwined. By supporting each other, we resist the isolation and helplessness that come with excessive individualism. Solidarity doesn't just offer an alternative way of thinking; it offers a force that drives transformative action, where success is measured not by personal gain, but by collective progress.

What Does Solidarity Require?

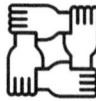

"Standing in solidarity" is a phrase we hear all the time, but what do we mean by this? Standing in solidarity requires more than just verbal support or symbolic gestures. It demands active engagement and a willingness to share in the struggles of others. One of the key elements is listening and learning—understanding the issues faced by those we are standing with and recognizing that our own perspectives might not fully encompass their experiences. This requires humility, openness, and a commitment to amplifying the voices of those directly affected rather than speaking over them. Solidarity is not about centering ourselves in someone else's struggle, but rather about supporting their leadership and aligning our actions with their needs and goals.

Solidarity often involves standing with others who have a similar identity or experience to us, as we naturally empathize with those who face similar challenges. This kind of solidarity can foster strong bonds within a community, whether it's based on race, gender, class, or shared struggles. But it is important to note that the kind of unity associated with solidarity is not based on shared identity or experience alone. It is also rooted in a common commitment to justice and mutual aid. People who stand in solidarity may come from different backgrounds, but they are bound by their shared values and goals. This unity is both moral and strategic, as it recognizes that systemic problems—such as racism, inequality, or environmental destruction—cannot be dismantled by individuals working alone.

Another crucial aspect of standing in solidarity is taking action. This might mean joining protests, engaging in advocacy, providing material support, or leveraging personal resources and networks to amplify a cause. The action taken will vary depending on the situation, but it must go beyond passive agreement. Solidarity often involves personal risk or sacrifice, whether it's facing backlash for speaking out or contributing time, money, or energy to a movement. True solidarity calls for standing by others, even when it is inconvenient or uncomfortable, because it is rooted in a sense of shared responsibility for addressing injustice.

A powerful example occurred in the 2023 SAG-AFTRA strikes, when actors in Hollywood went on strike demanding fair wages, better working conditions, and protections against the use of artificial intelligence in their work. The solidarity that was displayed was not just symbolic. People showed support by joining picket lines, organizing rallies, and using their platforms to spread awareness about the actors' demands. Crew members who weren't on strike refused to cross picket lines, halting production on numerous shows and films. Fans supported by boycotting new releases and amplifying the actors' messages on social media. This widespread solidarity helped to amplify the voices of the striking actors and put additional pressure on studios and production companies to address their concerns. The unity across different groups showed that the fight for fair treatment in the entertainment industry was a cause that resonated far beyond just those directly involved.

The last (and perhaps hardest) component of "standing in solidarity" involves consistency and long-term commitment. Solidarity isn't something that is performed momentarily during a crisis. It is an ongoing practice of showing up, offering support, and remaining engaged in the struggle for justice over time. This means continuing to support a cause even when it is no longer in the public spotlight or when the work becomes difficult. It involves being reliable allies and ensuring that we do not retreat when the struggle becomes hard or when our efforts are no longer as visible or celebrated. True solidarity is sustained—not fleeting—and it recognizes that meaningful change often takes time and perseverance.

The Challenges to Solidarity

While a powerful force for change, solidarity is not without its challenges. Standing together in support of a common cause often brings to light differences in priorities, approaches, and lived experiences that can create tension within communities and movements. Challenges to solidarity often emerge when internal disagreements or external pressures weaken a group's unity. Consider this scenario:

Workers in a large multinational corporation organize to demand better wages and working conditions. At first, the solidarity among employees is strong, with both office workers and factory workers joining forces to push for change. However, cracks begin to appear when management offers office workers a modest pay raise, leaving factory workers out of the deal.

Office workers, feeling that their concerns have been partially addressed, are now less motivated to continue the struggle, while factory workers—who face harsher working conditions and lower wages—are frustrated by the lack of collective pressure. As office workers begin to distance themselves from the protests, tensions grow. Factory workers feel abandoned, and accusations of privilege and betrayal emerge, further dividing the movement.

Then, management starts employing tactics to divide the workers further, such as promoting some office workers into management roles or threatening factory workers with layoffs if the protests continue. These pressures make it increasingly difficult for the workers to maintain their solidarity, even though they all originally sought the same improvements. In the end, internal divisions, unequal stakes, and external manipulation challenge the unity that once bound them together.

Maintaining solidarity within movements or communities can be difficult, as various challenges can weaken the bonds that hold groups together. Below are some key obstacles that groups may face.

Division Within Groups:

Differences in identity, ideology, or strategy can fragment movements. For example, disagreements over priorities or methods (e.g., peaceful vs. militant protest) may split groups that initially shared a common goal.

Power Imbalances:

Hierarchical structures within groups can create feelings of exclusion or resentment, leading to the breakdown of solidarity. Marginalized voices may feel unheard or sidelined.

Cultural & Social Differences:

Solidarity across diverse communities can be difficult when there are cultural misunderstandings, lack of trust, or competing interests, making cooperation less effective.

Economic Pressure & Scarcity:

In situations where resources are limited, competition for those resources may erode solidarity as people prioritize self-preservation over collective goals.

Oppression & Repression:

Governments or dominant powers often actively work to disrupt solidarity through propaganda, coercion, or direct repression. This can demoralize groups and deter participation.

Burnout & Fatigue:

Sustaining solidarity over time can be difficult when people become exhausted or disillusioned, especially if progress is slow or setbacks occur.

Overcoming challenges to solidarity requires intentional effort, open communication, and a commitment to inclusivity. One key strategy involves encouraging dialogue and making sure that all voices within the group are heard, especially those from marginalized or underrepresented communities. By creating spaces for everyone to contribute ideas and concerns, groups can build trust and address potential divisions before they escalate.

Clear, shared goals are also essential for maintaining solidarity. When everyone understands the overarching objective, it's easier to navigate differences in opinion or strategy. Leadership should emphasize the common purpose while respecting the diverse perspectives within the group, seeking compromises that uphold the broader mission.

The Give & Take of Reciprocity

Reciprocity refers to the exchange of resources, services, or favors with the expectation that what is given will eventually be returned in kind. It is a social norm that underpins many human relationships, fostering cooperation and mutual trust. In its most basic form, reciprocity can be seen as "you scratch my back, I'll scratch yours," but it goes beyond simple transactions. Reciprocity builds social bonds by creating a sense of obligation and connection between individuals or groups, encouraging people to work together for shared benefit. This exchange doesn't always need to be immediate or equal in value. Instead, it's often based on the understanding that helping others strengthens relationships and leads to future support when needed.

There are different types of reciprocity. *Generalized reciprocity* occurs when one gives without expecting a specific return. For example, a neighbor might help another fix their car, trusting that in the future, they can call on that person if they need help even if it's not directly related. *Balanced reciprocity*, however, involves a more direct and often equal exchange, where there's a clear expectation of a return in a relatively short time. And then there's *negative reciprocity*, which involves attempting to get something for less than what it's worth, such as in bargaining situations. This type can strain relationships if not handled carefully.

Generalized reciprocity is essential in creating social cohesion because it builds trust and reinforces the idea that cooperation benefits everyone involved. When people feel confident that their contributions will be returned in some way, they are more likely to invest in others and in their community. This cycle of giving and receiving can lead to deep, long-term relationships of mutual care, which help communities thrive by ensuring that no one person or group is left isolated or unsupported.

A scenario that illustrates generalized reciprocity could take place in a small community garden. One gardener may contribute extra seeds and tools to the group, while another offers their expertise in growing vegetables in challenging soil. As the season progresses, those who received help with their garden plots may later share their harvest with others, distributing fresh produce to members of the community who might not have the time or ability to grow their own. This system of mutual exchange—where contributions of effort, materials, and crops flow freely—demonstrates how everyone benefits from giving what they can and receiving when needed, creating a cycle of support that strengthens the entire garden and the relationships within it.

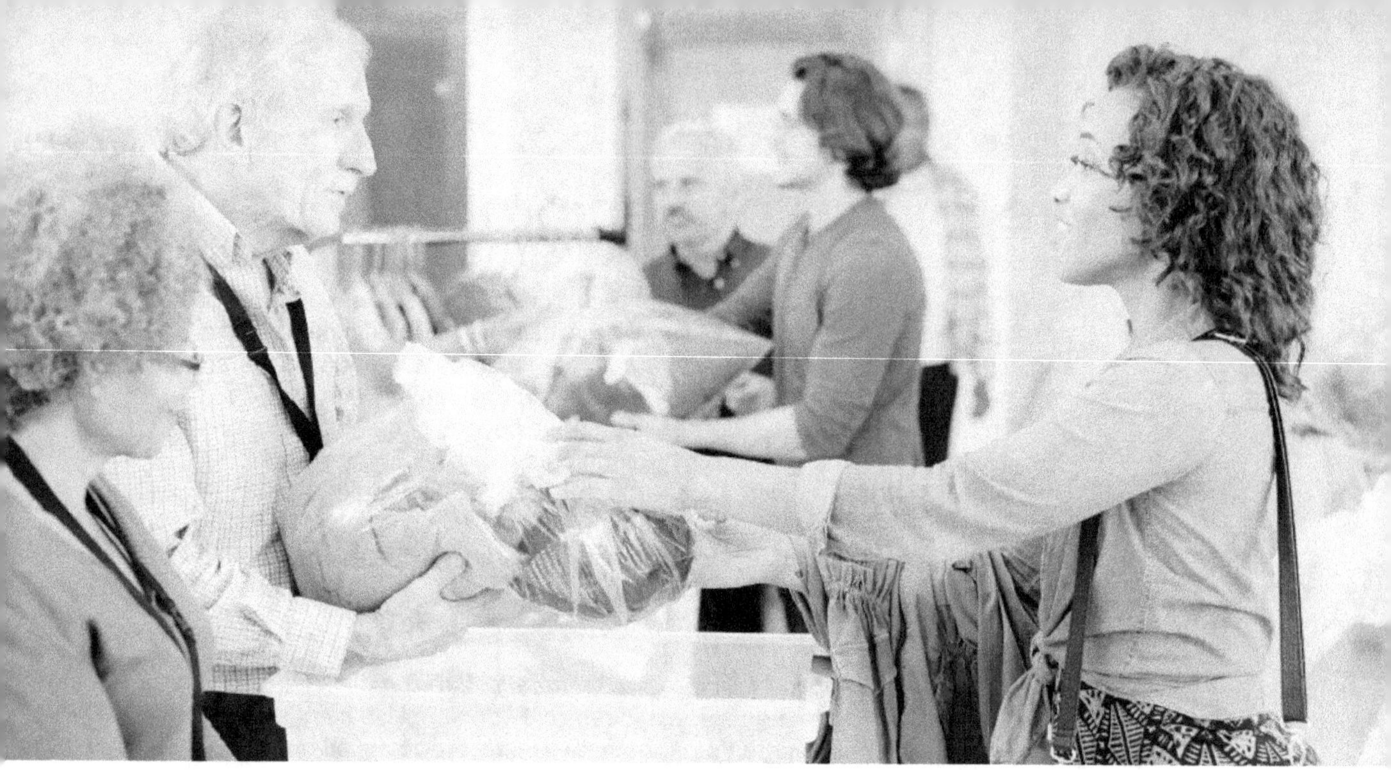

Beyond Transactional Relationships

In mutual aid, reciprocity functions not as a direct, transactional exchange but as a way of contributing to the well-being of the community with the understanding that benefits will come back to you, possibly at a later time and from a different source. This non-linear form of reciprocity emphasizes that everyone has something valuable to offer and that, at different points, each person will also need support. Instead of a one-for-one exchange, the focus is on creating a culture of mutual care where everyone gives according to their ability and receives according to their need. The strength of this system lies in its flexibility and its long-term approach to meeting the collective needs of the group.

For example, someone might contribute by offering their time to help distribute food to community members facing hardship. They don't do this with the expectation that those specific people will return the favor directly. Instead, they trust that by contributing to the community's overall well-being, they will, in turn, receive support when they are in need—whether it's through a future meal, assistance with a task, or emotional support from others in the group. This model works because it builds trust and a shared commitment to collective care, rather than focusing on individual transactions. Over time, these contributions create a robust network of interdependence, where everyone benefits from the resources and support that circulate within the community.

This kind of reciprocal exchange allows mutual aid networks to be sustainable and adaptable. By trusting in the long-term benefits of contributing to the collective good, people are more likely to offer what they can without feeling pressure to immediately receive something in return. This also helps to avoid the sense of indebtedness or imbalance that can sometimes arise in more transactional relationships. Mutual aid thrives on the idea that reciprocity is not about keeping score but about ensuring that everyone's needs are met over time.

In essence, reciprocity in mutual aid is about building a system where we contribute to the common good because we know that, when the time comes, the community will support us in return. It creates a sense of belonging and security, as we know we are part of a group that values and cares for us.

The Challenges to Reciprocity

While reciprocity is central to mutual aid, it can also face challenges, particularly in ensuring that contributions and benefits remain balanced over time. One common challenge is that people have different capacities to give and receive. In a mutual aid network, some members may have more time, resources, or skills to contribute than others, which can lead to imbalances in the perceived value of each person's contributions. This can create tension if some feel overburdened by the expectation to continually give or if those who cannot contribute as much begin to feel guilty or indebted. Maintaining a sense of equality within the group can become difficult when contributions are not evenly distributed, even when there's an understanding that everyone will receive support when needed.

Another challenge is that reciprocity in mutual aid relies heavily on trust. Since the expectation is not for immediate or direct repayment, people need to trust that the support they offer will eventually come back to them, either through the same person or from the community as a whole. If trust breaks down—whether due to unmet expectations, misunderstandings, or a lack of communication—reciprocity can falter. For example, if one person consistently gives to the group without seeing any tangible return, they might begin to feel taken advantage of or question the sustainability of their involvement. This can lead to burnout, frustration, or withdrawal from the network, which weakens the overall system of mutual support.

A scenario that illustrates this challenge might involve a community-run initiative where some volunteers regularly donate their time, while others primarily receive assistance. Over time, if volunteers begin to feel that they are carrying most of the burden without seeing others step up to help or contribute in different ways, resentment may build. The recipients, on the other hand, may feel uncomfortable or ashamed if they are unable to give back in equal measure due to their personal circumstances. This imbalance can strain relationships within the group and erode the sense of solidarity that mutual aid is built upon. Without open communication and a reaffirmation of the collective commitment to support everyone, the system can become strained.

Another challenge is navigating differences in values or priorities within the group. Mutual aid is often driven by diverse individuals with various perspectives on what support looks like and how resources should be distributed. In some cases, disagreements may arise over who deserves help or how much each person should contribute. For example, in a mutual aid network focused on housing assistance, some members might prioritize emergency shelter for those experiencing homelessness, while others may focus on long-term solutions for families. These differences in focus can lead to friction and make it difficult to maintain a cohesive system of reciprocity if members feel their contributions aren't being directed in ways that align with their values or the group's overall mission.

Finally, reciprocity in mutual aid faces challenges from external pressures, such as resource scarcity or societal systems that undermine cooperation. In times of crisis or scarcity, when people are overwhelmed by their own needs, the ability to give to others can be diminished. This can make it difficult for mutual aid networks to function smoothly, as people may prioritize their own survival over maintaining reciprocal relationships. Additionally, in capitalist societies where individualism and competition are highly valued, the idea of contributing to a collective effort without immediate personal gain can seem counterintuitive or even risky. Overcoming these cultural barriers requires ongoing education and trust-building, as well as efforts to ensure that the mutual aid network remains flexible and responsive to the changing needs of its members.

Ultimately, addressing these challenges requires open communication, flexibility, and a strong commitment to the principles of mutual aid. It's essential for members to regularly discuss their needs, contributions, and expectations to ensure that the system of reciprocity remains fair, inclusive, and sustainable. By recognizing the potential obstacles and working together to address them, mutual aid networks can continue to thrive, even in the face of these challenges.

The Power of Self-determination

Imagine a small town is hit by an economic downturn and unemployment is high. Rather than relying on government assistance or waiting for outside help, a group of laid-off workers decides to form a cooperative, or co-op. They pool their skills and resources to open a community-owned café, where each member has an equal say in decisions and shares in the profits. By organizing collectively and deciding their own future, they not only create sustainable employment for themselves, but they also build a business that reflects the needs and values of the community. This scenario illustrates **self-determination**, as the workers take control of their own destiny through cooperation and mutual support, rather than relying on external systems to solve their problems.

Self-determination is the right for people to make decisions about their own lives and futures, and it is a fundamental principle of mutual aid. It emphasizes autonomy, empowerment, and the belief that communities are best equipped to understand and address their own needs. In mutual aid, self-determination is essential because it promotes non-hierarchical forms of support, where those in need are active participants in both giving and receiving help. Unlike traditional charity, which often positions the recipient as passive and dependent on the aid provider, mutual aid encourages collective action and shared responsibility.

A key aspect of self-determination within mutual aid is that it rejects top-down approaches to assistance. Instead, it encourages people to identify their own challenges and work together to come up with solutions in ways that align with their unique circumstances and values. This empowers participants by acknowledging their ability to contribute meaningfully to their own well-being and that of their community.

For example, consider a mutual aid group formed in response to a housing crisis in a city. Rather than relying on government agencies or nonprofits to solve the issue, community members come together to share resources and expertise. Those facing eviction or housing insecurity collaborate with neighbors who may have legal knowledge or access to temporary housing solutions. Together, they organize rent strikes, offer legal aid, and create communal housing networks. The group's efforts are guided by the needs and decisions of those directly impacted, rather than external entities.

This focus on self-determination also creates resilience and long-term sustainability. When people are involved in shaping solutions that affect their lives, they are more likely to remain committed to those efforts and to develop the skills needed to maintain them over time. In mutual aid networks, self-determination helps build stronger, more interconnected communities where members support each other through challenges and work collectively to improve conditions for all. This contrasts with traditional forms of assistance, where beneficiaries might be left dependent on external aid without the tools to change their circumstances.

Ultimately, self-determination as a core principle of mutual aid ensures that individuals and communities retain control over their own futures. It rejects the notion of dependency or helplessness, instead promoting empowerment through collective action. By centering the voices and needs of those directly affected, mutual aid offers a model that is more just, equitable, and effective at addressing the root causes of social issues.

Embracing Grassroots Initiatives

The term "grassroots" refers to efforts that originate from and are driven by people within a community, rather than being led by political leaders, corporations, or traditional institutions. Grassroots initiatives are a powerful expression of self-determination, as they enable communities to actively address local needs on their own terms. One of their primary benefits is their responsiveness to the specific circumstances, needs, and desires of the people directly affected by an issue. Since these initiatives are led and organized by community members themselves, they are often more attuned to local realities and can create solutions that are more relevant and sustainable. In contrast, top-down approaches tend to impose solutions from above, which may not fully account for the unique context or needs of the affected community.

A key example of this difference is seen in disaster relief efforts. In the aftermath of Hurricane Katrina in 2005, government-led relief efforts were widely criticized for being slow and poorly coordinated. Many local communities, frustrated by the bureaucratic inefficiencies, organized their own grassroots relief networks (see photo). Neighborhoods came together to provide food, shelter, and aid to those in need long before official assistance arrived. These grassroots efforts were not only quicker but they were also more responsive to the immediate needs of the residents. Local knowledge and direct action can often outperform top-down strategies in times of crisis.

Another example can be seen in public health initiatives, particularly during the Ebola outbreak in West Africa between 2014 and 2016. While international organizations and governments initially struggled to contain the epidemic with large-scale, top-down interventions, local grassroots groups played a crucial role in turning the tide (see photo). Community-based health workers, religious leaders, and local organizations were instrumental in raising awareness, promoting safe burial practices, and providing accurate information to dispel myths about the disease. These grassroots efforts succeeded because they leveraged trust within the community and adapted their approaches to local cultural norms, making public health measures more effective.

The people in a community possess a deep understanding of their own challenges, needs, and resources, often developed through lived experience and cultural practices. This insider perspective is what allows grassroots initiatives to offer solutions that are highly relevant and practical, addressing problems in ways that outsiders or centralized authorities might overlook. By tapping into this localized wisdom, grassroots initiatives can craft strategies that are more attuned to the unique dynamics of the region, making their efforts not only more efficient but also more likely to succeed and be embraced by the community.

Decentralized Horizontal Leadership

Many modern institutions are organized as hierarchies with centralized power, reflecting a top-down structure where authority and decision-making are concentrated at the highest levels. This model often resembles a pyramid, with a small group of executives or leaders at the top setting strategic goals and policies, which are then implemented by lower-level managers and employees through a clear chain of command. The primary advantage of this approach is its efficiency in decision-making, as directives come from a central authority and are implemented in a structured manner. However, this model can also lead to many issues, such as a disconnect between leadership and on-the-ground realities.

In contrast, organizations with horizontal structures emphasize decentralization and collective decision-making. In these systems—which resemble a network or web—authority is distributed more evenly among participants, and decisions are made collaboratively rather than imposed from above. This approach encourages greater inclusivity and responsiveness, as all members have a voice and can contribute their unique perspectives and expertise.

In a system with horizontal leadership, self-determination is facilitated because people have the power to actively participate. Decisions are not handed down to them, but rather they have a seat at the table where the decisions are made. Below are some compelling reasons why a mutual aid group might want to be structured with horizontal leadership:

 ### Democratic Decision-Making:

Decisions are reached through collaboration and discussion, allowing the group to benefit from the collective wisdom of its members rather than relying on the directives of a select few.

 ### Prevention of Power Concentration:

By distributing leadership responsibilities, the group avoids potential imbalances and power dynamics that could arise in a more hierarchical structure. This helps create a more democratic and transparent decision-making process.

Inclusivity & Equal Participation:

Horizontal leadership allows people with diverse perspectives, backgrounds, and skills to contribute actively to the group's efforts, not just those with the most privilege.

Resilience & Redundancy:

No single individual holds all decision-making power, reducing the risk of disruptions caused by the absence or unavailability of a specific leader. The redundancy in roles ensures that the group can adapt to changes without significant disruption.

It's important to note that having a horizontal leadership structure does not mean there is an absence of leaders. Rather, it redefines leadership in a more collaborative and flexible way. In this model, leadership roles are often shared, rotated, or distributed based on the needs of the group and peoples' specific expertise. Instead of a single figure directing decisions from the top, multiple people may take on leadership responsibilities in different contexts, guiding the group with their knowledge or skills. Leaders in horizontal structures often act as facilitators, ensuring that everyone's voice is heard and that the group works collectively toward common goals. This approach emphasizes leadership as a dynamic and supportive role rather than one of power or authority.

Horizontal leadership models typically strive for **consensus** as a way to ensure that all members of a group have a voice in the decision-making process. Consensus refers to a collective agreement or shared understanding reached by a group on a particular course of action, solution, or outcome. This does not necessarily mean that every person within the group fully supports the decision, but rather that all members are willing to accept and abide by the agreed-upon solution for the sake of unity and cooperation. Consensus is characterized by:

Unanimity:

In its ideal form, consensus implies unanimous agreement among all members of the group. However, in practice, consensus may allow for a level of agreement where all members are sufficiently comfortable moving forward with the decision, even if there are some reservations or differing viewpoints.

Mutual Respect:

Consensus requires mutual respect among group members, even in the face of disagreement. It involves valuing every person's input and perspective, acknowledging differences, and working collaboratively to find common ground.

Commitment to Implementation:

Achieving consensus is not just about reaching an agreement; it also involves a commitment from all members to implement the decision effectively. Consensus implies shared responsibility and accountability for the outcomes of the decision.

———————

By striving for consensus, a mutual aid group embodies self-determination by ensuring that its members are active agents in deciding how their collective resources and efforts are utilized. With patience and a willingess to compromise, members will feel a sense of ownership over the group's actions, and the final decision will ultimately be one that reflects the collective will. This egalitarian approach reinforces the idea that the community is best equipped to decide its own future.

Chapter Review

Mutual aid operates on foundational principles that counteract the negative impacts of individualism prevalent in society. Solidarity, as a core principle, stands in stark contrast to the isolating nature of individualism. It promotes a sense of collective responsibility and interconnectedness, emphasizing the importance of supporting one another in communities. By practicing solidarity, mutual aid groups create spaces where people can come together, share resources, and address common challenges, thereby mitigating the alienation and disconnection often associated with individualism.

Reciprocity in mutual aid efforts emphasizes a balanced exchange of support and assistance among participants. Unlike charity, which can perpetuate unequal power dynamics and reinforce feelings of helplessness, reciprocity encourages people to contribute their own skills, resources, and support to the community. This reciprocal exchange of assistance builds a sense of self-reliance, as people actively engage in giving and receiving help, recognizing their own capacity to both contribute to and benefit from collective action.

Self-determination plays an important role in mutual aid by empowering people with autonomy over their own lives and actions. Within mutual aid groups, self-determination enables participants to assert control over the assistance they offer and receive, making decisions that align with their values, needs, and preferences. A horizontal leadership structure where power is shared equally, as opposed to a rigid hierarchy where all the power is concentrated at the top, allows mutual aid groups to implement more inclusive and adaptive solutions.

Discussion Questions

1. Think of a time when you relied on the support of others. How does that experience align with the core principles of mutual aid? Have you had an opportunity to return the support to those who were there for you?

2. How can shifting away from individualism as a society contribute to broader efforts towards social justice and equity? What are the potential benefits and challenges of transitioning towards a more collectivist society?

Chapter 3

Understanding Community Needs

A community is a living system comprised of the people who live in it, the relationships they build, and the shared spaces and resources they rely on. It includes infrastructure like homes, schools, parks, and roads, as well as services, such as healthcare, education, and public safety. A community is also defined by its social dynamics—the ways in which people come together to solve problems, celebrate achievements, and provide care.

In this chapter, we will explore the components that make up our communities. Regardless of the type of mutual aid work you want to do, having a good understanding of your community's strengths and weaknesses will help you decide where to focus your energy.

Community Assessment

Mutual aid projects—especially those that involve the public—are most effective when grounded in a deep understanding of community dynamics. To explore this, groups may want to conduct a **community assessment**, which is a systematic process of gathering and analyzing information to understand a community's strengths, needs, resources, and challenges.

The assessment involves collecting data, engaging with stakeholders, and evaluating factors affecting the community's well-being and quality of life. Its purpose is to inform the planning, decision-making, and resource allocation that will improve social, economic, health, and environmental conditions.

When conducting an assessment of your own community, be sure to examine it from all angles to gain a comprehensive understanding. Here are some of the most important factors to consider:

Demographic Characteristics:

Understand the demographic composition of the community, including age distribution, gender, race, ethnicity, household size, income levels, education levels, and employment status.

Community Assets & Resources:

Identify existing community assets and resources, including parks, libraries, community centers, schools, religious institutions, businesses, non-profit organizations, and other community-based organizations. Assess their accessibility, quality, and capacity to meet the needs of residents.

Community Needs & Priorities:

Engage with community members through surveys, focus groups, interviews, or town hall meetings to identify their needs, concerns, and priorities. Pay attention to diverse perspectives and voices.

Economic Vitality:

Evaluate the local economy, including employment opportunities, businesses, industries, income disparities, poverty rates, and economic development initiatives. Understand the economic challenges facing the community and potential opportunities for growth.

Health & Well-being:

Assess the overall health status and well-being of community members, including prevalence of chronic diseases, access to healthcare services, mental health resources, substance abuse issues, and other health-related concerns.

Safety & Security:

Consider factors related to public safety, crime rates, policing practices, emergency response capabilities, and access to legal services. Identify areas of concern and opportunities for improving community safety.

Cultural & Social Dynamics:

Recognize the cultural diversity and social dynamics within the community, including languages spoken, cultural traditions, social networks, and overall cohesion. Understand how these factors shape community interactions and relationships.

Educational Opportunities:

Evaluate the quality and accessibility of educational institutions, including schools, colleges, adult education programs, and vocational training centers. Consider learning disparities and opportunities for improving educational outcomes for all residents.

Environmental Sustainability:

Assess environmental factors such as air and water quality, access to green spaces, exposure to environmental hazards, and sustainability initiatives. Identify opportunities for promoting environmental health and sustainability within the community.

Technology & Connectivity:

Evaluate access to technology and digital resources, including internet connectivity, computer literacy, and availability of digital infrastructure. Addressing digital divides and promoting digital inclusion can improve opportunities for community members.

Historical & Cultural Context:

Understand the historical context and cultural heritage of the community, including Indigenous histories, migration patterns, and significant events that have shaped the community's identity.

By considering these factors comprehensively, an assessment can provide valuable insights for mutual aid groups to develop targeted programs that address the unique needs and strengths of the community.

Identifying Key Stakeholders

A **key stakeholder** is an individual, group, organization, or entity that has a vested interest in the well-being of a community. They are those who are directly affected by or can significantly influence the outcomes and decisions related to any change.

Key stakeholders may have specific interests, resources, expertise, or concerns that make their involvement essential for the success or sustainability of community initiatives. By engaging with key stakeholders, mutual aid groups can gather diverse insights and perspectives, create partnerships, and ensure that the priorities of all members are taken into account in the planning and decision-making process.

Key stakeholders can vary depending on the specific context and issues at hand. However, some common key stakeholders in many communities include the following:

Residents:

Community members are often the primary stakeholders, as they directly experience the impacts of community initiatives and decisions. Their voices, needs, and perspectives are essential for effective community engagement and decision-making.

Local Government Officials:

Elected and appointed officials at the municipal, county, or regional level play a significant role in shaping community policies and programs. They are responsible for providing essential services, enacting regulations, and allocating resources that affect community well-being.

Nonprofit Organizations:

Nonprofit organizations—including social service agencies, advocacy groups, and community-based organizations—are key stakeholders that provide vital services, resources, and advocacy efforts to address community needs and promote social change.

Businesses:

Local businesses and employers contribute to the economic vitality and employment opportunities within the community. They may also support initiatives through sponsorships, donations, and corporate social responsibility programs.

Utilities:

Utilities are key stakeholders as they provide essential services, such as electricity, water, gas, and telecommunications infrastructure. Their operations directly impact residents' daily lives, making their involvement crucial in community planning, development, and emergency response efforts.

Educational Institutions:

Schools, colleges, and universities are important stakeholders that contribute to education, workforce development, and community engagement. They provide learning opportunities, resources, and expertise that benefit both students and the broader community.

Healthcare Providers:

Hospitals, clinics, and healthcare organizations are the key stakeholders who promote community health and well-being. They provide medical services, public health programs, and education initiatives that address healthcare needs and disparities.

Faith-Based Organizations:

Churches, mosques, synagogues, temples, and other religious institutions play a significant role in providing spiritual support, social services, and community outreach programs.

Community Leaders & Advocates:

Community leaders, activists, and advocates represent the interests of specific populations or causes. They play a vital role in mobilizing resources, raising awareness, and advocating for policy changes that address social injustices and promote equity.

Media Outlets:

Local newspapers, radio stations, TV channels, and online media platforms serve as outlets for communication, information dissemination, and community engagement. They help shape public discourse, raise awareness of issues, and hold stakeholders accountable.

Civic & Neighborhood Associations:

Civic and neighborhood associations represent the interests of residents in specific geographic areas or communities. They often serve as forums for organizing, advocacy, and decision-making on local issues.

Identifying Threats

Communities face a multitude of complex and interconnected threats that span social, economic, environmental, and health domains. Understanding potential threats will allow your mutual aid group to prepare for emergencies or disasters that could jeopardize your safety. By being aware of threats, your group can take proactive measures to mitigate risks and protect people.

These threats include the impacts of climate change—such as extreme weather events, rising sea levels, and natural disasters—which pose significant risks to infrastructure and livelihoods. Additionally, communities grapple with socioeconomic challenges—including income inequality, poverty, and unemployment—which can exacerbate social tensions and crime. Emerging infectious diseases, such as COVID-19, are also threats to public health and well-being. On top of all this, communities must navigate technological disruptions, cybersecurity threats, and the rapid pace of globalization, which present both opportunities and risks for economic development and social stability.

Here are steps to assess threats to your community:

1. Identify Potential Threats:

Begin by compiling a list. This may include natural disasters (e.g., floods, wildfires, earthquakes), man-made hazards (e.g., industrial accidents, hazardous material spills), public health emergencies (e.g., pandemics, disease outbreaks), socio-economic challenges (e.g., unemployment, poverty), crime and violence, environmental degradation, or infrastructure failures.

2. Gather Data & Information:

Collect relevant data and information to inform the assessment process. This may include historical records, emergency response plans, hazard maps, community surveys, demographic data, vulnerability assessments, and input from local experts, stakeholders, and residents.

3. Conduct Risk Analysis:

Evaluate each potential threat based on its likelihood of occurrence and potential impact. Consider factors such as historical data, geographic location, climate patterns, socio-economic conditions, and infrastructure resilience. Prioritize threats based on their severity and likelihood to help focus assessment efforts.

4. Assess Vulnerabilities:

Identify vulnerabilities within the community that could exacerbate the impact of threats. This may include physical vulnerabilities (e.g., aging infrastructure, inadequate flood protection), social vulnerabilities (e.g., marginalized populations, limited access to healthcare), economic vulnerabilities (e.g., reliance on a single industry), and institutional vulnerabilities (e.g., lack of emergency preparedness plans).

5. Consider Interdependencies:

Recognize the interconnectedness of various systems and sectors. Assess how disruptions in one area (e.g., transportation, utilities, healthcare) could cascade and affect other areas. Consider dependencies on external resources and infrastructure that may be vulnerable to disruption.

Vulnerable Populations

Vulnerable populations in a community are people who are at increased risk of experiencing adverse outcomes or are facing significant challenges due to various factors. These factors may include socioeconomic status, age, race, ethnicity, gender identity, sexual orientation, disability, immigration status, health status, or geographic location. Vulnerable populations may face barriers to accessing resources, services, and opportunities, which can contribute to disparities in health, well-being, and quality of life.

By prioritizing support and resources for vulnerable groups, mutual aid efforts can work toward reducing disparities and improving outcomes for everyone. Some examples of vulnerable populations include:

Low-Income Individuals & Families:

People living below the poverty line or experiencing financial hardship may lack access to basic necessities, such as food, housing, healthcare, and education.

Children & Youth:

Children and adolescents are vulnerable due to their dependence on caregivers and their developmental stage. They may face risks related to poverty, abuse, neglect, inadequate education, and limited access to healthcare and support services.

Elderly Individuals:

Older adults may be vulnerable due to age-related health issues, limited mobility, social isolation, and financial insecurity. They may require assistance with activities of daily living and access to healthcare services.

People Experiencing Housing Insecurity:

Individuals and families experiencing homelessness or housing insecurity are vulnerable due to lack of stable shelter, which can lead to exposure to harsh weather conditions, violence, exploitation, and health issues.

Minority & Ethnic Communities:

Racial and ethnic minorities may face discrimination, marginalization, and disparities in access to healthcare, education, employment, housing, and other resources. They may also experience higher rates of poverty and health conditions.

People with Disabilities:

Individuals with physical, cognitive, sensory, or developmental disabilities may face barriers to accessing services, employment, education, transportation, and social participation.

Immigrants & Refugees:

Immigrants and refugees may face challenges related to language barriers, cultural adaptation, legal status, discrimination, and limited access to healthcare, education, and social services.

LGBTQ+ People:

Lesbian, gay, bisexual, transgender, queer, and other gender and sexual minorities may face stigma, discrimination, and violence based on their sexual orientation or gender identity. They may also experience disparities in healthcare, housing, employment, and legal rights.

Survivors of Violence & Trauma:

Individuals who have experienced domestic violence, sexual assault, child abuse, or other forms of trauma may face ongoing physical, emotional, and psychological challenges that impact their well-being and ability to access support services.

People with Chronic Health Conditions:

People who are immunocompromised or have chronic health conditions—such as diabetes, heart disease, cancer, HIV/AIDS, mental illness, or substance use disorders—may face challenges related to managing their health, accessing healthcare, and maintaining quality of life.

Acknowledging Privilege

Privilege refers to unearned advantages or benefits that individuals or groups receive based on their social identities, such as race, gender, class, sexual orientation, ability, religion, or other factors. These advantages are often inherent in social structures and institutions and are not earned or chosen by individuals themselves.

By acknowledging privilege, mutual aid groups can ensure their efforts do not inadvertently reinforce existing inequalities. Recognizing disparities allows for a more nuanced understanding of community dynamics and the unique challenges faced by marginalized populations. It promotes conscious efforts to include and uplift voices that are often overlooked, ensuring that support is distributed fairly and effectively. This awareness can lead to more empathetic and informed decision-making.

Privilege manifests in these forms:

Social Privilege:

Social privilege refers to advantages that people receive based on their membership in dominant social groups. For example, in many societies, being white, male, heterosexual, cisgender, or affluent confers social privileges, such as greater access to opportunities, resources, and recognition.

Structural Privilege:

Structural privilege refers to advantages embedded within societal structures and systems that benefit certain groups while disadvantaging others. For instance, structural privilege can be observed in educational, economic, legal, and healthcare systems that disproportionately favor dominant social groups and perpetuate systemic inequalities.

Interpersonal Privilege:

Interpersonal privilege refers to the advantages that people experience in their everyday interactions and relationships based on their social identities. This can include being treated with respect, dignity, and credibility, as well as being less likely to experience discrimination, harassment, or violence compared to marginalized groups.

Cultural Privilege:

Cultural privilege refers to the dominant cultural norms, values, and representations that reinforce the experiences and perspectives of privileged groups while diminishing those of marginalized groups. Cultural privilege can be seen in media, literature, art, and other forms of cultural production that center the narratives and experiences of dominant social groups.

It is important to note that privilege is often invisible or taken for granted by those who possess it, as it is normalized within society. However, recognizing one's own privilege is necessary if we are to understand how social inequalities are perpetuated.

Power Structures

Vulnerable populations are often excluded from power structures, leaving them without a voice in the decisions that affect their lives and perpetuating cycles of inequality. **Power structures** refer to the hierarchical relationships and systems of authority that exist within communities and societies. These structures determine who holds influence and decision-making authority, as well as who has access to resources, opportunities, and privileges.

Understanding power structures is essential when a mutual aid group conducts a community assessment, as it provides insight into the underlying dynamics that shape resource distribution, access to services, and decision-making processes. This knowledge enables the group to strategically navigate and engage with key stakeholders, ensuring that their initiatives address systemic issues rather than just symptoms.

Power structures can manifest in various forms, including:

Political Power:

This refers to the authority and influence wielded by government officials, elected representatives, and other political actors. Political power structures determine the laws, policies, and regulations that govern society, as well as the allocation of public resources and services.

Economic Power:

Economic power pertains to control over financial resources, wealth, and capital. It encompasses the influence exerted by corporations, banks, investors, and business owners who shape economic policies, markets, and the distribution of wealth within society.

Social Power:

Social power encompasses influence and authority derived from social status, prestige, and networks of relationships. It includes individuals or groups who hold sway over cultural norms, social institutions, and community dynamics, such as leaders, religious figures, and influencers.

Institutional Power:

Institutional power refers to the authority and influence wielded by formal organizations and institutions, such as schools, universities, hospitals, government agencies, and non-profit organizations. These institutions play a significant role in shaping social, educational, and healthcare practices.

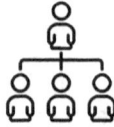

Structural Power:

Structural power refers to the underlying systems, norms, and structures that perpetuate inequalities and disparities within society. This includes systems of oppression—such as racism, sexism, classism, ableism, and homophobia—which shape the power dynamics and privilege of certain groups over others.

Cultural Power:

Cultural power relates to the ability to shape beliefs, values, and ideologies within society. It includes media outlets, entertainment industries, and cultural institutions that influence public discourse, perceptions, and attitudes toward different social groups.

Marginalized Groups

A **marginalized group** refers to a segment of society that experiences systematic social, economic, or political disadvantages and exclusion. Marginalization can occur due to various factors, such as race, ethnicity, gender, sexual orientation, disability, socioeconomic status, immigration status, religion, or other characteristics.

Marginalized groups often face discrimination, prejudice, stigma, and limited access to resources, opportunities, and decision-making power within society. This exclusion can lead to disparities in areas such as education, employment, healthcare, housing, and representation in political and social institutions. Recognizing and addressing the marginalization of these groups is essential for promoting equity and social justice.

Assessing the needs of a marginalized group in a community requires a thoughtful and inclusive approach. Here's how your mutual aid group can undertake this assessment:

Community Engagement:

Engage directly with members of the marginalized group through community meetings, focus groups, surveys, or one-on-one interviews. Create a safe and welcoming space for open dialogue and encourage participants to share their perspectives, experiences, and needs.

Cultural Competence:

Approach the assessment process with humility and sensitivity to the unique cultural, linguistic, and social context of the marginalized group. Respect diverse beliefs, practices, and customs, and ensure that assessment methods are culturally appropriate and accessible.

Participatory Approach:

Involve members of the marginalized group in all stages of the assessment process, from planning and design to data collection, analysis, and interpretation. Empower participants to shape the process, identify priorities, and co-create solutions that meet their needs.

Holistic Needs Assessment:

Take a holistic approach to assessing needs, considering physical, emotional, social, economic, and environmental dimensions of well-being. Explore a wide range of needs, including basic necessities (e.g., food, shelter, healthcare), social support, safety, education, employment, and access to services.

By including marginalized communities in discussions about issues that affect them—such as housing, healthcare, education, and employment—decision-makers can create more equitable and inclusive outcomes. A diverse range of perspectives leads to better solutions that benefit the entire community, ensuring that no one is left behind.

Recognizing Intersectionality

Intersectionality describes how various systems of oppression—such as racism, sexism, ableism, homophobia, and classism—intersect and impact people. At its core, intersectionality recognizes that people hold multiple social identities that influence each other, shaping experiences, opportunities, and challenges.

Here are some examples of intersectionality:

Race & Gender:

Black women may experience discrimination differently than white women or Black men, as they navigate the intersections of racism and sexism simultaneously. This can manifest in disparities in employment opportunities, healthcare access, and experiences of violence.

Class & Disability:

People with disabilities who come from low-income backgrounds may face compounded barriers to accessing healthcare, education, employment, and housing. They may experience intersectional discrimination due to both their disability and socioeconomic statuses.

Sexuality & Immigration Status:

LGBTQ+ immigrants may face unique challenges due to the intersection of their sexual orientation or gender identity with their immigration status. They may encounter discrimination and violence both within the immigrant community and from immigration authorities.

Religion & Ethnicity:

Muslim people who belong to marginalized ethnic groups may experience Islamophobia compounded with racism and xenophobia. They may face discrimination in employment, housing, and public spaces due to their religious identity and perceived ethnicity.

Age & Socioeconomic Status:

Older adults from low-income backgrounds may experience intersecting forms of ageism and poverty, leading to barriers in accessing healthcare, social services, and employment opportunities. They may also face discrimination in housing and healthcare.

Indigenous Identity & Gender:

Indigenous women and Two-Spirit individuals may experience intersecting forms of colonialism, sexism, and homophobia/transphobia. They may face disproportionately high rates of violence, poverty, and marginalization within both Indigenous and non-Indigenous communities.

By understanding intersectionality, your mutual aid group can better recognize the unique experiences and needs of marginalized people. This will help you avoid simplistic or reductionist approaches to social justice and work towards more inclusive and equitable solutions.

Evaluating Available Resources

Every community possesses a unique array of resources that affect the well-being of its members. From social services and healthcare facilities to educational institutions and recreational spaces, these resources are essential for ensuring that people can thrive and contribute to the community's overall success. That being said, alongside these assets, there are also gaps in access to essential services, which can disproportionately affect marginalized populations and hold communities back.

Why should your mutual aid group conduct a thorough evaluation of your resources and service gaps? Here are a few reasons:

Strategic Planning:

Knowledge of available resources informs decision-making processes. It helps groups set realistic goals, prioritize initiatives, and develop action plans that are responsive to the community's needs and assets.

Effective Resource Allocation:

By understanding the resources available, your group can allocate your time and effort more effectively. This ensures that you focus on addressing the most pressing needs in your community.

Promoting Collaboration:

Identifying available resources encourages collaboration and partnerships with local organizations, businesses, and government agencies. By working together, mutual aid groups can combine their strengths and expertise to address complex challenges more effectively.

Long-term Sustainability:

Understanding the resources available allows your group to plan for long-term sustainability. You can identify opportunities for fundraising and recruitment to ensure your initiatives continue to serve the community over time.

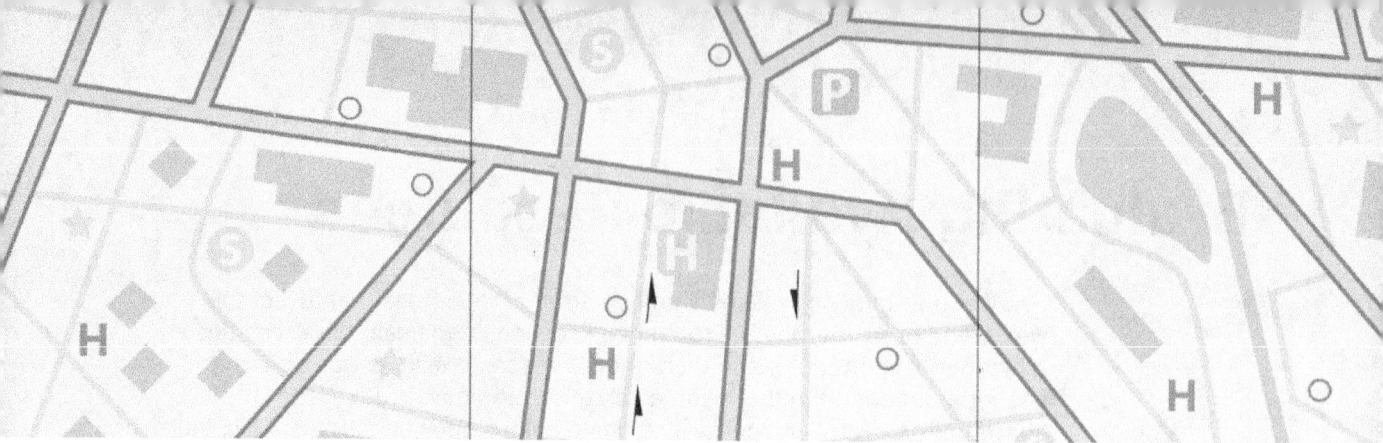

Mapping Community Assets

Mapping community assets involves identifying and visualizing the resources, strengths, and services available within a community that contribute to its well-being. This process starts with gathering information about the assets and then plotting them on a map to provide a visual overview. Some common categories of assets include:

Social Services:

Government agencies, nonprofit organizations, and community-based groups that provide social support services, such as food assistance, housing assistance, counseling services, childcare, and job support.

Healthcare Services:

Hospitals, clinics, pharmacies, and healthcare providers that offer medical, dental, mental health, and preventive care services.

Education & Learning:

Schools, libraries, educational institutions, tutoring programs, vocational training centers, and adult education classes that promote learning and skill development.

Financial Resources:

Banks, credit unions, financial counseling services, microfinance organizations, and loan programs that offer financial services, credit, and resources for economic empowerment and financial stability.

Employment & Job Training:

Job training programs, workforce development centers, vocational schools, and employment agencies that help community members acquire job skills, access employment opportunities, and achieve economic self-sufficiency.

Civic & Political Engagement:

Government agencies, elected officials, advocacy groups, community organizations, and civic institutions that engage in advocacy campaigns and coordinate efforts to address local issues and promote civic participation.

Cultural Opportunities:

Theaters, museums, art galleries, cultural centers, festivals, and events that promote cultural enrichment and artistic expression.

Transportation Services:

Public transit systems, bus routes, trains, ridesharing services, and community programs that provide transportation options.

Technology & Information Access:

Internet access points, libraries, computer labs, training programs, and digital literacy resources that promote access to information, communication tools, and technology skills.

Environmental Resources:

Parks, green spaces, community gardens, recycling programs, and organizations that promote environmental sustainability, conservation, and access to nature.

Community Centers & Recreation Facilities:

Facilities such as community centers, parks, recreational centers, sports clubs, and cultural centers that provide spaces for leisure, socialization, and activities.

Legal & Advocacy Support:

Legal aid services, pro bono clinics, advocacy organizations, and civil rights groups that provide support for community members facing legal issues.

These resources represent just a subset of the many assets that may exist within a community. Assessing and leveraging these resources can help your mutual aid group better understand and address any service gaps you find, which we discuss in detail below.

Identifying Service Gaps

Service gaps refer to discrepancies or inadequacies in the provision of essential services within a community or society. These gaps occur when the demand for certain services exceeds their availability or accessibility, resulting in unmet needs or disparities in access to resources and support.

Some examples of service gaps include:

Healthcare Access:

Limited access to affordable healthcare services, including primary care, mental health services, specialist care, and preventive services, particularly in underserved areas or among marginalized populations.

Education Disparities:

Disparities in access to quality education, including inadequate school facilities, insufficient resources for students with special needs, limited access to extracurricular activities, and disparities in academic achievement based on socioeconomic status or race/ethnicity.

Food Insecurity:

Limited access to healthy and affordable food options, including areas designated as food deserts with a lack of grocery stores or fresh produce, leading to food insecurity and malnutrition among community members.

Housing Affordability:

High rates of homelessness or housing instability due to inadequate affordable housing options, rising rents, insufficient support programs, and discrimination in housing access.

Transportation Barriers:

Limited access to reliable and affordable transportation options, including inadequate public transit services, long commute times, lack of sidewalks or bike lanes, and barriers for people with disabilities or limited mobility.

Employment Opportunities:

Limited access to quality job opportunities, vocational training programs, and workforce development initiatives, leading to high unemployment rates, underemployment, and economic insecurity.

Childcare Accessibility:

Insufficient availability of affordable and high-quality childcare options, including daycare centers, preschools, and after-school programs, creating barriers for working parents and affecting children's development and well-being.

Social Services Availability:

Limited availability of social services and support programs, including mental health counseling, substance abuse treatment, domestic violence shelters, and support services for vulnerable populations, like youth aging out of foster care or people experiencing homelessness.

Digital Divide:

Disparities in access to technology and digital resources, including limited access to high-speed internet, digital literacy programs, and computer hardware, which can hinder educational, economic, and social opportunities.

Cultural & Linguistic Accessibility:

Inadequate access to culturally competent and linguistically appropriate services, including interpretation and translation services, leading to barriers in accessing healthcare, education, legal services, and other essential resources for immigrant and minority communities.

There are several reasons why service gaps may exist, often reflecting systemic challenges, structural inequalities, and barriers to access. Some common reasons include:

Limited Funding:

Insufficient funding for public services and social programs can lead to service gaps, as resources may be allocated unevenly or inadequately to meet community needs.

Geographic Barriers:

Rural or remote communities may face challenges in accessing essential services due to geographic isolation, limited infrastructure, and transportation issues, leading to service gaps in healthcare and other areas.

Economic Disparities:

Socioeconomic disparities can contribute to service gaps, as low-income communities may lack access to quality healthcare, education, housing, and other essential services due to financial constraints and limited resources.

Market Forces:

Market forces and privatization of services may prioritize profit over community needs, leading to gaps in affordable housing, healthcare, childcare, and other essential services, particularly for marginalized populations.

Policy Decisions:

Policy decisions at the local, state, or national level can impact service provision and resource allocation, contributing to service gaps within communities.

Historical Disinvestment:

Historical disinvestment in certain communities—including redlining, segregation, and discriminatory policies—can result in long-standing service gaps and disparities in access to resources and opportunities.

Systemic Discrimination:

Discrimination based on race, ethnicity, gender, sexual orientation, disability, or other factors can result in unequal access to services and opportunities, perpetuating gaps and exacerbating social inequalities.

System Complexity:

Complex systems can create barriers, particularly for uninsured or underinsured individuals, contributing to gaps in healthcare access and outcomes.

Limited Awareness & Advocacy:

Lack of awareness about available services, eligibility criteria, and rights can prevent people from accessing needed support, highlighting the importance of community education to address service gaps.

These reasons underscore the complex interplay of factors contributing to service gaps and the importance of addressing systemic barriers to essential services. Understanding the specific needs of a community ensures that your efforts as a mutual aid group are targeted, relevant, and impactful.

Chapter Review

Mutual aid groups should conduct a comprehensive assessment to better understand the resources and needs of their community. This process begins with identifying key stakeholders and threats. Key stakeholders include local residents, leaders, government officials, businesses, nonprofits, and other groups with vested interests in the community's well-being. Assessing potential threats, such as economic instability, environmental hazards, health crises, and social inequalities helps in understanding the risks that could impact the community's future. This holistic view enables mutual aid groups to develop targeted strategies to mitigate these threats and improve community resilience.

Identifying vulnerable populations is another essential aspect of understanding community needs. Vulnerable populations—including low-income families, elderly individuals, marginalized groups, and people with disabilities—often face unique challenges and barriers to accessing resources. Understanding the specific needs of vulnerable groups allows for the creation of targeted support systems and services that address disparities and promote social justice.

Finally, evaluating community assets and service gaps is crucial for maximizing the impact of initiatives. Community assets can include physical infrastructure, local organizations, skilled individuals, and cultural resources that contribute to the community's strengths. Mapping these assets provides a visual guide that helps inform decisions. Simultaneously, identifying service gaps—areas where resources are insufficient or nonexistent—highlights critical needs that must be addressed. This dual approach ensures that development efforts are both resource-efficient and effective, targeting areas of greatest need while leveraging existing strengths.

Discussion Questions

1 What are some examples of vulnerable populations within your community, and what unique challenges do they face? What strategies can be implemented to ensure these groups are included and supported?

2 What are the most significant threats facing your community today, and how have they evolved over time? What strategies can be implemented to ensure a balanced and comprehensive approach to mitigating these threats?

IN THIS CHAPTER

>> Exploring ways to form a
foundation of trust as a group

>> How to create safe spaces that
encourage collaboration

>> Fair and transparent
decision-making, including
conflict resolution

Chapter **4**

Building Trust & Relationships

Getting a group of people together to start a mutual aid project can be particularly challenging, especially if they do not know each other beforehand. The initial unfamiliarity can lead to hesitancy, uncertainty, and a lack of cohesion. That is why it is important to invest time in building trust and developing relationships from the outset.

This chapter provides guidance on how you and your group members can successfully work together as a team by creating an inclusive and welcoming environment. We discuss how to practice active listening, how to overcome unconscious biases, and other useful strategies.

A Foundation of Trust

In any group project, trust is key to effective collaboration and achieving shared objectives. Trust is not something that develops overnight; rather, it is cultivated through consistent actions and behaviors that demonstrate reliability, integrity, and respect for one another. By prioritizing open communication and accountability, mutual aid groups can build trust with their members, creating a supportive environment where everyone feels empowered to contribute their best efforts.

To establish trust, every mutual aid group should make a conscious effort to engage in the following 4 behaviors:

Communicate Openly & Transparently:

By actively listening to your teammates' perspectives, concerns, and ideas, you show that their input is valued and respected. Encourage open dialogue and create a safe space where everyone feels comfortable expressing themselves without fear of judgment or criticism.

Demonstrate Reliability:

When you consistently follow through on your commitments, meet deadlines, and deliver high-quality work, you demonstrate reliability and dependability to your teammates. This reliability creates a sense of assurance among group members, as they know that they can count on you to contribute effectively to the project's success. Conversely, failing to uphold your responsibilities or being inconsistent in your actions can erode trust and undermine team cohesion.

Show Mutual Respect:

Treat your teammates with dignity, kindness, and empathy, regardless of differences in opinions, backgrounds, or working styles. Acknowledge and appreciate their contributions, expertise, and perspectives—recognizing the value that each member brings to the team. When everyone feels respected and valued for their unique strengths and abilities, it creates a sense of belonging and camaraderie within the group, strengthening trust and collaboration.

Take Ownership:

Take responsibility for mistakes or shortcomings, and be willing to learn and grow from feedback and constructive criticism. When team members hold themselves accountable and demonstrate a commitment to continuous improvement, it builds credibility and trustworthiness, enhancing team dynamics and cohesion. Show support and encouragement for your teammates' growth and development, offering assistance and guidance when needed.

Reliability & Accountability

Reliability refers to the quality of being trustworthy, consistent, and dependable. In the context of a mutual aid group, reliability means that members can rely on each other to fulfill their commitments, meet deadlines, and contribute effectively to the group's goals and activities.

People who are reliable demonstrate a track record of following through on their promises and obligations, thereby building trust and confidence with others. Reliability is essential for maintaining the integrity and effectiveness of mutual aid efforts, ensuring that members can depend on each other for support and collaboration.

Accountability refers to the obligation or willingness of people to accept responsibility for their actions, decisions, and commitments. In the context of a mutual aid group, this involves holding members accountable for fulfilling their roles, meeting expectations, and contributing to the group's objectives. This may include keeping accurate records, communicating openly and transparently, and addressing any issues or concerns that arise in a timely manner.

Accountability builds trust and transparency within the group, ensuring that everyone is held to the same standards and that resources are managed effectively. It also encourages a culture of integrity, where members are accountable not only to themselves but also to each other and the larger community.

Here are some ways these qualities can be demonstrated:

Consistency:

Members should consistently fulfill their commitments and obligations to the group. Whether it's attending meetings, completing assigned tasks, or contributing resources, reliability ensures that everyone can depend on each other to follow through on their responsibilities.

Transparency:

Open communication and transparency regarding group decisions, actions, and finances demonstrates accountability. Members should be informed about the group's activities, decision-making processes, and the allocation of resources to build trust and confidence in their operations.

Setting clear expectations:

Establishing clear expectations and roles for each member helps prevent misunderstandings and ensures that everyone understands their responsibilities. Clear guidelines for participation, communication channels, and decision-making procedures contribute to a productive group dynamic.

Tracking progress:

Implement systems for tracking and monitoring progress on group projects, tasks, and goals. Regularly reviewing progress reports and evaluating outcomes allow members to assess their contributions and hold themselves and others accountable for meeting objectives.

Admitting mistakes:

Encouraging a culture of accountability includes acknowledging and addressing mistakes or shortcomings openly and constructively. When errors occur, members should take responsibility, learn from the experience, and work collaboratively to rectify the situation and prevent similar issues in the future.

Feedback mechanisms:

Establish mechanisms for providing and receiving feedback within the group to address concerns, identify areas for improvement, and celebrate successes. Constructive feedback encourages a culture of continuous learning, growth, and accountability among members.

Active Listening

Active listening is more than just hearing words; it involves a conscious effort to fully understand, interpret, and respond to what is being communicated. In the context of mutual aid groups, active listening goes beyond a passive reception of information. It encompasses a genuine engagement with the thoughts, emotions, and needs expressed by others.

When people feel heard and understood, a sense of trust and rapport develops. In mutual aid groups where members may be facing diverse challenges, cultivating empathy and a supportive environment will create enduring relationships that sustain community well-being over time.

Here are some ways that a group can promote active listening:

Set the Tone:

Create a culture within the group that values and prioritizes hearing and respecting everyone's perspectives and experiences.

Establish Ground Rules:

Set clear guidelines for communication during group discussions. Encourage turn-taking, limit interruptions, and create a safe space where everyone feels comfortable expressing themselves without judgment.

Lead by Example:

Leaders and facilitators should model active listening behaviors in group interactions. Demonstrate attentive listening, maintain eye contact, and provide verbal and non-verbal cues to show engagement and understanding.

Encourage Open-ended Questions:

Instead of yes/no questions, promote open-ended inquiries that invite deeper reflection and sharing. These questions encourage more meaningful dialogue and help uncover underlying issues or concerns.

Use Reflective Techniques:

Encourage members to reflect back what they've heard to ensure they understand. Paraphrase or summarize others' statements before responding, which demonstrates active listening and validates their contributions.

Practice Empathy:

Encourage members to put themselves in others' shoes and consider their perspectives and feelings. Validate emotions and experiences without judgment, showing empathy and understanding.

Provide Feedback:

Offer constructive feedback to group members on their listening skills. Highlight examples of effective listening and suggest areas for improvement, creating a culture of continuous learning and growth.

Create Space for Silence:

Allow moments of silence during discussions to give members time to process information and formulate their thoughts. Silence can be a powerful tool for reflection and deeper understanding.

Evaluate & Reflect:

Periodically assess the group's listening practices and effectiveness. Solicit feedback from members on their experiences and identify areas for improvement to refine the group's communication processes.

Provide Training:

Offer workshops or training sessions on active listening techniques. Teach group members skills such as paraphrasing, summarizing, and asking clarifying questions to enhance their listening abilities.

Diversity, Equity & Inclusion

 A mutual aid group should prioritize diversity, equity, and inclusion (DEI) to ensure that all members of the community feel represented, respected, and supported. Practicing these principles helps break down barriers that often marginalize certain groups, ensuring that the aid provided truly reaches everyone in need, not just those with the most access or privilege. Here's what each term encompasses:

Diversity: refers to the variety of identities, perspectives, and experiences represented within a group. This includes differences in race, ethnicity, gender, sexual orientation, age, ability, religion, socioeconomic status, cultural background, and more. Embracing diversity means recognizing and celebrating these differences as valuable assets that contribute to a richer, more vibrant community.

Equity: involves ensuring fair treatment, access, and opportunities for all people, regardless of their background or identity. It recognizes that different groups may face systemic barriers and strives to address disparities by providing resources, support, and accommodations to level the playing field. Equity seeks to create inclusive environments where everyone has the support and resources they need to succeed.

Inclusion: refers to the practice of actively valuing, respecting, and involving all people within a group or organization. It goes beyond mere representation to create environments where everyone feels welcome, heard, and valued. Inclusive spaces create a sense of belonging, trust, and collaboration, where people can fully participate, contribute their perspectives, and thrive.

By embracing diverse perspectives and actively working to include voices from different backgrounds, experiences, and identities, mutual aid groups can create more equitable systems of support that address the specific needs of all community members.

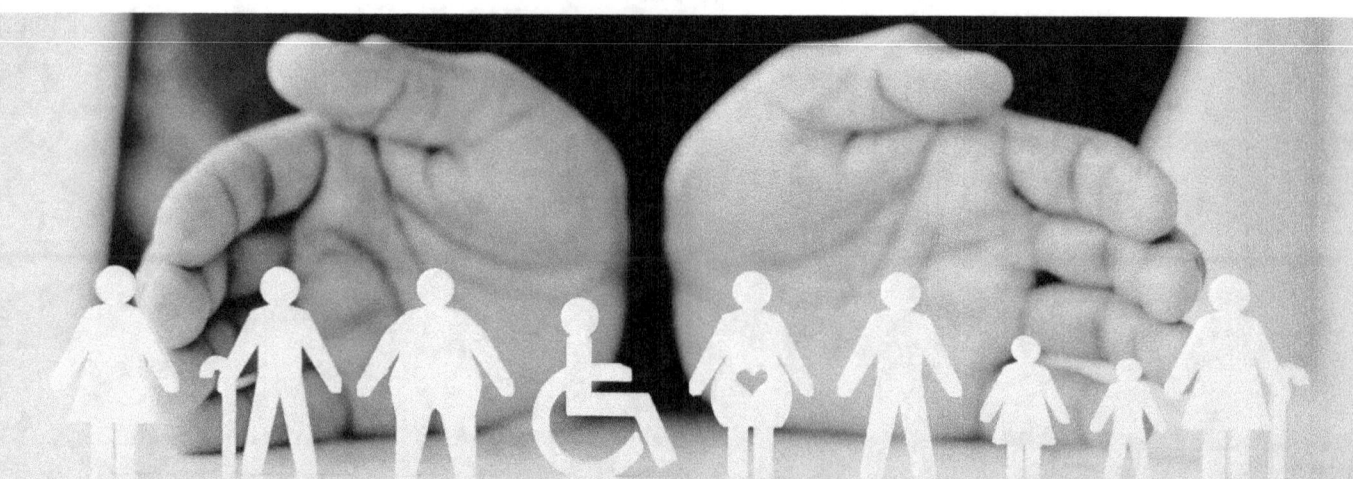

Creating Safe Spaces

A **safe space** is an environment where people feel comfortable expressing themselves authentically, without fear of judgment, discrimination, or harassment. It is a space that encourages inclusivity, respect, and empathy, allowing people to share their thoughts, feelings, and experiences openly and honestly.

Safe spaces can be physical locations—such as community centers, support groups, or classrooms—as well as virtual spaces, like online forums or social media groups. The concept of safe spaces originated as a response to the need for marginalized groups—such as LGBTQ+ individuals, people of color, or survivors of trauma—to have spaces where they could seek support, solidarity, and validation without facing prejudice or hostility.

By establishing safe spaces, mutual aid groups enable members to engage authentically, build meaningful connections, and work together effectively towards common goals, ultimately strengthening the group's capacity to address community needs and promote positive social change.

Here are a few key strategies to create safe spaces in mutual aid groups:

Establish Clear Guidelines:

Clearly outline and communicate guidelines for respectful and inclusive behavior within the group. This can include expectations around language use, active listening, and how to handle differing perspectives. Ensure that these guidelines are visible and easily accessible to all members.

Provide Training on Inclusivity:

Offer training sessions or workshops on inclusivity to educate members about the importance of creating a safe and welcoming environment. Address topics such as unconscious biases, cultural competence, and respectful communication. Training can enhance awareness and create a shared understanding of the value of diversity.

Address Microaggressions Promptly:

Act swiftly to address any instances of microaggressions or disrespectful behavior within the group. Establish a process for reporting and addressing such incidents, and make it clear that such behaviors will not be tolerated. This ensures a swift response to maintain a safe environment.

Create Confidential Spaces:

Establish confidential channels for people to share personal experiences, challenges, or concerns privately. This can be through one-on-one conversations with organizers or designated members. Confidential spaces provide an avenue for people who may not feel comfortable sharing openly in a group setting.

Implement Anti-Discrimination Policies:

Develop and communicate clear anti-discrimination policies within the group. These policies should explicitly state the group's commitment to fostering an environment free from discrimination based on race, gender, sexual orientation, religion, or any other protected characteristic. Ensure that consequences for violating these policies are known and enforced.

Promote Accessibility:

Ensure that all activities, events, and information are accessible to people with diverse needs. This includes physical accessibility, language accessibility, and accommodating different communication styles. Accessibility contributes to a sense of inclusivity and safety for all members.

Inclusive Language

Language plays a powerful role in shaping group dynamics and perceptions, and using **inclusive language** helps create an environment where people from diverse backgrounds feel valued and respected. When members hear themselves represented in the language used within the group, they are more likely to feel seen, heard, and understood, leading to stronger relationships and a greater sense of community.

Inclusive language also promotes equity and justice by avoiding language that reinforces stereotypes, biases, or discrimination. By choosing words and phrases that are inclusive and affirming of all identities, mutual aid groups can help dismantle barriers and create a safe space for everyone.

Here are some examples of using inclusive language in mutual aid groups:

1. Instead of using gender-specific terms like "guys" or "ladies," use gender-neutral alternatives like "everyone," "folks," or "friends."

2. Avoid assumptions about marital status or family structure by using terms like "partner" or "significant other" instead of "husband," or "wife."

3. Use person-first language to emphasize individuals' humanity over their conditions or identities. For example, say "person with a disability" instead of "disabled person."

4. Be mindful of cultural and religious diversity by using inclusive greetings and expressions that are respectful of different traditions and beliefs.

5. Avoid ableist language that reinforces negative stereotypes or assumptions about people with disabilities. For example, instead of saying "paralyzed with fear" or "crippled by doubt," use alternatives like "overwhelmed with fear" or "struggling with doubt."

6. Respect people's preferred pronouns and gender identities by asking and using the correct pronouns when addressing or referring to them.

7. Acknowledge and celebrate diversity by using inclusive terms that encompass a wide range of identities and experiences, such as "people of color," "LGBTQ+ community," or "neurodiverse individuals."

8. Avoid language that perpetuates racial stereotypes or biases and instead use terms that promote racial equity and justice.

Cultural Competence

One important component of mutual aid is **cultural competence,** which is the ability of individuals and organizations to effectively interact, work, and engage with people from diverse cultural backgrounds. It involves understanding, respecting, and appropriately responding to the cultural differences and similarities within, among, and between groups. This competence is developed through an ongoing process of learning about other cultures and being introspective about one's own cultural identity, which helps in understanding personal biases and perspectives.

Being culturally competent means having:

Awareness of one's own cultural worldview:

Recognizing one's own beliefs, values, and biases that are influenced by one's culture.

Knowledge of different cultural practices and worldviews:

Gaining factual information about the customs, values, beliefs, and practices of cultures different from one's own.

Skills in communication and interaction across cultures:

Being able to effectively communicate and interact with people across different cultures, which includes using appropriate language, non-verbal cues, and actively listening to understand others' perspectives.

Attitudes towards cultural differences:

Cultivating a positive attitude towards cultural differences, showing respect and openness to learn from others, and avoiding stereotyping.

Policy-making that reflects an understanding of diversity:

In organizational contexts, implementing practices and policies that are inclusive and responsive to the diverse groups within the community or organization.

Unconscious Bias

An **unconscious bias** is an automatic, ingrained stereotype or prejudice that individuals hold about certain groups of people. These biases can influence perceptions, attitudes, and behaviors in subtle ways, often without us being aware of them. In a mutual aid group, unconscious biases can manifest in various forms, such as assumptions about people's abilities, backgrounds, or worthiness of assistance.

Some common examples of unconscious bias include:

 Affinity Bias: Preferring or favoring people who share similar backgrounds, experiences, or interests as oneself. This bias can lead to favoritism and exclusion of those who are perceived as different.

 Confirmation Bias: Seeking out or interpreting information in a way that confirms pre-existing beliefs or stereotypes. This can lead to overlooking evidence that contradicts one's beliefs and reinforcing existing biases.

 Halo Effect: Forming a positive impression of someone based on one favorable attribute or characteristic, and extending that perception to other unrelated traits. This bias can lead to overestimating a person's abilities or qualities based on limited information.

 **Implicit Association:** Making unconscious associations between certain groups of people and specific traits or stereotypes. For example, associating women with nurturing or men with leadership roles, without conscious awareness.

 In-Group Bias: Favoring members of one's own social or identity group over those who are perceived as outsiders or belonging to different groups. This bias can lead to exclusionary behavior and unequal treatment of others.

 Attribution Bias: Making assumptions about the causes of someone's behavior based on their group membership rather than individual characteristics or circumstances. For example, attributing success to innate talent rather than effort or attributing failure to external factors rather than personal responsibility.

 Beauty Bias: Favoring people who are perceived as physically attractive or conforming to societal standards of beauty. This bias can lead to overlooking the abilities or contributions of people who do not fit these standards.

Everyone is susceptible to unconscious biases, and actively addressing them requires self-awareness, reflection, and ongoing effort to challenge and mitigate their impact.

To overcome unconscious biases in a mutual aid group, members can:

Raise Awareness:

Encourage members to reflect on their own biases and understand how they may impact their interactions with others. Provide education and training on unconscious bias to increase awareness and promote self-reflection.

Provide Feedback & Accountability:

Offer constructive feedback to members when biased behaviors or language are observed. Hold people accountable for their actions and encourage them to take responsibility for addressing and rectifying any harm caused by their biases.

Fair & Transparent Decision-making

Transparency in decision-making refers to the openness and clarity with which decisions are communicated and executed. In the context of mutual aid groups, transparency extends beyond merely sharing outcomes; it involves actively involving community members in the decision-making process, ensuring that the rationale, considerations, and implications are clear and accessible.

When members are informed about the decision-making process, they develop confidence in the group's intentions and actions. Transparency goes hand in hand with accountability. When processes are transparent, there is a clear line of responsibility. People within the mutual aid group and the broader community can understand who is accountable for specific decisions. This creates a culture of responsibility and ensures that decisions align with collective goals.

Here are some examples of how transparency plays a role in mutual aid groups:

Budgetary Decisions:

Transparent decision-making in budget allocation ensures that members are aware of how resources are distributed. This transparency is crucial for building trust and ensuring that financial decisions align with priorities and needs.

Project Planning & Implementation:

Transparent communication during the planning and implementation of mutual aid projects involves actively involving the group in decision-making. This can include decisions about project goals, timelines, and resource allocation. Community input ensures that projects resonate with the everyone's aspirations and are effectively implemented.

Implementing fair and transparent processes within a mutual aid group is crucial for maintaining trust. Here are several strategies that you can put into practice to keep everyone on the same page:

Consensus-Building:

Adopt a consensus approach to decision-making, where all members have a voice, and decisions are made only when there is broad agreement. This method ensures that all perspectives are considered and that no single person or small group dominates the decision-making process.

Clear Procedures:

Establish clear, documented procedures for how decisions are made, who makes them, and under what circumstances. Make these procedures accessible to all members to ensure everyone understands how their input will be incorporated into the group's decision-making process.

Regular Meetings:

Hold regular meetings with set agendas and provide minutes of each meeting to all members. This practice not only keeps members informed but also provides a structured opportunity for everyone to contribute to discussions and decision-making.

Honest Communication:

Communicate openly with all group members about decisions and the rationale behind them. This includes sharing both successes and challenges, as well as any changes in plans or strategies.

Diverse Representation:

Ensure that decision-making bodies within the group (like committees or leadership teams) are representative of the community's diversity in terms of demographics, expertise, and experience. This diversity helps to bring multiple viewpoints to the table, enriching the decision-making process.

Feedback Mechanisms:

Implement mechanisms for feedback, both structured and informal. Encourage members to express their views on decisions and the decision-making process, and use this feedback to make improvements.

Accountability Measures:

Set up accountability measures where decisions and actions are regularly reviewed, and leaders or decision-makers are held accountable to the other members. This could involve regular reporting, performance reviews, or other forms of evaluation.

Conflict Resolution

In any group setting, disagreements will likely occur due to differing perspectives, experiences, and priorities among members. However, it is crucial to approach these disagreements with a mindset focused on finding constructive solutions rather than escalating conflicts.

Conflict resolution refers to the process of addressing and resolving disagreements or disputes between people in a peaceful and constructive manner. It involves identifying the underlying issues, communicating effectively, and finding mutually acceptable solutions to resolve the conflict.

Mutual aid groups can employ various conflict resolution techniques to address disagreements and maintain harmony. Some effective techniques include:

Establishing ground rules:

Set clear guidelines for communication and behavior within the group to prevent conflicts from escalating. Ground rules may include respecting diverse opinions, refraining from personal attacks, and adhering to agreed-upon decision-making processes.

Collaborative problem-solving:

Encourage members to approach conflicts as opportunities to work together toward finding solutions that benefit everyone involved. Brainstorming ideas, considering different viewpoints, and exploring compromises can lead to innovative and inclusive outcomes.

Active listening:

Encourage members to listen attentively to each other's perspectives without interrupting or passing judgment. This demonstrates understanding and empathy, laying the groundwork for resolving conflicts.

Mediation:

Designate a neutral third party or a team of mediators within the group to facilitate discussions between conflicting parties. Mediators help identify common ground, clarify misunderstandings, and guide members toward mutually acceptable solutions.

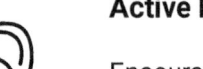

Taking breaks:

If tensions run high during discussions, suggest taking a short break to allow members to cool off and reflect on their emotions. Returning to the conversation with a fresh perspective can facilitate more productive dialogue.

By implementing these conflict resolution techniques, mutual aid groups can navigate disagreements constructively, promote cohesion among members, and maintain their focus on serving the community's needs.

Conflicts of Interest

Conflicts of interest in a mutual aid group can arise when individual members have interests or obligations that potentially interfere with the group's goals or the fair and impartial conduct of its activities. When conflicts of interest are left unaddressed, they can lead to biased decision-making, reduced transparency, and a loss of trust among members and the broader community.

By proactively identifying and managing these conflicts, the group ensures that all actions and decisions are made with the community's best interests in mind. This creates a culture of fairness and accountability.

Here are some scenarios where conflicts of interest might occur:

Personal Gain:

A member might make decisions that benefit them financially or professionally at the expense of the group's objectives. For example, a member might advocate for the group to purchase goods or services from a business they own or have a stake in, rather than seeking the best or most cost-effective option available.

Family & Friends:

Conflicts of interest can occur when members prioritize the needs and interests of family members or friends over the needs of the group. This might involve allocating resources or opportunities in a way that favors personal connections rather than based on need or merit.

Employment Conflicts:

Members who are employed by organizations that have a stake in the mutual aid group's activities might face conflicts between their professional responsibilities and their role in the group. For example, a member who works for a local government might have conflicting duties regarding resource allocation or policy decisions that affect the group.

Multiple Roles:

Members who serve in multiple roles within the community may encounter situations where their responsibilities conflict. For instance, a member who also serves on a local nonprofit board might face conflicts in deciding how to distribute resources or support between the two organizations.

Confidential Information:

Members who have access to confidential or proprietary information through their roles in the mutual aid group or their professional lives may face conflicts if they are tempted to use that information for personal gain or to benefit another organization or individual improperly.

Political or Ideological Beliefs:

Conflicts can also arise when members' personal political or ideological beliefs influence their decisions and actions within the group, potentially skewing priorities and activities away from the group's agreed-upon goals.

To avoid conflicts of interest in a mutual aid group, it is essential to establish clear guidelines and practices from the outset. Create a code of conduct (see Chapter 6) that explicitly outlines the procedures for disclosure. Require all members to openly declare any potential conflicts at the beginning of meetings or when relevant situations arise.

Maintaining Confidentiality

Confidentiality refers to the practice of keeping sensitive information private and only sharing it with authorized individuals. It ensures that personal details, conversations, or data shared in trust are not disclosed without permission.

Consider this scenario. A mutual aid group is helping a community member who is facing eviction. If the individual shares personal financial details, housing information, or reasons for their eviction, the group must ensure this information is kept private to protect the person's dignity and security. Sharing sensitive details without consent could lead to stigma, discrimination, or further hardship for them.

Here are categories of information that are typically kept confidential:

Personal Identifiable Information (PII):

This includes any data that can be used on its own or with other information to identify, contact, or locate a single person. Examples include names, addresses, phone numbers, email addresses, social security numbers, and any other personal details that can be linked to a specific individual.

Legal Matters:

Any information related to legal issues, including immigration status, involvement in legal proceedings, or interactions with law enforcement.

Health Information:

Any information pertaining to the medical history, mental or physical condition, or medical treatments or diagnoses must be kept confidential. This also includes any discussions around mental health support that members might seek or provide within the group.

Financial Information:

Details about an person's financial status, including their income, employment details, financial contributions to the group, bank account details, or any financial assistance they receive or need.

Personal Circumstances:

Sensitive details about peoples' personal lives, including family issues, housing situations, relationship status, or any other personal struggles that members might disclose within the safety of the group.

Meeting Details:

Conversations and minutes from meetings that may contain sensitive discussions or disclose the above types of information. Keeping these details private ensures that members can speak freely without concern that their words will be shared outside the group.

Communications:

Private correspondence between members or discussions that take place in confidence should also be treated as confidential. This includes emails, direct messages, and any other form of communication that is not meant for the public or broader group consumption.

Respecting and safeguarding this information not only builds trust and encourages participation but also aligns with legal standards and ethical practices. Ensuring confidentiality in these areas is critical to the integrity and effectiveness of mutual aid efforts, creating an environment where members feel secure and supported.

Chapter Review

Establishing a foundation of trust begins with creating an environment where all members feel valued and respected. This involves active listening, showing empathy, and being consistent in words and actions. Trust is built over time through reliable behavior, mutual respect, and a genuine commitment to the group's goals. Encouraging open communication and honesty allows members to express their ideas, concerns, and needs without fear of judgment.

Creating a safe space is crucial for nurturing trust and relationships within the group. Safe spaces ensure that all members feel comfortable sharing their thoughts and experiences. This involves setting clear guidelines for respectful communication, actively addressing any forms of discrimination or bias, and maintaining confidentiality when necessary. By establishing an inclusive atmosphere, the group can support diverse perspectives and create a sense of belonging for all members.

Fair and transparent decision-making is another key aspect of building trust. When decisions are made openly, members feel more invested and confident in the group's direction. This involves clearly communicating the decision-making process, seeking input from all members, and ensuring that everyone has an opportunity to participate. Transparency in decision-making helps to prevent misunderstandings and reduces the potential for conflicts.

Discussion Questions

1 Think about a time when someone else's biases impacted your participation in a group or project. How did you navigate the situation?

2 How can a mutual aid group balance the need for open, inclusive participation with the practicalities of efficient decision-making? What methods can be employed to ensure that all voices are heard without slowing down the group's progress?

Chapter **5**

Organizing a Mutual Aid Group

Joining or starting a mutual aid group offers many practical and emotional benefits. You are likely to experience a profound sense of connection and community as you address shared challenges and support one another. It's a chance to connect with others who share your values and to work together toward making a real impact in people's lives.

Whether you're organizing food drives, offering rides, or providing resources in times of crisis, mutual aid creates a sense of solidarity and common purpose. In this chapter, we dive into the steps you can take to get started.

Before You Begin

Joining or starting a mutual aid group can be driven by a complex interplay of emotions—including, but not limited to, empathy, solidarity, or possibly, isolation—all rooted in a desire to support others and receive support in return. Witnessing or experiencing hardship can cause people to seek out mutual aid groups, as well as frustration or even rage toward governments and systemic issues. These feelings not only motivate some to take action, but they also serve as the foundation for building strong, inclusive, and resilient mutual aid networks that prioritize collective well-being.

Before joining or starting a mutual aid group, it is a good idea to ask yourself a series of reflective questions to assess your readiness, commitment, and alignment with a group's goals and values. Here are some to consider:

What are my motivations for joining or starting a mutual aid group?

Reflect on your reasons for wanting to participate in mutual aid efforts. Are you driven by a desire to support your community, address specific needs, or promote social justice? How are your own personal needs not being met by the community?

What skills, resources, and experiences can I contribute to the group?

Assess your strengths, talents, and resources that you can bring to the mutual aid group. Consider how your unique skills and experiences can complement those of other group members and contribute to the collective effort.

Am I willing to commit time and effort to the group's activities?

Consider the level of time and energy you are able and willing to dedicate to projects. Mutual aid groups often require active participation and engagement, including attending meetings, volunteering, and contributing to ongoing efforts.

What are my values and principles?

Reflect on what matters most to you and what guides your decisions and actions. Take time to explore your beliefs, priorities, and aspirations, and consider how they influence your behavior and relationships.

Am I comfortable collaborating with others and sharing responsibilities?

Assess your ability to work collaboratively with others and share responsibilities. Mutual aid efforts require teamwork and communication.

What are my expectations for the group, and are they realistic?

Manage your expectations by considering what you hope to achieve through your involvement. Be realistic about what the group can accomplish and understand that progress may take time and effort.

How do I handle conflict and disagreement?

Reflect on your conflict resolution skills and ability to navigate disagreements constructively within a team setting. Mutual aid groups may encounter challenges or disagreements, and it is important to be able to address conflicts respectfully and collaboratively.

Am I open to learning and growth?

You'll need to maintain an open mindset and be willing to learn from others, adapt to new ideas and perspectives, and grow personally and professionally through your involvement in the mutual aid group.

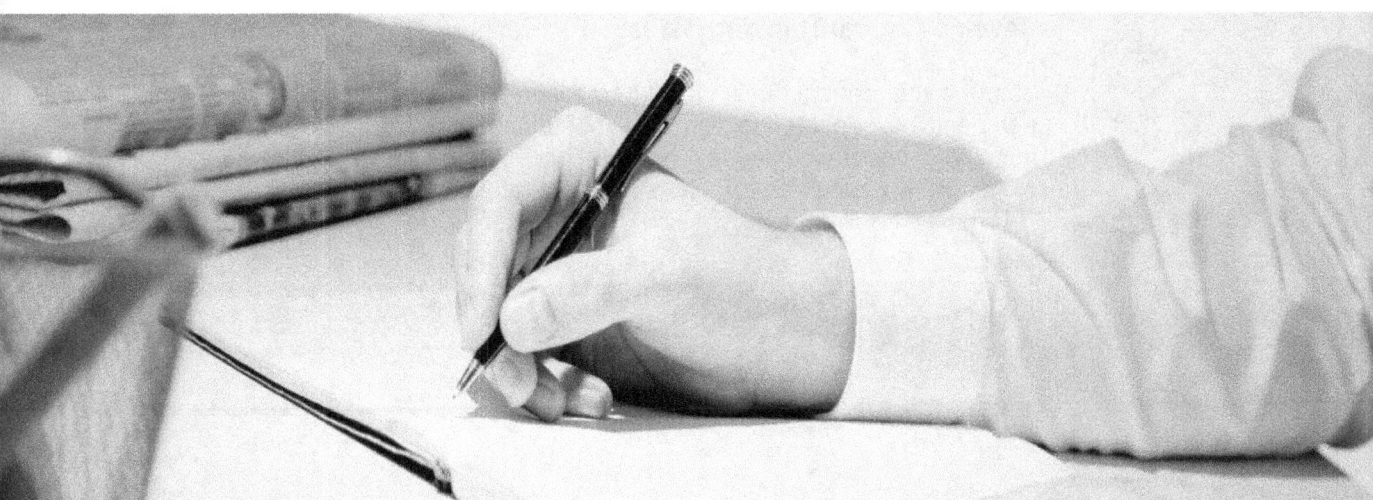

Adopting a Constructive Mindset

When getting involved in mutual aid, it is crucial not only to identify the challenges and issues within a community but also to adopt a constructive mindset that enables you to offer creative solutions. Merely pointing out problems without seeking solutions can lead to feelings of helplessness and stagnation. By cultivating a constructive mindset, group members can approach challenges with optimism and resilience, viewing them as opportunities for growth.

This mindset encourages collaboration, creativity, and resourcefulness, empowering participants to explore new ideas and approaches to address community needs. Rather than becoming overwhelmed by obstacles, a constructive mindset enables members to work together to devise practical, effective, and sustainable solutions.

Here are some strategies to achieve a constructive mindset:

Seek Creative Solutions:

Approach problems with creativity and innovation by exploring alternative options, brainstorming ideas, and thinking outside the box. Encourage experimentation and be open to trying new strategies or methods to achieve desired outcomes.

Define Goals & Priorities:

Clearly define your goals and priorities to provide clarity and direction when faced with challenges. Break down large goals into smaller, actionable steps and prioritize tasks based on their importance and impact.

Develop Critical Thinking Skills:

Sharpen your critical thinking skills by evaluating problems from multiple perspectives, considering potential consequences and implications, and identifying underlying causes. Analyze information objectively, question assumptions, and seek evidence-based solutions.

Be Open to Growth:

Cultivate a belief that challenges are opportunities for growth and learning rather than insurmountable obstacles. Embrace setbacks as learning experiences and focus on developing skills, knowledge, and resilience.

Take Initiative:

Take proactive steps to address challenges rather than waiting for solutions to come to you. Always work toward identifying problems, initiating action, and seeking out resources, support, and expertise as needed.

Collaborate & Communicate:

Foster collaboration and communication with others to leverage diverse perspectives, expertise, and resources in solving problems. Work cooperatively with team members, seek feedback and input, and communicate openly and transparently to ensure everyone is aligned and working towards common goals.

Researching Existing Groups

Before deciding to initiate a mutual aid group, it is wise to conduct thorough research on existing groups to understand the landscape of similar efforts in your community or broader area. By understanding existing initiatives, you can identify potential gaps or opportunities for collaboration, ensuring that your efforts complement rather than duplicate existing work. Researching existing groups also provides valuable insights into best practices, resources, and networks that can inform the development of your own mutual aid initiative should you choose to go that route.

Keep in mind that the grassroots nature of mutual aid groups often means they operate at a local level and may not always have a significant online presence or extensive documentation. As community-led initiatives, these groups may rely on informal networks, word-of-mouth communication, and in-person interactions to coordinate activities and support community members. This informal approach can make it challenging to find information about mutual aid groups through traditional research methods.

Here are some ways you can go about researching existing mutual aid groups:

Online Search:

Start by conducting an online search using search engines like Google or social media platforms like Facebook, X, Instagram, or TikTok. Use keywords such as "mutual aid [your city or region]" to find relevant groups. Explore community forums, neighborhood groups, and local news websites for information on mutual aid efforts.

Community Directories:

Check community directories, nonprofit organizations, or local government websites for listings of mutual aid groups and grassroots organizations in your area. Some cities or regions may have directories specifically focused on community resources and support networks.

Community Centers & Libraries:

Visit local community centers, libraries, or civic organizations to inquire about mutual aid initiatives operating in your area. Staff members may have information about groups and resources available to support residents in times of need.

Word of Mouth:

Reach out to friends, family members, neighbors, and colleagues to ask if they are aware of any mutual aid groups or networks in the community. Personal connections can often lead to valuable insights and recommendations.

Attend Community Events:

Attend community events, rallies, or meetings where mutual aid groups or organizers may be present. Engaging with community members and participating in local gatherings can provide opportunities to learn about mutual aid efforts and connect with like-minded people.

How to Know if a Mutual Aid Group Is a Good Fit

Researching existing mutual aid groups and determining if they are a good fit involves several steps to ensure alignment with your values, interests, and community needs.

Here's how you can approach this process:

Review Mission & Values:

Once you have identified potential groups, review their mission statements, values, and objectives. Pay attention to the group's goals, principles, and approach to mutual aid. Consider whether their mission aligns with your own values and interests, and whether their focus areas match the needs of your community.

Assess Activities & Projects:

Explore the activities and projects that the group is involved in. Look for information about past and ongoing initiatives, events, and campaigns. Consider whether the group's projects address issues that are meaningful to you and resonate with your desire to contribute to community solidarity and support.

Evaluate Organizational Structure:

Assess the group's organizational structure, decision-making processes, and membership guidelines. Understand how the group operates, how decisions are made, and how members are involved in planning and implementation. Consider whether the group's structure and processes align with your preferences and comfort level.

Engage with Members:

Talk with current members of the mutual aid group to learn more about their experiences and perspectives. Attend group meetings, events, or activities to get a sense of the group dynamics and culture. Ask questions, share your interests, and listen to the experiences of others to gauge whether the group is a good fit for you.

Consider Accessibility & Inclusivity:

Evaluate the accessibility and inclusivity of the group, including factors such as meeting locations, language accessibility, and accommodation for diverse needs. Consider whether the group fosters a welcoming and inclusive environment where all members feel valued and respected.

Assess Personal Commitment:

Finally, assess your own level of commitment and capacity to engage with the group. Consider factors such as time availability, skills and expertise, and personal boundaries. Determine whether you are able to contribute meaningfully to the group's activities and goals while also prioritizing your well-being and other responsibilities.

When deciding if a mutual aid group is a good fit for you, it's important to give people a chance and to embrace the diversity within the group. A good group will include members from different backgrounds and life experiences—people you might not interact with in your normal circles. This diversity can enrich the group's perspectives and approaches to problem-solving. By being open to forming connections with people who are different, you not only broaden your own understanding and empathy but also you contribute to a more inclusive and cohesive group environment.

However, if your research shows that no mutual aid groups currently exist in your community or the ones that do exist are not a good fit for you, then you should consider starting one of your own. Read on!

Becoming an Organizer/Facilitator

An **organizer** is someone who coordinates and mobilizes groups toward achieving common goals, typically within social, political, or professional contexts. Organizers are key in planning activities, rallying support, and building sustainable systems that encourage participation and collective action. They often play a crucial role in initiating campaigns, setting agendas, and facilitating communication among stakeholders.

An organizer's responsibilities include identifying and addressing the needs of the community, strategizing on action plans, and managing resources effectively to ensure that objectives are met. They are instrumental in creating cohesion and motivating people to contribute to a cause.

We discussed in Chapter 2 how decentralized horizontal leadership in mutual aid groups ensures community initiatives do not fall victim to the same problems that come with rigid hierarchies and their concentration of power at the top. When leadership is shared by all members, everyone has equal power. Because of this, if you decide to organize your own mutual aid group, it would be wise to think of yourself more as a facilitator instead of the boss who calls all the shots.

A **facilitator** is someone who guides a group of people to understand their common objectives and assists them in planning how to achieve these objectives. In doing so, this person enables smoother interactions among group members, often by encouraging participation, fostering a conducive environment for dialogue, and managing the flow of conversation to ensure productive outcomes. Their main goal is to help participants reach a consensus or actionable solution in a cooperative and harmonious manner.

Here are some additional responsibilities you should expect when you initiate your own mutual aid group:

Leadership & Vision Setting:

As an organizer, you will be responsible for setting the vision and direction of the group. This involves articulating clear goals, defining the group's purpose, and establishing how it will operate. You'll need to inspire and motivate others to join and contribute to the group's objectives.

Community Engagement:

You will need to actively engage with community members to understand their needs, concerns, and how best the group can serve them. This might involve outreach activities, attending community events, and facilitating open dialogues.

Resource Management:

Organizers must manage both human and material resources. This includes coordinating volunteers, overseeing the distribution of aid, and ensuring that resources such as food, clothing, or funding are obtained and used efficiently. Financial transparency and accountability are also crucial in maintaining trust within the group and the broader community.

Conflict Resolution:

In any group dynamic, conflicts can arise. As an organizer, you will need skills in mediation and conflict resolution to handle disagreements within the group effectively and maintain a cooperative atmosphere. This includes being impartial and providing a safe space for members to express concerns.

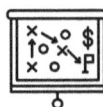

Logistics & Planning:

Organizing events, meetings, and aid distributions requires careful planning and logistical management. This includes scheduling, venue selection, ensuring accessibility, and possibly coordinating with other organizations or stakeholders.

Communication:

You will need to facilitate clear and open communication channels within the group and ensure that information is disseminated effectively to all members and stakeholders. This might involve regular meetings, email updates, social media management, and creating promotional materials.

Education & Training:

Providing training and educational resources to volunteers can be vital, especially if your group deals with specific issues such as healthcare, legal aid, or disaster response. It is important to ensure that all members are well-prepared and informed.

Sustainability & Growth:

Long-term planning is essential for the sustainability of the group. This includes developing strategies for funding, expanding community impact, and possibly formalizing the structure of the group if it grows significantly.

———————————

Being an organizer of a mutual aid group requires a broad skill set and a high level of commitment, but it can also be incredibly rewarding as it provides direct, meaningful impact within your community.

Recruiting Members

A **core team** in a mutual aid group typically consists of committed and dedicated members who take on leadership roles, coordinate activities, and push the group's mission and objectives forward. The core team is responsible for guiding the overall direction of the mutual aid efforts, mobilizing resources and ensuring the group's sustainability and effectiveness over time.

Members of the core team often work closely together to plan and implement initiatives, engage with community members, and address challenges and opportunities as they arise. They serve as the driving force behind the mutual aid group, providing vision, direction, and support to achieve the group's goals and make a positive impact in the community.

When forming a core team, it is important to seek out people with a diverse range of skills and experiences to ensure the group's effectiveness and inclusivity. Here are some skills and attributes to consider when recruiting new members to promote diversity within the team:

Organizational Skills:

Look for ipeople who excel in organization and planning, as they can help coordinate logistics, manage resources, and streamline group activities effectively.

Communication Skills:

Seek out members who possess strong communication skills, including verbal and written communication abilities. Effective communicators can convey ideas clearly, facilitate discussions, and maintain open lines of communication within the team and with the broader community.

Leadership Abilities:

Identify people with leadership potential who can inspire, motivate, and empower others. Leadership skills are essential for guiding the team, making decisions, and mobilizing resources to achieve mutual aid goals.

Cultural Competence:

Prioritize candidates who demonstrate cultural competence and sensitivity to diverse perspectives, backgrounds, and experiences. Cultural competence promotes respect and understanding within the team and when engaging with community members from different cultural backgrounds.

Community Engagement Experience:

Look for people with experience in community engagement, outreach, and relationship-building. These members can help establish and maintain connections with diverse communities, stakeholders, and organizations to ensure that the group's initiatives are inclusive and responsive to community needs.

Problem-Solving Skills:

Seek out people who are adept at critical thinking and problem-solving. These members can analyze complex issues, develop creative solutions, and navigate challenges effectively, enhancing the group's ability to address community needs and adapt to changing circumstances.

Diversity of Background & Experience:

Aim to recruit members with diverse backgrounds, experiences, and perspectives, including but not limited to race, ethnicity, gender, age, socioeconomic status, and professional expertise. Diversity enriches team dynamics, fosters innovation, and ensures that the group can effectively serve the needs of a broad range of community members.

Flexibility & Adaptability:

Look for people who are flexible, adaptable, and open-minded. Flexibility allows team members to adjust to changing priorities, unforeseen challenges, and evolving community needs, ensuring that the group remains responsive and resilient in dynamic environments.

Professional Skills:

Based on the type of mutual aid work you anticipate, you may want to recruit members who have specific skills that require a high level of education or professional experience, such as legal, financial, or medical. Also, graphic design, social media, and website building experience may come in handy.

———————————

By prioritizing these skills and attributes when recruiting new members for your core team, you can cultivate a diverse and dynamic group that is well-equipped to make a positive impact in the community.

Finding People to Join You

The prospect of recruiting members to help you form a mutual aid group can indeed feel daunting. But rather than fixating on assembling a large group from the outset, it can be more manageable and effective to focus on finding just one person who shares your vision and passion—a **partner** who can collaborate closely with you in laying the foundation for the group.

This individual can serve as a trusted ally with whom you can brainstorm ideas, strategize, and refine the group's mission and objectives. By building a strong partnership with this initial teammate, you can develop a solid framework and approach for your mutual aid efforts, which can then serve as a magnet for attracting additional members as the group gains momentum and visibility within the community.

It is often beneficial to start by looking within your existing network to identify potential partners who share similar values and interests. However, this can sometimes pose challenges, as conversations about societal issues and community activism may not always occur within our immediate circles. In such cases, it may require branching out and engaging with broader communities, attending local events, and participating in online forums dedicated to social justice and mutual aid.

By actively seeking out like-minded people beyond your immediate networks and making connections with those who are passionate about collective action, you can expand your pool of potential collaborators. Once you have found an initial partner to join you, cooperation becomes key. Working together as a team, you can brainstorm strategies and approaches to reach out to others.

Making a Pitch to Others

When sharing your idea to start a mutual aid group with someone, it will be natural for them to be curious, as opportunities to engage in such initiatives do not often come along. They may not be familiar with the concept of mutual aid, so you might need to provide some explanation about what it entails and offer insights from the ideas outlined in this book. Despite any initial uncertainty, people will likely be receptive and honored to be considered for such meaningful endeavors.

Keep in mind, though, potential partners may need some time to consider the commitment involved. Give them space to reflect on the opportunity and assure them that you are available to address any questions or concerns they may have along the way. You may have to meet more than once before they sign on.

When approaching a potential partner to join you in starting a mutual aid group, you'll want to communicate your vision clearly and compellingly. Here are some points you may want to incorporate in your pitch:

You could begin by expressing your passion for addressing community needs and your belief in the power of people coming together to bring about positive change. Share specific examples of the challenges you have observed in your community and articulate how a mutual aid group could make a meaningful difference in addressing those challenges.

Emphasize the collaborative nature of the project and the opportunity for both of you to contribute your unique skills, perspectives, and resources. Be ready to talk about decentralized horizontal leadership (See Ch.2) and to explain how everyone has equal authority. This will assure them that they have power setting the direction of the group from the get-go. Highlight the potential impact your group could have on your community.

Invite them to join you on this journey, emphasizing that their involvement will be valued and that together, you can make a tangible difference in not only the community, but also your own lives. Be open to discussing any questions or concerns they may have, and be prepared to listen actively and address any hesitations they may express. By approaching the conversation with sincerity, enthusiasm, and a genuine commitment to shared values, you can inspire them to join you in launching the mutual aid group.

If someone you have approached is not receptive or unable to commit, it is important to respect their decision and maintain a positive attitude. Thank them for considering the opportunity and express your understanding of their circumstances. Reassure them that there are no hard feelings and that you remain open to collaborating in the future if their circumstances change.

Meanwhile, continue your efforts to recruit potential partners by reaching out to others who may share your vision and commitment. Remember that building a mutual aid group is a collaborative effort, and setbacks or rejections are a natural part of the process. Stay persistent and focused on finding people who align with your goals and are enthusiastic about joining forces to make a difference.

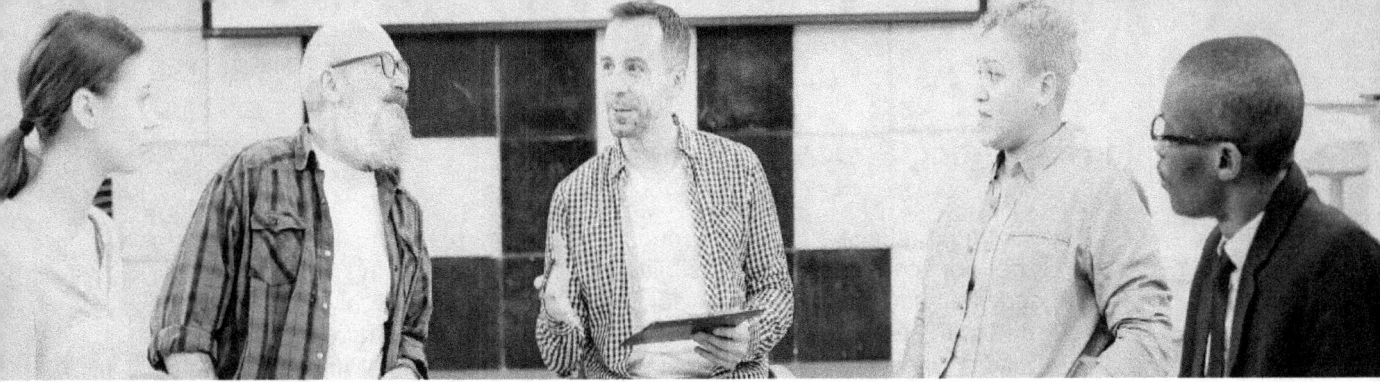

Section 3

The First Meeting

Once you have successfully recruited a few members, you are ready to hold your first meeting! As you prepare, it is important to acknowledge and validate the range of emotions that members may be experiencing. Some may be excited about the prospect of coming together to address shared needs, while others may feel curious, skeptical, or even hesitant due to past experiences or uncertainty about what to expect. Recognizing and respecting these diverse feelings is essential for creating an inclusive and supportive environment for all members.

During the first meeting, take time to establish a welcoming atmosphere where everyone feels comfortable expressing their thoughts and ideas. Begin by introducing yourselves and sharing your motivations for joining the mutual aid group. Encourage members to share their personal experiences and insights, as this will help build trust and rapport. Be mindful of power dynamics and ensure that everyone has an equal opportunity to participate in the discussion.

As the meeting progresses, outline the goals of the mutual aid group. Discuss the specific needs and challenges facing your community and brainstorm potential strategies and initiatives for addressing them. Encourage members to contribute their unique perspectives and skills, emphasizing the collective nature of the group and the value of working together towards common goals.

It is important to be patient and understanding during this initial phase, as some members may need time to adjust to the dynamics of the group and feel comfortable sharing their thoughts and ideas. Establish a culture of empathy, respect, and openness, and emphasize the importance of active listening and constructive communication. By creating a supportive and inclusive environment from the outset, you can lay the foundation for a successful and impactful mutual aid group that benefits both its members and the community at large.

Choosing a Meeting Space

Hosting mutual aid group meetings remotely via platforms like Zoom can offer convenience and accessibility, especially considering various scheduling conflicts or health concerns. However, it is highly recommended to host in-person gatherings whenever feasible. Face-to-face interactions build stronger bonds and deeper understanding among group members, allowing for richer discussions and more effective collaboration. In-person meetings also facilitate nonverbal communication and spontaneous brainstorming, enhancing the overall dynamics and synergy of the group.

When selecting a meeting space for a mutual aid group, several factors should be taken into consideration to ensure that it meets everyone's needs and facilitates productive discussions. Some of these factors include:

Accessibility:

Choose a location that is easily accessible to all members, taking into account factors such as proximity to public transportation, parking availability, and any mobility issues that members may have. Ensure that the meeting space is wheelchair accessible and has appropriate facilities for people with disabilities.

Safety:

Choose a meeting space in a safe and well-lit area. Remember, people want to feel personally secure in situations where they are meeting strangers. Also, keep in mind other safety protocols, such as wearing face masks to protect anyone who is immunocompromised.

Noise level:

Assess the noise level in the meeting space and choose a location that is conducive to focused discussions. Avoid spaces that are too noisy or distracting, such as busy cafes or public parks, and opt for quieter environments where members can engage in meaningful dialogue without interruptions.

Amenities:

Evaluate the amenities available at the meeting space, such as audiovisual equipment, Wi-Fi access, and restroom facilities. Ensure that the space has everything needed to facilitate a productive meeting, including tables, chairs, and any other necessary supplies.

Capacity:

Select a meeting space that can comfortably accommodate the expected number of attendees. Ensure that the space has adequate seating and room for members to move around comfortably.

Affordability:

Consider the cost of using the meeting space, and choose an option that is affordable for the group. Look for free or low-cost meeting spaces, such as community centers, libraries, or religious institutions.

Privacy:

Consider the level of privacy offered by the meeting space, especially if sensitive or confidential topics will be discussed. Choose a location where members feel comfortable sharing their thoughts and experiences without fear of judgment or intrusion.

Community connection:

Look for meeting spaces that are located within or have strong connections to the community. Choosing a space that is familiar and accessible can help encourage greater participation.

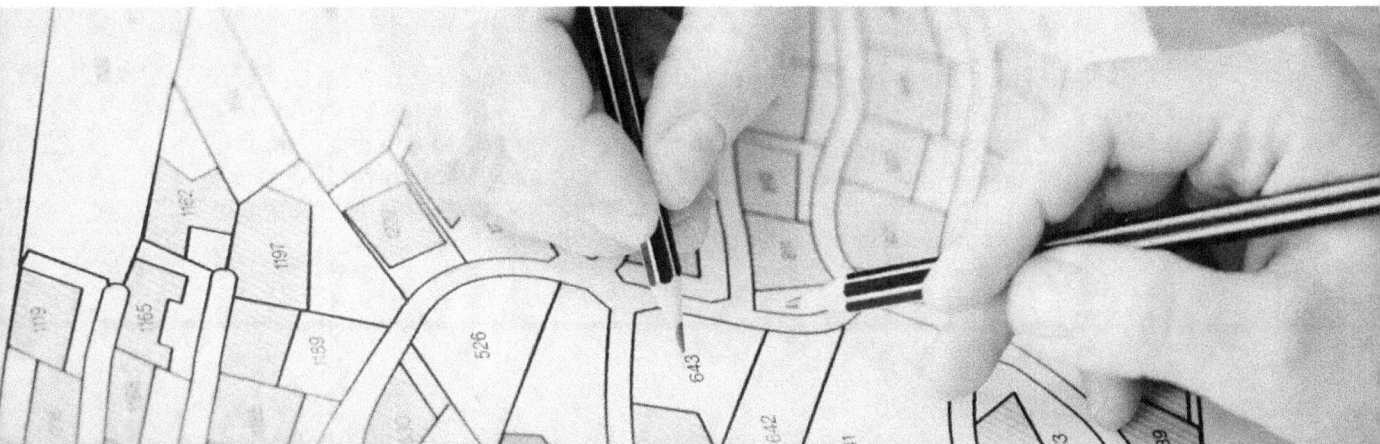

First Impressions

First impressions can have a lasting impact on how people engage with a group. A positive first impression builds trust and openness, while a negative one can create tension or even discourage participation. Here are some tips to help you make a positive impact at a mutual aid group meeting:

Arrive early:

Being punctual shows respect for the group's time and demonstrates your commitment to the cause. Arriving early also allows you to familiarize yourself with the meeting space and greet other members as they arrive.

Dress appropriately:

Dressing neatly and appropriately for the occasion can help you feel more confident. Choose attire that reflects the tone of the meeting and makes you feel comfortable and prepared to engage with others.

Be attentive & engaged:

During the meeting, actively listen to what others have to say and participate in discussions with enthusiasm and respect. Maintain eye contact, nod in agreement, and ask thoughtful questions to show your interest and engagement in the conversation.

Introduce yourself:

Take the opportunity to introduce yourself to the group and share a bit about your background and reasons for joining. Be concise and genuine, and focus on highlighting your skills, experiences, and interests that align with the group's goals.

Show empathy & compassion:

Mutual aid groups are often formed to support people facing various challenges or crises. Show empathy and compassion towards others by offering words of encouragement, sharing personal experiences when appropriate, and offering to help in any way you can.

Demonstrate humility & openness:

Approach the meeting with humility and a willingness to learn from others. Acknowledge that everyone brings valuable perspectives and experiences to the table, and be open to new ideas and approaches.

Follow up:

After the meeting, consider following up with other members to express your appreciation for their insights and contributions. Connect with them on social media or via email to continue the conversation and explore opportunities for collaboration outside of the group setting.

In group settings, it's important to give each other a chance when making first impressions, as these initial judgments can often be incomplete or based on assumptions. People may be nervous, quiet, or unfamiliar with the group dynamic at first, and what they present in that moment might not reflect their true selves. Be sure to give people space to show who they are over time.

First Meeting Agenda

Sending the agenda to members via email ahead of the first meeting is a great way to ensure everyone is on the same page and prepared to contribute meaningfully. By providing an overview of the topics to be discussed and setting a specific time limit for the meeting, you can maximize efficiency and respect everyone's commitments. This proactive approach conveys a sense of professionalism and organization, setting a positive tone for collaborative efforts moving forward.

It is important not to cram too much into the first meeting. An initial meeting should focus on setting a comfortable pace, encouraging open communication, and building foundational relationships among participants. Overloading the agenda with too many topics or decisions can lead to a sense of urgency that stifles genuine dialogue.

Instead, providing ample time for introductions, sharing individual motivations, and discussing broad goals can create a more relaxed and inclusive atmosphere. This approach helps members feel heard and valued, laying the groundwork for productive collaboration and trust. By pacing the meeting thoughtfully, the group can better navigate its discussions and build a strong, cohesive foundation for future actions.

Here is an example of what your email to members might say. You will obviously want to modify this to reflect your own style:

Dear Members,

Thank you for your interest in joining our new mutual aid group! We're excited to gather together for our first meeting on [DATE, TIME, at LOCATION] to discuss our shared vision for supporting each other and our community. The attached agenda outlines the topics we'll cover during our time together, including: exploring community needs, identifying our responsibilities and skills, discussing our motivations for participation, and planning our next steps. We value your input and participation, and we look forward to collaborating with each of you to make a positive impact in our community.

Cheers,
[Your Name]

Here is an example of an agenda for the first meeting of a mutual aid group. Adjust the timing and content of each agenda item as needed to accommodate the group's size, dynamics, and specific objectives.

Welcome & Introductions (10 minutes)

Welcome everyone to the first meeting of the mutual aid group. Briefly introduce the purpose of the meeting and the goals for the session. Ask each participant to introduce themselves, sharing their name, background, and what motivated them to join the group.

Discussion on Community Needs (20 minutes)

Facilitate a discussion on the pressing needs and challenges facing the community. Encourage participants to share their observations and experiences regarding community needs, including issues related to health, housing, food security, and social support. Take notes and identify common themes or priorities that emerge from the discussion.

Identification of Responsibilities & Skills (10 minutes)

Discuss the various roles and responsibilities needed to effectively run the mutual aid group. Invite participants to identify their skills, expertise, and interests that they can contribute. Create a list of potential roles within the group, such as organizing events, outreach, fundraising, communications, and logistics.

Setting Initial Goals (10 minutes)

Collaboratively establish initial, achievable goals for the mutual aid group. Consider including a discussion about this book in each meeting going forward. The group could read a chapter every week to ensure that everyone fully understands mutual aid and is on the same page.

Next Steps & Closing (10 minutes)

Summarize key points discussed during the meeting and review the agreed-upon goals. Outline the next steps for the group, including scheduling regular meetings, establishing communication channels, and setting up working groups. Encourage participants to stay engaged and follow up with any additional thoughts or questions. Thank everyone for their participation and commitment to collective action.

Meeting Minutes

Meeting minutes are official written records that document the discussions, decisions, and actions taken during a meeting. They serve as a historical record of the proceedings and are typically prepared by a designated individual, such as the secretary or note-taker. Here's why mutual aid groups should take meeting minutes:

Reference:

Minutes serve as a reference tool for members who were unable to attend the meeting or need to review what was discussed. They help keep everyone informed and aligned with the group's objectives and progress.

Legal & Compliance Requirements:

Meeting minutes may be required for legal purposes, especially for formal organizations such as non-profits. They demonstrate that proper procedures were followed, decisions were duly recorded, and actions were taken in accordance with the group's bylaws or governing documents.

Accountability:

By documenting action items, meeting minutes hold members accountable for their commitments and provide a basis for tracking progress on assigned tasks. They help ensure that discussions are translated into tangible outcomes and that responsibilities are clearly defined.

Memory Aid:

Meeting minutes serve as a memory aid for future reference, helping members recall past discussions, decisions, and agreements. They prevent misunderstandings or discrepancies by providing an accurate record of what was said and done during the meeting.

Ideally, someone should be designated at the beginning of each meeting to take minutes, or, for consistency, they could be appointed for a set period. When selecting a note-taker, it's important to choose someone who is attentive, organized, and able to capture key points accurately. To facilitate this process, the group can rotate the responsibility among members to share the workload and allow everyone to develop their skills. Clear guidelines should be provided on what to include, such as decisions made, action items, and any significant discussions.

The designated note-taker should distribute the minutes promptly after the meeting, ensuring all members are informed and can follow up on tasks and discussions. This practice helps maintain transparency, keeps everyone on the same page, and provides a valuable record of the group's progress.

Roles & Responsibilities

Identifying key roles in a mutual aid group involves understanding the diverse tasks and responsibilities required for successful community support. While some groups may benefit from people filling specific roles to ensure smooth functioning, others may operate with an informal structure, where tasks are delegated as needed.

The group may initially designate just one person to take on a specific role, such as facilitating meetings, to keep the structure simple and manageable. This approach allows the group to establish a basic organizational framework and ensures that meetings run smoothly. As the group grows and begins to take action and engage in fundraising efforts, it will become necessary to designate additional roles. These might include coordinators for various projects, a treasurer for managing funds, and communication officers to handle outreach.

Each group must assess its unique needs, resources, and objectives to determine the most effective allocation of roles and responsibilities. Flexibility and adaptability are key, allowing groups to evolve and tailor their approach based on changing circumstances and community dynamics. Consider the following roles on the next few pages:

Organizer/Coordinator:

Responsibilities:
Oversee & coordinate all aspects of the mutual aid project
Develop & maintain project timelines & schedules
Serve as the main point of contact for the team & the community

Skills:
Leadership & project management
Strong organizational & communication skills
Ability to delegate tasks effectively

Community Liaison:

Responsibilities:
Build & maintain relationships with the community
Act as a bridge between the project & community members
Gather feedback & input from the community to inform decisions

Skills:
Excellent interpersonal & communication skills
Cultural competency & community engagement experience
Empathy & active listening skills

Communications Coordinator:

Responsibilities:
Develop & implement a communication strategy
Manage social media accounts, newsletters, & other communications
Disseminate information about project updates, events, & community needs

Skills:
Writing & content creation
Social media management
Public relations & community outreach

Logistics & Operations Manager:

Responsibilities:
Ensure the smooth execution of day-to-day operations
Manage the distribution of resources & supplies
Coordinate transportation, storage & logistics for events or distributions

Skills:
Attention to detail & organizational skills
Problem-solving & logistical coordination
Ability to adapt to changing circumstances

Treasurer & Fundraising Coordinator:

Responsibilities:
Develop & manage the project budget
Explore & implement fundraising strategies
Track & report on financial transactions

Skills:
Financial management & budgeting
Grant writing & fundraising
Record-keeping & financial reporting

Legal & Compliance Advisor:

Responsibilities:
Ensure compliance with relevant laws & regulations
Provide legal guidance on organizational structure & activities
Address any legal challenges or concerns that may arise

Skills:
Legal expertise or access to legal support
Knowledge of nonprofit regulations & compliance (if applicable)
Problem-solving & risk management

Technology & Data Manager:

Responsibilities:
Oversee the use of technology tools & platforms, including a website
Manage data collection & analysis for reporting purposes
Ensure the security & privacy of sensitive information

Skills:
Proficiency in technology tools & platforms
Data management & analysis
Information security & privacy

Volunteer Coordinator:

Responsibilities:
Recruit, train & manage volunteers
Match volunteers with tasks based on their skills & interests
Maintain a database of available volunteers & their capacities

Skills:
Volunteer management & recruitment
Communication & interpersonal skills
Organization & logistical coordination

Research & Needs Assessment Specialist:

Responsibilities:
Conduct ongoing needs assessments within the community
Research best practices & innovative solutions for mutual aid projects
Inform project decisions based on data & community input

Skills:
Research & data analysis
Community needs assessment
Critical thinking & problem-solving

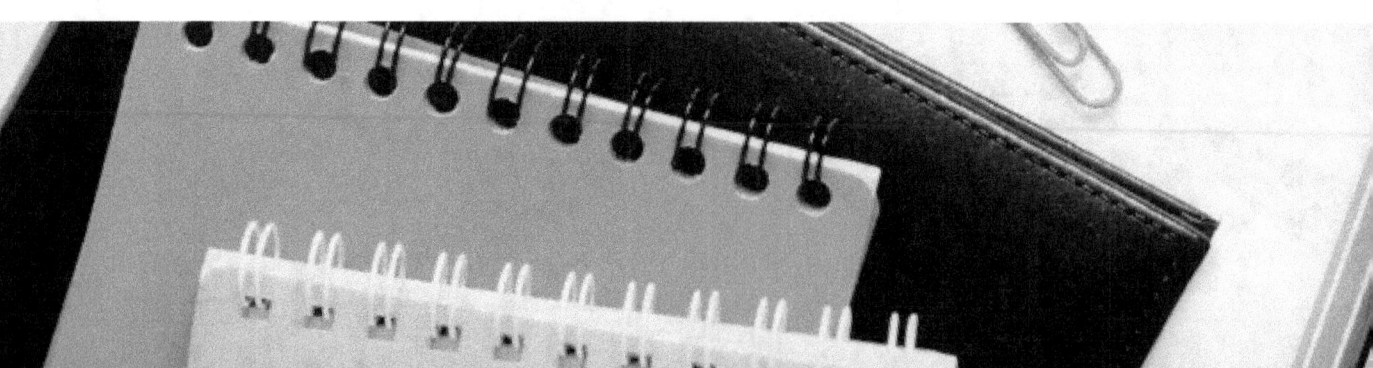

Wellness & Mental Health Coordinator:

Responsibilities:
Address the mental health and well-being of team & community members
Provide resources and support for individuals facing emotional challenges
Implement strategies for creating a supportive and positive environment

Skills:
Knowledge of mental health resources
Compassion and empathy
Crisis intervention skills

Evaluation & Impact Assessment Specialist:

Responsibilities:
Develop and implement an evaluation framework for the project
Assess the impact of the mutual aid efforts on the community
Provide regular reports on project outcomes & areas for improvement

Skills:
Evaluation & impact assessment
Data analysis & reporting
Continuous improvement mindset

Graphic Designer:

Responsibilities:
Create logos & other artwork for the group
Prepare designs for flyers, website & social media
Presenting creative ideas & concepts to the group for input

Skills:
Knowledge of design software
A "good eye" for design
Comfortable receiving feedback & making adjustments

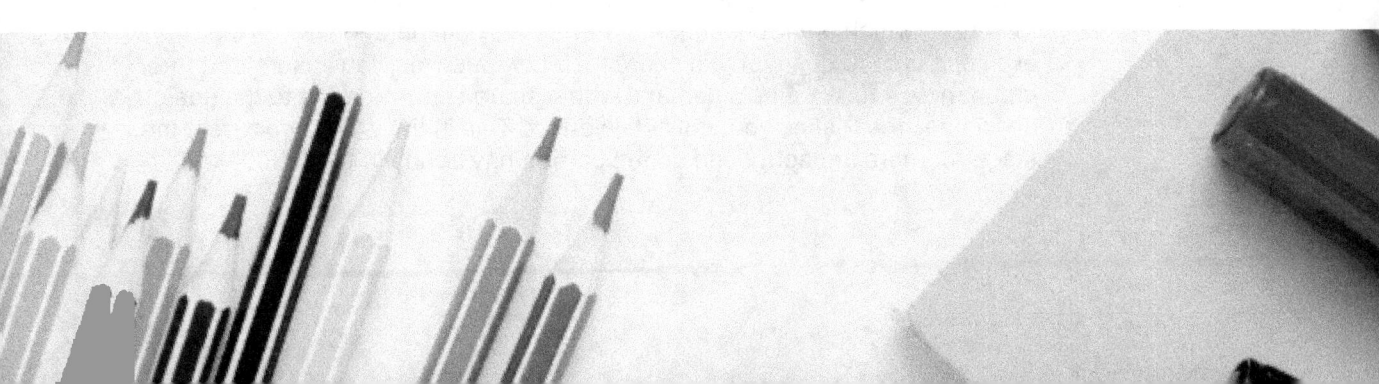

The Next Meeting & Beyond

When forming a new mutual aid group, the initial excitement might make you want to dive right into coordinating community actions. Groups that are formed in response to urgent crises will obviously require a fast pace, but in most other mutual aid projects it is beneficial to exercise patience and restraint during the first few meetings. A slower pace allows members to thoroughly understand and align with the group's mission.

Initiating actions without a solid plan can lead to disorganization, decreased effectiveness, and potentially negative consequences. Proper training ensures that all members understand their roles and responsibilities, creating a cohesive team that can respond effectively to community needs.

This period is a critical time for building relationships and trust among members, which are foundational for effective collaboration. By giving everyone time to connect and share their perspectives, you ensure that the group moves forward as a unit and with a shared commitment to the goals and values that define your collective effort. This initial groundwork sets the stage for more impactful and united community action in the future.

It is recommended that the group's first two projects are the following:

Craft a Mission Statement:

The mission statement articulates the purpose and aims of the group, guiding every decision and action. A clear, well-thought-out mission statement ensures that all members are aligned and motivated by a common goal. It should be concise and inspiring, capturing the essence of what the group intends to achieve and why. This statement will also be critical when communicating the group's purpose to the community and potential new members. Tips on writing a great mission statement are in the next subsection.

Conduct a Community Assessment:

Before diving into projects, it is essential to understand the environment in which you are operating. As discussed in Chapter 3, a community assessment involves collecting and analyzing data about the community's strengths, weaknesses, needs, and resources. This could include demographic information, economic conditions, social issues, and existing community resources. Understanding these elements helps the group identify where they can make the most significant impact and avoid duplicating efforts that other organizations are already addressing. This assessment should be an ongoing process, regularly updated to adapt to the changing needs of the community.

By aligning the mission statement with the findings of the community assessment, the group can ensure that its efforts are targeted and effective, directly addressing the most pressing issues.

Writing a Mission Statement

Crafting a **mission statement** should be a priority for a mutual aid group as it sets the foundation for the group's purpose, values, and goals. This statement serves as a guiding light, informing decisions and actions, and providing clarity and direction for members.

A well-crafted mission statement reflects the group's commitment to addressing shared needs and articulates its core principles and priorities. It also helps communicate the group's identity to potential members, partners, and the broader community. Therefore, is essential for your group to dedicate time and effort into developing a clear and concise mission statement early on.

Here are the key components of a great mission statement:

Purpose:

Clearly state the reason for the group's existence and what it aims to achieve. This helps members and stakeholders understand the group's focus and direction.

Values:

Articulate the core principles and beliefs that guide the group's actions and decisions. These values should reflect the group's commitment to equity, solidarity, collaboration, and community empowerment.

Goals:

Outline the specific objectives or outcomes that the group seeks to accomplish. These goals should be realistic, measurable, and aligned with the group's purpose and values.

Audience:

Consider the intended audience of the mission statement, which may include group members, stakeholders, and the broader community. The language and tone should resonate with these audiences and inspire engagement and support.

Conciseness:

Keep the mission statement succinct and to the point. Avoid overly complex language or jargon that may obscure the group's message.

Memorability:

Craft a mission statement that is memorable and impactful, making it easier for members and stakeholders to internalize the group's purpose and values.

Here are some examples of mission statements for mutual aid groups:

Example 1:
"We are committed to addressing food insecurity in our community by providing weekly grocery deliveries to low-income families, organizing community gardens for sustainable food production, and advocating for policy changes to increase access to nutritious food options."

Example 2:
"Empowering our community through mutual aid, we seek to support unhoused residents by providing emergency shelter, hygiene kits, and job training programs. We also work to combat housing discrimination and promote affordable housing policies."

Example 3:
"Driven by a spirit of solidarity and grassroots activism, we are dedicated to supporting marginalized youth through mentorship programs, educational scholarships, and mental health resources. We also organize community events to amplify their voices and advocate for equitable educational opportunities."

Example 4:
"Our mission is to build a more resilient community by providing disaster relief assistance, emergency preparedness training, and neighborhood resource centers. Through collaborative partnerships with local organizations and government agencies, we aim to enhance community resilience and response capabilities during times of crisis."

Writing the mission statement should be a collaborative endeavor within the group, involving input and feedback from all members. This inclusive approach ensures that the statement reflects collective values, aspirations, and priorities. While the process may take some time as members discuss and refine ideas, it is essential to achieve consensus and craft a statement that resonates with everyone. By actively engaging in this process, members will contribute their perspectives and develop a sense of ownership and commitment to the mission.

Roberts' Rules of Order

As a mutual aid group grows in size, it may become useful to implement **Robert's Rules of Order** to maintain structure and ensure that key items are addressed efficiently during meetings. Robert's Rules of Order is a widely recognized framework to ensure that meetings run smoothly, fairly, and efficiently. Their purpose is to facilitate orderly, democratic discussion and decision-making, giving all members a voice while maintaining focus.

At its core, Robert's Rules outlines various types of motions that can be made during a meeting. These motions range from basic proposals (main motions) to amendments, procedural motions, and motions that address the meeting's conduct, such as calling for a recess or adjourning. Each motion has specific rules for how it is introduced, debated, and voted upon. For instance, main motions introduce new business, while subsidiary motions modify or dispose of main motions.

One of the key benefits of using Robert's Rules is that it ensures everyone has an equal opportunity to participate. The rules protect the rights of the majority to decide, the minority to be heard, and individual members to express their views. This structured approach helps prevent meetings from becoming chaotic or dominated by a few voices. By adhering to these rules, organizations can maintain order, make clear decisions, and keep comprehensive records of their proceedings.

However, it is important to note that while Robert's Rules can be highly effective for larger, more formal organizations, they might be overly rigid for smaller, informal groups. In such cases, adopting a simplified version or focusing on the key principles of fairness and order may be more appropriate. The group could consider running the first half of meetings more formally using Robert's Rules to handle essential business and decisions. The second half could then transition into a more conversational format, allowing members to freely brainstorm, share ideas, and discuss issues in a relaxed, open environment. This hybrid approach ensures that the group remains organized while also encouraging the collaborative and creative spirit that mutual aid thrives on.

Running a meeting using Robert's Rules of Order involves a specific process to ensure orderly and efficient decision-making. Here is an overview of the key steps:

Roberts' Rules of Order

Call to Order: The chairperson (or presiding organizer) starts the meeting by calling it to order at the designated time. This signals that the meeting is officially beginning.

Roll Call/Attendance: The secretary or designated individual takes roll call to document who is present. This ensures that a quorum (the minimum number of members required to conduct business) is present.

Approval of Minutes: The minutes from the previous meeting are reviewed and approved. Members can suggest corrections, which are then voted on. Once any corrections are made, the minutes are formally approved by a majority vote.

Reports of Officers & Committees: Officers (e.g., organizer, treasurer) and committee chairs present their reports. These reports provide updates on activities, financial status, and other relevant matters. After each report, members may ask questions or make comments.

Unfinished Business: Any business or agenda items that were not completed in previous meetings are addressed. This ensures continuity and that important matters are not overlooked.

New Business: Members introduce new topics or proposals for discussion and decision. This is typically done through main motions. A member makes a motion, another seconds it, and then it is opened for discussion.

Debate & Discussion: Members discuss the motion on the floor. Members should be recognized by the chair before speaking. Each member has the opportunity to speak, typically within time limits, and debate should be relevant to the motion.

Voting: Once discussion is complete, the chair puts the motion to a vote. Voting can be conducted in various ways, such as voice vote, show of hands, roll call, or secret ballot. The method depends on the organization's rules and the type of motion.

Announcements: The chair or members may make any necessary announcements about upcoming events, deadlines, or other matters.

Adjournment: The meeting is formally closed with a motion to adjourn. A member moves to adjourn, another seconds it, and a vote is taken. If the motion passes, the meeting ends.

Discussion Topics

By meeting regularly, mutual aid group members will have the opportunity to connect on a deeper level, share experiences, and develop a sense of camaraderie. These meetings provide a platform for open communication, where people can voice their concerns, share ideas, and work collaboratively towards common goals.

Discussions during these meetings may cover a wide range of topics. Here are some that are worth exploring on a regular basis:

Community Needs:

Discuss the results of recent assessments and identify emerging needs or trends within the community.

Project Planning & Coordination:

Brainstorm ideas for upcoming projects or initiatives, assign responsibilities, and establish timelines.

Skill-sharing & Capacity Building:

Share expertise and resources among group members, discuss training opportunities, and identify areas for skill development.

Reflection & Evaluation:

Reflect on past projects or events, evaluate their effectiveness, and identify lessons learned for future improvements.

Outreach & Collaboration:

Explore opportunities for collaboration with other organizations or community stakeholders, discuss outreach strategies, and plan engagement activities.

Book Clubs & Continuous Learning

Ensuring that every member of your mutual aid group is well-informed and educated about the principles and practices of mutual aid is important for the group's effectiveness and cohesion. Incorporating a **book club** into regular activities can be a valuable strategy to achieve this goal. By selecting a relevant book on mutual aid–such as this one–and assigning chapters for weekly reading, members can deepen their understanding of the concept and its applications.

Engaging in discussions about the assigned chapters during group meetings allows people to share their insights, questions, and reflections, creating a collective learning experience. These discussions serve as opportunities for members to clarify any misconceptions, explore different perspectives, and identify practical strategies for applying mutual aid principles in community initiatives.

These discussions will no doubt spark creativity and innovation within the group. As members delve into the material and exchange ideas, they may uncover new insights and approaches to addressing community needs.

Flexibility & Adaptability

Flexibility and adaptability are essential qualities for a mutual aid group. In the dynamic landscape of community needs and resources, situations can change rapidly, requiring the group to adjust its approach and strategies accordingly. Here's why flexibility and adaptability are crucial:

Responding to Emerging Needs:

Community needs can evolve over time, especially during times of crisis or uncertainty. A flexible mutual aid group can quickly pivot to address emerging needs as they arise, ensuring efforts remain relevant and effective.

Adapting to Changing Circumstances:

External factors such as economic conditions, policy changes, or natural disasters can impact the community environment. A group that can adapt its plans and activities in response to these changes demonstrates resilience and agility in navigating unpredictable circumstances.

Maximizing Impact:

Being flexible allows a mutual aid group to seize opportunities and leverage resources more effectively. By adjusting your approach based on feedback and evaluation, the group can optimize its impact on the community.

Building Trust & Engagement:

Flexibility demonstrates a willingness to listen to community members and respond to their needs and preferences. This builds trust and engagement, as people see the group as responsive and committed to their well-being.

Learning & Growth:

By reflecting on past experiences and incorporating lessons learned into future actions, the group can refine strategies and become more effective over time.

Project Management

Project management in a mutual aid group involves coordinating and overseeing tasks to ensure projects are completed effectively. This includes planning, organizing resources, setting timelines, assigning roles, and monitoring progress. Effective project management helps the group stay focused, meet objectives, and adapt to changing circumstances while maximizing impact. Here are key steps and considerations for allocating tasks in a mutual aid project:

Define Project Goals:

Clearly articulate the goals and objectives of the project. This provides a foundational understanding of the tasks that need to be undertaken to achieve these objectives.

Identify Key Areas & Needs:

Break down the project into key areas or categories, such as logistics, communication, community outreach, fundraising, and operations. Identify specific tasks within each category.

Assess Team Skills & Strengths:

Conduct an inventory of the skills and strengths of each team member. Identify areas of expertise, professional backgrounds, and personal interests that align with the needs of the project.

Considerations for Task Allocation:

Assign tasks based on team members' skills and expertise to ensure that they are working in areas where they can contribute most effectively. Consider their interests and passion for specific aspects of the project. Assigning tasks aligned with personal interests often leads to higher motivation and commitment. Provide opportunities for members to take on tasks that align with their professional or personal development goals, allowing for skill-building and growth.

Ensure Diversity in Task Assignment:

Encourage diversity in task assignment to ensure that team members have the opportunity to contribute based on their unique perspectives and backgrounds.

Roles & Responsibilities:

Clearly define roles and responsibilities for each team member, including specifying the tasks they are responsible for and the expected outcomes. Empower team members by delegating appropriate authority with their assigned tasks. This creates a sense of ownership and accountability.

Flexibility & Adaptability:

Be open to adapting task assignments as the project progresses. Team members may discover new skills or interests, and project needs may evolve, requiring adjustments in task allocation.

Regular Check-Ins & Communication:

Conduct regular check-ins to discuss progress, challenges, and upcoming tasks to ensure team members stay informed and can provide input. Maintain open lines of communication to address any concerns, questions, or suggestions. Encourage team members to express their preferences and seek clarification when needed.

Collaboration & Cross-Functional Teams:

Build collaboration among team members by assigning tasks that require cooperation and joint efforts. Consider forming cross-functional teams where people from different areas of expertise work together on specific initiatives.

Training & Support:

Provide training and support for team members who may be taking on new or unfamiliar tasks. This ensures that everyone feels equipped and confident in their assigned roles.

Rotate Responsibilities:

Consider rotating responsibilities over time to prevent burnout and provide opportunities for team members to gain experience in different areas of the project.

Celebrate Achievements:

Acknowledge and celebrate individual and team achievements. Recognizing efforts and successes builds a positive and motivated working environment.

The Challenge of Unequal Participation

Unequal participation in a mutual aid group can have detrimental effects on the group's cohesion, effectiveness, and inclusivity. When a few voices dominate discussions and decision-making processes, it can lead to feelings of disenfranchisement and disengagement among other members. This imbalance undermines the principle of collective effort and shared responsibility that is central to mutual aid. It can also result in decisions that do not fully reflect the diverse needs and perspectives of the entire group.

Unequal participation can also take the form of members not making a commitment to put in time and effort to help the group accomplish its objectives. A lack of commitment from some members can place a disproportionate burden on the more active participants, leading to burnout and frustration. This imbalance can also slow down the progress of projects and create gaps in the group's efforts, weakening overall effectiveness.

To avoid unequal participation, it is essential to establish clear and inclusive communication practices from the outset. This can involve setting ground rules that encourage everyone to contribute, such as using a talking stick or round-robin format during discussions to ensure each person has a chance to speak. Facilitators can play a role in moderating conversations, actively inviting quieter members to share their thoughts and ensuring that no single individual monopolizes the dialogue. Creating smaller working groups or committees can provide more opportunities for all members to participate meaningfully, allowing them to focus on specific tasks or projects that align with their interests and strengths.

Establishing clear expectations and flexible roles can help accommodate varying levels of commitment, ensuring that all members can participate in ways that align with their abilities and schedules. By addressing these challenges proactively, mutual aid groups can sustain their initiatives over time.

Evaluating Impact & Effectiveness

Key Performance Indicators (KPIs) are specific metrics used to evaluate the effectiveness of a mutual aid group in achieving its objectives. These indicators are quantifiable measures that help assess progress, track performance, and determine whether goals are being met. KPIs are typically aligned with the group's strategic priorities and are used to monitor success over time.

A mutual aid group would want to use KPIs to help demonstrate its value to the community and build credibility with stakeholders, including donors, volunteers, and partners. KPIs enable the group to set realistic goals, monitor progress, and make data-driven decisions that enhance their overall efficiency and impact.

When developing KPIs, it's important to ensure that they meet the SMART criteria to increase their effectiveness and utility. SMART is an acronym that stands for Specific, Measurable, Achievable, Relevant, and Time-bound.

Specific KPIs are clearly defined and focused on a specific aspect of performance, making them easier to understand and track.

Measurable KPIs are quantifiable and can be objectively measured, allowing for accurate assessment of progress and success.

Achievable KPIs are realistic and attainable within the resources and capabilities of the organization or project.

Relevant KPIs are aligned with the group's objectives and priorities, ensuring that they contribute directly to their mission and goals.

Time-bound KPIs have a defined timeframe or deadline for achievement, providing a sense of urgency and accountability.

In the context of a mutual aid group, some examples of KPIs may include:

Number of People Served:
This KPI measures the reach and impact of the mutual aid group by quantifying the number of individuals who have received support from the group.

Response Time:
This KPI measures the speed and efficiency of the mutual aid group's response to requests for assistance or support. It assesses how quickly the group can mobilize resources and provide aid to those in need.

Participant Satisfaction:
This KPI evaluates the satisfaction levels of participants who have received support from the mutual aid group. It may involve collecting feedback through surveys, interviews, or other means to gauge participant experiences and perceptions.

Volunteer Engagement:
This KPI assesses the level of engagement and involvement of volunteers within the mutual aid group. It may include metrics such as the number of volunteers recruited, hours contributed, tasks completed, and retention rates.

Partnerships & Collaborations:
This KPI measures the extent of partnerships and collaborations established by the mutual aid group with other organizations, agencies, or stakeholders. It evaluates the effectiveness of these partnerships in expanding the group's reach, resources, and impact.

Resource Utilization:
This KPI tracks the efficient use of resources—including financial resources, supplies, facilities, and volunteer efforts—by the mutual aid group. It assesses how effectively resources are allocated and managed to achieve desired outcomes.

By tracking KPIs, your mutual aid group can assess its effectiveness, identify areas for improvement, and demonstrate its impact to stakeholders.

Chapter Review

Before starting or joining a mutual aid group, it is important to adopt a positive, constructive mindset. Researching existing groups in your area can provide insights into effective practices and help avoid duplicating efforts. If no suitable group exists, consider becoming an organizer. Preparing to lead means understanding the principles of mutual aid, and being ready to guide discussions and create an inclusive environment.

Next, think about recruitment. Start by reaching out to your existing networks to gauge interest. Use social media platforms, community bulletin boards, and local events to spread the word. Crafting a compelling pitch is essential; highlight the benefits of mutual aid, such as creating a supportive community and addressing shared challenges. Emphasize how the group values diverse perspectives and skills. Clear communication about the group's purpose and potential impact can inspire others to join and contribute.

Holding the first group meeting is about setting a solid foundation. Begin by welcoming everyone and facilitating introductions to create a sense of camaraderie. Outline the basic principles of mutual aid and discuss the initial goals of the group. Encourage open dialogue and invite members to share their motivations and expectations. It's important to establish ground rules for respectful communication and decision-making processes. Designate a note-taker to record key points and decisions, ensuring transparency and accountability. Keep the agenda manageable to avoid overwhelming participants and allow for natural conversation flow.

The next meeting and beyond should focus on building momentum and structure. Consider crafting of a mission statement and conducting a community assessment. This foundational work will inform the group's initiatives and ensure you are addressing real needs. As the group grows, continue to designate roles as needed.

Discussion Questions

1 Think about a group project you were involved in that was particularly successful. What factors contributed to its success, and how might these be applied to your mutual aid group?

2 Reflect on a challenging experience you had while working in a group. What did you learn that could be useful in a mutual aid context?

Chapter **6**

Legal & Ethical Considerations

In this chapter, we explore the key legal and ethical challenges your mutual aid group may face in its operations. From managing donations to navigating liability and privacy concerns, your group must be aware of the administrative responsibilities that come with community organizing. We also discuss the specific obligations required of non-profits, should your group decide to register as a charitable organization.

Organizational Structure

Depending on the scale of your mutual aid operations, you may decide to establish a formal organizational structure and implement policies and procedures to ensure ethical operations and legal compliance. These foundational elements provide a framework for the group's activities, decision-making processes, and interactions with members, beneficiaries, and the broader community.

The type of formal organizational structure chosen by a mutual aid group significantly influences its legal obligations and compliance requirements. For instance, opting for a non-profit organization status entails adhering to specific IRS regulations—such as filing annual reports and maintaining tax-exempt status eligibility.

We discuss some common types of organizational structures over the next few pages:

Unincorporated Association:

An unincorporated association is a simple and flexible organizational structure where members come together voluntarily to pursue a common purpose or goal. It typically requires minimal formalities—such as adopting a constitution or bylaws—and does not involve official registration with government authorities. This structure provides autonomy and ease of operation, but it may offer fewer legal protections and benefits compared to incorporated entities. Donations are not tax-deductible.

501(c)(3) Non-profit Charitable Organization:

A 501(c)(3) non-profit organization is a tax-exempt entity recognized by the Internal Revenue Service (IRS) under section 501(c)(3) of the Internal Revenue Code. To obtain tax-exempt status, the group must incorporate at the state level and apply for recognition of tax-exempt status from the IRS. This structure offers benefits such as tax-deductible donations, expanded eligibility for grants, and limited liability protection for officers and directors. However, it involves more administrative requirements, including compliance with non-profit regulations and reporting obligations.

501(c)(4) Social Welfare Organization:

Similar to a 501(c)(3) organization, a 501(c)(4) social welfare organization is tax-exempt but serves a broader purpose related to the promotion of social welfare and community advocacy. While contributions to 501(c)(4) organizations are not typically tax-deductible, these organizations have more flexibility to engage in lobbying and political activities to advance their goals. Like 501(c)(3) organizations, they must incorporate at the state level and apply for tax-exempt status from the IRS.

Cooperative:

A cooperative, or co-op, is a business or organization owned and operated by its members for their mutual benefit. In a cooperative structure, members pool resources, share decision-making authority, and distribute profits or benefits equitably among themselves. While cooperatives are more commonly associated with economic enterprises—such as worker cooperatives or consumer cooperatives—they can also be applied to mutual aid initiatives focused on community support and solidarity.

Unincorporated Associations

An **unincorporated association** is a group of people who come together for a common purpose without formally registering as a legal entity with the government. In the context of a mutual aid group, structuring as an unincorporated association offers several advantages and disadvantages.

PROS

Simplicity:
Forming an unincorporated association is relatively straightforward and requires minimal paperwork compared to establishing a formal non-profit organization. This simplicity makes it an attractive option for smaller mutual aid groups with limited resources and administrative capacity.

Flexibility:
Unincorporated associations have greater flexibility in their operations and decision-making processes. They are not bound by the strict regulatory requirements imposed on non-profit organizations, allowing them to adapt more easily to changing circumstances and community needs.

Cost-effectiveness:
Since unincorporated associations do not need to comply with the formal registration and reporting requirements of non-profit organizations, they incur fewer administrative costs and ongoing obligations. This cost-effectiveness allows mutual aid groups to allocate more resources towards their mission and activities.

CONS

Limited liability protection:
One of the main drawbacks of structuring as an unincorporated association is the lack of legal separation between the group and its members. As a result, members may be personally liable for the group's debts, liabilities, and legal actions, putting their personal assets at risk in the event of a lawsuit or financial dispute.

Credibility & fundraising challenges:
Donors and grantmakers may be hesitant to support unincorporated groups due to concerns about transparency, accountability, and legal status.

Starting out as an unincorporated association can be a good approach for a new mutual aid group. You can begin operations quickly without the administrative burden and legal requirements associated with formal non-profit status. As the group grows and solidifies its mission and activities, you can then consider applying for non-profit status if this aligns with your long-term goals. Transitioning to non-profit status later provides flexibility and allows the group to gauge its sustainability and impact before committing to the additional regulatory obligations and expenses of formal incorporation.

501(c)(3) Non-Profit Charitable Organizations

A **501(c)(3) organization** is a type of non-profit organization that is recognized by the Internal Revenue Service (IRS) as exempt from federal income tax under section 501(c)(3) of the Internal Revenue Code. These organizations are commonly referred to as charitable organizations because they operate exclusively for charitable, religious, educational, scientific, literary, or similar purposes.

In addition to being exempt from federal income tax, donations made to 501(c)(3) organizations are typically tax-deductible for donors. These organizations must adhere to specific IRS regulations and reporting requirements to maintain their tax-exempt status.

Becoming a 501(c)(3) non-profit organization offers several advantages and disadvantages for your mutual aid group:

<u>PROS</u>

Eligibility for grants & donations:
Many foundations, corporations, and individuals prefer to donate to tax-exempt organizations, making it easier to secure funding for the mutual aid group's activities.

Tax-exempt status:
As mentioned above, 501(c)(3) organizations are exempt from federal income tax, as well as some state and local taxes, which can save money and make fundraising efforts more effective.

Increased credibility:
Being recognized as a 501(c)(3) non-profit can enhance the group's credibility and legitimacy in the eyes of the public, potential donors, and partner organizations.

Limited liability protection:
Non-profit status can provide some degree of limited liability protection for board members and volunteers, reducing personal risk.

Ability to offer tax deductions:
Donors to 501(c)(3) organizations can typically receive tax deductions for their contributions, which may incentivize larger donations.

CONS

Compliance requirements:
Obtaining and maintaining 501(c)(3) status requires adherence to complex regulations and reporting requirements, which can be time-consuming and costly.

Restrictions on political activities:
Non-profits classified as 501(c)(3) organizations are subject to strict limitations on political lobbying and advocacy, which may limit the group's ability to engage in certain types of activism.

Limited revenue-generating activities:
Non-profits must primarily serve a charitable purpose, and income-generating activities that are unrelated to the organization's mission may be subject to unrelated business income tax (UBIT).

Public scrutiny:
501(c)(3) organizations are subject to public disclosure requirements, including the annual filing of Form 990, which provides detailed financial information to the IRS and is accessible to the public.

Risk of mission drift:
Non-profit organizations may face pressure to prioritize fundraising, potentially leading to a drift away from their original mission or a lack of focus on community needs.

We discuss the application process and specific obligations for non-profits in Section 4 of this chapter.

501(c)(4) Non-Profit Social Welfare Organizations

A mutual aid group might pursue **501(c)(4) non-profit** status to actively engage in political activities aimed at promoting social welfare and advancing their advocacy goals. By obtaining this classification, the group gains the ability to participate in lobbying, advocacy campaigns, and political campaigns, allowing them to more effectively influence public policy and address systemic issues impacting their community. This designation offers the flexibility to combine direct aid with advocacy efforts, amplifying the group's impact and enabling them to address root causes of social problems through legislative and policy change. Here are some examples of 501(c)(4) organizations:

Environmental advocacy groups:
Organizations like the Sierra Club and the League of Conservation Voters operate as 501(c)(4) entities to advocate for environmental protection, climate action, and conservation policies at local, state, and federal levels.

Civil rights & social justice organizations:
Groups such as the American Civil Liberties Union (ACLU) and the NAACP Legal Defense Fund use their 501(c)(4) status to advocate for civil rights and racial justice through litigation, lobbying, and education campaigns.

Gun control advocacy groups:
Organizations like Everytown for Gun Safety are organized as 501(c)(4) entities to advocate for gun violence prevention measures, lobby for stronger gun laws, and mobilize public support for firearms regulation.

Healthcare advocacy organizations:
Entities like Planned Parenthood Action Fund and the American Cancer Society Cancer Action Network use their 501(c)(4) status to advocate for access to healthcare services, reproductive rights, and public health policies.

Political advocacy organizations:
Groups such as the Human Rights Campaign and the National Rifle Association (NRA) operate as 501(c)(4) organizations to advance their respective political agendas, influence elections, and support candidates who align with their policy priorities.

Here are some of the pros and cons of your mutual aid group registering as a 501(c)(4) non-profit:

PROS

Tax-exempt status:
Like 501(c)(3) organizations, 501(c)(4) organizations enjoy tax-exempt status for federal income tax purposes, which can reduce financial burdens and allow more resources to be directed toward programs.

Ability to engage in political advocacy:
Unlike 501(c)(3) organizations, which have restrictions on engaging in partisan political activities, 501(c)(4) groups can participate in lobbying, advocacy, and political campaigns to advance their policy objectives.

Flexibility in activities:
501(c)(4) organizations have broad latitude to engage in a wide range of activities related to promoting social welfare, including public education, advocacy campaigns, community organizing, and direct aid.

Less stringent IRS oversight:
While 501(c)(4) organizations are still subject to IRS regulations and reporting requirements, they generally face less scrutiny and regulatory oversight compared to 501(c)(3) organizations, allowing for greater operational flexibility.

CONS

Limited tax-deductible donations:
Contributions to 501(c)(4) organizations are not tax-deductible for donors, which may make fundraising more challenging compared to 501(c)(3) organizations that can offer tax benefits to donors.

Funding restrictions:
Some foundations and grant-making entities may have policies that restrict funding to 501(c)(4) organizations. As a result, a mutual aid group may have fewer opportunities to secure grants and institutional funding compared to a 501(c)(3) non-profit.

Perception of partisanship:
Because 501(c)(4) organizations are allowed to engage in political advocacy and lobbying, there may be a perception that they are more partisan or ideological in nature, which could affect their credibility and appeal to certain stakeholders.

Complexity of compliance:
While 501(c)(4) organizations have more flexibility in their activities, they also face additional compliance requirements related to political spending, reporting, and disclosure, which can involve administrative burdens and legal risks.

Overall, the decision to pursue 501(c)(4) status should be carefully weighed against the specific goals, activities, and funding needs of your mutual aid group, taking into account the potential benefits and drawbacks of this organizational structure.

Cooperatives (Co-ops)

A **cooperative**, often referred to as a co-op, is an association of individuals or businesses who voluntarily come together to meet their common economic, social, and cultural needs and aspirations through a jointly-owned and democratically-controlled enterprise. In a cooperative, members pool their resources—such as capital, labor, or expertise—to provide goods, services, or benefits to themselves and their community.

Key characteristics of cooperatives include:

Voluntary Membership:

Members choose to join and participate in the cooperative on a democratic basis.

Democratic Control:

Members have equal voting rights and participate in decision-making processes, such as electing representatives, setting policies, and approving major decisions.

Member Ownership:

Members collectively own and control the cooperative enterprise—typically through purchasing shares or contributing equity capital—with ownership rights and benefits allocated based on member participation or patronage.

Shared Benefits:

Cooperatives operate for the mutual benefit of their members, striving to maximize member value, rather than generating profits for external shareholders or investors.

Social Responsibility:

Cooperatives adhere to principles of social responsibility, community engagement, and sustainable development—prioritizing people and planet over purely financial objectives.

Cooperatives can operate in various sectors—including agriculture, consumer goods, housing, finance, energy, healthcare, and education—providing a wide range of products and services to their members and communities.

Here are some of the financial considerations related to starting a co-op:

Initial Investment:
Establishing a cooperative requires initial capital investment for incorporation fees, legal expenses, organizational development, and infrastructure setup, which can be substantial depending on the scale and complexity of the cooperative.

Administrative Expenses:
Cooperatives must comply with legal, regulatory, and accounting requirements, which may involve administrative expenses for recordkeeping, reporting, audits, and professional services.

Member Equity Contributions:
Members may be required to contribute equity capital or purchase shares in the cooperative to finance its operations and expansion, which can represent a significant financial commitment and risk for members.

Profit Distribution:
Cooperatives distribute profits among members based on their participation or patronage, which may result in variable returns depending on member activity and cooperative performance, compared to fixed dividends or returns in other business models.

Financial Constraints:
Cooperatives may face challenges in accessing external funding sources or investment capital, as investors may perceive cooperative enterprises as riskier or less profitable compared to conventional businesses, limiting growth and expansion opportunities.

If a mutual aid group is considering transitioning into a cooperative, there are co-op development organizations that can provide guidance and support throughout the process. These are specialized organizations that provide technical assistance, training, and consulting services to groups interested in forming or converting into co-ops. Examples include the Cooperative Development Foundation (CDF), the National Cooperative Business Association (NCBA CLUSA), and local cooperative development centers or networks.

Policies & Procedures

Establishing policies and procedures will enable your mutual aid group to operate in accordance with ethical principles and legal requirements. These policies should cover a range of areas—including financial management, conflict resolution, data privacy, and resource distribution. By articulating standards of conduct and defining acceptable practices, your group can uphold integrity, fairness, and respect in all your interactions and activities.

Having clear policies and procedures also helps mitigate risks and ensures compliance with relevant laws and regulations. For example, financial policies can help safeguard assets, prevent fraud or misuse of funds, and maintain accurate records for reporting and accountability purposes. Policies related to volunteer screening, confidentiality, and safety protocols demonstrate a commitment to safeguarding the well-being of participants and stakeholders.

A structured approach to governance and operations enhances your group's credibility and reputation in the community. When people perceive the mutual aid group as well-organized, responsible, and accountable, they are more likely to trust and support your initiatives, collaborate on projects, and contribute resources. This positive reputation can strengthen your ability to attract volunteers, secure funding, and forge partnerships with other community entities.

Articles of Association

Writing the **articles of association** for a mutual aid group is a important step in formally establishing the organization. This document serves as the foundation upon which your group is legally recognized and outlines its fundamental characteristics. When drafting the articles, it is essential to clearly define the group's name, purpose, and objectives. The name should be unique and reflective of your mission, while the purpose should succinctly describe the group's primary goals and activities. This clarity ensures that all stakeholders—including members, donors, and regulatory bodies—understand the group's intent and scope.

The articles of association must also specify the group's registered office address, which is the official location where legal documents can be sent and received. This address provides a point of contact and anchors the group within a specific jurisdiction, which is important for legal and operational purposes. The document should include the names of the incorporators or founding members, who are responsible for the initial setup and organization of the group. These details lend legitimacy and accountability to your formation.

Another component of the articles of association is the description of your governance structure. This includes outlining the roles and responsibilities of the board of directors, officers, and any other key positions. It should also detail how directors and officers are elected or appointed, the length of their terms, and procedures for their removal if necessary. Establishing a clear governance framework helps ensure that the group operates smoothly and transparently, with well-defined lines of authority and accountability.

Finally, the articles of association should include provisions for amending the document in the future. This allows the mutual aid group to adapt and evolve over time in response to changing circumstances or new challenges. Typically, amendments require a vote by the membership or board of directors, ensuring that changes are made democratically and with broad consensus. By thoughtfully drafting the articles of association, you can lay a solid legal and operational foundation that supports your mission and facilitates your growth.

On the following pages is an example of articles of association for a mutual aid group that is organized as a non-profit. You will need to modify this to suit your own group's structure and preferences.

Example: Articles of Association for "Community Solidarity Mutual Aid"

Article I: Name

The name of the organization shall be Community Solidarity Mutual Aid, hereinafter referred to as "the Group."

Article II: Purpose

The Group is established as a not-for-profit organization with the primary purpose of providing mutual aid and support to members of the community.

The Group aims to:

- Provide food, clothing, and other basic necessities to those in need.
- Facilitate skill-sharing and resource exchange among members.
- Organize community initiatives to promote solidarity and mutual support.
- Advocate for social and economic justice within the community.

Article III: Registered Office

The registered office of the Group shall be located at:
[Registered Office Address]

Article IV: Incorporators

The names and addresses of the incorporators of the Group are as follows:

[Name of Incorporator 1], [Address]
[Name of Incorporator 2], [Address]
[Name of Incorporator 3], [Address]

Article V: Governance Structure

<u>Section 1: Board of Directors</u>
The Group shall be governed by a Board of Directors, which shall consist of no fewer than five (5) and no more than eleven (11) members. Directors shall be elected by the membership at the annual meeting.

Section 2: Officers
The officers of the Group shall be a President, Vice President, Secretary, and Treasurer. Officers shall be elected by the Board of Directors from among its members at the first meeting following the annual meeting.

Section 3: Terms of Office
Directors shall serve for a term of two (2) years and may be re-elected. Officers shall serve for a term of one (1) year and may be re-elected.

Section 4: Removal and Vacancies
A director or officer may be removed by a two-thirds (2/3) vote of the Board of Directors. Vacancies on the Board or among the officers shall be filled by the Board for the remainder of the term.

Article VI: Membership

Section 1: Eligibility
Membership is open to all individuals who support the purposes of the Group and are willing to contribute to its activities.

Section 2: Dues
The Board of Directors shall determine the annual membership dues, if any. Dues shall be used to support the activities of the Group.

Section 3: Voting Rights
Each member in good standing shall be entitled to one vote on each matter submitted to a vote of the members.

Article VII: Meetings

Section 1: Annual Meeting
The annual meeting of the members shall be held on [specific date or month] at a time and place determined by the Board of Directors.

Section 2: Regular Meetings
Regular meetings of the Board of Directors shall be held at least quarterly, at times and places determined by the Board.

Section 3: Special Meetings
Special meetings of the members or the Board of Directors may be called by the President or by a majority of the Board.

Article VIII: Amendments

These Articles of Association may be amended by a two-thirds (2/3) vote of the members present and voting at any duly called meeting, provided that notice of the proposed amendment has been given to all members at least thirty (30) days in advance.

Article IX: Dissolution

Upon the dissolution of the Group, any remaining assets shall be distributed to one or more organizations with similar purposes, as determined by the Board of Directors.

Incorporators:

[Name], [Signature], [Date]
[Name], [Signature], [Date]
[Name], [Signature], [Date]

Organization Bylaws

The **bylaws** of a mutual aid group serve as the internal rules and guidelines that govern the day-to-day operations and overall governance of the organization. While the articles of association establish the group's fundamental principles and legal existence, the bylaws provide detailed procedures for how the group functions. They cover a wide range of topics, including membership criteria, meeting procedures, the roles and responsibilities of officers and directors, financial management, and the process for amending the bylaws themselves.

One of the key components of the bylaws is a section on membership. This part of the document defines who can become a member, the rights and responsibilities they have, and any required dues or fees. It also outlines the process for admitting new members and for handling situations where membership might need to be revoked. By clearly defining these aspects, the bylaws help ensure that all members are aware of their roles within the group and the benefits and obligations that come with membership.

The bylaws also detail the governance structure of the mutual aid group, specifying the composition and duties of the board of directors and officers (if applicable). This section typically includes information on how directors and officers are elected or appointed, the length of their terms, and the procedures for their removal if necessary. It may also outline the frequency and format of board meetings, as well as the quorum required for decision-making. By providing a clear governance framework, the bylaws help maintain order and accountability within the organization, ensuring that decisions are made transparently and democratically.

Another important aspect covered by the bylaws is financial management. This section includes guidelines for budgeting, financial reporting, and the handling of funds. It may also specify procedures for conducting audits and ensuring financial transparency. By establishing robust financial management practices, the bylaws help safeguard the group's resources and build trust among members and donors.

Lastly, the bylaws should include provisions for amending the document. This ensures that the mutual aid group can adapt to changing circumstances and evolving needs. Typically, amendments require a vote by the board of directors or the general membership, and the process for proposing and approving changes is clearly outlined. By including these provisions, the bylaws provide a mechanism for continuous improvement and responsiveness to the community.

Code of Ethics

 A **code of ethics** is a set of principles or guidelines that specify the expected behavior and values of individuals within an organization. It serves as a moral compass, guiding members on how to act ethically and responsibly in their interactions with each other and with the community. For a mutual aid group, implementing a code of ethics can help maintain trust and ensure accountability to the members and the broader community.

Here is an example of a code of ethics for a mutual aid group:

CODE OF ETHICS

Solidarity & Respect:
We value the dignity and worth of all individuals and communities. We commit to building relationships based on mutual respect, empathy, and solidarity, regardless of race, ethnicity, gender, sexual orientation, religion, disability, or socioeconomic status.

Integrity & Accountability:
We strive to act with honesty, transparency, and integrity in all our interactions. We hold ourselves accountable to our members and the communities we serve, ensuring that our actions align with our shared values and principles.

Inclusivity & Diversity:
We embrace diversity and inclusivity as essential strengths of our organization. We recognize the importance of amplifying marginalized voices and perspectives, and we are committed to creating spaces that are safe, welcoming, and inclusive for all.

Confidentiality & Privacy:
We respect the privacy and confidentiality of our members and the people we serve. We handle sensitive information with discretion and confidentiality, ensuring that personal data is protected and used only for its intended purpose.

Non-Discrimination & Anti-Oppression:
We reject all forms of discrimination, oppression, and injustice. We actively challenge systemic inequalities and work towards creating a more equitable and just society for all.

Conflict Resolution & Mediation:
We are committed to resolving conflicts and disagreements through open communication, dialogue, and mediation. We seek to address conflicts constructively and respectfully, with a focus on finding mutually agreeable solutions and maintaining positive relationships.

Social Responsibility & Advocacy:
We recognize our responsibility to advocate for social change and address the root causes of inequality and injustice. We engage in advocacy efforts to promote policies and practices that advance social justice, human rights, and collective well-being.

Continuous Learning & Growth:
We are dedicated to ongoing learning and self-reflection. We acknowledge that we may make mistakes and commit to learning from them, seeking feedback, and continuously improving our practices to better serve our communities.

Writing a code of ethics involves a collaborative process that includes input from all members of the mutual aid group. The process typically begins with a series of discussions or workshops where members identify and articulate the core values and ethical standards that will guide their actions. Drafting the code involves synthesizing these discussions into a clear, concise document. Finally, the code is formally adopted by the group, often through a consensus or majority vote.

Anti-Discrimination Policy

An **anti-discrimination policy** is a set of guidelines and principles aimed at preventing discrimination and promoting equality within an organization. Mutual aid groups may choose to implement an anti-discrimination policy to ensure that all people are treated fairly and respectfully, regardless of their race, ethnicity, gender, sexual orientation, religion, disability, or other characteristics.

Having an anti-discrimination policy helps create an inclusive environment where everyone feels safe and respected. It sets clear expectations for behavior and establishes procedures for addressing incidents of discrimination or harassment if they occur. By promoting diversity and inclusion, mutual aid groups can better serve their communities and work towards social justice and equity.

Here is an example of an anti-discrimination policy for a mutual aid group:

Conflict-of-Interest Policy

 A **conflict-of-interest policy** provides guidelines for identifying, disclosing, and managing situations where personal interests may conflict with the interests of a mutual aid group. Such a policy helps ensure transparency, integrity, and trust within the organization by preventing situations where people could benefit personally at the expense of the group or its mission. By having a clear policy in place, the mutual aid group demonstrates its commitment to ethical conduct and accountability, encouraging a culture of fairness and professionalism.

Here is an example of a conflict-of-interest policy for a mutual aid group:

CONFLICT-OF-INTEREST POLICY

Disclosure: All members of the mutual aid group are required to disclose any potential conflicts of interest that may arise in the course of their involvement with the organization. This includes financial interests, personal relationships, and other situations where there may be a divergence between personal and organizational interests.

Evaluation: The mutual aid group's board of directors or governing body will evaluate any disclosed conflicts of interest to determine their significance and potential impact on the organization. This evaluation will consider factors such as the nature of the conflict, the magnitude of the financial or personal interest involved, and whether the conflict could compromise the group's mission or objectives.

Recusal: In cases where a conflict of interest is deemed significant, the individual involved will be required to recuse themselves from any discussions or decisions related to the matter in question. This may include abstaining from voting on certain issues or refraining from participating in specific activities where their personal interests could unduly influence the outcome.

Transparency: The mutual aid group will maintain transparency regarding conflicts of interest by documenting disclosures, evaluations, and any actions taken to address them. This information will be made available to members of the organization and relevant stakeholders as appropriate, ensuring accountability and trust.

Annual Review: The conflict-of-interest policy will be reviewed annually by the mutual aid group's leadership to ensure its effectiveness and relevance. Any updates or revisions to the policy will be communicated to all members and implemented accordingly.

By adhering to this conflict-of-interest policy, the mutual aid group demonstrates its commitment to upholding ethical standards and safeguarding the interests of its members and the broader community.

Data Protection & Privacy Policy

 A **data protection & privacy policy** outlines how a mutual aid group collects, uses, stores, and protects personal information obtained from its members, volunteers, and community members. It establishes guidelines for handling sensitive data in accordance with legal requirements and ethical standards.

Key components of a data protection and privacy policy may include:

Data Collection: Clearly specify the types of personal information collected by the mutual aid group, such as names, contact details, and demographic data, and the purposes for which it will be used.

Consent: Describe the process for obtaining consent from individuals before collecting their personal information, including the right to withdraw consent at any time.

Data Use & Sharing: Outline how personal data will be used, stored, and shared, ensuring that it is only accessed by authorized individuals for legitimate purposes related to the group's activities.

Data Security: Implement measures to safeguard personal information against unauthorized access, disclosure, alteration, or destruction, including encryption, password protection, and secure data storage systems.

Data Retention: Establish guidelines for the retention and deletion of personal data, specifying the period for which it will be kept and the circumstances under which it will be securely disposed of.

Individual Rights: Inform individuals of their rights regarding their personal data, such as the right to access, rectify, or erase their information, and provide mechanisms for exercising these rights.

Compliance & Accountability: Commit to complying with applicable data protection laws and regulations, appointing a designated individual or team responsible for overseeing data protection practices and addressing data privacy inquiries or concerns.

Having a data protection and privacy policy demonstrates the mutual aid group's commitment to respecting people' privacy rights and maintaining the confidentiality and security of their personal information. It helps create trust and confidence among stakeholders and ensures compliance with legal and regulatory requirements.

Here is an example of a data protection and privacy policy for a mutual aid group:

DATA PROTECTION & PRIVACY POLICY

[Organization Name] is committed to protecting the privacy and personal data of its members, volunteers, donors, and other stakeholders. This Data Protection & Privacy Policy outlines how we collect, use, disclose, and protect personal information in accordance with applicable data protection laws and regulations.

1. Collection & Use of Personal Information:
We collect personal information directly from individuals when they register as members, volunteer for our activities, make donations, or interact with us through our website or other channels. Personal information may include names, contact details, demographic information, and other relevant data necessary for our organizational activities. We use personal information to communicate with individuals, provide services, process donations, manage memberships, and fulfill our organizational objectives.

2. Disclosure of Personal Information:
We do not disclose personal information to third parties without consent, except as required by law or as necessary for the purposes stated in this policy. In some cases, we may share personal information with trusted service providers who assist us in carrying out our activities, such as payment processors or email service providers. We ensure that these third parties comply with applicable data protection laws and regulations.

3. Data Security & Retention:
We implement appropriate technical and organizational measures to protect personal information from unauthorized access, disclosure, alteration, or destruction. Personal information is retained only for as long as necessary to fulfill the purposes for which it was collected or as required by law.

4. Individual Rights:
Individuals have the right to access, correct, or delete their personal information held by [Organization Name]. Requests to exercise these rights should be submitted in writing to the Data Protection Officer. We will respond to such requests in accordance with applicable data protection laws and regulations.

continues ...

5. Consent:
By providing personal information to [Organization Name], individuals consent to the collection, use, and disclosure of their information as described in this policy. Individuals may withdraw consent at any time by contacting the Data Protection Officer.

6. Updates to the Policy:
This Data Protection and Privacy Policy may be updated from time to time to reflect changes in legal or regulatory requirements or our organizational practices. Any updates will be posted on our website, and individuals will be notified of significant changes.

Contact Information:
For inquiries about our Data Protection and Privacy Policy or to exercise your rights under applicable data protection laws, please contact:

[Data Protection Officer's Name]
[Organization Name]
[Address]
[Email Address]
[Phone Number]

This is a basic example and should be customized to reflect the specific practices and requirements of the mutual aid group.

Criteria for Distributing Resources

 Establishing criteria for distributing resources is important to ensure fairness and equity within a mutual aid group. To achieve this, the group should carefully consider the diverse needs of the community and prioritize those who are most vulnerable and marginalized. Factors such as income level, housing stability, access to healthcare, and other basic needs should be taken into account when determining eligibility for assistance.

Additionally, the group should strive to be transparent and accountable in its decision-making process, seeking input from community members and maintaining clear communication about the criteria and allocation process. By prioritizing fairness and inclusivity in resource distribution, the mutual aid group can effectively support those who need it most while creating a sense of trust and solidarity within the community.

When determining who to distribute resources to, a mutual aid group might consider the following criteria:

- **Needs Assessment:** Prioritizing individuals or families based on the severity of their needs, such as lack of access to basic necessities like food, shelter, clothing, and medical care.

- **Vulnerability:** Focusing on vulnerable populations, including the elderly, children, disabled individuals, single-parent households, and those with chronic illnesses or mental health conditions.

- **Income Level:** Assisting those with low or no income, unemployed individuals, and underemployed workers who cannot meet their basic living expenses.

- **Geographic Location:** Targeting residents in specific geographic areas that are particularly affected by crises, such as neighborhoods with high poverty rates, disaster-stricken areas, or regions with limited access to public services.

- **Community Input:** Consulting with community members to identify and prioritize those in need, ensuring the aid is distributed in a way that reflects the community's perception of who is most in need.

- **Equity Considerations:** Ensuring equitable distribution by taking into account historical and systemic inequities that may affect certain groups more than others, such as racial, ethnic, and gender disparities.

- **Urgency:** Responding to urgent requests for aid, such as immediate food and shelter needs, to prevent further harm or deterioration of the individual's situation.

- **Availability of Resources:** Balancing the distribution based on the availability of resources, ensuring that aid is given in a sustainable manner and can reach as many people as possible.

- **Engagement & Participation:** Giving priority to community members who are actively engaged with the mutual aid group or those who have contributed to the group's activities, promoting a reciprocal and supportive community dynamic.

- **Referrals & Recommendations:** Considering referrals from trusted community organizations, social workers, or other mutual aid groups that have firsthand knowledge of peoples' circumstances.

Disciplinary Policy

While the primary focus of mutual aid is collaboration and support, instances may arise where disciplinary action becomes necessary to maintain the integrity and effectiveness of the group. A **disciplinary policy** outlines the procedures and consequences for conflicts or breaches of conduct within the mutual aid group. It establishes clear expectations for behavior and provides a framework for handling situations where people violate the organization's rules or code of ethics.

The policy typically includes details such as the types of behavior that warrant disciplinary action, the steps involved in addressing misconduct, and the potential consequences. The primary purpose of a disciplinary policy is to promote accountability, maintain order, and uphold the values and standards of the organization.

One scenario that might warrant disciplinary action is when a member engages in behavior that compromises its mission and values. This could include actions such as harassment, discrimination, dishonesty, or disruptive behavior during meetings or activities. Another scenario may involve misuse or misappropriation of group resources—such as funds, supplies, or information—for personal gain or purposes unrelated to the group's objectives.

The specific procedures for disciplinary action typically involve a series of steps designed to address the issue and resolve conflicts constructively. These steps may include informal discussions or mediation to address concerns and provide opportunities for reconciliation. If informal resolution attempts are unsuccessful or if the misconduct is severe or recurrent, the group may proceed to formal disciplinary measures—such as warnings, probationary periods, or removal from the group.

Here is an example of a disciplinary policy for a mutual aid group:

DISCIPLINARY POLICY

1. Purpose
The purpose of this disciplinary policy is to maintain a positive, respectful, and safe environment within the Community Solidarity Mutual Aid (the "Group"). This policy outlines the procedures for addressing behaviors that are inconsistent with the Group's values and objectives.

2. Scope
This policy applies to all members, volunteers, and participants of the Group.

3. Code of Conduct
All members are expected to:

- Treat others with respect and dignity
- Refrain from any form of harassment, discrimination, or violence
- Act with integrity and honesty
- Follow the Group's bylaws, policies, and procedures
- Contribute to a supportive and inclusive community

4. Violations
Violations of the Code of Conduct include, but are not limited to:

- Harassment or discrimination based on race, gender, sexual orientation, religion, or any other protected characteristic
- Physical or verbal abuse
- Theft, fraud, or misuse of the Group's resources
- Disruptive behavior that undermines the Group's activities or meetings
- Consistent failure to fulfill agreed-upon responsibilities

5. Reporting Violations
Members who witness or experience a violation of the Code of Conduct should report the incident to a member of the Board of Directors or the designated Ethics Officer. Reports should be made in writing and include detailed information about the incident.

continues...

6. Investigation

Upon receiving a report of a violation, the Board of Directors or the Ethics Officer will:

- Acknowledge receipt of the report within five (5) business days
- Conduct a fair and impartial investigation, including interviews with the parties involved and any witnesses
- Maintain confidentiality to the extent possible, consistent with conducting a thorough investigation

7. Disciplinary Actions

Based on the findings of the investigation, the Board of Directors may take one or more of the following actions:

- Verbal or written warning
- Suspension of membership or volunteer duties for a specified period
- Requirement to complete specific corrective actions (e.g., training)
- Permanent termination of membership or volunteer duties

8. Appeal Process

Members who are subject to disciplinary action have the right to appeal the decision. To initiate an appeal, the member must submit a written request to the Board of Directors within ten (10) business days of receiving the disciplinary decision. The Board will review the appeal and provide a written response within fifteen (15) business days.

9. Record Keeping

The Board of Directors will maintain records of all reports, investigations, and disciplinary actions. These records will be kept confidential and secure.

10. Review & Amendment

This disciplinary policy will be reviewed annually by the Board of Directors and may be amended as necessary to ensure its effectiveness and alignment with the Group's values and objectives.

11. Communication

This policy will be communicated to all members upon joining the Group and will be readily accessible on the Group's website and at all Group meetings.

Adopted this [Date]

Signatures of Board Members:

[Name], [Signature]

Risk Management & Liability

Risk management is the process of identifying, assessing, and mitigating risks to minimize their potential impact on an organization or project. It involves analyzing potential hazards, determining the likelihood and severity of their occurrence, and implementing strategies to reduce or eliminate their negative consequences. Risk management aims to protect an organization's assets, reputation, and stakeholders by proactively addressing potential threats and vulnerabilities.

A mutual aid group should identify risks related to volunteer activities, transportation services, food preparation and distribution, fundraising events, and other activities. Once potential risks have been identified, the group can develop risk management strategies to minimize exposure to liability. This may involve implementing safety protocols and procedures, providing training and resources to volunteers, securing appropriate insurance coverage, or establishing emergency response plans.

Liability is another important consideration for mutual aid groups, as they may be held legally responsible for any harm or damages that occur as a result of their activities. To mitigate liability risks, mutual aid groups should ensure that they operate in accordance with applicable laws and regulations, obtain necessary permits and licenses, and adhere to industry best practices. Additionally, having clear policies and procedures in place–such as waivers of liability for volunteers and participants (see next page)–can help protect the group from potential legal claims.

It is important for mutual aid groups to consult with legal experts to assess their specific liability risks and develop appropriate strategies to address them. By prioritizing risk management and liability mitigation, mutual aid groups can create a safer environment for their members and the broader community, ultimately enhancing their ability to fulfill their mission effectively and responsibly.

Here is an example of a waiver of liability for mutual aid group participants:

WAIVER OF LIABILITY

1. Introduction
This Waiver of Liability (the "Waiver") is executed by the undersigned participant (the "Participant") in favor of [Mutual Aid Group Name], its directors, officers, members, volunteers, and agents (collectively, the "Group"). The Participant desires to engage voluntarily in activities organized by the Group, including but not limited to community service, distribution of goods and services, meetings, events, and any other related activities (the "Activities").

2. Acknowledgment of Risk
The Participant acknowledges that participation in the Activities may involve inherent risks, including but not limited to physical injury, illness, property damage, and other potential hazards. The Participant voluntarily assumes all such risks, both known and unknown, even if arising from the negligence of the Group or others.

3. Release & Waiver
In consideration of being permitted to participate in the Activities, the Participant hereby releases, waives, discharges, and covenants not to sue the Group for any and all liability, claims, demands, actions, and causes of action arising out of or related to any loss, damage, or injury, including death, that may be sustained by the Participant or to any property belonging to the Participant, whether caused by the negligence of the Group or otherwise, while participating in the Activities or while on the premises where the Activities are conducted.

4. Indemnification
The Participant agrees to indemnify and hold harmless the Group from any and all claims, actions, suits, procedures, costs, expenses, damages, and liabilities, including attorney's fees, brought as a result of the Participant's involvement in the Activities and to reimburse the Group for any such expenses incurred.

5. Medical Treatment

The Participant consents to receive medical treatment that may be deemed advisable in the event of injury, accident, and/or illness during the Activities. The Participant releases and discharges the Group from any claim whatsoever that arises or may arise on account of any first aid, treatment, or service rendered in connection with the Participant's involvement in the Activities.

6. Voluntary Participation

The Participant acknowledges that they are voluntarily participating in the Activities and that they have read and understand the terms of this Waiver. The Participant further acknowledges that they are not relying on any representations, statements, or inducements apart from the terms of this Waiver.

7. Governing Law

This Waiver shall be governed by and construed in accordance with the laws of the state in which the Group is based, without regard to its conflict of laws principles.

8. Severability

If any term or provision of this Waiver is held to be invalid or unenforceable, the remaining terms and provisions shall remain in full force and effect.

9. Entire Agreement

This Waiver constitutes the entire agreement between the Participant and the Group with respect to the subject matter contained herein and supersedes all prior agreements, understandings, and negotiations regarding the same.

IN WITNESS WHEREOF, the Participant has executed this Waiver as of the date set forth below.

Participant's Name: _____

Participant's Signature: _____

Date: _____

Participant Address: _____

Participant Phone Number: _____

Emergency Contact Name/Phone: _____

Recordkeeping & Bookkeeping

Recordkeeping and bookkeeping are foundational practices for the successful operation of mutual aid groups. These practices encompass the thoughtful documentation of various aspects of the group's activities, ensuring transparency, accountability, and efficiency in its operations.

Recordkeeping involves keeping track of financial documents—such as income and expenditure statements, receipts, and bank statements. These documents provide a clear picture of the group's financial transactions, ensuring that donations are properly recorded, expenses are accounted for, and funds are allocated responsibly. Maintaining detailed financial records enables the group to adhere to legal and regulatory requirements and facilitates the preparation of financial reports for stakeholders.

Beyond financial records, maintaining documentation of meetings is also important. This includes taking minutes that capture key discussions, decisions, and action points. Minutes serve as an official record of the group's proceedings, ensuring that members have a clear understanding of the topics discussed and the outcomes of the meeting. Additionally, minutes provide a historical record of the group's activities, aiding in continuity and accountability.

Mutual aid groups should also maintain records of important decisions, agreements, and policies. This may include documents such as bylaws, codes of conduct, conflict-of-interest policies, and data protection protocols. These documents outline the group's guiding principles, operational procedures, and ethical standards, serving as a reference for members and stakeholders alike.

Legal Compliance

Compliance with federal, state, and local laws is crucial for a mutual aid group to ensure its sustainability and effective operation. Navigating these legal requirements can safeguard the group against potential legal issues and enhance its credibility and effectiveness in serving the community.

Depending on the size and operations of the group, it may be advantageous to seek out legal advice from a professional. Initially, the group should identify the key areas where legal advice is necessary—such as organizational structure, tax compliance, fundraising regulations, or employment law. Once these areas are pinpointed, the group can explore various avenues for obtaining legal counsel.

One effective approach is to reach out to local legal aid organizations that offer pro bono services to community and non-profit groups. Many lawyers and law firms provide free legal services as part of their community service efforts and may be interested in supporting causes that benefit the community directly. Additionally, contacting law schools nearby can also be beneficial, as many have legal clinics where law students, supervised by licensed attorneys, provide legal advice to non-profits and community organizations at no cost.

Another avenue is through professional networks or referrals from other mutual aid groups or non-profits. Often, these networks can recommend attorneys who specialize in non-profit law and are familiar with the unique needs and challenges of community-based groups. For ongoing legal needs, it might be worth setting aside a budget for legal fees or negotiating reduced rates with a law firm that aligns with the group's mission and values.

Federal/State/Local Laws

For mutual aid groups, navigating the legal landscape involves understanding and complying with a variety of laws at the federal, state, and local levels. The following pages provide a breakdown of some key areas where these laws typically apply.

FEDERAL LAWS

Tax Regulations: For groups seeking non-profit status, such as 501(c)(3) organizations, compliance with IRS regulations is crucial. This includes maintaining eligibility for tax-exempt status by adhering to rules regarding political activities, lobbying, and the use of funds for charitable purposes only.

Labor Laws: Federal laws such as the Fair Labor Standards Act (FLSA) regulate wage and hour standards for employees, while the Volunteer Protection Act provides certain protections for volunteers.

Anti-Discrimination Laws: Laws such as the Civil Rights Act, the Americans with Disabilities Act (ADA), and Equal Employment Opportunity laws must be followed to ensure there is no discrimination in hiring, volunteering, or serving the community based on protected characteristics.

Privacy & Data Protection: Compliance with the Health Insurance Portability and Accountability Act (HIPAA) if dealing with health information, and understanding the implications of the Federal Trade Commission (FTC) regulations on data privacy and security.

STATE LAWS

Charitable Solicitation: Most states require registration before a non-profit can legally solicit donations within that state. The requirements vary widely, so it's essential to check the specific laws in each state where funds are raised.

Incorporation & Reporting: State laws dictate the process for incorporating as a non-profit or other entity and what annual or periodic reporting is necessary to maintain legal status.

State Labor Laws: These may include minimum wage laws, state-specific worker compensation laws, and unemployment insurance obligations.

Fundraising & Financial Regulations: State laws also govern financial audits, fundraising practices, and the management of funds, often overseen by the state's attorney general or a specific department of charitable affairs.

LOCAL LAWS

Zoning & Use Permits: Local zoning laws may affect where a mutual aid group can operate, especially if it involves physical facilities like offices, shelters, or food distribution centers.

Health & Safety Codes: Depending on the activities involved, local health and safety codes must be followed, particularly if food preparation or distribution is involved.

Business Licenses: Some local jurisdictions may require specific licenses for activities, even if they are charitable in nature.

Event Permits: If organizing events, local permits may be required, especially for large gatherings or use of public spaces.

COMPLIANCE STRATEGIES

Legal Consultation: Regular consultation with legal experts, particularly those specializing in nonprofit law, can help navigate the complexities of applicable laws.

Education & Training: Educating staff and volunteers on compliance requirements specific to their roles can prevent unintentional violations.

Regular Reviews: Periodically reviewing compliance with all relevant laws, including new legislation that might affect operations, is essential.

Mutual aid groups can utilize various free resources to ensure compliance with federal, state, and local laws. Online platforms like the IRS website provide extensive information on tax obligations and requirements for non-profit organizations, including downloadable forms and guidelines. Many state and local government websites offer free resources and toolkits specific to non-profit compliance, including registration processes, reporting requirements, and legal obligations. Public libraries and community centers often have access to legal databases and can provide assistance or direct groups to free legal clinics and workshops. Additionally, organizations such as the National Council of Nonprofits and local bar associations frequently offer free webinars, guides, and consultation services to help community organizations navigate the legal landscape.

Volunteer Protection Act

The Volunteer Protection Act (VPA) of 1997 is a federal law in the United States designed to promote volunteerism by offering liability protections to volunteers serving nonprofit organizations and governmental entities. Under this act, volunteers are shielded from liability for harm caused by their acts or omissions on behalf of the organization or entity, provided certain conditions are met. Here are key aspects of the Volunteer Protection Act:

Liability Protection: The VPA provides immunity to volunteers from civil liabilities for any harm they cause while performing duties or activities within the scope of their volunteer responsibilities—unless the harm was caused by willful, criminal, or grossly negligent misconduct, or a conscious, flagrant indifference to the rights or safety of the individual harmed by the volunteer.

Exclusions: The protection does not apply in cases of harm caused by a volunteer operating a motor vehicle, vessel, aircraft, or other vehicle for which the state requires the operator or the owner of the vehicle to possess an operator's license or maintain insurance.

State Law Preemption: The Act preempts state laws that are less protective of volunteers from liability but allows states to enact laws that provide additional protection from liability. This means that the VPA sets a baseline level of protection, and states can choose to offer more but not less.

Insurance: If a volunteer is covered by an insurance policy (like the organization's policy), the liability protection applies only to the amount of damages in excess of the insurance coverage.

Scope of Work: The protection only applies when volunteers are acting within the scope of their responsibilities at the time of the act or omission.

No Affect on Organization Liability: While the VPA protects individual volunteers from liability, it does not protect the nonprofit organizations themselves from being sued. Organizations can still be held liable for the actions or inactions of their volunteers.

The VPA encourages individuals to volunteer their time for the benefit of their communities by providing a legal safeguard against the fear of litigation. By understanding the protections afforded and the limitations of these protections, volunteers can engage more freely in public service activities, knowing they are generally protected from legal liability.

Solicitation Laws

Solicitation laws are regulations that govern the act of asking for donations or funds from individuals, businesses, or organizations. These laws vary depending on the jurisdiction and can apply to both nonprofit and for-profit entities. In the context of mutual aid groups or nonprofits, solicitation laws typically cover activities such as fundraising events, online crowdfunding campaigns, direct mail appeals, and door-to-door canvassing.

Key aspects of solicitation laws may include requirements for obtaining permits or licenses before conducting fundraising activities, rules regarding the disclosure of information to donors, restrictions on deceptive or misleading fundraising practices, and guidelines for the use of funds raised. Additionally, there may be specific regulations governing how funds must be managed, reported, and disbursed.

Failure to comply with solicitation laws can result in legal consequences, such as fines, penalties, or restrictions on future fundraising activities. Therefore, it is essential for mutual aid groups to familiarize themselves with the solicitation laws applicable in their area and ensure that their fundraising efforts adhere to all legal requirements. Seeking legal advice or consulting with experts in nonprofit law can help mutual aid groups navigate these regulations effectively and avoid potential pitfalls.

Permits & Licenses

Mutual aid groups may need to obtain permits or licenses for various activities depending on local regulations and the nature of their operations. Some examples include:

Fundraising Events: If the group plans to organize events such as bake sales, charity dinners, or auctions, they may need permits or licenses from local authorities or regulatory agencies. These ensure compliance with fundraising regulations and may involve fees or documentation.

Street Collections: If the group intends to conduct street collections or solicit donations in public spaces, they may need permits or licenses from municipal authorities. These permits often outline specific guidelines for collecting funds in public areas and may require advance approval or coordination with local law enforcement.

Food Preparation & Distribution: If the mutual aid group plans to prepare or distribute food to community members, they may need permits or licenses related to food safety and sanitation. These permits ensure compliance with health regulations and may involve inspections of food preparation facilities or adherence to specific guidelines for handling and serving food.

Transportation Services: If the group provides transportation services to community members–such as shuttle services for medical appointments or grocery delivery services–they may need permits or licenses related to transportation regulations. These permits ensure compliance with safety standards and may involve vehicle inspections or insurance requirements.

Public Events or Gatherings: If the group organizes public events or gatherings–such as community meetings, rallies, or marches–they may need permits from local authorities to use public spaces or facilities. These permits often outline guidelines for crowd management, security, and other logistical considerations.

It is important for mutual aid groups to research and understand the specific permit and licensing requirements applicable to their activities in their local jurisdiction. Consulting with legal experts or regulatory agencies can help ensure compliance and avoid potential legal issues.

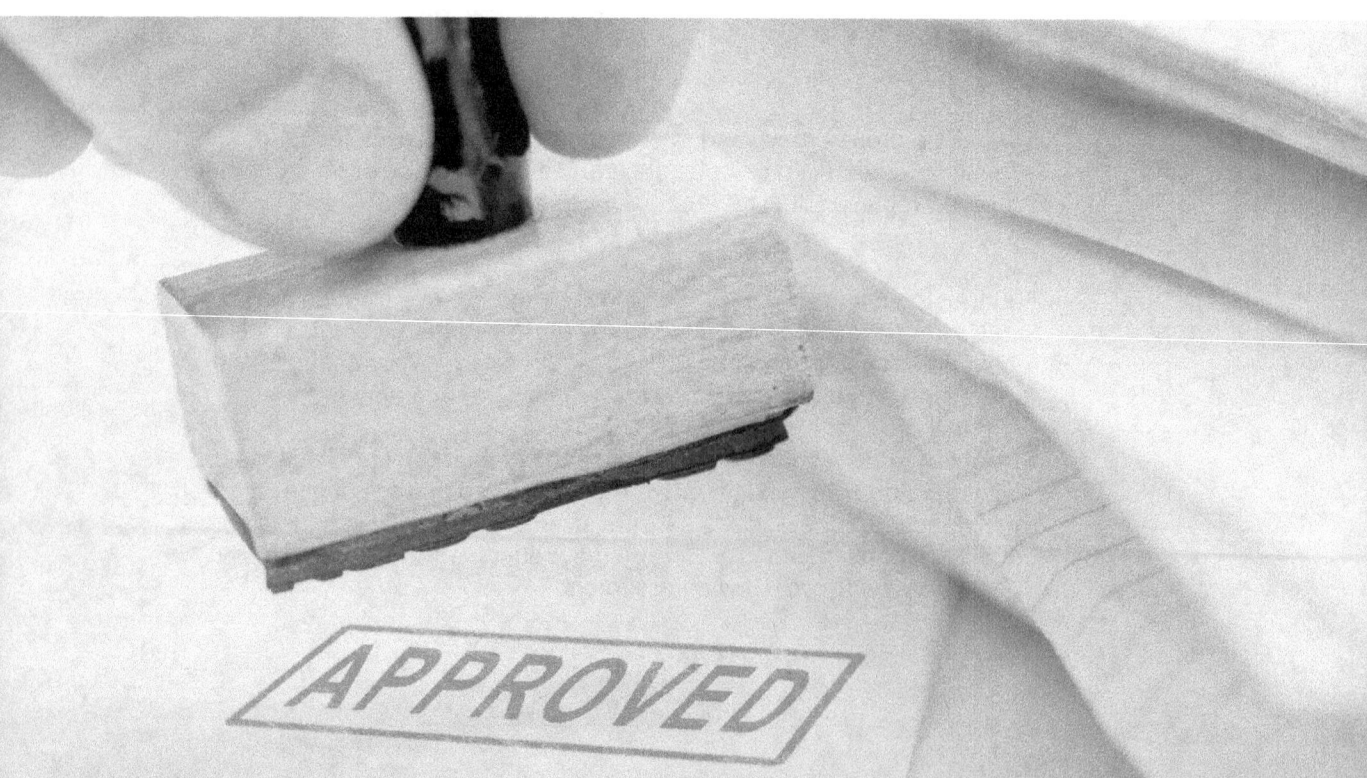

Filing Taxes

The tax obligations of a mutual aid group largely depend on how the group is structured. One common structure is the unincorporated association, which is typically a group of individuals working together towards a common goal without forming a legal entity. While unincorporated associations can operate informally, they are not exempt from tax obligations and must carefully navigate these requirements.

For unincorporated associations, the first step is recognizing that, unlike incorporated entities or recognized nonprofits, they do not automatically qualify for tax-exempt status. This means that any income the group receives—whether from donations, grants, or sales—may be subject to federal, state, and local taxes. The group must report all income and expenses accurately and may need to file a tax return, depending on how the IRS views the association's financial activities.

Unincorporated associations should also be aware of their state and local tax obligations. Each state has different rules regarding the taxation of unincorporated groups. Some states may require these groups to register and file periodic reports, while others might impose specific taxes on income or sales. Additionally, local jurisdictions may have their own regulations, including business licenses and local taxes. Understanding and complying with these requirements is important to avoid penalties.

Maintaining detailed and accurate financial records is essential for managing tax obligations. This includes keeping track of all income, donations, grants, and expenditures. Proper bookkeeping practices not only help in filing accurate tax returns but also enhance transparency and accountability within the group. This is particularly important when dealing with donors and supporters who expect their contributions to be managed responsibly.

Consulting with a tax professional or legal advisor who understands the nuances of tax law for community-based groups can be invaluable. These experts can provide guidance on what forms to file, how to maximize potential tax benefits, and ensure compliance with all relevant laws. By being proactive and informed about their tax obligations, mutual aid groups can focus more effectively on their mission, confident that their financial and legal bases are covered.

Non-Profit Obligations

While becoming an official non-profit organization can provide certain benefits—such as tax-exempt status and eligibility for grants—it also comes with a significant level of government oversight and regulation. For mutual aid groups who are deeply involved in social activism and who may even protest government actions, the idea of being closely monitored by government agencies may not align with their strategic interests.

As mentioned earlier, non-profit organizations are subject to strict rules and regulations set forth by the Internal Revenue Service (IRS) and other government bodies. Mutual aid groups who prioritize autonomy and flexibility in their operations may find the non-profit regulatory burden to be overly restrictive.

Obtaining and maintaining non-profit status requires considerable time, effort, and resources. Non-profit organizations must comply with complex application processes, annual reporting requirements, and ongoing compliance obligations. For mutual aid groups who are primarily focused on direct community support and activism, dedicating energy to regulatory compliance may not be the most effective use of their limited resources.

Official non-profit status can also potentially limit a mutual aid group's ability to engage in certain types of advocacy or political activities. 501(c)(3) non-profit organizations are subject to restrictions on lobbying and political campaigning, which may hinder their ability to advocate for systemic change or challenge government policies.

Overall, while non-profit status offers certain advantages, mutual aid groups should carefully weigh the benefits and drawbacks before pursuing official non-profit status. For groups that prioritize autonomy, flexibility, and grassroots activism, maintaining independence from government regulation may better align with their mission and values.

Application for 501(c)(3)

 Applying for non-profit status involves several steps, and the process may vary depending on your jurisdiction. However, here are the general steps a mutual aid group would typically take to apply for 501(c)(3) status:

1. Determine Eligibility:
Ensure that your mutual aid group meets the eligibility criteria for non-profit status under section 501(c)(3) of the Internal Revenue Code. Generally, organizations must operate exclusively for religious, charitable, scientific, literary, or educational purposes, among others.

2. Incorporate:
Decide on the legal structure of your organization and incorporate it at the state level. Most states require non-profits to incorporate before applying for federal tax-exempt status. Choose a name for your organization and file articles of incorporation with the appropriate state agency.

3. Draft Bylaws:
Develop bylaws that outline the internal rules and procedures governing your organization's operations, including the structure of the board of directors, decision-making processes, and membership criteria.

4. Obtain an Employer Identification Number (EIN):
Apply for an Employer Identification Number (EIN) from the IRS. This unique nine-digit number is used to identify your organization for tax purposes.

5. File Form 1023 or 1023-EZ:
Prepare and submit either Form 1023 (Application for Recognition of Exemption Under Section 501(c)(3)) or Form 1023-EZ (Streamlined Application for Recognition of Exemption Under Section 501(c)(3)). Form 1023-EZ is a shorter and simpler application form available for certain eligible organizations with less than $50,000 in annual gross receipts.

6. Pay the Application Fee:
Include the required application fee with your Form 1023 submission. The fee amount varies depending on the organization's gross receipts and the form used.

7. Wait for Determination:
After submitting your application, wait for the IRS to review it. The processing time can vary, but it typically takes several months. During this period, the IRS may request additional information or clarification.

Receive Tax-Exempt Status:
Once the IRS approves your application, you will receive a determination letter recognizing your organization's tax-exempt status under section 501(c)(3). This letter confirms that donors can make tax-deductible contributions to your organization, and your group can enjoy other benefits of tax-exempt status.

Maintain Compliance:
Ensure ongoing compliance with IRS regulations and reporting requirements to maintain your organization's tax-exempt status. This includes filing annual information returns (Form 990) and adhering to any state regulations.

It is important to consult with legal and financial professionals experienced in non-profit law and tax matters to navigate the application process effectively and ensure compliance with all relevant regulations.

Board of Directors

A **board of directors** serves as the fundamental governance body of a non-profit organization. It is responsible for overseeing the organization's activities, ensuring legal compliance, and advancing its mission.

One of the primary functions of the board is to provide strategic direction and guidance to the organization. Board members are typically chosen for their expertise, diverse perspectives, and commitment to the organization's mission. They bring a range of skills, knowledge, and networks that can help steer the organization toward its goals.

The board of directors operates through regular meetings where key decisions are made, policies are developed, and progress is monitored. These meetings serve as forums for discussing organizational priorities, assessing performance, and addressing emerging challenges. Board members may also serve on committees or task forces focused on specific areas such as finance, governance, or fundraising.

Additionally, the board plays an important role in ensuring compliance with legal and regulatory requirements. This includes overseeing financial management, reviewing annual budgets and financial statements, and ensuring that the organization operates in accordance with its mission and values. The board is also responsible for hiring and evaluating the performance of the organization's executive leadership, such as the executive director or CEO.

Financial Reporting

Financial reporting for non-profit organizations plays an important role in demonstrating the stewardship of funds, building trust with stakeholders, and fulfilling regulatory requirements. It involves documenting and communicating the financial activities and health of the organization to stakeholders. Here's a general overview of the types of reporting that should be expected:

Income Statement (or Statement of Activities):
This report shows the organization's revenues and expenses over a specific period, typically a fiscal year. It provides insight into how funds are generated and utilized to support the organization's operations.

Balance Sheet (or Statement of Financial Position):
This report presents the organization's financial position at a specific point in time. It lists the organization's assets (such as cash, investments, and property), liabilities (such as loans and accounts payable), and net assets (the difference between assets and liabilities).

Cash Flow Statement:
This report details the organization's cash inflows and outflows during the reporting period, categorizing them into operating, investing, and financing activities. It provides insight into how cash moves in and out of the organization and helps assess its liquidity and ability to meet financial obligations.

Notes to the Financial Statements:
These are additional disclosures accompanying the financial statements, providing more details about specific accounting policies, significant transactions, and other relevant information.

Annual Report:
Many non-profit organizations prepare an annual report, which includes financial highlights, program achievements, impact stories, and messages from leadership. It serves as a communication tool to engage donors, supporters, and the community.

IRS Form 990:
Most non-profit organizations are required to file IRS Form 990 annually. This form provides detailed information about the organization's mission, programs, governance, finances, and compliance with tax regulations. It is publicly available and helps ensure transparency and accountability.

Chapter Review

The organizational structure of a mutual aid group is a fundamental consideration that impacts many legal aspects of its operation. The group must decide whether to remain an unincorporated association, form a cooperative, or seek non-profit status as a 501(c)(3) or 501(c)(4) organization. Each structure has its own legal implications, including liability, tax obligations, and regulatory requirements. For example, while an unincorporated association may offer simplicity and flexibility, it may also expose members to personal liability. Conversely, incorporating as a non-profit can provide liability protection and potential tax exemptions but requires adherence to stricter regulatory standards and governance.

Establishing clear policies and procedures is essential for maintaining ethical operations. Transparent policies help prevent conflicts of interest, promote fair treatment, and provide a framework for resolving disputes. Having a code of conduct can guide members' behavior and ensure that the group's activities align with its values and mission.

Depending on the group's structure and activities, various federal, state, and local laws may apply. This can include registration requirements, tax filings, and adherence to labor laws if the group employs staff. 501(c)(3) non-profits, in particular, must comply with regulations governing charitable organizations, such as reporting financial activities, maintaining tax-exempt status, and avoiding political activities that could jeopardize their standing. Ensuring compliance often requires consulting with legal professionals who specialize in non-profit law to navigate these complexities and avoid potential legal pitfalls.

Discussion Questions

1 Can you recall a time when clear policies and procedures helped resolve a conflict or prevent misunderstandings in a group or organization you were part of? What specific policies were most effective?

2 Have you ever encountered legal challenges while participating in a group project? How did you address these challenges, and what did you learn from the experience?

Chapter **7**

Fundamentals of Resource Mobilization

Resources can take many forms, from food and clothing to volunteer labor and financial contributions. In mutual aid, the goal is to pool these resources in a way that strengthens the community and ensures that help is available where it's needed most.

In this chapter, we discuss how your mutual aid group can mobilize resources efficiently. Whether responding to natural disasters, addressing food insecurity, or organizing transportation services, access to the right resources can make the difference between success and failure.

Human Resources

Mutual aid is fundamentally about people helping people. It's the collaboration and solidarity between individuals that allows mutual aid to thrive. Whether someone is organizing logistics, offering emotional support, or sharing their specific skills, every contribution is valuable. Unlike many formal organizations, mutual aid groups often operate with a horizontal structure, meaning there's less hierarchy and more shared responsibility. This makes human resources especially important, as the success of the group relies on each member's commitment and participation in sustaining the collective effort.

The value of human resources goes beyond just physical work—each person's unique abilities, knowledge, and connections add to the group's overall strength. They are the lifeblood of any mutual aid project, and organizers must always prioritize the needs and preferences of the people who volunteer their time and energy.

The human resources involved in mutual aid include:

Organizers & Leaders:

People who take on leadership roles—coordinating activities, facilitating meetings, and guiding the overall direction of the group's efforts.

Volunteers:

Community members who contribute their time and effort to support various tasks and projects organized by the group, such as distributing resources, providing assistance to vulnerable populations, or participating in events.

Specialists & Professionals:

People with specialized skills or expertise—such as healthcare professionals, legal advisors, social workers, or educators—who offer their services to address specific needs within the community.

Advocates & Activists:

People who advocate for social justice, equity, and systemic change, leveraging their voices and resources to address underlying issues contributing to community challenges.

Collaborators & Partners:

External organizations or businesses that collaborate with the mutual aid group to amplify their impact, share resources, or provide additional support to community members.

Recipients of Aid:

People who benefit from the mutual aid group's efforts, including individuals facing financial hardship, housing insecurity, food insecurity, or other forms of adversity.

Why People Volunteer

From organizing community events to providing direct assistance to those in need, volunteers play an important role in driving the mission and impact of mutual aid groups. In the spirit of solidarity and cooperation, mutual aid relies on the collective efforts of caring people working together towards shared goals.

People volunteer for various reasons, which are discussed in greater detail below. By acknowledging and being sensitive to these diverse motivations, mutual aid groups can tailor their volunteer opportunities to align with their interests and values.

Sense of Purpose:
Many volunteers are driven by a sense of purpose and a desire to contribute to the well-being of others. They may feel compelled to take action in response to social, economic, or environmental challenges facing their communities and seek opportunities to address these issues through collective action.

Community Connection:
Volunteers often have strong ties to their communities and feel a sense of responsibility to support their neighbors. They may be motivated by a desire to strengthen community resilience through mutual aid initiatives.

Empathy & Compassion:
Volunteers are often characterized by their empathy and compassion for others. They may feel deeply moved by the struggles and hardships faced by people in their communities and are driven to offer support to those in need.

Skill & Expertise:
Many volunteers possess valuable skills, expertise, and resources that they are eager to contribute to mutual aid efforts. Whether it's professional expertise, technical skills, or lived experience, volunteers bring diverse talents and perspectives to the table, enriching the collective capacity of mutual aid groups to address complex challenges.

Personal Growth & Fulfillment:
Volunteering in a mutual aid group can offer people opportunities for personal growth, fulfillment, and self-discovery. They may derive a sense of satisfaction, purpose, and fulfillment from their volunteer work, gaining valuable experiences, skills, and relationships along the way.

Desire for Impact:
Volunteers are often motivated by a desire to make a tangible impact and see meaningful results from their efforts. They may be drawn to mutual aid groups that prioritize direct service provision, community organizing, or advocacy work, where they can actively participate in initiatives that have a real and measurable impact on the lives of others.

Team Spirit:
Mutual aid volunteers believe in the power of collective action and recognize that by working together as a team, they can pool their resources, talents, and energy to address shared challenges and create positive change.

Here are a few examples of mutual aid groups effectively deploying volunteers:

Food Distribution Teams:
Some mutual aid groups organize teams of volunteers to collect, package, and distribute food to community members in need. These teams often coordinate with local food banks, farms, and businesses to source donations and organize delivery routes. Volunteers may be assigned specific tasks such as sorting food items, packing bags, or making doorstep deliveries.

Community Care Networks:
Mutual aid groups often establish community care networks to provide assistance to vulnerable people, such as the elderly or people with disabilities. Volunteers in these networks offer various forms of support, including grocery shopping, medication delivery, transportation to medical appointments, and companionship. By matching volunteers with people in need based on proximity and availability, these networks bring personalized and compassionate care to the community.

Emergency Response Teams:

During crises or natural disasters, mutual aid groups mobilize emergency response teams to provide immediate assistance and relief. Trained volunteers may perform tasks such as conducting wellness checks, distributing emergency supplies, setting up shelters, and assisting with evacuation procedures. By rapidly deploying volunteers to affected areas and coordinating with local authorities and relief agencies, these emergency response teams help mitigate the impact of disasters and support affected communities in their recovery efforts.

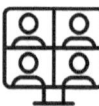

Virtual Support Networks:

With the rise of remote work and online communication platforms, some mutual aid groups have established virtual support networks to connect volunteers with people in need of remote assistance. Volunteers may offer virtual tutoring, mentorship, counseling, or technical support to help community members navigate challenges such as remote learning, job searching, mental health issues, or technology-related issues. These virtual support networks provide accessible and flexible support options for people unable to access in-person services.

Language Support Teams:

In diverse communities, mutual aid groups may create language support teams to assist non-native speakers with accessing essential services and information. Volunteers fluent in multiple languages offer interpretation and translation services for tasks, such as filling out forms, scheduling appointments, and navigating government websites. These language support teams play a crucial role in breaking down language barriers and ensuring equitable access to resources for all community members.

Menu of Opportunities

 When someone approaches and asks how they can help your mutual aid group, you may want to have a **menu of opportunities** ready to show them. This is a structured list or catalog of various ways in which individuals or organizations can engage with or support the group. It typically includes a range of options tailored to different interests, skills, resources, and levels of commitment—allowing stakeholders to choose the level and type of involvement that best suits them.

For example, a menu of opportunities for volunteers may include options like participating in direct service activities, providing professional expertise or specialized skills, assisting with fundraising or outreach efforts, serving on committees or task forces, or offering in-kind donations or other forms of support. Similarly, a menu of opportunities for potential partners or donors may outline different levels of collaboration or sponsorship—such as financial contributions, event sponsorship, or strategic partnerships.

By presenting a menu of opportunities, a mutual aid group can effectively communicate the various ways in which people can contribute to its mission. It provides a framework for organizing and coordinating volunteer efforts, partnerships, and fundraising activities.

Here is a an example of a menu of opportunities for a mutual aid group:

MENU OF OPPORTUNITIES

Direct Service Volunteers:
- Distributing food, clothing, or other essential items to those in need
- Assisting with transportation
- Providing childcare or eldercare support

Skilled Professionals:
- Legal assistance for navigating housing issues, immigration matters, or other legal concerns
- Medical or mental health professionals offering telehealth consultations or wellness check-ins
- Financial advisors providing budgeting assistance or financial literacy workshops

continues...

Community Organizers:
- Leading outreach efforts to raise awareness about the mutual aid group's services and resources
- Organizing community events or workshops on topics such as disaster preparedness, self-care, or mutual aid principles
- Facilitating neighborhood meetings or forums to identify community needs and priorities

Fundraising & Development:
- Planning and executing fundraising campaigns or events to support the group's programs
- Researching and applying for grants from foundations, corporations, or government agencies
- Cultivating relationships with individual donors or corporate sponsors to secure financial support

Administrative Support:
- Assisting with data entry, record-keeping, or database management tasks
- Providing virtual or in-person logistical support for meetings, events, or volunteer activities
- Helping to maintain the group's website, social media channels, or email communications

In-Kind Donations:
- Donating food, clothing, personal hygiene items, or other essential supplies for distribution to community members
- Offering access to facilities or equipment for group meetings, events, or storage of donated items
- Providing professional services such as graphic design, printing, or photography for promotional materials

Strategic Partnerships:
- Collaborating with local businesses, schools, faith-based organizations, or other community groups to expand outreach and impact
- Forming alliances with advocacy organizations, grassroots movements, or government agencies to address systemic issues affecting the community
- Participating in coalitions or networks focused on mutual aid, social justice, or disaster response at the regional or national level

Offering a menu of opportunities to new supporters creates a welcoming first impression, demonstrating the group's flexibility and commitment to engaging members according to their interests and capacities.

Orientation & Training

Providing a comprehensive orientation and training program for volunteers will ensure everyone understands the mutual aid group's mission, goals, and values, as well as their roles and responsibilities. During orientation, volunteers should be introduced to the group's history, structure, and current projects, allowing them to gain a deeper understanding of how their efforts contribute to the overall objectives. Volunteers should also be briefed on any relevant policies, procedures, and safety protocols to ensure smooth and safe operations.

Training sessions should equip volunteers with the necessary skills and knowledge to perform their roles effectively. This may include specific training on tasks they will be undertaking—such as disaster response techniques, community organizing strategies, or communication skills. Training sessions can also provide volunteers with opportunities to practice their skills in simulated scenarios or role-playing exercises, allowing them to gain confidence and competence before engaging in real-world activities.

Organizers should provide ongoing support and mentorship to volunteers throughout their tenure with the group. This can include regular check-ins, feedback sessions, and opportunities for skill development and growth. By investing in the orientation, training, and support of volunteers, mutual aid groups can ensure that their members are well-prepared and empowered to make meaningful contributions to the community.

Volunteer training for a mutual aid group can cover a wide range of topics tailored to the specific needs and activities of the organization. Some examples of training topics include:

Organization Overview: Providing volunteers with an understanding of the mutual aid group's mission, goals, and history.

Role-specific Training: Training volunteers on the specific tasks and responsibilities associated with their roles, such as disaster response, community outreach, fundraising, or administrative duties.

Safety Protocols: Educating volunteers on safety measures and protocols relevant to their activities, including first aid procedures, emergency evacuation plans, and the proper use of personal protective equipment.

Communication Skills: Offering training on effective communication strategies, active listening, conflict resolution, and cultural competency to facilitate positive interactions with the community and other volunteers.

Legal & Ethical Considerations: Informing volunteers about relevant laws and ethical guidelines governing their activities, such as confidentiality requirements, data protection laws, and anti-discrimination policies.

Cultural Sensitivity: Providing training on cultural awareness and inclusion to ensure that volunteers respect and value the diversity of their community.

Volunteer Code of Conduct: Reviewing the organization's code of conduct and expectations for volunteer behavior, including respect, integrity, and accountability.

Practical Skills: Offering hands-on training sessions or workshops to develop practical skills relevant to the group's activities, such as map reading, navigation, inventory management, or community organizing techniques.

Emotional Support: Equipping volunteers with strategies for self-care and stress management, as well as resources for accessing emotional support if needed.

Ongoing Support: Providing volunteers with information about ongoing support structures, such as mentorship programs, peer support networks, and access to resources and tools for continued learning and development.

Skill Matching

 **Skill matching** involves identifying the specific skills, expertise, and interests of volunteers and matching them with the tasks and needs of the group. By creating a skill bank—a database of volunteer skills and expertise—mutual aid groups can efficiently identify and leverage the talents within their volunteer pool to address community needs and carry out their activities effectively. To engage in skill matching and create a skill bank, mutual aid groups can take these steps:

1. Volunteer Skills Assessment:
Conduct a comprehensive assessment of volunteers' skills, experiences, interests, and availability. This may involve distributing surveys, conducting interviews, or hosting skill assessment sessions to gather information about volunteers' backgrounds and expertise.

2. Skill Inventory:
Compile a comprehensive inventory of volunteer skills, categorizing them based on relevant categories such as technical skills (e.g., medical, construction, counseling), language proficiency, cultural competencies, leadership abilities, and specialized knowledge areas.

3. Skills Mapping:
Match volunteers' skills and expertise with the specific needs and tasks of the mutual aid group. Identify areas where volunteers' skills can be effectively utilized to address community needs, such as disaster response, food distribution, organizing, fundraising, or administrative support.

4. Skill Bank Development:
Create a centralized skill bank or database to document volunteers' skills, preferences, and availability. This can be in the form of a spreadsheet, online platform, or database accessible to volunteer coordinators and team leaders.

5. Volunteer Engagement:
Regularly communicate with volunteers to inform them about available opportunities, projects, and roles that align with their skills and interests. Encourage volunteers to update their skills profiles and preferences regularly to ensure the accuracy of the skill bank.

6. Skill Utilization:
Assign volunteers to tasks, projects, or teams based on their skills, expertise, and availability. Provide opportunities for volunteers to utilize and develop their skills while contributing to the organization's mission and objectives.

7. Training & Development:
Offer training, workshops, and resources to support volunteers in developing new skills, enhancing existing ones, and staying informed about best practices and emerging trends in their areas of expertise.

Volunteer Coordination

Volunteer coordination refers to the process of organizing and managing volunteers to ensure their efforts are directed efficiently toward a common goal. In mutual aid, this involves assigning tasks, setting schedules, providing necessary information or resources, and maintaining communication.

The goal is to make sure volunteers know their roles, can work effectively together, and are supported throughout their efforts. Good coordination ensures that the mutual aid initiative runs smoothly, with tasks being completed on time and resources being used efficiently.

Communicating effectively with volunteers is essential for mutual aid groups to maintain engagement. Here are some best practices:

Clear & Timely Communication:

Provide clear and timely communication about volunteer opportunities, expectations, and organizational updates. Use multiple channels, such as email, social media, and messaging apps to reach volunteers and ensure that important information reaches them in a timely manner.

Personalized Outreach:

Tailor communication to the preferences and interests of individual volunteers whenever possible. Recognize volunteers for their contributions, celebrate milestones, and express gratitude for their time and effort. Personalized messages demonstrate appreciation and strengthen relationships with volunteers.

Two-Way Communication:

Encourage open dialogue and feedback. Create opportunities for volunteers to share their ideas, concerns, and suggestions for improvement. Actively listen to their feedback and incorporate it into decision-making processes when appropriate.

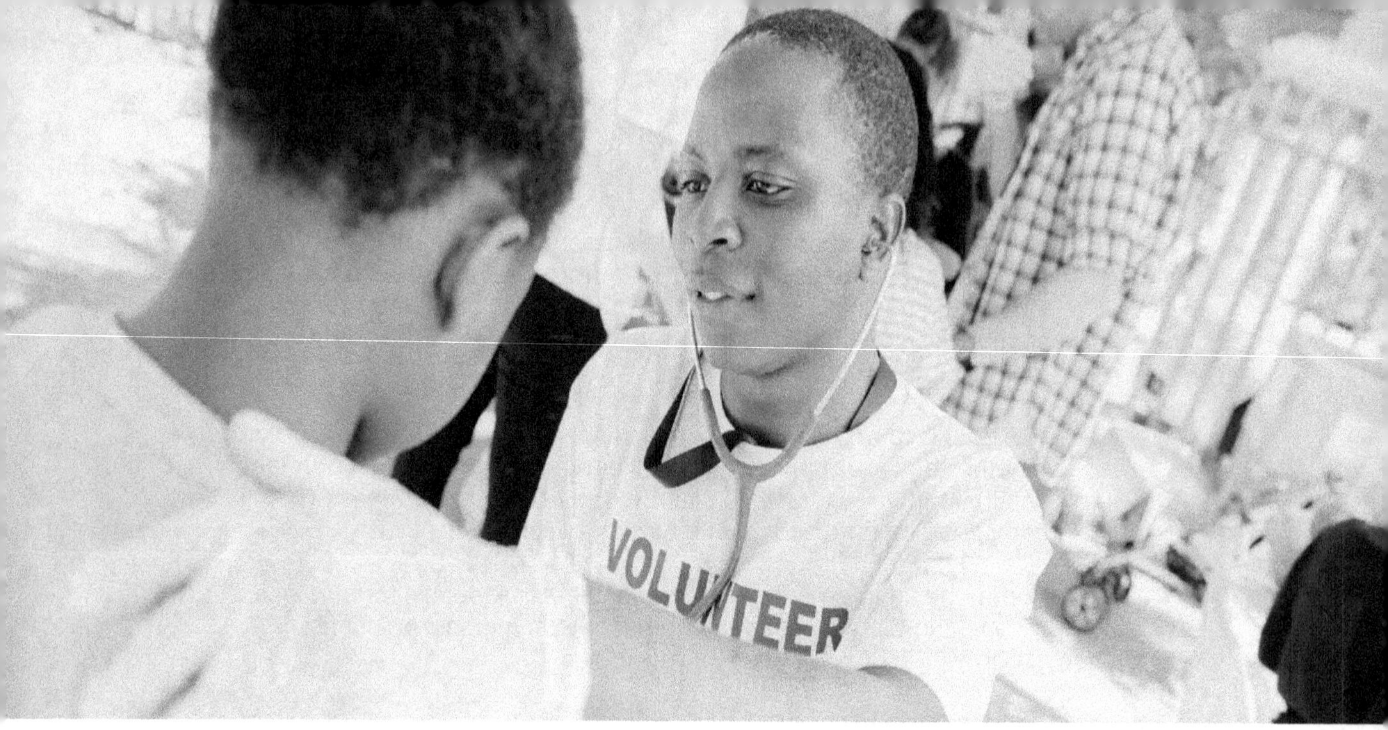

Provide Clear Instructions:

Clearly communicate tasks, responsibilities, and expectations for volunteers. Provide detailed instructions, resources, and training materials to help them succeed in their roles. Clarify any questions or concerns they may have to ensure they feel confident and supported.

Regular Updates & Check-Ins:

Provide regular updates and check-ins to keep volunteers informed and engaged. Schedule regular meetings, webinars, or newsletters to share information about organizational activities, upcoming events, and volunteer opportunities. Check in with volunteers individually to assess their well-being and address any challenges they may be facing.

Respect Volunteer Time & Boundaries:

Respect volunteers' time and boundaries by being mindful of their availability, preferences, and personal commitments. Avoid overloading them with excessive tasks or communication. Provide flexibility and autonomy for them to manage their volunteer activities according to their schedules and priorities.

Transparent & Honest Communication:

Be honest in all communications with volunteers. Provide updates on the organization's activities, challenges, and decision-making processes. Transparency builds trust.

Provide Opportunities for Growth & Development:

Offer opportunities for volunteers to learn new skills and gain experience. Provide training, mentorship, and networking opportunities to support them in their personal and professional goals. Empower volunteers to take on leadership roles and contribute to decision-making processes.

Regular Evaluation & Feedback:

Evaluate volunteer programs, activities, and communication strategies regularly. Solicit feedback from volunteers through surveys or one-on-one conversations to identify areas for improvement and make necessary adjustments. Continuous assessment will help ensure that communication with volunteers remains effective and responsive to their needs.

Celebrate Successes:

Recognize and celebrate the contributions and achievements of volunteers. Highlight individual and team accomplishments, share success stories, and publicly acknowledge volunteer efforts through social media, newsletters, or awards ceremonies. Celebrating successes reinforces volunteer commitment and motivation.

Depending on the scale of your operations, you may choose to utilize a **centralized volunteer management system**, which is a structured approach or software platform to efficiently recruit, onboard, schedule, track, and communicate with volunteers. It provides a centralized hub where volunteer information, preferences, availability, and tasks are managed. This system enables mutual aid groups to streamline their processes—including volunteer registration, background checks, training, assignment of tasks, and tracking hours.

Financial Resources

Mutual aid groups may adopt an anti-capitalist stance due to their recognition of the systemic inequalities perpetuated by capitalist structures. Capitalism—as an economic system—is often critiqued for prioritizing profit over people, perpetuating wealth disparities, and exacerbating social injustices. Groups may come to view capitalism as inherently exploitative, particularly for marginalized communities who are disproportionately affected by its consequences.

While mutual aid groups may hold reservations about engaging in capitalistic practices, current economic reality often requires raising financial resources to sustain their initiatives. Groups must recognize that their efforts to support marginalized communities and address systemic inequities often require some level of funding to be effective. Whether it is providing direct assistance to people in need, organizing community events, or advocating for policy changes, financial resources play a critical role in enabling groups to achieve their objectives.

In navigating this tension between ideological values and practical needs, mutual aid groups may adopt creative approaches to fundraising that align with their principles and goals. Rather than relying solely on traditional capitalist models, they may prioritize grassroots fundraising efforts that emphasize community solidarity and collective support. This can involve organizing donation drives, hosting fundraising events, or launching crowdfunding campaigns that mobilize resources within their networks.

Mutual aid groups may also explore alternative funding sources that align with their values—such as seeking grants from philanthropic foundations or partnering with ethical businesses that share their commitment to social justice. By diversifying their funding streams and remaining transparent about their financial practices, groups can maintain their integrity while ensuring the sustainability of their initiatives.

Group Bank Account

Establishing a bank account is a fundamental step for any mutual aid group to manage its finances effectively. Having a dedicated bank account allows you to separate personal and group funds, ensuring transparency and accountability in financial transactions. To open a bank account, you will typically need to provide certain documentation, such as the group's formation documents (e.g., Articles of Association or Bylaws), meeting minutes, identification documents for authorized signatories, and proof-of-address for the group's principal place of business.

When selecting a bank or credit union, you should consider factors such as fees, accessibility, and services offered. Some banks may offer specific accounts tailored to non-profit organizations or community groups, which may include benefits such as waived fees or discounted services. It is essential to research and compare options to find a banking partner that aligns with the group's needs and values. Once the account is opened, you should establish clear procedures for managing finances, including who has access to the account and how funds are deposited, withdrawn, and documented. Regular monitoring of the account and keeping detailed records of transactions are crucial for financial oversight and reporting.

Lastly, some banks may require the group to obtain an Employer Identification Number (EIN) from the Internal Revenue Service (IRS) if you plan to hire employees or engage in certain financial activities. It is important to familiarize yourself with any legal or regulatory requirements related to banking and financial management to ensure compliance.

Fundraising Basics

When your mutual aid group delves into fundraising, there are several basics you should keep in mind to ensure your efforts are effective and aligned with your values and goals.

Here are some key fundamentals:

Understand Your Legal Requirements:

Before beginning any fundraising activities, it is important you understand the legal landscape. This includes complying with solicitation laws and fulfilling any tax obligations. Compliance will help avoid legal pitfalls and maintain trust with supporters.

Define Clear Goals & Objectives:

Your mutual aid group should set clear, specific goals for what you hope to achieve with the funds raised. This could include purchasing supplies, covering operational costs, or funding specific projects. Clear goals help in crafting targeted fundraising appeals and provide transparency for donors.

Develop a Fundraising Strategy:

A strategy should encompass various fundraising methods tailored to your capacity and community. Options might include online fundraising campaigns, grant writing, community events, or crowdfunding. It is important to consider what resources are available and what methods will resonate with potential donors.

Engage the Community:

Mutual aid is fundamentally about community engagement and support. Fundraising should be approached as a community-building exercise, not just a financial necessity. Engaging community members in the planning and execution of fundraising activities can strengthen ties and improve participation.

Transparency & Accountability:

Being transparent about how funds are raised and spent builds trust and credibility. Regular updates to donors and community members about the impact of their contributions reinforce the value of their support and encourage ongoing engagement.

Use of Technology:

Leveraging technology can streamline fundraising efforts. Tools like social media, fundraising platforms, and payment processing services can expand reach and make it easier for people to donate.

Cultivate Donor Relationships:

Building and maintaining relationships with donors is crucial. This means regular communication, recognition of their support, and providing them with opportunities to stay engaged with the group's activities. A strong relationship can turn one-time donors into long-term supporters.

Evaluate & Adapt:

After each fundraising campaign, evaluate what worked and what didn't. This reflection allows your group to learn from your experiences and adapt your strategies to improve future efforts.

Donations & Sponsorships

Donations and sponsorships are often key sources of funding that enable mutual aid groups to carry out their missions. To manage these resources efficiently and ethically, mutual aid groups should consider the following practices:

Establish Clear Policies & Procedures:

It's important for mutual aid groups to have clear policies and procedures in place for accepting and managing donations and sponsorships. These policies should outline what types of donations are acceptable, under what conditions the group will accept sponsorships, and how conflicts of interest will be avoided. This helps to ensure that all contributions align with the group's values and goals.

Transparent Record-Keeping:

Effective record-keeping is essential not only for organizational transparency but also for donor trust. Every donation and sponsorship should be recorded in detail, including the amount, source, date, and any restrictions specified by the donor. This transparency helps in reporting, ensures compliance with donor wishes, and aids in financial management.

Acknowledge & Thank Donors:

Recognizing contributors not only fosters goodwill but also encourages future support. Sending thank you letters, providing acknowledgments on social media, or even hosting appreciation events are ways to acknowledge donors and sponsors. These gestures show gratitude and reinforce the value of contributions to the group's activities.

Regular Communication:

Keeping donors and sponsors informed about how their contributions are being used and the impact they are making is crucial. Regular updates through newsletters, reports, social media posts, or direct communications can keep supporters engaged and invested in the group's work.

Ethical Considerations:

Mutual aid groups should carefully consider the sources of their donations and sponsorships. Accepting funds from sources that contradict the group's principles can undermine its credibility and mission. Groups should set ethical guidelines to determine acceptable funding sources, considering the broader impacts on their community and objectives.

Leverage Sponsorships Strategically:

When it comes to sponsorships, it's beneficial to seek partners that align with the group's values and can offer more than just financial support. This might include in-kind donations, access to networks, or shared platforms for advocacy. Strategic sponsorships can amplify the group's reach and effectiveness beyond the monetary value.

Plan for Sustainability:

While donations and sponsorships can provide essential funding, relying solely on these can be risky. Mutual aid groups should also explore other revenue streams to ensure financial stability and sustainability. This might include memberships, service fees, or merchandise sales.

By implementing these practices, you can manage donations and sponsorships effectively, ensuring that they contribute positively to your mission while maintaining the trust and support of your stakeholders.

Here are some approaches that can help groups solicit donations:

Online Fundraising Campaigns:

Utilizing digital platforms like crowdfunding sites can help reach a wider audience. Platforms such as GoFundMe, Kickstarter, or specialized non-profit tools like Donorbox and Fundly allow groups to create targeted campaigns with specific financial goals. These platforms also provide tools for sharing the campaigns via social media, email, and other online channels.

Social Media Engagement:

Social media is a powerful tool for reaching potential donors and raising awareness about the group's activities and needs. Regular updates, impactful stories, and clear calls to action can encourage followers to contribute financially. Some platforms offer tools for direct donations and fundraisers.

Community Events:

Hosting events such as workshops, talks, or cultural activities can serve dual purposes: they raise awareness about the group's mission and work, and they can be used to solicit donations. Events can include a ticket fee, a donation box, or a specific fundraising goal announced at the event.

Direct Appeals:

Personalized letters or emails to potential donors can be very effective, especially when they clearly communicate the group's needs, goals, and the direct impact of donations. Tailoring the message to highlight specific projects or urgent needs can increase the response rate.

Crowdfunding Campaigns

Crowdfunding is a method of raising many small amounts of money from a large number of people for a project or venture. This approach taps into the collective efforts of a big pool of individuals—primarily online via social media and crowdfunding platforms—and leverages their networks for greater reach and exposure.

Crowdfunding platforms—such as Kickstarter, GoFundMe, Indiegogo, and others—offer a place where people can create campaigns to solicit financial contributions from the public. Each campaign is set up with a specific financial goal and a deadline, and creators typically offer rewards or incentives to backers in exchange for their contributions.

There are several types of crowdfunding:

Donation-based crowdfunding: People give money to enterprises or organizations because they believe in the cause or mission. No financial return is expected.

Rewards-based crowdfunding: Backers receive a tangible item or service in return for their funds. This is common for product launches, creative projects, and entrepreneurial ventures.

Equity crowdfunding: Investors receive a stake in the company, usually in the form of equity.

Debt crowdfunding: Investors receive their money back as a loan with interest. This is also known as peer-to-peer (P2P) lending.

Crowdfunding is used for a wide range of purposes—including startup funding, charity, medical expenses, disaster relief, personal projects, and more. It provides an alternative to traditional forms of financing such as bank loans, capturing a wider audience and utilizing digital platforms to reach potentially thousands of contributors.

Organizing an effective crowdfunding campaign involves several strategic steps that a mutual aid group can undertake to ensure success:

1. Define Clear Objectives:
Before launching a crowdfunding campaign, the group should clearly define what the funds will be used for. This could be anything from purchasing supplies for the community, funding a specific project, or covering operational costs. Clear, specific goals help potential donors understand the impact of their contributions.

2. Choose the Right Platform:
Select a crowdfunding platform that aligns with the group's values and goals. Popular platforms like GoFundMe, Kickstarter, and Indiegogo cater to different types of projects and audiences. Some platforms are more suitable for nonprofit fundraising, offering tools and features that can enhance donation efforts.

3. Create a Compelling Campaign Page:

The campaign page should tell a compelling story, highlighting the group's mission, the people involved, and the community's needs. High-quality images, videos, and testimonials can enhance the narrative and engage potential donors. The page should clearly articulate how the funds will be used and the difference they will make.

4. Set a Realistic Funding Goal & Timeline:

Establish a realistic funding goal based on the group's financial needs and the average donation amounts expected. The timeline for the campaign should also be considered; shorter campaigns tend to create a sense of urgency, while longer campaigns might be necessary to reach larger goals.

5. Leverage Social Media & Community Networks:

Share the campaign across social media channels, email newsletters, and through community networks. Regular updates and engagement with supporters throughout the campaign can keep the momentum going and encourage sharing and repeat donations.

6. Offer Rewards or Incentives:

For some types of campaigns, offering rewards or incentives based on the donation size can motivate larger contributions. These could range from simple thank-you notes to merchandise or exclusive experiences related to the group's activities.

7. Monitor & Adapt the Campaign:

Keep an eye on the campaign's progress and be ready to adapt strategies if necessary. This could mean adjusting marketing techniques, addressing donor questions promptly, or even extending the campaign duration if needed to meet the goal.

8. Express Gratitude & Report Back:

Once the campaign concludes, it is important to thank donors and provide updates on how their contributions are being used. Regular updates about the project's progress or the impact of the aid provided can build trust and foster a long-term relationship with donors, which is beneficial for future fundraising.

By meticulously planning and executing these steps, your mutual aid group can significantly increase the likelihood of conducting a successful crowdfunding campaign, thereby securing essential funds for your initiatives.

Collecting "Dues" from Members

Implementing membership dues can be a strategic decision for a mutual aid group to ensure sustainable financial support for its activities. (Groups may wish to avoid negative connotations with the words "dues" and "fees" by calling them "investments" or "contributions.") Dues can help cover operational expenses, fund community initiatives, and maintain the group's long-term viability. However, before implementing dues, the group should consider its financial needs, member demographics, and the perceived value of membership.

To establish dues, the group may need to conduct a financial assessment to evaluate its operating costs and funding requirements. This assessment can help determine an appropriate dues structure that balances affordability for members with the group's financial sustainability goals. Dues can be set at a fixed amount, tiered based on membership levels or income brackets, or offered on a sliding scale to accommodate varying financial circumstances.

Communicating the rationale behind dues and the benefits of membership is essential to garnering support from members. The group should clearly outline what dues cover—such as access to resources, participation in activities, or voting rights—to demonstrate the value of membership. Providing transparency around how dues are used and the impact they have on the group's mission can help build trust and member engagement.

When collecting dues, the group should establish clear procedures for payment, such as online payment platforms, automatic bank transfers, or in-person cash payments. Offering flexibility in payment options and deadlines can accommodate members' preferences and circumstances. The group should also keep accurate records of payments and provide regular updates on its financial status and use of funds.

It is important for the group to periodically review its dues structure and adjust as needed based on changing financial needs, member feedback, and evolving community priorities. By effectively managing membership dues, your mutual aid group can ensure financial stability and continue making a positive impact in your community.

Selling Merchandise

Selling merchandise can be an effective way for your mutual aid group to raise funds and increase visibility in the community. To start, the group should first design or source items that align with your mission and resonate with your target audience. This could include t-shirts, tote bags, stickers, or other items featuring the group's logo or messaging. When designing merchandise, the group should consider incorporating imagery that communicates your values and goals.

Once the merchandise has been selected or designed, you will need to determine how they will produce and distribute it. You may choose to work with a local printing company or manufacturer to produce the items, or you could explore options for dropshipping.

Print-on-demand is a retail fulfillment method where a store does not keep the products it sells in stock. Instead, when a store sells a product, it produces the item to the customer's specifications, adding designs or other customizations. This approach allows for lower overhead costs and reduced risk, as the seller only produces items when there is demand from customers. Printful, Printify, and Gelato are popular print-on-demand services.

Selling merchandise at a physical location requires an initial purchase of inventory, which may not be feasible for a mutual aid group with limited resources. That is why having an online store is a good option. It provides accessibility to a broader audience beyond the constraints of a specific geographical location. An online store offers convenience for customers to browse and purchase items from the comfort of their homes.

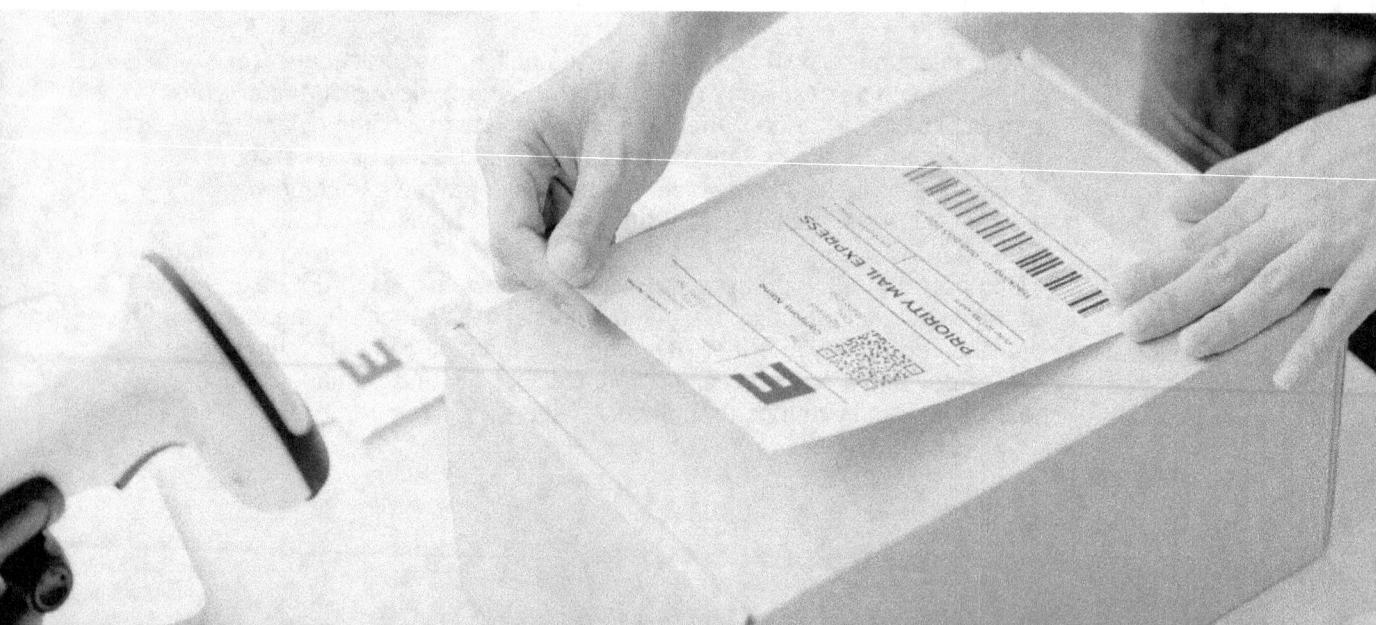

Setting up an online store for a mutual aid group involves several key steps:

1. Choose an e-commerce platform:
Research and select an e-commerce platform that aligns with the group's needs, budget, and values. Popular options include Shopify, WooCommerce (for WordPress websites), BigCommerce, and Squarespace. Consider factors such as ease of use, features, pricing, and customization options when making a decision.

Set up the store:
Sign up for an account on the chosen e-commerce platform and follow their instructions to set up the store. This typically involves providing basic information about the group and selecting a template or theme for the store design.

Add products:
Create product listings for the merchandise the group wants to sell. Include high-quality images, detailed descriptions, pricing information, and any other relevant details. Organize products into categories or collections to make it easy for customers to browse and find what they're looking for.

Configure payment & shipping settings:
Set up processing options to accept payments from customers. Most e-commerce platforms offer integrations with popular payment gateways like PayPal, Stripe, and Square. Configure shipping settings to determine shipping rates, methods, and delivery times for orders.

Customize the store:
Customize the store's design and layout to reflect the group's branding and aesthetic preferences. This may involve customizing colors, fonts, and imagery, adding a logo or banner, and arranging the layout of product pages and navigation menus.

Test & launch the store:
Once the store is set up and configured, thoroughly test it to ensure that everything is functioning correctly. Test the ordering process, payment processing, and shipping calculations to identify and resolve any issues. Once everything is working smoothly, officially launch the store and make it live to the public.

Promote the store:
Promote the online store to the group's community and target audience to drive traffic and sales. Utilize social media, email newsletters, website banners, and other marketing channels to spread the word about the store and encourage people to visit and make purchases.

Monitor & optimize:
Regularly monitor the store's performance and sales metrics to identify areas for improvement and optimization. Use analytics tools provided by the e-commerce platform to track traffic, sales, and customer behavior, and use this data to make informed decisions about marketing strategies, product offerings, and store improvements.

Operating an online store requires an ongoing commitment from a mutual aid group, necessitating a dedicated member to manage store communications, including customer service and support. This individual will need to handle inquiries, resolve issues, and ensure that customers have a positive experience. Effective communication will involve promptly addressing questions about products, order statuses, and returns or exchanges.

It is also worth noting that even if your mutual aid group offers exceptional products, without effective marketing your efforts may go unnoticed. By strategically promoting your merchandise through social media, email newsletters, website banners, and community events, the group can raise awareness and generate interest. Engaging content, compelling visuals, and clear calls-to-action can help capture the attention of supporters and encourage them to make purchases, ultimately driving the success of the fundraiser.

Applying for Grants

While many grants are specifically targeted towards non-profits, there are also grants available to other types of organizations, including grassroots community groups and social enterprises. However, the eligibility criteria for grants can vary widely depending on the funding source and the specific grant program. It is essential for mutual aid groups to carefully review the requirements of each grant opportunity to determine if they qualify and to ensure that their grant application aligns with the funder's priorities and objectives.

Here's how your mutual aid group might approach the grant application process:

1. Research & Identify Grant Opportunities:
The first step is to research and identify grant opportunities that align with the mission and objectives of your group. This may involve exploring government grants, foundation grants, corporate grants, and other sources of funding. It's essential to carefully review the eligibility criteria, application requirements, and deadlines for each grant opportunity.

2. Develop a Grant Proposal:
Once potential grant opportunities have been identified, you will need to develop a compelling grant proposal. This involves outlining the specific project or program to be funded, detailing its goals, objectives, activities, and expected outcomes. The proposal should clearly articulate the need for funding, the target population to be served, and the group's capacity to effectively implement the project.

3. Gather Required Documentation:
Grant applications often require various supporting documents, such as financial statements, organizational budgets, letters of support, and project budgets. You will need to gather and organize these documents to include with the grant proposal.

4. Submit the Grant Application:
With the grant proposal and supporting documentation prepared, you can submit the grant application according to the guidelines provided by the funding organization. This may involve completing an online application form, submitting materials via email or mail, or using a grant management platform.

5. Follow-Up & Communication:
After submitting the grant application, follow up with the funding organization as needed. This may include providing additional information or clarification requested by the funder, attending meetings or site visits, and maintaining open communication throughout the review process. If the grant application is successful and funding is awarded, you will need to effectively manage the grant funds and adhere to any reporting requirements specified by the funder.

Entrepreneurial Investments

It is unlikely for mutual aid groups to accumulate surplus funds, given their focus on immediate community needs and often lean operational structures. However, in scenarios where surplus funds do arise, groups may consider entrepreneurial investments as a strategic option to further their mission. Such investments could include funding local startups, social enterprises, or community projects that align with the group's goals.

By directing excess funds into entrepreneurial ventures, a mutual aid group not only encourages local economic development but also creates sustainable sources of income that can support ongoing activities. This approach allows the group to maintain its commitment to the community while potentially expanding its impact through strategic financial growth.

For a mutual aid group looking to invest surplus funds in socially responsible ways, the process involves several key steps to ensure that their investments contribute both to their financial stability and their mission of community support. Here's how a group might approach this:

1. Define Investment Goals & Criteria

The first step is to clearly define what the group aims to achieve with its investments. This involves setting specific, measurable objectives that align with the group's values, such as supporting environmental sustainability, promoting social equity, or boosting local economic development. The group should also determine the level of risk they are willing to take and the expected returns.

2. Establish an Investment Committee

Forming a committee dedicated to managing investments can help in making informed decisions. This committee should include members with financial expertise as well as representatives from the community or group who understand its mission and goals. This committee would be responsible for research, decision-making, and ongoing monitoring of investments.

3. Research Socially Responsible Investment (SRI) Options

The committee can then explore various socially responsible investment vehicles. This might include:

- Socially responsible mutual funds or ETFs, which are funds that invest in companies with strong environmental, social, and governance (ESG) practices
- Community development financial institutions (CDFIs), which are banks, credit unions, and other financial bodies that provide financial services to underserved communities
- Direct investments in local businesses or startups, especially those that are aligned with the group's mission
- Green bonds or social bonds, which are issued to finance projects with environmental or social benefits

4. Evaluate & Select Investments

Each potential investment should be evaluated not only for its financial return and risk level but also for its impact on the community and alignment with the group's values. The investment committee should conduct due diligence to ensure these criteria are met.

5. Monitor & Review Investments

Once investments are made, they should be monitored regularly to assess performance against the expected financial and social outcomes. This should involve regular reporting to the wider group and periodic reassessment of the investment portfolio.

Material Resources

Material resources are the tangible assets, supplies, equipment, and infrastructure that are necessary for carrying out the activities, operations, and projects of an organization. By effectively managing and mobilizing material resources, mutual aid groups can ensure the efficient delivery of assistance and support to community members in need. This enhances their capacity to respond to emergencies and crises, and contribute to the overall well-being and resilience of their communities.

Material resources for mutual aid groups may include but are not limited to:

Food & Water: Supplies of food, water, and other essential items for distribution to community members in need, especially during emergencies, crises, or disaster situations.

Personal Protective Equipment (PPE): Equipment such as masks, gloves, face shields, and sanitizers to ensure the safety and protection of volunteers and recipients during interactions and activities.

Medical Supplies: Basic medical supplies, first aid kits, and hygiene products to address health-related needs and emergencies within the community.

Clothing & Shelter: Clothing, blankets, tents, and other shelter-related items to provide temporary relief and support to individuals and families experiencing homelessness, displacement, or adverse living conditions.

Transportation: Vehicles, bicycles, or other modes of transportation to facilitate the delivery of goods, services, and assistance to community members across different locations.

Tools & Equipment: Tools, equipment, and machinery required for various projects, such as construction, repairs, gardening, or infrastructure development.

Communication Devices: Phones, radios, walkie-talkies, or other communication devices to enable effective coordination and collaboration among volunteers and team members.

Office Supplies: Stationery, printing materials, computers, and other office supplies necessary for administrative tasks, documentation, and communication within the organization.

Storage Facilities: Warehouses, storage units, or designated spaces to safely store and organize material resources, supplies, and equipment before distribution or use.

Financial Resources: Funds, grants, donations, or financial assistance to procure material resources, cover operational expenses, and support the sustainability of mutual aid initiatives and projects.

Figuring Out Logistics

Logistics refers to the process of planning, implementing, and coordinating the efficient movement and storage of resources from one location to another to meet the needs of an organization. It encompasses transportation, inventory management, warehousing, packaging, and distribution.

In the context of mutual aid groups, logistics play a crucial role in ensuring that material and human resources are effectively mobilized, deployed, and utilized to provide assistance and support to community members in need. Effective logistics management helps optimize resource allocation, minimize costs, reduce delays, and enhance the overall effectiveness of mutual aid projects.

Here are some best practices in handling logistics:

Inventory Management:

Maintain detailed records of available resources, including quantities, types, and expiration dates, using inventory management software or spreadsheets. Regularly update inventory levels and track incoming and outgoing donations to prevent shortages or overstocking.

Storage & Organization:

Establish designated storage areas or warehouses equipped with shelves, bins, and labeling systems to store material resources safely and efficiently. Arrange items logically based on categories, accessibility, and frequency of use to streamline inventory management and retrieval processes.

Distribution Planning:

Develop clear distribution plans and protocols outlining how material resources will be allocated, distributed, and tracked to ensure equitable access and prevent waste or misuse. Consider factors such as geographic distribution, population demographics, and specific needs when planning distribution efforts.

Volunteer Training:

Provide comprehensive training and orientation sessions for volunteers involved in handling material resources, covering topics such as inventory management, safety procedures, and customer service skills. Ensure that volunteers understand their roles, responsibilities, and the importance of accurate record-keeping and accountability.

Collaboration & Partnerships:

Collaborate with local organizations, businesses, government agencies, and community stakeholders to leverage resources, share expertise, and coordinate logistics effectively. Establish formal partnerships or memorandums of understanding (MOUs) to clarify roles, responsibilities, and mutual support arrangements.

Communication & Coordination:

Establish clear communication channels to facilitate real-time information sharing, decision-making, and problem-solving among team members, volunteers, and partner organizations. Use communication tools such as email, messaging apps, and regular meetings to keep stakeholders informed and engaged.

Safety & Compliance:

Prioritize safety measures and compliance with relevant regulations and guidelines when handling material resources, particularly those related to food, medical supplies, and hazardous materials. Implement safety protocols, hygiene practices, and sanitation procedures to protect volunteers and recipients from potential risks or health hazards.

Evaluation & Feedback:

Conduct regular evaluations and feedback sessions to assess the effectiveness of logistics processes, identify areas for improvement, and solicit input from volunteers and community members. Use feedback to refine logistics strategies, address challenges, and enhance overall operational efficiency.

Goods Exchanges & Free Stores

A **goods exchange**, often referred to as a swap, is an event where people exchange goods they no longer need for items they do need. It operates on the principle of mutual benefit, allowing participants to trade possessions without the use of money.

Goods exchanges can take various forms, including physical events where people bring items to swap, online platforms or forums for virtual trading, or organized systems within communities or organizations. When a goods exchange is formally set up to run in a retail space it is referred to as a **free store**. The goal of these exchanges is to promote sharing resources, reducing waste, and building community connections.

Setting up a goods exchange can offer several benefits to your mutual aid group:

Sharing Resources:
A goods exchange enables members to share items they no longer need with others who may find them valuable. This promotes resource sharing within the community and reduces waste by giving items a second life.

Meeting Basic Needs:
For people facing financial challenges, access to free or low-cost items through the exchange can help meet basic needs, such as clothing, household goods, and food.

Building Community:
The exchange fosters connections and relationships among members by creating opportunities for interaction and collaboration. It strengthens community bonds as people come together to support one another.

Environmental Sustainability:
By promoting reuse and recycling, the goods exchange contributes to environmental sustainability by diverting items from landfills and reducing the consumption of new resources.

Empowerment & Self-Reliance:
Participating in the exchange empowers people to take control of their own needs and resources. It promotes self-reliance and resilience within the community by providing access to essential items without relying on traditional market systems.

Here are some steps your mutual aid group could take to establish a goods exchange:

1. Establish Guidelines:
Start by defining the guidelines and rules for the goods exchange. Determine what types of items are eligible for exchange, any restrictions or limitations (e.g., no hazardous materials), and guidelines for quality and condition of items.

2. Designate a Space:
Choose a physical location where people can drop off and pick up items for the exchange. This could be a designated area within a community center, local library, or even a member's home. Ensure the space is accessible and has adequate storage for items.

3. Create an Inventory System:
Develop a simple inventory system to keep track of items available for exchange. This could be a spreadsheet or online platform where people can list items they have available and browse items offered by others.

4. Promote the Exchange:
Spread the word about the goods exchange within the mutual aid group and the broader community. Use social media, email newsletters, and word-of-mouth to encourage participation and increase visibility.

5. Organize Exchange Events:

Host regular exchange events where people can come together to swap items in person. These events can be themed (e.g., clothing swap, book exchange) or open to all types of items. Provide clear instructions for how the exchange will operate and any safety protocols that need to be followed.

6. Facilitate Communication:

Establish channels for communication between people participating in the exchange. This could include online forums, messaging groups, or a dedicated email address where people can coordinate exchanges, ask questions, and provide feedback.

7. Monitor & Evaluate:

Regularly monitor the success of the goods exchange and gather feedback from participants. Evaluate what is working well and where improvements can be made to enhance their exchange experience.

Partnering with Local Businesses

Forming partnerships with local businesses can be mutually beneficial for both the businesses and the mutual aid group. These partnerships can provide the group with access to resources, expertise, and support, while offering businesses opportunities for community engagement and positive publicity. Here are some scenarios of how a mutual aid group can partner with local businesses:

Donation Drives:

The mutual aid group collaborates with a local grocery store to organize a food or clothing donation drive. The store provides collection bins and promotes the drive to its customers, while the group coordinates the collection, sorting, and distribution of donated items to those in need.

Sponsorship:

A mutual aid group hosts a community event, such as a neighborhood cleanup or a health fair, and seeks sponsorship from local businesses to cover event expenses. In exchange for sponsorship, businesses receive recognition in event promotions, signage, and press releases, enhancing their visibility and reputation in the community.

Volunteer Engagement:
A mutual aid group partners with a restaurant to provide meals for volunteers participating in a project, such as building a community garden or repairing homes for elderly residents. The restaurant donates food or offers discounted catering services, while volunteers enjoy a meal together as a token of appreciation for their contributions.

Skill Sharing Workshops:
A mutual aid group collaborates with a local hardware store to host workshops on home repair, gardening, or sustainable living practices. The store provides space for the workshops and offers discounts on supplies, while the group recruits skilled volunteers to lead the sessions and share their expertise with community members.

Fundraising Events:
A mutual aid group teams up with a brewery or coffee shop to organize a fundraising event, such as a benefit concert or a trivia night. The business provides the venue, beverages, and promotional support, while the group sells tickets and manages event logistics. Proceeds from the event go towards supporting the group's programs and initiatives.

Promotional Partnerships:
A mutual aid group partners with a local bookstore or art gallery to promote community art projects or literary events. The business showcases artwork or hosts book signings by local authors, attracting customers and fostering a sense of community pride. In return, the group helps promote the business through social media, newsletters, and word-of-mouth marketing.

When approaching a potential business partner, your mutual aid group should consider providing a **mutual benefit proposition**, which is a proposal that outlines the advantages and value that both parties stand to gain from collaborating. It articulates how the partnership will benefit not only your group but also the business, creating a win-win scenario.

For example, the proposition might highlight opportunities for your group to increase community impact, expand reach and visibility, and gain access to resources. For the local business, the proposition might emphasize benefits such as positive brand exposure, improved community relations, increased customer loyalty, and potential business growth or revenue.

By clearly outlining the benefits of the partnership, your mutual aid group can demonstrate to the business why it makes sense to collaborate and how the partnership aligns with both organizations' goals and values.

Chapter Review

Resource mobilization is a fundamental aspect of sustaining and growing a mutual aid group, beginning with the effective engagement of human resources. Volunteers are the lifeblood of mutual aid initiatives, providing the energy, skills, and commitment necessary to carry out the group's mission. Volunteers need clear roles, training, and ongoing support to perform their tasks efficiently. Creating a sense of community among volunteers builds loyalty and enhances productivity, ensuring the group can consistently meet its objectives.

Financial resources are also important to the viability of a mutual aid group. A comprehensive fundraising strategy should incorporate diverse income streams, such as individual donations, grants, and community fundraising events. Transparency in financial management builds trust among donors and members, ensuring that funds are used responsibly and effectively. Regular financial reporting and open communication about the group's financial status and needs can motivate continued support and investment.

Material resources—such as food, clothing, medical supplies, and other essentials—are crucial for directly addressing the needs of the community. To secure these resources, mutual aid groups can forge partnerships with local businesses, non-profit organizations, and community members willing to offer in-kind donations. Establishing a reliable supply chain for these materials involves identifying potential donors, clearly communicating the group's needs, and creating systems for their efficient collection, storage, and distribution. By strategically mobilizing human, financial, and material resources, a mutual aid group can build a solid foundation for ongoing support and impactful community service.

Discussion Questions

1 Have you ever encountered challenges or obstacles while volunteering? How did you address them, and what did you learn from the experience?

2 Reflect on a time when you participated in a fundraising event or campaign. What methods were used to raise funds, and what made the campaign successful or unsuccessful?

IN THIS CHAPTER

>> How to build a "brand" identity
   for a mutual aid group, including
   logo and website design and
   social media strategies

>> Discussing outreach campaigns

>> How to prepare for press
   coverage

>> Handling criticism and negativity

Chapter **8**

Communicating with the Public

Your mutual aid group may choose to engage with the broader public through community events, social media outreach, partnerships with other organizations, or participation in local initiatives. These interactions can help spread awareness, attract new members, and build community support.

It is important that while engaging with people in the community that you maintain a positive public image. In this chapter, we discuss stategies on how to successfully build a brand for your mutual aid group and how to handle both positive and negative attention.

A "Brand" Identity

A mutual aid group might not initially see itself as a "brand" in the commercial sense because its primary focus is on community support and solidarity, not profit. However, understanding and embracing some branding principles can be incredibly beneficial.

A **brand identity** is the collection of all elements that an organization creates to portray the right image to the public. It is more than just a logo or a visual motif. A brand identity encompasses the entire aesthetic and communicative approach an organization uses to present itself to the outside world. This identity helps in shaping the perception of the organization by conveying its values, personality, and promises through various forms of representation.

Key components of a brand identity include:

Logo & Name:

These are often the most immediate visual symbols of a brand. A logo needs to be distinctive, recognizable, and reflective of the its values. The name, similarly, should be unique and memorable, and often it is created to communicate something about the brand's purpose or values.

Color Palette:

Colors play an important role in differentiation and emotional appeal. Each color can evoke different feelings and associations. A brand chooses specific colors as part of its identity to consistently convey these emotions across all its materials.

Typography:

The choice of fonts and how they are used contribute significantly to the character of the brand. Typography can express seriousness, whimsy, sophistication, or simplicity, helping to set the tone of the brand's communications.

Imagery:

This includes the style of photography, graphics, icons, and illustrations used by the brand. Consistent imagery helps create a recognizable visual language that enhances the brand's narrative.

Voice:

This is about how the brand communicates in written and spoken word. The brand's voice can be professional, friendly, authoritative, or conversational— among other styles—and is key in connecting with the target audience on an emotional level.

Overall Design Style:

This is the composite of all visual and verbal elements. It should be distinctive and coherent to ensure that all communications are unified and instantly recognizable as belonging to the brand.

Deciding on the elements of a brand identity can serve as an excellent early project for a new mutual aid group, as it encourages creative thinking and facilitates discussions about the group's vision and goals. By brainstorming ideas for logos, color schemes, typography, and messaging, members can collaboratively explore different ways to visually and verbally represent the group's mission and values.

This process not only sparks creativity, but it also develops a deeper understanding of the group's identity and how it wants to be perceived by the community. Through open dialogue and consensus-building, the group can establish a cohesive brand identity—one that resonates with its members and aligns with its overarching vision.

It is worthwhile for a mutual aid group to take some time working together to craft a brand identity for the following reasons:

Trust & Credibility:

In the context of mutual aid, the brand helps establish trust and credibility within the community. It signals a commitment to certain values such as solidarity, inclusivity, and direct action. A strong, clear brand helps reassure community members and potential donors that the group is reliable and effective in its efforts to address specific needs.

Visibility & Awareness:

A well-defined brand helps a mutual aid group become more visible in a crowded non-profit space. It helps in differentiating the group from other organizations, highlighting its unique approach and focus. This is especially important when seeking to attract volunteers, beneficiaries, and donors who are bombarded with messages from numerous sources.

Consistency:

A consistent brand identity across various platforms (social media, flyers, emails, etc.) helps in maintaining a coherent message that is easily recognizable. This consistency ensures that every time someone comes across the group—whether online or in print—they immediately associate the materials with the group's efforts and values.

Fundraising & Resource Mobilization:

For mutual aid groups that rely on community donations and grants, a strong brand can be an asset in fundraising efforts. It can help convey the importance and impact of the group's work, making it more appealing to potential donors and grant-making organizations.

Scalability & Partnership:

As mutual aid groups grow or seek to collaborate with other organizations, a strong brand can facilitate partnerships and broader community involvement. It provides a clear idea of what the group stands for, making it easier for others to see alignment in values and objectives.

Community Engagement:

Branding can play a pivotal role in how a mutual aid group communicates and engages with its community. A brand that resonates with the community's values and aesthetics can enhance participation and activism.

Group Name

When your mutual aid group sets out to choose a name, the process involves careful consideration of several key factors to ensure it accurately reflects the your mission, values, and the broader community. The goal is to select a name that not only resonates with potential members and beneficiaries but also encapsulates the spirit and purpose of the group's efforts. Here are some things to consider:

Reflecting Core Values & Mission:

The first step in naming a mutual aid group is to deeply understand its core mission and the values. For instance, if the group is focused on food security in a specific neighborhood, the name might include words like "pantry," "food," "nourish," or "community" to directly reflect this focus. This approach helps in immediately communicating the group's purpose to the public. Members should brainstorm keywords that are relevant to their goals and activities, which can be a good starting point for a name.

Simplicity & Memorability:

The name should be easy to remember, pronounce, and spell. This accessibility ensures that people can easily share information about the group, whether by word-of-mouth or through digital and printed materials. A straightforward and memorable name can go a long way in helping the group's activities become more widely recognized and easily communicated.

Uniqueness & Legal Considerations:

It's important to choose a name that is not already in use by another organization, especially within the same region or sector. This uniqueness helps avoid confusion and potential legal complications. A quick search on the internet and a check with local business registries can help ascertain if the name is indeed unique. Securing a relevant domain name for a website is also an important factor to consider.

Cultural Sensitivity & Inclusivity:

Finally, the name should be culturally sensitive and inclusive, reflecting the diversity of the community the group aims to serve. This consideration helps ensure that the name is welcoming to all potential members and does not inadvertently exclude or offend. This is especially important in diverse communities where the impact of language and cultural nuances can be significant.

───────────

Through this thoughtful and inclusive approach, your mutual aid group can come up with a name that not only embodies your mission and values but also strengthens your appeal and effectiveness within the community. Rushing this process can lead to a name that lacks impact or fails to connect with the target audience, potentially hindering the group's efforts to build a strong and cohesive brand. By thoughtfully deliberating and seeking input from all members, the group can choose a name that truly represents its collective vision and aspirations.

Designing a Logo

Coming up with a logo for a mutual aid group is a creative and collaborative process that involves capturing the essence of the group's mission, values, and aspirations in a visual symbol. Members should engage in discussions and creative exercises to identify themes and imagery that resonate with the group's identity. Here is the general process for creating a logo:

1. Brainstorming & Concept Development:
Initiate discussions within the group to brainstorm ideas and concepts that reflect the mutual aid group's mission, values, and objectives. Encourage members to share their perspectives and insights on what symbols, imagery, or themes resonate most strongly with the group's identity. Explore various avenues for inspiration, including shared experiences, community traditions, and collective goals.

2. Sketching & Mood Boards:
Translate brainstormed ideas into visual representations by sketching rough designs or creating mood boards. This phase allows for experimentation and exploration of different visual directions. Group members can collaborate to refine initial concepts and explore how graphic elements can be combined to convey the desired message and emotions.

3. Feedback & Iteration:
Share the initial design concepts with the broader community to gather feedback and insights. Encourage constructive criticism and suggestions for improvement. Use this feedback to iterate on the designs, making adjustments to better align with the group's values and resonate with the intended audience. Iterate as needed until a consensus is reached on a design direction that accurately represents the mutual aid group's identity.

4. Professional Collaboration:
Once a final design direction has been chosen, collaborate with a graphic designer to refine and finalize the logo. Work with the professional to ensure that the design meets industry standards, is scalable, legible, and versatile across various platforms and applications. Leverage their expertise to bring the concept to life, while still staying true to the group's vision and values. If a group member possesses graphic design expertise and is willing to volunteer their time, this can significantly reduce costs; otherwise, the group should be prepared to budget for hiring a professional designer.

5. Openness to Revision:

Maintain an open and flexible approach throughout the design process. Be willing to incorporate feedback, make revisions, and iterate on the design as necessary to ensure that the final logo accurately represents the mutual aid group's identity and resonates with the community. Stay committed to the collaborative spirit of the project, valuing diverse perspectives and input.

Several factors contribute to making a good logo:

Simplicity:
A good logo should be simple and easy to recognize, even at a glance. Simple logos are memorable and versatile across different applications.

Memorability:
A successful logo leaves a lasting impression on viewers. It should be unique and distinctive, standing out from others and making a strong impression in the minds of the audience.

Relevance:
A good logo should be relevant to the brand it represents, reflecting its values, mission, and identity. It should evoke the right emotions and associations that align with the brand's messaging.

Versatility:
A well-designed logo should be versatile enough to work across various mediums and sizes, from digital platforms to print materials. It should maintain its integrity and legibility whether scaled up or down, and it should work well in both color and black-and-white formats.

Timelessness:
The best logos withstand the test of time. They avoid trends and fads, remaining relevant and effective for years to come. Timeless logos have a classic appeal that transcends passing design trends.

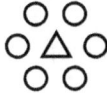

Uniqueness:
A good logo should be distinct and original, setting the brand apart from others in the field. It should avoid clichés and generic symbols, opting for a design that is fresh and memorable.

The logo should be prominently featured on all official communications, including the group's website, social media profiles, newsletters, and printed materials. This consistent use helps to create a visual connection that supporters and community members can easily identify and trust.

Setting Up a Website

Once a mutual aid group is ready to engage with the public, it is worth exploring setting up a website that can serve as a centralized hub for communication, coordination, and outreach. A website provides a platform to showcase the group's mission, values, and ongoing initiatives to a wider audience. It also offers an opportunity to articulate their goals and impact in a comprehensive and accessible manner, which encourages greater understanding and engagement from potential supporters, volunteers, and beneficiaries.

When setting up a website, your group should consider several key factors to ensure it effectively serves your purposes and meets the needs of the community:

Clear Communication of Mission & Goals:

The website should clearly articulate the group's mission, values, and objectives. Visitors should understand what the group stands for and how they can get involved or benefit from its activities.

User-Friendly Design & Navigation:

The website should be easy to navigate, with clear menus, intuitive organization, and quick access to important information. Users should be able to find what they need easily, whether they are seeking assistance, volunteering, or learning more about the group.

Accessibility:

Ensure that the website is accessible to all users, including those with disabilities. This includes using alt text for images, providing captions for videos, and using a design that is compatible with screen readers.

Mobile Compatibility:

With a large number of users accessing the internet from mobile devices, it's essential that the website is mobile-friendly and responsive. This ensures a seamless experience for visitors regardless of the device they are using.

Resource Repository:

The website should serve as a repository for important resources, guidelines, and contact information. This may include FAQs, downloadable forms, contact details for key personnel, and links to external resources.

Donation & Volunteer Opportunities:

Make it easy for visitors to donate funds or volunteer their time by providing clear calls to action and streamlined processes for getting involved. This may include online donation forms, volunteer sign-up forms, and information about upcoming events or initiatives.

Community Engagement:

Incorporate features that encourage community engagement and interaction, such as forums, discussion boards, or social media integration. This creates a sense of belonging and facilitates communication among members.

Privacy & Security:

Ensure that the website complies with data protection regulations and follows best practices for privacy and security. This includes using secure connections (HTTPS), implementing strong password policies, and protecting sensitive information.

Regular Updates & Maintenance:

Assign responsibility for regularly updating and maintaining the website to ensure that content remains current and relevant. This may include adding new information, updating event calendars, or responding to inquiries from visitors.

Feedback Mechanisms:

Provide ways for visitors to give feedback or ask questions, such as contact forms or surveys. This allows the group to gather insights from the community and continually improve the website's effectiveness.

Setting up a website for a mutual aid group may incur costs, including domain registration fees, web hosting expenses, and website design and development costs if professional assistance is needed. Domain registration fees typically involve an annual payment to secure the group's chosen website address (URL). Web hosting fees are recurring costs associated with storing the website's files and making them accessible on the internet.

Opting for a simple website design using templates available on a web hosting platform offers numerous benefits. By avoiding the need for a professional web designer and their associated costs, the group can save valuable resources while still establishing a functional online presence. Templates provide easy-to-use frameworks that streamline the website creation process, allowing group members with minimal technical expertise to build and maintain the site. Embracing simplicity ensures quicker deployment of the website, enabling the group to start engaging with the public sooner.

Social Media Presence

A social media presence allows your mutual aid group to expand its reach and visibility. By maintaining active profiles on social platforms, the group can connect with a broader audience, including people who may not be aware of its activities through other channels. Regularly sharing updates, stories, and calls to action on social media helps keep the group top-of-mind and encourages community members to get involved or seek assistance when needed.

Social media also serves as a powerful advocacy tool, allowing the group to raise awareness about pressing issues, mobilize support for campaigns and initiatives, and amplify the voices of marginalized communities. These platforms enable the group to share compelling visual content, personal stories, and multimedia campaigns that resonate with diverse audiences and inspire action. By leveraging social media platforms for advocacy, the group can drive positive change, challenge systemic injustices, and build solidarity within the community.

When using social media, mutual aid groups can employ several best practices to effectively engage with their community, advocate for their cause, and maximize their impact:

Consistent Branding:

Maintain a cohesive brand identity across all social media platforms, including profile pictures, cover photos, and bios. Consistency helps build recognition and credibility.

Regular Updates:

Post regular updates about the group's activities, initiatives, and accomplishments. Consistent posting keeps the audience informed and engaged while maintaining visibility.

Visual Content:

Incorporate visual content such as photos, videos, and infographics to make posts more engaging and shareable. Visual content tends to attract more attention and can effectively convey key messages.

Interactive Content:

Encourage interaction and engagement by posting polls, questions, and calls to action. Respond promptly to comments, messages, and inquiries to foster dialogue and build relationships with followers.

Hashtags:

Use relevant hashtags to increase the visibility of posts and reach a wider audience. Research trending hashtags related to mutual aid, community support, and relevant social issues to maximize exposure.

Community Involvement:

Highlight community members, volunteers, and beneficiaries in posts to showcase their contributions and stories. Tag people and organizations when appropriate to acknowledge their support and create a sense of community.

Advocacy & Education:

Use social media to raise awareness about issues related to mutual aid, social justice, and community resilience. Share informative articles, resources, and educational content to empower followers with knowledge and encourage advocacy.

Transparency & Accountability:

Practice transparency by sharing information about the group's finances, activities, and decision-making processes. Be open about successes, challenges, and lessons learned to build trust and accountability with followers.

Diverse Content:

Ensure diversity and inclusivity in content by featuring voices and perspectives from a variety of backgrounds and identities. Represent the diversity of the community and amplify marginalized voices.

Measure & Adapt:

Monitor social media analytics to track engagement, reach, and other metrics. Use insights to refine content strategies, identify trends, and optimize performance over time.

The key to social media is consistency. Regular updates and content keep the group's activities and mission in the public eye, creating a sense of community and ongoing interest. It's important not to be discouraged by low engagement on some posts, as social media algorithms can be unpredictable and views can fluctuate. All it takes, though, is one post to resonate widely and potentially go viral, dramatically increasing the group's reach and bringing global attention to your efforts. By staying consistent and persistent, the group can steadily build a robust online presence, ensuring that your message has the best chance of reaching a broad audience.

Outreach Campaigns

An **outreach campaign** is a targeted effort to engage a specific audience or community for a particular purpose. It involves reaching out to people through various channels and methods to raise awareness, provide information, and encourage action around a particular issue or initiative.

Outreach campaigns can take many forms, including digital marketing, community events, and media. The goal of an outreach campaign is to effectively communicate messages, build relationships, and mobilize support to achieve desired outcomes—such as increasing participation, driving behavior change, or advocating for a specific cause. Successful outreach campaigns are strategic, well-planned, and tailored to the needs and preferences of the target audience.

Running an effective outreach campaign requires careful planning, coordination, and execution. Here are the steps a mutual aid group can take to effectively run an outreach campaign:

1. Define Objectives:
Clearly define the objectives of the outreach campaign. Determine what the group hopes to achieve, whether it's raising awareness, increasing participation, driving action, or advocating for a specific cause.

2. Identify Target Audience:
Identify the target audience or community that the outreach campaign aims to reach. Understand their demographics, interests, preferences, and needs to tailor messaging and strategies accordingly.

3. Develop Key Messages:
Develop clear, compelling messages that resonate with the target audience and align with the objectives of the campaign. Craft messages that highlight the benefits of participating in the mutual aid group, address community needs, and inspire action.

4. Choose Outreach Channels:
Select the most appropriate outreach channels and methods to reach the target audience effectively. This may include social media, email newsletters, community events, door-to-door canvassing, local media outlets, and partnerships with other organizations.

5. Create Outreach Materials:
Develop outreach materials, such as flyers, posters, brochures, social media graphics, and emails to support the campaign. Ensure that materials are visually appealing, informative, and consistent with the group's branding and messaging.

6. Engage Community Partners:
Collaborate with community partners, organizations, and influencers to amplify the reach of the campaign. Leverage existing networks and relationships to access new audiences.

7. Train Volunteers:
Provide training and support to volunteers who will be involved in outreach activities. Equip them with the knowledge, skills, and resources needed to effectively communicate messages, engage with the community, and address questions or concerns.

8. Launch Campaign:
Implement the outreach campaign according to the planned timeline and strategy. Monitor progress, track key metrics, and make adjustments as needed to optimize performance and ensure effectiveness.

9. Evaluate & Adjust:
Evaluate the success of the campaign by analyzing key metrics, such as reach, engagement, and impact. Gather feedback from participants, volunteers, and community members to identify strengths, weaknesses, and areas for improvement. Use insights to refine future efforts.

By following these steps, your mutual aid group can run an effective outreach campaign that raises awareness, engages the community, and drives meaningful action in support of its mission and objectives.

Emails & Newsletters

Emails and newsletters are powerful tools for mutual aid groups to engage with supporters, share updates, and mobilize action. By building an email list and regularly communicating with supporters through newsletters, groups can create stronger connections, inspire involvement, and amplify their impact.

Whether it's announcing upcoming events, sharing success stories, or calling for volunteers, email provides a direct line of communication that ensures important information reaches supporters quickly and efficiently. By sending newsletters on a consistent basis, the group stays top-of-mind and maintains visibility among supporters, ensuring that they remain engaged and connected to the group's work over time. However, be mindful not to send too many emails, as recipients may quickly become annoyed by an inundated inbox and unsubscribe from the mailing list.

When sending newsletters, mutual aid groups can follow these best practices to maximize engagement:

Clear Subject Lines:

Use clear and concise subject lines that accurately convey the content of the newsletter and entice recipients to open it. Avoid spammy or misleading language that may decrease open rates.

Compelling Content:

Provide valuable and engaging content that resonates with your audience. Include stories, updates, testimonials, and calls to action that highlight the impact of your work and inspire supporters to get involved.

Visual Appeal:

Use eye-catching visuals, such as images, graphics, and videos to enhance the visual appeal of your newsletter. Visual content helps break up text, capture attention, and convey information more effectively.

Mobile Optimization:

Ensure that your newsletter is optimized for mobile devices, as many recipients read emails on their smartphones or tablets. Use responsive design, legible fonts, and appropriately sized images to ensure a seamless viewing experience on all devices.

Consistent Branding:

Maintain consistent branding across your newsletters, including colors, fonts, logos, and messaging. Consistency helps reinforce your brand identity and helps recipients recognize your organization.

Clear Call to Action (CTA):

Include a clear and prominent call to action that prompts recipients to do something, such as donating, volunteering, or visiting your website. Make the CTA stand out visually and use persuasive language.

Personalization:

Personalize your newsletters whenever possible by addressing recipients by name and incorporating personalized content based on their interests or past interactions with your group. Personalization helps strengthen connections and increases engagement.

A/B Testing:

Experiment with different elements of your newsletter–such as subject lines, content, or calls-to-action–through A/B testing. Test variations to see which performs better and use insights to optimize future newsletters.

Analytics & Tracking:

Track key metrics such as open rates, click-through rates, and conversions to measure the performance of your newsletters. Use analytics data to identify trends, understand recipient behavior, and refine your strategy.

Direct Mail

Engaging with supporters through direct mail can be a valuable complement to a mutual aid group's digital outreach efforts, providing a tangible and personalized way to connect with the community. By sending letters, postcards, or other printed materials via postal mail, groups can reach people who may not be active online or who prefer offline communication methods.

One effective strategy for engaging supporters through direct mail is to send personalized thank-you notes or appreciation letters to donors, volunteers, and community partners. Personalized messages expressing gratitude for their support and contributions can strengthen relationships, foster loyalty, and encourage continued engagement with the group's activities. Including handwritten elements or signatures can add an extra touch of authenticity and sincerity.

Direct mail can also be used to share updates, stories, and impact reports with supporters, providing them with a tangible reminder of the group's ongoing efforts and accomplishments. Newsletters or brochures arriving in their mailbox can make them feel more connected to the group.

Virtual Events

Virtual events are online gatherings that bring remote participants together to interact, collaborate, and engage with content or activities. Hosted on virtual platforms—such as video conferencing software, webinars, or social media platforms—these events offer opportunities for networking, learning, and community building without the need for attending in person.

Hosting virtual events can offer several benefits for a mutual aid group:

Accessibility:

Virtual events allow participants to join from anywhere with an internet connection, making them accessible to a wider audience. This inclusivity can increase participation and engagement, especially for people who may face barriers to attending in-person events, such as transportation issues or mobility limitations.

Cost-Effectiveness:

Hosting virtual events can be more cost-effective than in-person events, as they eliminate expenses associated with venue rental, catering, and travel. This cost savings allows mutual aid groups to allocate resources more efficiently and maximize the impact of their events.

Flexibility:

Virtual events offer flexibility in scheduling and format, allowing mutual aid groups to host them at convenient times. Virtual platforms provide flexibility in event formats, enabling groups to host webinars, panel discussions, workshops, fundraisers, and social gatherings with ease.

Community Building:

Virtual events provide opportunities for community building and networking, allowing participants to connect with each other, share experiences, and build relationships. These connections can strengthen solidarity and create a sense of belonging.

Scalability:

Virtual events can be scaled to accommodate large numbers of participants without the limitations of physical space. This scalability allows mutual aid groups to reach a broader audience and amplify the impact of their events.

While virtual events offer numerous benefits, they also come with some limitations. One is the potential for technical difficulties, such as poor internet connections, audio/video lag, or platform glitches, which can disrupt the flow of the event and negatively impact the experience. Virtual events may also lack the personal connections and spontaneous interactions that often occur in face-to-face settings, leading to reduced engagement.

Despite these limitations, mutual groups can improve the experience of their virtual events with careful planning, effective communication, and by leveraging appropriate technology.

Live Events

A mutual aid group may choose to host live events as they offer valuable opportunities for in-person connection, collaboration, and community building. Live events—such as workshops, forums, or fundraising gatherings—allow participants to engage directly with one another, share experiences, and build relationships.

Live events provide a platform for dynamic and interactive experiences, enabling mutual aid groups to deliver impactful content, facilitate meaningful discussions, and mobilize action around important issues. While live events require careful planning and logistical coordination, the benefits of in-person engagement and connection make them a valuable component the group's broader outreach efforts.

Here's a step-by-step guide to organizing a live event:

1. Define the Purpose & Audience:
Determine the objective of the event and identify the target audience. Is it a fundraiser, community gathering, awareness campaign, or celebration? Understanding the purpose will guide subsequent decisions.

2. Select a Venue:
Choose a venue that can accommodate the expected number of attendees and aligns with the event's theme and logistics. Consider factors such as accessibility, amenities, parking, and cost. Reserve the venue well in advance to secure the desired date. Depending on the size and location of the event, you may also need to obtain a permit.

3. Set a Date & Time:
Select a date and time that maximizes attendance and minimizes conflicts with other events. Consider factors like holidays, local events, and peak attendance times. Ensure the chosen date works for key stakeholders and partners.

4. Plan the Program:
Develop a detailed program agenda outlining the sequence of activities, speakers, performances, and any special presentations. Allocate sufficient time for each segment and include breaks for networking, refreshments, and audience engagement.

252

5. Secure Speakers & Performers:
Invite relevant speakers, performers, and special guests to participate in the event. Confirm their availability and provide them with guidelines or expectations for their contributions. Coordinate logistics such as travel arrangements and accommodations if necessary.

6. Promote the Event:
Create a comprehensive marketing and promotional plan to generate buzz and attract attendees. Utilize a mix of online and offline channels, including social media, email newsletters, press releases, flyers, posters, and community outreach. Leverage partnerships with local organizations and media outlets to spread the word.

7. Manage Logistics:
Attend to logistical details such as event registration, ticketing, seating arrangements, audiovisual equipment, signage, catering, and volunteer coordination. Create a timeline and assign responsibilities to ensure smooth execution on the day of the event.

8. Ensure Safety & Accessibility:
Prioritize the safety and accessibility of all attendees by adhering to relevant regulations and guidelines. Provide clear directions, signage, and support for people with disabilities. Implement measures to address emergencies and medical needs.

9. Engage Volunteers:
Recruit and train volunteers to assist with various tasks before, during, and after the event. Assign roles such as registration, ushering, guest assistance, setup, cleanup, and media support. Conduct briefings to ensure volunteers understand their responsibilities.

10. Execute the Event:
Execute the event according to the planned agenda, adapting as necessary to unforeseen circumstances. Maintain open communication among team members and stakeholders to address any issues promptly. Capture feedback and insights for future improvements.

11. Follow Up & Evaluate:
After the event, follow up with attendees to express gratitude, share highlights, and gather feedback through surveys. Evaluate the event's success based on predefined goals and metrics, identifying strengths and areas for improvement.

By following these steps and exercising careful planning and execution, a mutual aid group can host a successful live event that encourages community engagement, raises awareness, and advances its mission.

Press Coverage

Securing press coverage can be highly beneficial for a mutual aid group, as it will expand their reach and garner support from a wider audience. Media coverage provides an opportunity for groups to raise awareness about their initiatives, highlight their impact, and attract volunteers, donors, and community partners.

Press coverage can also play a role in shaping public perception and generating interest in mutual aid initiatives. Media stories can humanize the work of mutual aid groups by sharing stories of people who have been positively impacted by their help and solidarity. These human-interest stories help to connect with audiences on an emotional level, eliciting empathy, compassion, and support for the group's mission.

Being covered by the press can also help mutual aid groups attract the attention of policymakers, influencers, and other stakeholders, potentially leading to increased resources and partnerships. This increased visibility can help groups advocate for systemic change and policy reforms to address underlying issues contributing to inequality and injustice.

Press coverage brings numerous benefits to a mutual aid group, but there are also potential negative consequences to be aware of:

Misrepresentation:
The media may misrepresent the goals, activities, or impact of the mutual aid group. Misinterpretation or sensationalization of information could distort the group's message, undermine its credibility, and lead to misunderstandings among the public.

Political Bias:
Media outlets may have political biases or agendas that influence their coverage of mutual aid groups and related issues. Groups should be cautious of potential distortions in media reporting.

Privacy Concerns:
Press coverage may inadvertently expose sensitive information about people who have sought assistance from the mutual aid group. Protecting the privacy and confidentiality of beneficiaries is crucial, and media attention could potentially compromise their anonymity.

Increased Scrutiny:
With increased visibility comes increased scrutiny, as the actions and decisions of the mutual aid group may be subject to greater public criticism. Negative coverage or backlash from the media or public could damage the group's reputation and hinder its ability to effectively carry out its mission.

Dependency:
Excessive media attention may lead to a sense of dependency on external support or validation, rather than fostering self-reliance and empowerment within the community. Mutual aid groups should be cautious of becoming overly reliant on media coverage as a measure of success and focus instead on maintaining grassroots support and engagement.

Distracted Focus:
Managing media inquiries, interviews, and public relations activities can be time-consuming and resource-intensive, diverting attention and resources away from the group's core mission and activities. Mutual aid groups should carefully balance the benefits of media exposure with the need to prioritize their primary objectives and responsibilities.

Overall, while press coverage can be a valuable tool for raising awareness and mobilizing support, mutual aid groups should approach media engagement strategically and thoughtfully–taking proactive steps to mitigate potential risks and negative consequences. By maintaining transparency, protecting privacy, and staying true to their values and mission, groups can navigate media attention effectively and maximize the positive impact of their work.

Press Releases

A mutual aid group may choose to write a **press release** as a strategic communication tool to effectively disseminate important information, promote upcoming events, or highlight significant achievements to the media and the broader public. Press releases offer a formal and structured format for conveying key messages in a concise and newsworthy manner, making them more likely to be picked up by journalists and media outlets for coverage. Several key components contribute to a good press release:

Headline: A compelling and attention-grabbing headline that succinctly summarizes the main news or announcement being communicated.

Dateline: The city and date of the press release's issuance, providing context and timeliness to the news.

Lead Paragraph (or "Lede"): The opening paragraph, which contains the most important information and answers the "who, what, where, when, why, and how" of the news story.

Body: The main body of the press release provides additional details, quotes, and background information to support the news being communicated. It may include relevant statistics, facts, or anecdotes to enhance the story's credibility and relevance.

Quotes: Incorporating quotes from key stakeholders, such as organization leaders, spokespersons, or beneficiaries, adds authenticity and human interest to the press release. Quotes should be relevant, concise, and attributed to the appropriate source.

Boilerplate & Contact Information: A brief paragraph at the end that provides background information about the group, including its mission, history, and achievements. Add the name, title, and contact of a designated spokesperson who can answer additional questions.

Here is an example of a press release for a mutual aid group:

[Embargoed until April 30, 2024]

[City, State] – April 30, 2024

[Mutual Aid Group Name] Launches Innovative Food Redistribution Program to Address Food Insecurity in Pandemic

[City, State] – [Mutual Aid Group Name], a grassroots organization serving the greater metro area, is proud to announce the launch of its groundbreaking food redistribution program aimed at addressing food insecurity exacerbated by the COVID-19 pandemic.

As the economic fallout from the pandemic continues to impact vulnerable populations, access to nutritious food has become increasingly challenging for many individuals and families. Recognizing this urgent need, [Mutual Aid Group Name] has developed an innovative solution to redistribute surplus food from local businesses, farms, and community partners to those in need.

"Our goal is to ensure that no one in our community goes hungry, especially during these challenging times," said [Spokesperson Name], member of [Mutual Aid Group Name]. "Through our new food redistribution program, we aim to leverage existing resources and partnerships to maximize the impact of our collective efforts and provide much-needed support to those facing food insecurity."

The food redistribution program will involve partnerships with local restaurants, grocery stores, and farms to collect excess perishable and non-perishable food items that would otherwise go to waste. [Mutual Aid Group Name] volunteers will then sort, package, and distribute the donated food to people in need through a network of distribution centers and community organizations.

"We believe that everyone deserves access to nutritious food, regardless of their circumstances," said [Volunteer Name], a dedicated volunteer with [Mutual Aid Group Name]. "By working together as a community, we can make a meaningful difference in the lives of those who are struggling to put food on the table."

continues...

In addition to addressing immediate food needs, [Mutual Aid Group Name] aims to raise awareness about food insecurity issues, advocate for systemic change, and build long-term resilience within the community.

For more information about [Mutual Aid Group Name]'s food redistribution program and how to get involved, please visit [Organization Website] or contact [Spokesperson Name] at [Phone Number] or [Email Address].

About [Mutual Aid Group Name]:
[Mutual Aid Group Name] is a grassroots organization dedicated to fostering solidarity, support, and mutual aid within the community. Through collective action, [Mutual Aid Group Name] strives to address pressing social issues, empower individuals and families, and help build a more resilient and equitable society.

Media Contact:
[Spokesperson Name]
[Title]
[Organization Name]
[Phone Number]
[Email Address]

[Note: Customize the information within brackets with specific details relevant to the mutual aid group and its initiatives.]

Once your mutual aid group has a final press release ready, you can take several steps to attract media attention and increase the likelihood of coverage:

1. Media List Building:
Compile a list of relevant media outlets, journalists, bloggers, and influencers who cover topics related to mutual aid, community initiatives, or social causes. Research their contact information and areas of interest to ensure targeted outreach.

2. Press Release Distribution:
Send the press release directly to journalists and media outlets on the media list via email. Include a personalized pitch that highlights the newsworthiness of the story, emphasizes its relevance to their audience, and explains why they should consider covering it.

3. Media Outreach:

Follow up with journalists and media contacts to ensure they received the press release and offer to provide additional information, interviews, or visuals to support their coverage. Building relationships with media professionals can increase the likelihood of coverage and future collaboration.

4. Press Release Wire Services:

Consider distributing the press release through reputable distribution services or newswire services, which can help reach a broader audience of journalists, editors, and news organizations.

5. Social Media Promotion:

Share the press release on the mutual aid group's social media channels, website, and other online platforms to increase visibility and encourage community members to share it with their networks.

6. Follow-Up & Persistence:

Be persistent in following up with journalists and media contacts to gauge their interest in covering the story. Offer to provide additional information, arrange interviews with spokespersons or beneficiaries, and accommodate their deadlines and preferences.

7. News Hooks & Timeliness:

Emphasize any timely or relevant angles of the press release that may appeal to journalists, such as current events, trends, or local issues. Providing a compelling news hook can increase the newsworthiness and appeal of the story.

By implementing these strategies and approaches, your mutual aid group can effectively promote your press release, attract media attention, and increase the likelihood of securing coverage for your initiatives. Be ready to answer follow-up questions or for a journalist to reach out for an interview. The next sections will help you prepare.

Interviews with Journalists

Journalists seek interviewees who can contribute meaningful and compelling content to their stories, enriching the narrative and providing valuable insights and perspectives to their audience. By understanding what journalists are looking for, mutual aid groups can better prepare for interviews and effectively communicate their message to the media.

Journalists are typically looking for several key elements to create a compelling and informative story:

Accuracy:

Journalists seek accurate and reliable information from their interviewees. They expect people to provide truthful and factual responses to their questions, supported by evidence or firsthand knowledge.

Relevance:

Journalists look for interviewees who can speak knowledgeably and insightfully about the topic at hand. They seek people with relevant expertise, experience, or perspectives that add value to the story and help provide context and depth.

Clarity:

Interviewees should communicate their ideas and viewpoints clearly and succinctly. Journalists prefer responses that are easy to understand and articulate, avoiding jargon or technical language that may confuse or alienate the audience.

Perspective:

Journalists value interviewees who offer unique perspectives, insights, or angles on the topic being discussed. They seek diverse viewpoints that enrich the story and provide a well-rounded understanding of the subject matter.

Engagement:

Interviewees who are enthusiastic, passionate, and engaging during the interview are more likely to captivate the audience and hold their attention. Journalists appreciate interviewees who are willing to share personal anecdotes, stories, or examples that bring the topic to life and make it relatable to the audience.

Credibility:

Journalists assess the credibility and trustworthiness of their interviewees based on their background, expertise, and track record. They look for people who are credible sources of information and can provide valuable insights or firsthand experiences relevant to the story.

Cooperation:

Journalists appreciate interviewees who are cooperative, responsive, and willing to provide additional information or context as needed. They value interviewees who respect deadlines, boundaries, and professional standards of conduct during the interview process.

When being interviewed by a journalist, keep the following considerations in mind to ensure a successful and effective interaction:

Prepare Key Messages:
Before the interview, identify and prepare key messages that align with the group's mission, goals, and initiatives. Be clear, concise, and consistent in communicating these messages throughout the interview.

Know Your Audience:
Understand the audience of the media outlet and journalist conducting the interview. Tailor your responses to resonate with their audience's interests, concerns, and values.

Be Transparent & Honest:
Maintain transparency and honesty in your responses to the journalist's questions. Avoid providing misleading or inaccurate information, as this can damage your mutual aid group's credibility and reputation.

Stay On Message:
Stay focused on your key messages and objectives during the interview. Avoid getting sidetracked or drawn into unrelated topics that may detract from your main points.

Be Prepared for Tough Questions:
Anticipate and be prepared to address tough or challenging questions from the journalist. Stay calm, composed, and respectful in your responses, even when faced with difficult inquiries.

Bridge to Key Messages:
If asked a question that does not directly align with your key messages, use bridging techniques to transition back to your main points. For example, acknowledge the question briefly and then pivot to a related topic that aligns with your key messages.

Speak Clearly & Concisely:
Speak clearly and concisely, avoiding jargon or technical language that may be difficult for the audience to understand. Use plain language and simple explanations to convey your message effectively.

Provide Examples & Stories:
Use examples, anecdotes, and real-life stories to illustrate your points and make them more relatable and engaging for the audience.

Respect Deadlines & Boundaries:
Respect the journalist's deadlines and boundaries during the interview process. Be punctual, responsive, and cooperative in providing information and accommodating their needs.

After the interview, follow up with the journalist to express gratitude for the opportunity and offer any additional information or resources that may be helpful for their story. By keeping these considerations in mind, your mutual aid group can effectively navigate interviews with journalists, share your message, and raise awareness about your initiatives and impact.

Televised Interviews

Television coverage allows mutual aid groups to share their stories, showcase their work, and highlight the importance of solidarity in times of need. By appearing on TV, groups can inspire viewers to get involved, mobilize support, and create a sense of collective action and empathy.

Before being interviewed on television, it's essential to be prepared and aware of several key considerations to ensure a successful and effective appearance:

Understand the Format:
Familiarize yourself with the format of the TV interview, whether it's a live broadcast, recorded segment, panel discussion, or one-on-one interview. Understand the length of the segment, the interviewer's style, and any technical aspects, such as camera angles and lighting.

Know Your Message:
Identify and prepare key messages that you want to convey during the interview. These messages should align with your objectives and the topic being discussed. Practice delivering your messages clearly, concisely, and confidently.

Dress Appropriately:
Choose appropriate attire that aligns with the tone and setting of the interview. Avoid patterns, logos, or colors that may distract from your message or clash with the television studio's background.

Body Language:
Pay attention to your body language, posture, and facial expressions during the interview. Maintain eye contact with the interviewer, sit or stand with good posture, and avoid fidgeting or distracting mannerisms that may convey nervousness or discomfort.

Speak Clearly & Concisely:
Speak clearly and enunciate your words to ensure that your message is easily understood by the audience. Keep your responses concise and to the point, avoiding rambling or tangential explanations that may lose the viewer's interest.

Stay Calm & Composed:
Remain calm, composed, and focused throughout the interview, even if you encounter unexpected questions or challenges. Take deep breaths, pause if necessary to collect your thoughts, and respond confidently.

Be Authentic:
Be yourself during the interview and communicate authentically. Speak from your personal experience, expertise, and perspective, and avoid trying to memorize scripted responses or sound overly rehearsed.

Anticipate Questions:
Anticipate potential questions that the interviewer may ask and prepare responses in advance. Consider how you will address challenging or controversial topics while staying true to your message and objectives.

Stay On Message:
Stay focused on your key messages throughout the interview. Use bridging techniques to transition back to your main points if the conversation veers off track or if you encounter unrelated questions.

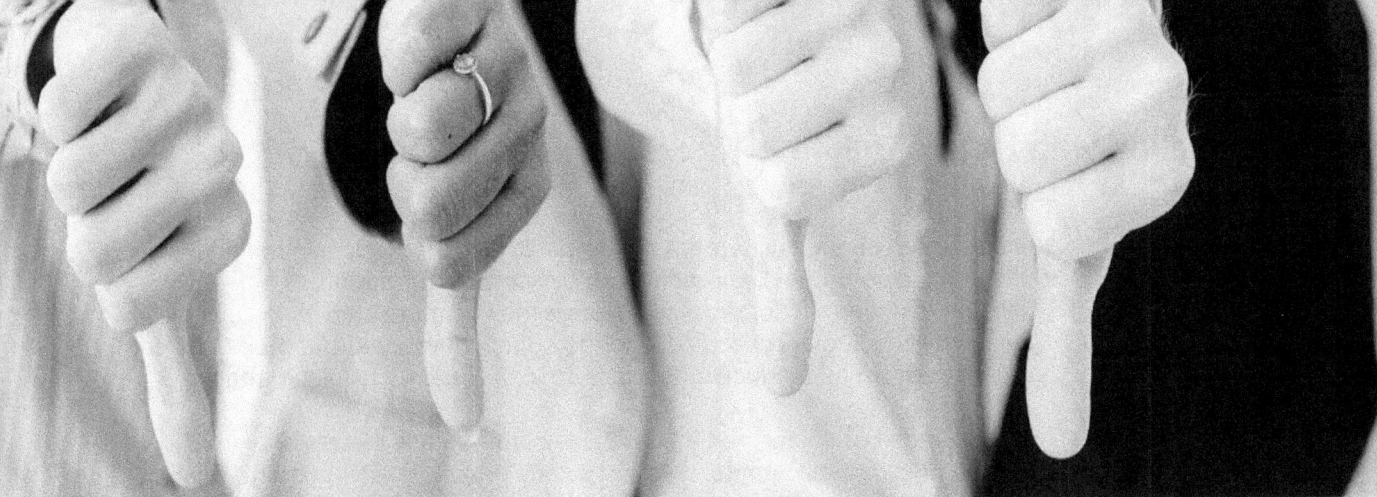

Handling Criticism & Negativity

As your mutual aid group gains visibility and expands its reach within the community, you may inevitably encounter criticism and negative press coverage at some point. While these challenges can be disheartening, they also present opportunities for growth, reflection, and improvement.

Criticism and negativity may arise from various sources, including misunderstandings, differing perspectives, or genuine concerns about the group's actions, decisions, or impact. It's essential for mutual aid groups to approach criticism and negative press coverage with a constructive mindset, acknowledging the feedback, and taking proactive steps to address any valid concerns or issues raised.

When faced with criticism and negative press, groups should prioritize transparency, accountability, and responsiveness in their communications and actions. Listen to the concerns raised, engage in open dialogue, and provide clear and honest explanations or solutions where necessary. By demonstrating a willingness to address criticism and learn from feedback, you can build trust and credibility within the community.

Additionally, your mutual aid group can leverage positive relationships with media outlets and journalists to mitigate the impact of negative press coverage and ensure that your perspectives are accurately represented. This may involve proactively reaching out to media contacts to provide context, clarification, or additional information related to the coverage. By maintaining open lines of communication with the media, you can help shape the narrative surrounding your initiatives and create more balanced and nuanced coverage.

Dealing with Haters Online

 **Haters** often engage in derogatory or hostile behavior–such as making disparaging comments, spreading rumors or misinformation, or actively seeking to undermine or discredit. Haters may be motivated by jealousy, insecurity, ideological differences, or personal grievances, and their behavior can range from mild criticism to more aggressive and malicious attacks.

In the context of social media and online communities, haters may troll, harass, or cyberbully others, creating a toxic or hostile environment. Dealing with haters requires patience, resilience, and a strategic approach to managing negative feedback and maintaining a positive online presence. When interacting with haters, mutual aid groups should approach the situation with patience and empathy while prioritizing their mission and values. Here are some strategies for effectively managing these interactions:

Remain Calm & Composed:
Avoid engaging in heated arguments or retaliatory behavior, as this can escalate the situation and reflect poorly on the group.

Focus on Facts & Positivity:
Respond to haters with factual information, positivity, and respect. Acknowledge their concerns or criticisms, and provide accurate and transparent explanations or clarifications where necessary.

Set Boundaries:
Delete or hide comments that are abusive, offensive, or violate community guidelines, and consider blocking repeat offenders if necessary to maintain a positive and respectful online environment.

Empathize & Educate:
Use the opportunity to educate the hater about the group's work, objectives, and impact, and address any misconceptions in a constructive manner.

Don't Feed the Trolls:
In some cases, it may be more productive to ignore or disengage from negative comments rather than fueling further hostility.

Turn Negativity into Opportunity:
Consider whether there are valid concerns or areas for improvement that the group can address to improve its credibility. Turn negative experiences into opportunities for learning and adaptation.

PR Crisis Management

Crisis management, in terms of public relations, involves the strategic handling of negative or potentially damaging media attention that could adversely affect a mutual aid group's reputation, credibility, or public perception. It encompasses the proactive planning, rapid response, and effective communication strategies employed by organizations to mitigate the impact of unfavorable press coverage and safeguard their reputation during times of crisis.

An example of negative press coverage of a mutual aid group could involve a news story that alleges mismanagement of funds or resources within the organization. For instance, suppose a local newspaper publishes an article claiming that a mutual aid group–known for its efforts to support vulnerable community members during a pandemic–has been mishandling donations and failing to distribute aid effectively. The article may cite anonymous sources or testimonies from disgruntled volunteers who allege instances of favoritism, misallocation of funds, or lack of transparency in the group's operations.

The negative press coverage could lead to public scrutiny, questioning the integrity and credibility of the mutual aid group and its leadership. Community members, donors, and supporters may express concerns about the group's financial accountability, ethical standards, and overall effectiveness in addressing the needs of those it aims to serve.

In response to the negative press coverage, the mutual aid group may issue a statement denying the allegations and providing evidence to refute the claims made in the article. They may also conduct an internal investigation or audit to address any legitimate concerns raised and implement measures to improve transparency, accountability, and oversight in their operations.

Despite the challenges posed by the negative press coverage, the mutual aid group can use the experience as an opportunity to strengthen its governance, communication, and operational processes. By addressing the issues raised in the article transparently and proactively, the group can rebuild trust and credibility within the community and continue its mission of providing support.

Chapter Review

Should your mutual aid group choose to engage with the broader public, effective communication is key. One of the foundational steps in this process is building a strong brand identity, which includes creating a recognizable logo, a memorable name, and an overall style that reflects the group's values and mission. Consistent use of visual and verbal elements across all platforms ensures that the group's presence is cohesive and professional.

Outreach campaigns are an important component of communicating with the public. These can include social media posts, email newsletters, and virtual/live community events. The goal might be to raise awareness about the group's mission, recruit volunteers, or mobilize resources. Effective outreach campaigns are well-planned and target specific audiences, using tailored messages that resonate with different segments of the community.

Getting covered by the press can significantly amplify your reach and impact, and press releases can facilitate this process. Once a journalist or reporter agrees to cover the story, you should prepare some talking points so you make a positive impression on the public.

Handling criticism and negativity is an inevitable part of public engagement. It's important to approach criticism constructively and use it as an opportunity for growth. Addressing concerns transparently and thoughtfully can build trust and demonstrate a commitment to the community's well-being.

Discussion Questions

1 Reflect on an organization that you believe has a strong and effective brand identity. What specific elements of their brand make it successful, and how can these elements be applied to a mutual aid group?

2 Consider the unique characteristics and needs of your community. What types of outreach campaigns do you believe would be most successful in engaging and mobilizing people in your area, and why?

IN THIS CHAPTER

>> How to promote a culture of
continuous learning

>> Adult education initiatives,
including skill-sharing workshops
and leadership training

>> Initiatives involving children and
youth, including mentorship and
scholarship programs

Chapter **9**

Education &
Skill-Sharing Programs

Mutual aid education programs provide opportunities for lifelong learning
that are often unavailable through conventional systems. Many
communities face barriers to education due to economic disparities,
geographic isolation, or institutional biases. Mutual aid groups can bypass
these barriers by creating flexible, community-driven learning programs that
meet the specific needs of their participants. This chapter will explore how
these programs work and why they are essential to strengthening
community resilience.

A Culture of Continuous Learning

In today's rapidly changing and uncertain world, the challenges faced by communities demand adaptability, resilience, and innovation. Communities are constantly confronted with complex and interconnected issues that require creative solutions. In response to these challenges, mutual aid groups should embrace a culture of continuous learning as a strategic imperative.

By cultivating a mindset of curiosity, exploration, and growth, mutual aid groups can adapt more effectively to changing circumstances, anticipate emerging needs, and identify new opportunities for collaboration and impact. A culture of continuous learning enables groups to leverage the collective wisdom, experiences, and insights of their members. As the landscape of community needs continues to evolve, groups that prioritize learning and adaptation will be better equipped to navigate uncertainty, build stronger relationships, and achieve lasting positive change.

Mutual aid groups can promote continuous learning through various strategies and initiatives tailored to the needs and preferences of their community.

Here are some examples that enable members to develop their skills, knowledge, and capacities:

Workshops & Training Sessions:
Skill-building workshops and training sessions can cover a wide range of subjects, including crisis response, community organizing, conflict resolution, communication skills, and cultural competency.

Peer Learning Circles:
These informal gatherings provide opportunities for members to come together to discuss key issues, share insights and experiences, and learn from one another.

Guest Speakers & Experts:
Guest lectures or panel discussions can offer valuable insights, perspectives, and expertise from external sources, enriching the learning experience for members and stimulating thought-provoking discussions.

Online Resources & Webinars:
Providing access to educational materials and digital learning opportunities—like articles, podcasts, and webinars—allows members to engage in self-directed learning at their own pace and convenience.

Reflection & Evaluation:
Facilitating discussions or conducting surveys to gather feedback from members and stakeholders helps identify lessons learned, areas for improvement, and opportunities for growth.

Partnerships & Collaborations:
Collaborative initiatives with other organizations, institutions, or experts enable mutual aid groups to leverage external expertise, networks, and resources to enhance their learning and capacity-building efforts.

Creating Learning Spaces

A **learning space** refers to any physical or virtual environment intentionally designed to facilitate learning, collaboration, and knowledge-sharing among individuals or groups. Learning spaces can take various forms—including classrooms, libraries, conference rooms, online platforms, and community centers—and they are characterized by their flexibility, accessibility, and conducive atmosphere for learning and engagement.

In a physical sense, learning spaces may feature adaptable furniture, technology-enabled infrastructure, and interactive tools to support different learning activities and styles. These spaces are designed to promote active participation, creativity, and critical thinking, fostering a dynamic learning environment where people feel comfortable exploring ideas, asking questions, and collaborating with others.

In a virtual context, learning spaces encompass online platforms, forums, and digital communities where individuals can access educational resources, engage in discussions, and collaborate with peers regardless of geographical location. These virtual learning spaces leverage technology to facilitate communication, interaction, and knowledge-sharing in a flexible and scalable manner, catering to diverse learning needs and preferences.

When creating a learning space, mutual aid groups should consider several factors to ensure that it effectively supports the needs and preferences of its members. Here are some key considerations:

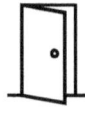

Accessibility:

Ensure that the learning space is accessible to all members of the community, including those with disabilities or special needs. Consider factors such as physical accessibility, transportation options, and language accessibility to ensure that the space is welcoming and inclusive.

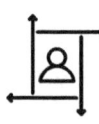

Flexibility:

Design the space to be flexible and adaptable to accommodate a variety of learning activities, formats, and group sizes. Incorporate movable furniture, modular layouts, and multi-functional spaces that can be easily reconfigured to support different types of learning experiences.

Technology & Resources:

Equip the space with appropriate technology, tools, and resources to facilitate learning and collaboration. This may include audiovisual equipment, multimedia tools, internet access, and learning materials relevant to the group's focus areas and objectives.

Comfort & Ergonomics:

Prioritize the comfort and well-being of learners by providing comfortable seating, adequate lighting, temperature control, and ergonomic furnishings. Create a welcoming and inviting atmosphere that encourages engagement, concentration, and participation.

Safety & Security:

Ensure that the space is safe, secure, and conducive to learning. Implement safety protocols, emergency procedures, and security measures to protect participants and minimize risks associated with physical and environmental hazards.

Cultural Sensitivity & Diversity:

Consider the cultural backgrounds, values, and preferences of the community when designing the learning space. Create an environment that respects and celebrates diversity, promotes cultural sensitivity, and fosters inclusivity and belonging for all participants.

Community Partnerships:

Explore opportunities to collaborate with local organizations, educational institutions, or community centers to leverage existing resources, expertise, and networks in creating and maintaining the learning space. Forge partnerships that enhance access, reach, and sustainability while maximizing the impact and effectiveness of the initiatives.

By carefully considering these factors, mutual aid groups can create a learning space that serves as a vibrant hub for education, collaboration, and community-building.

Flexible Learning Formats

Flexible learning formats refer to educational approaches and methodologies that allow for customization, adaptability, and personalized learning experiences to meet the diverse needs, preferences, and circumstances of learners. These formats are designed to accommodate different learning styles, schedules, and contexts, providing learners with greater autonomy, choice, and control over their education.

A mutual aid group should consider using flexible learning formats to ensure that its educational initiatives are accessible, inclusive, and responsive to the needs of its members and the community. Some examples of flexible learning formats include:

Blended Learning:

Blended learning combines traditional face-to-face instruction with online learning activities, allowing learners to access course materials, participate in discussions, and complete assignments both in-person and remotely. This approach offers flexibility in terms of time, location, and pace of learning, while still providing opportunities for interaction and collaboration with peers and instructors.

Flipped Classroom:

In a flipped classroom model, learners engage with instructional content—such as videos, readings, or interactive modules—independently outside of class time, freeing up in-person class sessions for active learning, discussions, and hands-on activities. This format allows learners to review and digest content at their own pace while maximizing face-to-face interaction and engagement during class sessions.

Self-Paced Learning:

Self-paced learning allows learners to progress through course materials and activities at their own speed, independently of fixed schedules or timelines. Learners have the flexibility to study and review content according to their individual needs and preferences, enabling them to take ownership of their learning and focus on areas where they need additional support or reinforcement.

Modular Courses:

Modular courses break down complex subjects or topics into smaller, manageable units or modules that can be completed sequentially or independently. Learners have the flexibility to choose which modules to focus on based on their interests, goals, and prior knowledge, allowing for a more customized and adaptive learning experience.

Project-Based Learning:

Project-based learning involves engaging learners in real-world projects or tasks that require them to apply and integrate knowledge, skills, and concepts from multiple disciplines. This format fosters creativity, critical thinking, and problem-solving skills while providing flexibility in terms of project scope, timeline, and collaboration opportunities.

Microlearning:

Microlearning delivers short, focused learning activities or resources—such as videos, quizzes, or interactive simulations—that can be completed in brief, digestible segments. Learners can access microlearning modules on-demand and integrate them into their daily routines, making it easy to fit learning into busy schedules.

Flexible Assessment Options:

Flexible learning formats also include a variety of assessment options that accommodate different learning preferences and styles. These may include traditional exams, essays, projects, presentations, portfolios, or peer assessments, allowing learners to demonstrate their knowledge and skills in ways that align with their strengths and interests.

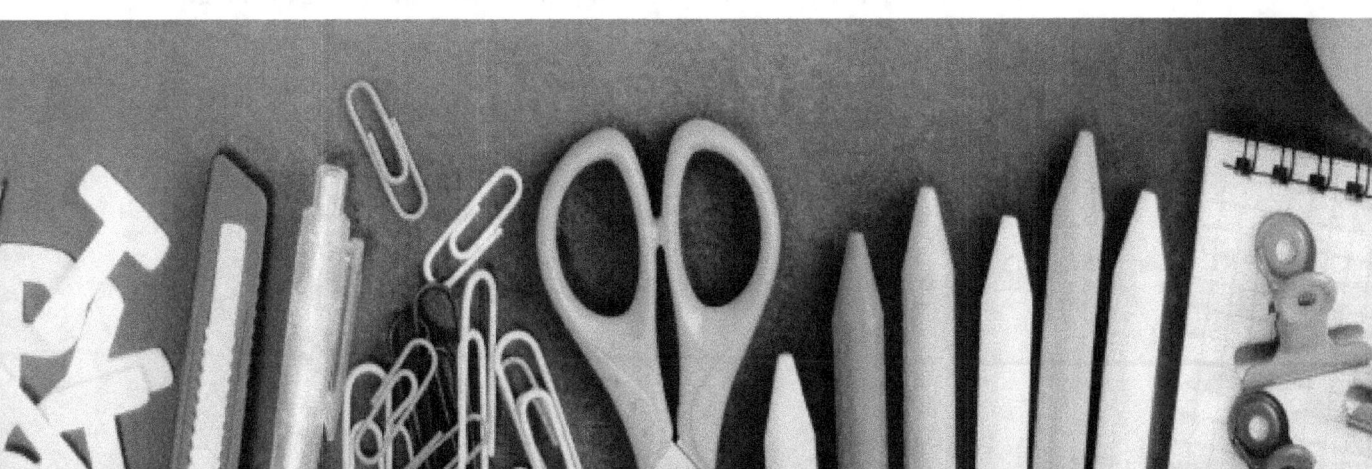

Adult Education Initiatives

Adult education initiatives encompass a wide range of educational programs, courses, and activities designed specifically for adult learners to acquire new knowledge, skills, and competencies or enhance existing ones. These initiatives may include literacy programs, vocational training, language courses, financial literacy workshops, or personal development seminars, among others.

By investing in adult education, mutual aid groups can make a meaningful difference in the lives of adults and contribute to building a more equitable, inclusive, and thriving society. Groups may choose to undertake adult education initiatives for a variety of reasons:

Empowerment & Self-Sufficiency:

By providing adult education opportunities, mutual aid groups empower people to build their capabilities, confidence, and self-sufficiency. Education equips adults with the knowledge and skills they need to navigate life's challenges, pursue opportunities, and achieve their goals.

Community Development:

Adult education initiatives contribute to the overall development and well-being of the community by strengthening members' capacities and fostering a culture of lifelong learning. As adults acquire new knowledge and skills, they become more active and engaged members of the community, contributing to its social, economic, and cultural vitality.

Social Inclusion & Equity:

Adult education initiatives promote social inclusion and equity by ensuring that all members of the community have access to educational opportunities regardless of their background, circumstances, or previous educational experiences. By removing barriers to participation and addressing the diverse learning needs of adults, mutual aid groups promote inclusivity and create opportunities for upward social mobility.

Skill Development & Employment Opportunities:

Many adult education initiatives focus on skill development and vocational training to enhance participants' employability and job prospects. By offering courses and workshops that align with labor market demands and industry needs, mutual aid groups can help adults acquire the skills and credentials they need to access better job opportunities and achieve financial stability.

Personal Growth & Fulfillment:

Adult education initiatives provide opportunities for personal growth, enrichment, and fulfillment, enabling participants to explore new interests, hobbies, and passions outside of their professional or academic pursuits. Lifelong learning contributes to overall well-being and quality of life by fostering intellectual stimulation, creativity, and a sense of purpose.

Skill-Sharing Programs

Skill-sharing refers to the exchange of knowledge, expertise, and abilities between individuals or groups, often in an informal or collaborative setting. It involves people sharing their skills, experiences, and talents with others who are interested in learning or developing similar competencies.

Skill-sharing can take various forms, including workshops, classes, mentorship programs, peer-to-peer learning sessions, and online tutorials. It is a reciprocal process where both the teachers and the learners benefit from the exchanges. Skill-sharing encourages a sense of community, collaboration, and empowerment, enabling participants to learn from one another, build connections, and expand their capabilities in a supportive and inclusive environment.

There are numerous examples of skill-sharing programs that cater to a wide range of interests, needs, and demographics. Some specific examples include:

Language Exchange Clubs:

Language exchange clubs bring together people who are interested in learning and practicing different languages. Participants take turns teaching each other their native languages, providing opportunities for learners to practice speaking, listening, and conversing in a supportive and immersive environment.

DIY Workshops:

DIY workshops offer hands-on learning experiences in various crafts, hobbies, or practical skills—such as woodworking, sewing, gardening, or home repair. Participants learn from skilled instructors or experienced enthusiasts who share their expertise and provide guidance on specific projects or techniques.

Coding Bootcamps:

Coding bootcamps provide intensive training programs in computer programming and software development. Participants learn coding languages, programming concepts, and software engineering skills through project-based learning experiences led by experienced instructors.

Cooking Classes:

Cooking classes offer opportunities for people to learn culinary skills, techniques, and recipes from professional chefs or culinary enthusiasts. Participants explore different cuisines, cooking methods, and ingredients while gaining hands-on experience in preparing and cooking meals.

Financial Literacy Workshops:

Financial literacy workshops educate participants about personal finance, budgeting, investing, and money management. These workshops often cover topics like saving for retirement, managing debt, understanding credit scores, and making informed financial decisions.

Artist Workshops:

Artist workshops provide instruction and guidance in various artistic mediums—such as painting, drawing, pottery, photography, or sculpture. Participants learn artistic techniques, develop their creative expression, and explore different styles under the guidance of skilled instructors.

Fitness & Wellness Classes:

Fitness and wellness classes offer opportunities for people to learn and practice exercise routines, mindfulness techniques, and healthy lifestyle habits. These classes may include yoga, meditation, dance, martial arts, or group fitness sessions led by certified instructors or fitness enthusiasts.

These are just a few examples of skill-sharing programs that exist in communities. Skill-sharing initiatives cater to diverse interests, preferences, and learning styles, providing opportunities for people to acquire new skills, connect with others, and pursue their passions in collaborative and supportive environments.

By equipping individuals with valuable skills and knowledge, a mutual aid group enhances the resilience and self-sufficiency of its community—empowering members to address challenges, pursue opportunities, and thrive in their personal and professional lives.

Leadership Training

The prevalence of bad leadership is unfortunately a widespread issue in many organizations and industries. Poor leadership can manifest in various forms—including micromanagement, lack of communication, favoritism, lack of empathy, and a failure to provide direction or support. These ineffective leadership practices can lead to decreased morale, disengagement among team members, high turnover rates, and ultimately, diminished performance.

When a mutual aid group provides leadership and management training to its members, the impact extends beyond the organization itself to the broader community. Equipping members with the skills and knowledge needed to effectively lead and manage not only enhances the group's internal operations but also empowers people to take on leadership roles in other aspects of their lives. As these trained leaders apply their newfound skills in their workplaces, schools, neighborhoods, and other community settings, they can inspire positive change, foster collaboration, and drive collective action.

Good leaders and managers exhibit a range of practices that contribute to their effectiveness in guiding and empowering their teams. Some key practices include:

Clear Communication:

Effective leaders communicate clearly and transparently with their team members, ensuring that everyone understands goals, expectations, and responsibilities.

Empathy & Emotional Intelligence:

Good leaders demonstrate empathy and emotional intelligence, understanding the perspectives and feelings of others and encouraging a supportive and inclusive team environment.

Delegation:

Effective leaders delegate tasks and responsibilities appropriately, leveraging the strengths and skills of team members while also providing opportunities for growth and development.

Decision-Making:

Strong leaders make informed decisions based on data, input from team members, and consideration of potential outcomes. They are decisive yet open to feedback and adaptability.

Conflict Resolution:

Good leaders are skilled at managing conflicts and resolving disputes within the team, fostering a culture of collaboration, respect, and understanding.

Vision & Strategic Thinking:

Effective leaders have a clear vision for the future and the ability to develop and communicate strategic plans to achieve organizational goals.

Accountability:

Strong leaders hold themselves and their team accountable for their actions and outcomes, encouraging a culture of responsibility and integrity.

Continuous Learning & Development:

Good leaders prioritize their own ongoing learning and development, seeking opportunities to improve their skills and knowledge while also supporting the growth and development of their team members.

Adaptability:

In today's rapidly changing environment, good leaders are adaptable and resilient. They are able to navigate uncertainty and complexity with grace and confidence.

Empowerment & Support:

Effective leaders empower their team members by providing them with the resources, autonomy, and support they need to succeed, while also offering guidance and encouragement along the way.

———————

By embodying these practices, leaders can create environments where team members feel valued, motivated, and empowered to contribute their best work toward achieving shared goals.

Coordinating a Workshop

When organizing a workshop, a mutual aid group can follow these steps to ensure a successful and meaningful event:

1. Identify the Topic:
Determine the specific skill or subject matter that the workshop will focus on based on the interests, needs, and expertise of the community members. Consider conducting surveys to gather input on potential workshop topics.

2. Find a Facilitator:
Identify individuals within the community or external experts who have the knowledge, experience, and willingness to facilitate the workshop. Reach out to potential facilitators and discuss the workshop objectives, format, and logistics to ensure alignment with the group's goals and expectations.

3. Set the Date & Venue:
Determine the date, time, and location for the workshop, taking into account the availability of participants and facilitators, as well as logistical considerations, such as space requirements and accessibility. Secure a venue that can accommodate the workshop format and participants' needs.

4. Plan the Workshop Format:
Decide on the format and structure of the workshop, including the agenda, activities, and duration. Consider whether the workshop will be interactive, hands-on, or lecture-based, and plan accordingly.

5. Promote the Workshop:

Create promotional materials—such as flyers, posters, and social media posts—to advertise the workshop to the community. Utilize the group's communication channels—such as email newsletters, website, and social media accounts—to spread the word and encourage participation. Consider collaborating with local organizations or community partners to reach a broader audience.

6. Gather Supplies & Materials:

Prepare any necessary supplies, materials, or equipment needed for the workshop activities. Ensure that the venue is equipped with the necessary facilities—such as tables, chairs, audiovisual equipment, restrooms, and Wi-Fi access—to support the workshop requirements.

7. Manage Registration:

Set up a registration process to track participant attendance and manage logistics, such as seating arrangements, catering, and materials distribution. Provide clear instructions for registering for the workshop and communicate any deadlines or requirements to participants.

8. Facilitate the Workshop:

On the day of the workshop, welcome participants and introduce the facilitator(s) and agenda. Facilitate the workshop activities, encourage participation and interaction among attendees, and ensure that the workshop stays on schedule. Be prepared to address any questions, concerns, or technical issues that may arise during the event.

9. Collect Feedback:

After the workshop, solicit feedback from participants to evaluate the effectiveness of the event and identify areas for improvement. Use feedback surveys, post-event evaluations, or informal discussions to gather insights on the workshop content, format, facilitation, and overall experience.

10. Follow Up:

Follow up with participants after the workshop to provide additional resources, support, or opportunities for further learning and skill development. Share any materials, handouts, or recordings from the workshop with participants who may have missed the event or want to review the content.

Educational Content Creation

Creating educational content for YouTube and other social media is a powerful way for a mutual aid group to reach and engage with its community members and a wider audience. Content can be easily accessed and shared, making it an effective tool for spreading knowledge and empowering people.

To start, the group can identify relevant topics based on community feedback, emerging issues, or common questions and concerns. These topics can range from practical skills—like budgeting or gardening—to broader subjects, such as mental health awareness or social justice advocacy.

Once the topics are determined, the group can leverage the multimedia capabilities of YouTube and other platforms to create engaging and visually appealing content. This may include short explainer videos, tutorials, interviews with experts or community members, or animated infographics. By presenting information in a dynamic and interactive format, the group can capture the attention of its audience and make complex concepts more accessible and understandable.

Once the content is produced, the group can share it across its social media channels. By optimizing the content for each platform and using relevant hashtags and keywords, the group can increase visibility and reach a wider audience. Encouraging community members to like, share, and comment on the content can further amplify its impact.

Eventually, a mutual aid group may reach the thresholds necessary to qualify for creator programs on social media platforms, allowing them to monetize their content. This additional income stream can help sustain the group's operations, fund community initiatives, and expand its reach and impact.

Youth Programs

Offering youth programs can be a valuable initiative for a mutual aid group, providing numerous benefits for both the organization and the community. Engaging with young people allows the group to invest in the future by empowering the next generation with the skills, knowledge, and resources they need to succeed. By offering educational, recreational, and developmental programs tailored to the needs and interests of young people, the group can support their personal growth, academic success, and social-emotional well-being.

Youth programs enable the mutual aid group to build strong relationships and connections with younger members of the community—creating a sense of belonging, trust, and community pride. By providing a supportive and inclusive environment where young people can learn, explore, and connect with peers and mentors, the group can help combat social isolation, promote positive social interactions, and strengthen community bonds.

Here are some of the types of youth programs that a mutual aid group may choose to offer:

Tutoring & Homework Assistance: Providing academic support to help students succeed in their studies.

Mentorship Programs: Connecting young people with positive role models and mentors to guide them in personal and professional development.

Sports & Recreation Activities: Organizing sports leagues, fitness classes, and recreational activities to promote physical health and teamwork.

Arts & Crafts Workshops: Offering creative outlets through art classes, music lessons, and craft workshops to encourage self-expression and creativity.

Career Exploration & Job Skills Training: Providing career counseling, job shadowing opportunities, and workshops on resume writing, interview skills, and job search strategies.

Life Skills Education: Teaching essential life skills such as financial literacy, cooking, time management, and conflict resolution.

Youth Leadership Programs: Encouraging leadership development through training sessions, volunteer opportunities, and youth-led community projects.

Mental Health Support: Offering counseling services, peer support groups, and workshops on stress management, emotional well-being, and resilience.

Environmental Stewardship: Engaging young people in community gardening, recycling initiatives, and environmental conservation projects to promote sustainability.

Cultural & Diversity Programs: Celebrating cultural diversity through events, discussions, and activities that promote understanding and inclusion.

Technology & Coding Classes: Teaching digital literacy, coding, and other technology skills to prepare young people for the digital world.

Mentorship Programs

Organizing a mentorship program for young people in the community is a meaningful endeavor for a mutual aid group, offering opportunities for guidance, support, and personal development. A mentor serves as a trusted advisor and role model—providing insights, advice, and perspective based on their own experiences and expertise. Mentees can learn from their mentor's wisdom and mistakes—gaining valuable advice to navigate challenges and make informed decisions.

Having a mentor provides mentees with a supportive and encouraging presence in their lives, someone who believes in their potential and champions their success. Mentors offer encouragement, motivation, and constructive feedback—helping mentees build confidence, resilience, and belief in their own abilities. Mentees can also benefit from the mentor's network and connections, gaining access to valuable resources, opportunities, and introductions that can support their personal and professional development.

To initiate a mentorship program, a mutual aid group can begin by defining clear objectives and goals, outlining what it hopes to achieve through the program and how it will benefit both mentors and mentees. Identifying the specific needs and interests of youth participants is crucial in tailoring the program to their preferences and aspirations.

Once the objectives are established, the group can recruit suitable mentors from within the community who possess relevant skills, experiences, and a genuine desire to support young people. Mentors can be volunteers from diverse backgrounds—including professionals, educators, entrepreneurs, or community leaders—who are willing to commit their time and expertise to mentorship activities.

Next, the group can develop a structured framework for the mentorship program, outlining the roles and responsibilities of mentors and mentees, as well as guidelines for communication, goal setting, and accountability. Establishing clear expectations and boundaries helps ensure a productive and mutually beneficial mentorship relationship.

Finally, the group can facilitate matches between mentors and mentees based on shared interests, goals, and compatibility. Regular check-ins, evaluations, and feedback mechanisms can help monitor the progress of mentorship relationships and identify any challenges or areas for improvement.

Scholarship Programs

 Offering scholarships to young people in the community demonstrates a mutual aid group's commitment to investing in the future of its members and promoting educational opportunities. By providing financial assistance and support to young people, the group can empower them to pursue their academic goals, realize their full potential, and contribute positively to their communities and society as a whole. Here are some general steps a mutual aid group can take to establish a scholarship:

1. Define Objectives and Criteria:
Begin by defining clear objectives and criteria for the scholarship program. This includes outlining specific goals and outcomes the group hopes to achieve—such as academic achievement, financial need, community involvement, or leadership potential.

2. Develop Application Process:
Develop a structured application process—establishing guidelines, deadlines, and requirements for submission. Clear instructions and resources are provided to applicants to ensure fairness and transparency.

3. Secure Funding:
Secure funding through various sources—possibly donations, grants, fundraising events, or partnerships with local businesses and organizations. Leveraging community resources maximizes the program's impact.

4. Establish Selection Committee:
Create a selection committee or panel of volunteers to review scholarship applications. Committee members assess candidates based on established criteria and make informed decisions regarding scholarship awards. Diversity and representation on the committee ensure fairness and equity in the selection process.

5. Selecting Recipients:
Notify scholarship recipients of their awards and make arrangements for an award ceremony or recognition event to celebrate their achievements.

6. Providing Ongoing Support:
Offer to provide ongoing support and mentorship to scholarship recipients throughout their academic journey. This includes additional resources, guidance, and mentorship to ensure recipients' success in their educational pursuits.

Chapter Review

Communities are constantly confronted with complex and interconnected issues that require creative solutions. In response to these challenges, mutual aid groups must embrace a culture of continuous learning as a strategic imperative. By encouraging members to exchange their expertise, groups create a dynamic environment where people feel empowered to contribute and grow.

Adult education initiatives can play an important role in addressing gaps left by traditional educational systems. These programs offer opportunities for adults to gain new skills and knowledge that can improve their economic prospects and overall well-being. Classes might include literacy and numeracy, vocational training, financial planning, or health education. By tailoring these initiatives to the specific needs and interests of the community, mutual aid groups can ensure that adults have access to relevant and practical education that empowers them to take control of their lives.

Youth programs aim to provide young people with the skills, knowledge, and support they need to thrive. Activities might include tutoring, mentorship, extracurricular activities, and workshops on topics such as technology, arts, and leadership. By investing in the education and development of young people, mutual aid groups help to build a foundation for a stronger future community. These programs not only enhance the educational outcomes for young people but also create a sense of belonging and responsibility, encouraging them to become active, engaged members of society.

Discussion Questions

1. Reflecting on your own experiences, can you recall any successful adult education initiatives you have been a part of or observed that could inspire similar efforts in a mutual aid group?

2. Consider both adults and young people in your community. What types of educational programs are most needed and why?

IN THIS CHAPTER

» Discussing the dynamic nature
of crises in the 21st century

» Forming an emergency plan,
including how to coordinate
with first responders

» Useful trainings and simulations,
including first aid, de-escalation
& self-defense

Chapter **10**

Emergency Preparedness & Response

Crises have become increasingly prevalent in the 21st century. From natural disasters to acts of domestic terrorism, we are continuously confronted with threats to our well-being and survival. This heightened frequency underscores the need for communities to be ready and resilient, making emergency preparedness an important aspect of mutual aid activism.

In this chapter, we'll explore how your mutual aid group can create comprehensive emergency plans to ensure you're ready to respond effectively when the need arises.

The Dynamic Nature of Crises

The 21st century has seen an unprecedented proliferation of crises across the globe, ranging from natural disasters and public health emergencies to economic downturns and social upheavals. These crises—often interconnected and overlapping—have posed significant challenges for individuals, communities, and nations. The term **polycrisis** refers to a situation where multiple crises or emergencies occur simultaneously or in rapid succession, often compounding one another and creating complex obstacles for societies to overcome.

Crises are dynamic in several key ways, which can challenge those tasked with managing the response and heightening the need for adaptive strategies:

Unpredictability:

Crises often arise without warning and can develop in unexpected ways. The initial cause may be clear—such as a natural disaster like an earthquake or a human-made event like a financial collapse—but the cascade of effects that follow can be difficult to predict and manage.

Variability in Scale & Scope:

The impact of a crisis can vary greatly, affecting small communities or entire regions. A crisis can also escalate quickly, expanding from a local issue to a national or even global concern. The scope can broaden, moving from affecting a single sector (like healthcare during a pandemic) to impacting multiple facets of life, including the economy and governance.

Evolution Over Time:

What starts as an acute emergency can turn into a long-term or chronic situation. For instance, a hurricane can lead to immediate needs for rescue and relief, followed by long-term rebuilding and recovery efforts. This evolution requires responses to adapt over time, shifting resources and strategies to meet changing needs.

Complex Interactions with Existing Conditions:

Crises often interact with and are compounded by existing social, economic, and environmental conditions. For example, a drought might exacerbate existing water scarcity issues, or an economic downturn might hit harder in areas already experiencing high unemployment. These interactions can deepen a crisis and create new challenges to address.

Feedback Loops:

The actions taken to manage a crisis can themselves change the situation, sometimes in unintended ways. Relief efforts might alleviate immediate suffering but could also lead to dependency or disrupt local economies. Understanding and managing these feedback loops is crucial to effective crisis response.

In times of extraordinary emergency, the sheer scale and complexity of the situation can overwhelm government agencies and institutions, leading to delays or gaps in the response. In such circumstances, mutual aid groups can play a vital role in filling these gaps and providing much-needed assistance to affected communities. With their grassroots networks, community connections, and nimble organizational structures, mutual aid groups are often able to mobilize quickly and respond to emerging needs on the ground.

Whether it's distributing essential supplies, providing shelter and support to displaced individuals, or coordinating volunteers for relief efforts, mutual aid groups can step in where traditional government responses fall short, offering immediate and localized assistance to those most in need. With thorough preparation, groups can enhance their readiness to face crises, serving their communities more effectively when emergencies occur. A proactive approach not only strengthens the group's capacity to assist but also deepens the trust and reliance the community places in these groups. Here are three strategies groups can employ to get ready:

Preparation & Planning:

Effective preparation is essential for mutual aid groups to respond efficiently when a crisis strikes. This involves creating flexible response plans that can be adapted to different types of emergencies, whether they are natural disasters, economic hardships, or public health crises. Such plans should include identifying key resources—such as food, medical supplies, and emergency shelter locations—and establishing clear communication channels both within the group and with external partners like local authorities and other nonprofit organizations. Training volunteers in emergency response, first aid, and crisis management is also crucial so that they are ready to act effectively under stressful conditions.

Building Networks:

Beyond internal preparations, mutual aid groups should build strong networks with other community stakeholders. These relationships are invaluable during a crisis, allowing for the rapid mobilization of resources and coordinated efforts across different organizations. By making these connections before a crisis occurs, mutual aid groups can ensure a more unified and effective response when the community is in need.

Adaptability & Learning:

Crises are dynamic, so responses must be equally adaptable. Mutual aid groups should continuously learn from each crisis situation to improve their preparedness and response strategies. This involves debriefing after events to identify what worked well and what did not, and then updating plans accordingly. Emphasizing a culture of learning and adaptability within the group ensures that the organization can evolve and maintain its relevance and effectiveness in changing circumstances.

Environmental Disasters

Mutual aid groups may find themselves responding to a variety of environmental disasters, each presenting unique challenges and requiring tailored response strategies. These events can cause widespread destruction to homes, infrastructure, and natural habitats, displacing communities and disrupting essential services like water, electricity, and transportation. Here are four common environmental disasters:

Extreme Weather

Mutual aid groups may be called upon to respond to the impacts of extreme weather like tornados, storms, and hurricanes. This may involve providing emergency shelter, distributing supplies like food and water, and assisting with evacuation and rescue efforts.

Earthquakes

In regions prone to seismic activity, mutual aid groups may be tasked with responding to the aftermath of earthquakes, which can cause extensive damage to buildings and infrastructure, as well as trigger secondary hazards like landslides and tsunamis. Groups may help in search and rescue operations, medical assistance, and humanitarian aid distribution.

Wildfires

Mutual aid groups may need to respond to wildfires, particularly in areas with a high risk due to drought, high temperatures, and vegetation density. Groups may assist with evacuation efforts, provide support to displaced individuals, and offer assistance to firefighters and emergency responders.

Human Accidents

Mutual aid groups may need respond to environmental disasters caused by human activities, such as industrial accidents, oil spills, and toxic chemical releases. These incidents can have devastating consequences for communities and ecosystems, requiring specialized expertise and resources to mitigate their impacts and facilitate recovery.

Economic Downturns

The cyclical nature of capitalism generates periodic downturns characterized by fluctuations in economic activity, employment, and consumer spending. What are often referred to as "boom and bust cycles" are the result of various factors—such as changes in consumer confidence or investment, shifts in government policy, and economic trends.

During boom periods, economic growth and prosperity prevail, leading to increased consumption, investment, and employment. However, this growth eventually leads to overproduction, speculation, and inflation—culminating in a peak followed by a downturn. Recessions or depressions ensue, marked by declining output, rising unemployment, and reduced consumer spending.

Mutual aid groups can play an important role in these challenging times by providing vital support to individuals and communities adversely affected by economic downturns, offering assistance such as food, job training, and financial counseling to help mitigate the impacts of these cycles on vulnerable populations.

Here are some types of economic downturns that mutual aid groups may encounter:

Recessions:

Recessions are periods of economic decline characterized by reduced consumer spending, declining business investment, and rising unemployment rates. Mutual aid groups may respond to recessions by providing assistance to individuals and families who have lost jobs or are struggling to make ends meet. This may include food assistance, rental assistance, utility bill support, and access to affordable healthcare services.

Financial Crises:

Financial crises occur when there is a sudden and severe disruption in financial markets, leading to instability in banking systems, stock markets, and currency values. Mutual aid groups may respond to financial crises by providing financial education and counseling to individuals and families facing foreclosure, bankruptcy, or other financial hardships. They may also offer support to small businesses and entrepreneurs struggling to access credit or stay afloat during turbulent economic times.

Unemployment Spikes:

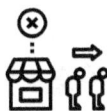

Unemployment spikes occur when there is a rapid increase in the number of people who are unemployed, often due to factors like technological advancements, industry shifts, or external shocks like pandemics. Mutual aid groups may respond to unemployment spikes by offering job training programs, career counseling services, and networking opportunities to help individuals reenter the workforce or transition to new industries.

Market Disruptions:

Market disruptions can occur when there are sudden changes in supply and demand dynamics, leading to price volatility, shortages, or surpluses of goods and services. Mutual aid groups may respond to market disruptions by organizing community food cooperatives, bulk purchasing programs, or barter networks to help people access essential goods and services during times of scarcity or uncertainty.

Public Health Emergencies

The 21st century has seen a significant increase in the prevalence of public health emergencies, as evidenced by outbreaks of SARS, influenza, Ebola, and COVID-19. Urbanization has led to densely populated areas where infectious diseases can spread quickly, while climate change has contributed to the emergence of new pathogens and the resurgence of old ones–as well as exacerbating health disparities and environmental health risks. Antimicrobial resistance also poses a growing threat to global health security, further complicating efforts to control infectious diseases.

Mutual aid groups play a crucial role in responding to public health emergencies by providing support to affected communities, disseminating accurate information, promoting preventive measures, and assisting with vaccination campaigns, testing, and contact tracing efforts. Here are some types of public health emergencies that mutual aid groups may encounter:

Infectious Disease Outbreaks:

Infectious disease outbreaks—such as pandemics or epidemics—occur when a contagious disease spreads rapidly within a community, region, or country. Mutual aid groups may respond to infectious disease outbreaks by providing support to affected individuals and communities, promoting public health measures such as vaccination campaigns and hygiene practices, and disseminating accurate information to combat misinformation and stigma.

Natural Disasters with Health Impacts:

Natural disasters like hurricanes, earthquakes, floods, and wildfires can have significant health consequences—including injuries, waterborne diseases, and mental health issues. Mutual aid groups may respond to natural disasters by providing medical assistance, distributing hygiene kits and personal protective equipment, and offering mental health support and counseling services to affected individuals and communities.

Environmental Hazards:

Environmental hazards—such as air pollution, water contamination, and chemical spills—can pose serious risks to public health. Mutual aid groups may respond by advocating for environmental justice and pollution control measures, conducting community health assessments, and providing support to people affected by environmental disasters or pollution-related health issues.

Bioterrorism Events:

Bioterrorism events involve the intentional release of biological agents—such as bacteria, viruses, or toxins—to cause harm to individuals or populations. Mutual aid groups may respond to bioterrorism events by assisting with emergency response efforts, providing medical treatment and decontamination services, and collaborating with public health authorities and law enforcement agencies to mitigate the impact of the attack.

By working together with government agencies, healthcare providers, and other community organizations, mutual aid groups help ensure a coordinated and effective response to public health crises.

Political Clashes

The 21st century has been marked by significant political instability across the globe–characterized by polarization, social unrest, and geopolitical tensions. In many regions, political divisions have deepened, leading to gridlock within governments. Economic inequality, social injustice, and dissatisfaction with established systems have fueled mass protests and demonstrations demanding reform.

Geopolitical tensions have been exacerbated by competition for resources, territorial disputes, and ideological conflicts. Rising nationalism, populism, and authoritarianism have further strained international relations–leading to diplomatic standoffs, trade disputes, and military conflicts. In this volatile environment, mutual aid groups play an important role in supporting communities affected by political instability, offering solidarity, resources, and assistance to vulnerable populations, and advocating for social justice and human rights.

Political clashes can manifest in a variety of ways, including violence, discrimination, displacement, and oppression. Here are some types of political clashes that mutual aid groups may have to respond to:

Armed Conflicts:

Armed conflicts–including wars, civil wars, and insurgencies–can result in widespread violence, destruction, and displacement. Mutual aid groups may respond to armed conflicts by providing humanitarian assistance to affected populations–including food, shelter, medical care, and psychosocial support. They may also advocate for peacebuilding efforts and promote dialogue and reconciliation between conflicting parties.

Political Repression:

Political repression involves the suppression of dissent, freedom of speech, and civil liberties by authoritarian regimes or oppressive governments. Mutual aid groups may respond to political repression by providing support to political prisoners and their families, documenting human rights abuses, and advocating for political reform and democratic governance.

Dissemination of Propaganda:

Propaganda is a powerful tool often employed in political clashes to manipulate public perception and sway opinions. By leveraging media channels, social networks, and public figures, those in power can control the flow of information, making it difficult for the public to discern truth from fabrication. Mutual aid groups may respond by disseminating accurate information and promoting media literacy.

Refugee & Migration Crises:

Refugee and migration crises occur when large numbers of people are forced to flee their homes due to persecution, conflict, or environmental disasters. Mutual aid groups may respond to refugee and migration crises by providing support to displaced individuals and families, including shelter, food, medical care, and legal assistance. They may also advocate for refugee rights and support policies that promote refugee integration and protection.

Domestic Terrorism

The 21st century has witnessed a concerning rise in domestic terrorism, characterized by acts of violence perpetrated by individuals or groups within their own countries with the intent to instill fear, cause harm, or advance ideological agendas. Motivations for domestic terrorism vary widely and can include extreme beliefs, racial or religious hatred, anti-government sentiments, or grievances against specific social groups. The proliferation of extremist groups—fueled by online radicalization and echo chambers—has contributed to the spread of domestic terrorism worldwide.

Advancements in technology have also made it easier for individuals to access information, disseminate propaganda, and coordinate attacks, amplifying the threat posed by lone actors and small cells. Mutual aid groups play a critical role in addressing the impacts of domestic terrorism by providing support to victims and communities affected by these attacks, promoting unity and resilience, and advocating for policies that address the root causes of extremism and violence.

Here are some types of domestic terrorism that mutual aid groups may encounter:

Mass Shootings:

Mass shootings involve the use of firearms to target innocent civilians in public spaces such as schools, workplaces, or community events. Mutual aid groups may respond to these incidents by providing immediate assistance to victims and their families, supporting mental health services for survivors, and advocating for gun violence prevention measures and community safety initiatives.

Hate Crimes & Extremist Violence:

Hate crimes and extremist violence target individuals or groups based on their race, religion, ethnicity, sexual orientation, or other characteristics. These acts can include assaults, vandalism, arson, and other forms of violence intended to intimidate or terrorize specific communities. Mutual aid groups may respond to hate crimes by providing support to affected communities, promoting intergroup dialogue and understanding, and advocating for policies that address the root causes of extremism and discrimination.

Cyberattacks:

Cyberattacks involve the use of computer networks and digital technology to disrupt or damage critical infrastructure, communication systems, or government operations. As a result, essential utilities and services may become inaccessible to individuals and communities. Mutual aid groups may respond to the impacts of cyberattcks by setting up support hubs to provide food, water, or medical care to those affected by the disruption.

In the face of domestic terrorism, mutual aid groups can serve as a vital source of comfort and resilience for affected communities. By offering immediate support such as food, shelter, and emotional counseling, these groups help to alleviate the immediate distress and fear that follows such traumatic events. They create safe spaces where individuals can share their experiences and find solace in solidarity, creating a sense of connection and mutual understanding.

Emergency Planning

An **emergency plan** is a structured document that outlines specific procedures and protocols to follow in the event of a crisis. It serves as a roadmap for how individuals, organizations, or communities should respond to various types of emergencies, including natural disasters, public health incidents, accidents, and other unforeseen events.

Emergency plans typically include information on roles and responsibilities, communication protocols, evacuation procedures, resource allocation, and coordination with external agencies and stakeholders. The goal of an emergency plan is to ensure a coordinated, efficient, and effective response, with the primary objective of protecting lives, minimizing damage, and facilitating recovery.

As an example, here is an outline of a mutual aid group's emergency plan for a hurricane:

Risk Assessment:
Identify the potential risks and vulnerabilities associated with hurricanes, including flooding, high winds, power outages, and road closures. Assess the group's readiness to respond to these risks and prioritize actions to mitigate their impact.

Communication Plan:
Establish clear communication protocols for disseminating emergency alerts, updates, and instructions to members, volunteers, and the community. Designate communication channels–such as email, text messaging, social media, and phone trees–and ensure that contact information for key personnel is up-to-date.

Evacuation Procedures:
Develop evacuation procedures for members and volunteers in the event of mandatory evacuations or unsafe conditions. Identify evacuation routes, assembly points, and transportation options, and provide guidance on what to bring and how to secure property before leaving.

Shelter & Safety:
Identify shelter locations within the community and in neighboring areas where members and volunteers can seek refuge during the storm. Ensure that shelters are equipped with supplies–such as food, water, first aid kits, and bedding–and establish protocols for managing occupancy and safety.

Resource Mobilization:
Develop plans for mobilizing resources and support from within the group and from external partners, such as local government agencies, non-profit organizations, and businesses. Coordinate the acquisition and distribution of emergency supplies, equipment, and personnel, and establish mechanisms for tracking inventory and resource allocation.

Post-Disaster Recovery:
Develop plans for assessing damage, conducting needs assessments, and coordinating recovery efforts in the aftermath of the hurricane. Identify priorities for rebuilding and recovery, including addressing immediate needs, restoring infrastructure, and providing long-term support to affected individuals and communities.

By having an emergency plan in place, mutual aid groups can ensure that they are prepared to respond effectively to crises, protect the safety and well-being of their community, and contribute to the overall resilience and recovery of the affected area.

Coordinating with Local Emergency Services

When responding to an emergency, mutual aid groups should coordinate with local emergency services in order to maximize their impact and ensure a cohesive response. By collaborating closely with firefighters, police officers, paramedics, and other first responders, mutual aid groups can gain valuable insights into the nature and scope of the emergency, as well as access to critical information and resources. This collaboration enables groups to align their efforts with the overall response strategy, avoid duplication of services, and fill gaps in assistance where needed.

Mutual aid groups can also provide valuable support to local emergency services by augmenting their capacity during times of high demand or resource shortages. For example, groups can assist with tasks such as traffic control, crowd management, search and rescue operations, and distribution of relief supplies. By leveraging the skills, knowledge, and resources of both volunteers and professional responders, mutual aid groups can help alleviate the strain on emergency services and ensure a more robust and resilient response to crises.

In addition to providing immediate assistance during the initial response phase, mutual aid groups can also play a crucial role in long-term recovery and rebuilding efforts. By working with local government agencies, non-profit organizations, and businesses, groups can help coordinate recovery efforts, provide support to individuals and families affected by the emergency, and facilitate the restoration of essential services and infrastructure. This collaborative approach fosters community resilience and ensures that the impacts of the emergency are addressed comprehensively.

Here are some ways that mutual aid groups can take to facilitate coordination with local emergency services:

Establish Relationships:

Build relationships with key stakeholders in local emergency services, including fire departments, police departments, emergency medical services (EMS), and government agencies responsible for emergency management. Attend meetings, introduce yourself and your organization, and express your willingness to collaborate.

Understand Roles & Responsibilities:

Familiarize yourself with the roles and responsibilities of local emergency services during different types of emergencies. Understand their protocols, chains of command, and standard operating procedures to ensure that your efforts align with their overall response strategy.

Share Information:

Maintain open lines of communication with local emergency services, sharing relevant information about your organization, capabilities, and resources. Provide contact information for key personnel and establish communication protocols for sharing updates, requests for assistance, and situational awareness during emergencies.

Collaborate on Planning & Training:

Collaborate with local emergency services on emergency planning and training exercises. Participate in joint drills and simulations to practice coordination, communication, and response protocols. This will help build trust, familiarity, and confidence in working together during real emergencies.

Identify Points of Contact:

Establish designated points of contact within your mutual aid group and with local emergency services for coordination purposes. Designate liaisons who will serve as the primary communication link between the two organizations and ensure timely exchange of information and coordination of efforts.

Respect Chain of Command:

Recognize and respect the chain of command within local emergency services. Follow their lead during emergencies and defer to their expertise and authority in decision-making processes. Clear communication and mutual respect are key to effective coordination.

Offer Support & Assistance:

Be proactive in offering support and assistance to local emergency services during emergencies. Clearly communicate the capabilities and resources your mutual aid group can provide—such as volunteers, supplies, equipment, or specialized skills. Be prepared to respond promptly to requests for assistance.

Establish Memorandums of Understanding (MOUs):

Consider formalizing your partnership with local emergency services through memorandums of understanding (MOUs). These agreements outline the roles, responsibilities, and expectations of both parties during emergencies, providing a framework for collaboration and coordination.

―――――――――――

By taking these steps to coordinate with local emergency services, mutual aid groups can enhance their effectiveness, strengthen their partnerships, and ensure a more coordinated and integrated response to crises.

Communication Protocols

Establishing communication protocols is an essential step for mutual aid groups to prepare for emergency situations effectively. Clear and reliable communication ensures that information is disseminated promptly, coordination is streamlined, and resources are deployed efficiently during times of crisis.

In particularly acute emergencies or critical situations, it may be advantageous for a mutual aid group to establish a **communications hub**, which is a centralized location or system for coordinating communication activities. It is a designated space—either physical or virtual—where information is received, processed, and disseminated among stakeholders, response teams, and the community.

A communications hub should be equipped with the necessary infrastructure, technology, and personnel to support emergency response activities—such as telecommunication devices, computers, radios, internet access, and trained staff. Its primary function is to ensure the efficient and effective exchange of information, coordination of response efforts, and dissemination of critical updates and instructions.

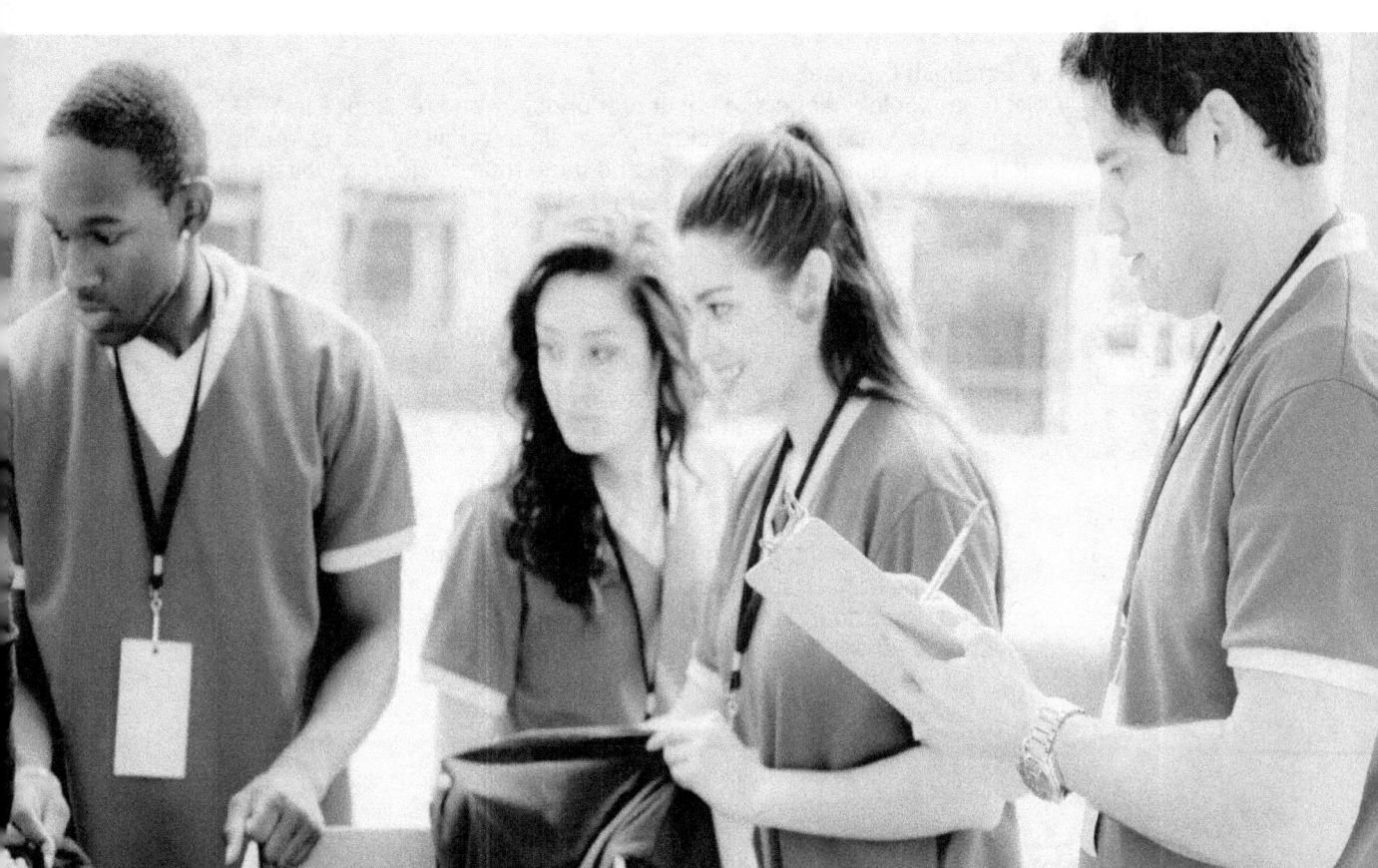

Here's how a mutual aid group can establish a communications hub:

1. Identify a Central Location:
Choose a central location that serves as the hub for communication activities during emergencies. This could be a physical space such as a community center, office, or designated command post, or it could be a virtual space such as an online platform or communication app.

2. Equip the Hub:
Equip the hub with the necessary infrastructure and equipment to support communication activities. This may include telecommunication devices such as phones, computers, radios, and internet access, as well as office supplies, whiteboards, maps, and other resources to facilitate coordination and sharing information.

3. Designate Roles:
Assign specific communication roles and responsibilities to volunteers who will staff the hub. This may include roles such as coordinator, radio operator, social media manager, and information officer, each responsible for different aspects of communication and information dissemination.

4. Establish Channels:
Set up multiple channels to ensure redundancy and resilience in communication. This may include phone lines, email accounts, group chat platforms, social media channels, and radio frequencies, as well as backup systems in case primary channels fail.

5. Develop Protocols:
Develop clear protocols and procedures for how information will be relayed, received, and disseminated within the hub. Establish guidelines for incident reporting, message prioritization, escalation procedures, and sharing information with external stakeholders.

6. Train & Prepare Staff:
Provide training and orientation sessions for staff members who will be operating the hub. Ensure that they are familiar with equipment and protocols, understand their roles and responsibilities, and are prepared to respond effectively as the emergency unfolds.

7. Maintain Continual Operations:
Ensure that the hub operates continuously throughout the duration of the emergency, with staff members rotating shifts as needed to maintain coverage and support response efforts around the clock.

Resource Inventory

Conducting a **resource inventory** is a vital step for mutual aid groups to ensure they can effectively respond to community needs, particularly during emergencies. A thorough resource inventory helps groups understand what they have, what they need, and how quickly they can mobilize assets when required.

By ensuring they have these essential resources on hand, mutual aid groups can enhance their capacity to provide timely and effective support to their communities in times of crisis. Here are some specific resources that are essential for groups to have on hand:

Food & Water Supplies:

Stockpiling non-perishable food items (such as canned goods, grains, and dried fruits) and potable water ensures that the group can provide immediate assistance to individuals and families affected by emergencies, especially in situations where access to food and water is disrupted.

Medical & First Aid Kits:

Equipping the group with medical supplies and first aid kits allows volunteers to administer basic medical care and address minor injuries or illnesses during emergencies. This includes bandages, disinfectants, over-the-counter medications, and essential medical equipment.

Emergency Shelter Equipment:

Having supplies to set up temporary shelters is necessary for providing safe refuge to displaced individuals during emergencies. This may include tents, tarps, sleeping bags, blankets, and portable heaters for warmth in cold weather.

Communication Devices:

Reliable communication devices enable mutual aid groups to coordinate their response efforts and stay connected with volunteers and community members. This includes mobile phones, two-way radios, satellite phones, and portable chargers.

Transportation Vehicles:

Access to transportation vehicles (such as vans or trucks) allows the group to transport supplies, equipment, and volunteers to affected areas quickly and efficiently, facilitating the delivery of aid and support.

Personal Protective Equipment (PPE):

Providing volunteers with PPE—including masks, gloves, goggles, and protective clothing—helps ensure their safety and reduces the risk of exposure to hazards during emergency response activities, such as natural disasters or disease outbreaks.

Power Generation Equipment:

Portable generators and solar-powered chargers can provide emergency power supply, enabling the group to operate essential equipment, maintain communication channels, and provide lighting in areas without electricity.

Community Maps & Information:

Access to detailed maps and information about local infrastructure, key facilities, vulnerable populations, and evacuation routes enhances the group's ability to plan and execute effective emergency response strategies.

Financial Resources:

Maintaining financial reserves or establishing emergency funds allows mutual aid groups to procure additional resources, cover operational expenses, and respond promptly to emerging needs during crises.

Training & Educational Materials:

Providing training materials, manuals, and educational resources on emergency preparedness and response equips volunteers with the knowledge and skills needed to effectively assist their communities during emergencies.

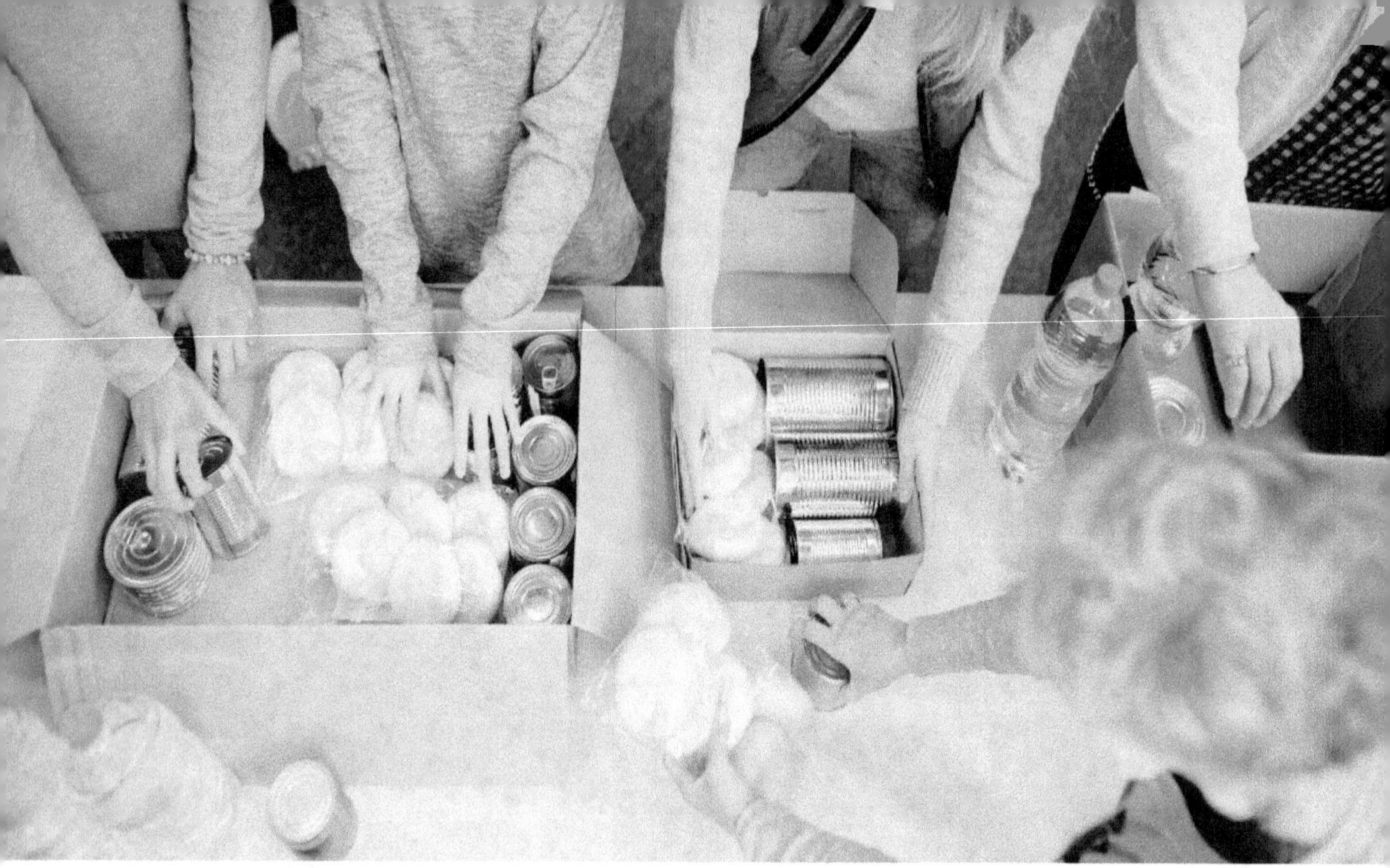

Resource Distribution

 Preparing for resource distribution in an emergency situation is an important part of the planning process for mutual aid groups. By establishing clear protocols and procedures in advance, groups can ensure the efficient and equitable distribution of resources to people in need during times of crisis.

Mutual aid groups should develop a system for prioritizing distribution based on the severity of need and the available resources. This may involve categorizing individuals or households according to factors such as vulnerability, proximity to the emergency, and specific needs (e.g., medical conditions, disabilities, or lack of access to basic necessities).

Once priorities have been established, the group should devise a plan for how resources will be distributed efficiently and fairly. This may involve setting up distribution centers in strategic locations, coordinating with local authorities and community organizations, and implementing protocols for verifying eligibility and tracking.

Communication is key during the resource distribution process. Mutual aid groups should establish clear channels of communication with affected individuals, as well as with partner organizations, volunteers, and local emergency services. Providing timely updates, instructions, and information about available resources helps to alleviate uncertainty and ensure transparency in the distribution process. Groups should also be prepared to adapt their distribution plans in real-time based on changing circumstances and emerging needs.

Finally, mutual aid groups should document their resource distribution efforts for accountability and evaluation purposes. Keeping records of the where resources go, the individuals served, and any challenges or lessons learned during the process helps to improve future response efforts and build trust with the community. By carefully planning and preparing for resource distribution in advance, groups can maximize their effectiveness in responding to emergencies and providing critical support to those in need.

DISTRIBUTING FOOD

When distributing food in an emergency situation, mutual aid groups must consider several factors to ensure the safe and equitable allocation of resources.

Nutrition: Assess the nutritional needs of the affected population, taking into account dietary preferences, cultural considerations, and any specific dietary restrictions or medical conditions.

Perishability: Prioritize the distribution of perishable items to minimize waste and foods with a long shelf life that require minimal preparation.

Accessibility: Ensure that distribution points are easily accessible to all community members, including those with mobility issues or disabilities.

Communication: Establish clear channels to inform the community about the availability of food distribution points, operating hours, and any eligibility criteria.

Safety: Implement measures to maintain safety and hygiene standards during food distribution, including proper handling and storage practices, sanitation protocols, and adherence to public health guidelines to prevent the spread of foodborne illnesses or contamination.

Shelters & Transitional Housing

People can become displaced in emergency situations due to various factors that disrupt their ability to remain in their homes or communities safely. Natural disasters such as hurricanes, floods, wildfires, earthquakes, and severe storms can force people to evacuate their homes to escape imminent danger posed by environmental hazards. Human-made disasters like industrial accidents, chemical spills, terrorist attacks, armed conflict, or civil unrest can also result in displacement as people flee areas affected by violence, insecurity, or hazardous conditions.

Other factors contributing to displacement in emergencies include structural damage to homes, loss of utilities such as water and electricity, contamination of water supplies, and infrastructure failures that render communities uninhabitable or unsafe. As a result, people may find themselves without shelter, basic necessities, or access to essential services, requiring immediate assistance from mutual aid groups and emergency responders.

Mutual aid groups may offer various types of shelters and transitional housing to meet the diverse needs of individuals and families during emergencies. Some common types include:

Disaster Relief Housing:

In the aftermath of natural disasters or large-scale emergencies, mutual aid groups may establish disaster relief housing solutions such as temporary shelters, tent cities, mobile housing units, or emergency housing vouchers to provide accommodation and support to affected individuals.

Overnight Shelters:

Overnight shelters provide temporary lodging for individuals experiencing homelessness or housing insecurity, particularly during cold weather months or extreme weather conditions. These shelters may offer sleeping accommodations, meals, hygiene facilities, and support services to help people access resources and transition to more stable housing solutions.

Transitional Housing Programs:

Transitional housing programs offer longer-term housing solutions for people who are homeless or at risk of homelessness. These programs provide safe and stable housing with supportive services, case management, and life skills training to help participants address underlying issues, stabilize their lives, and transition to permanent housing.

Family Shelters:

Family shelters specifically cater to families with children who are experiencing homelessness or housing instability. These shelters may offer family-friendly accommodations, childcare services, educational resources, and parenting support to help families overcome barriers to housing stability and achieve self-sufficiency.

Women's Shelters:

Women's shelters provide safe and supportive housing for women and children fleeing domestic violence, intimate partner abuse, or other forms of gender-based violence. These shelters offer confidential accommodations, counseling services, legal advocacy, and referrals to community resources to help survivors rebuild their lives free from violence.

Youth Shelters:

Youth shelters offer temporary housing and support services for unaccompanied youth and young adults who are experiencing homelessness or housing instability. These shelters may provide age-appropriate accommodations, counseling, educational support, and resources to help young people transition to independence and secure housing.

It is important to provide privacy and security to those who have become displaced, in addition to emotional and psychological support. Losing a home is a traumatic and stressful experience, so counseling services can help people cope during their transition. By addressing these considerations, mutual aid groups can offer safe and compassionate support to those in need.

Providing shelter and transitional housing in an emergency situation requires careful planning, coordination, and resource mobilization. Here are some steps mutual aid groups can take to make preparations:

1. Assess Community Needs:
Conduct a thorough assessment of the community's needs for shelter and transitional housing during emergencies. Identify vulnerable populations–such as individuals who are already experiencing homelessness, families with children, elderly residents, and people with disabilities–who may require specialized support and accommodations.

2. Identify Potential Shelter Sites:
Identify potential shelter sites within the community that can be used to provide temporary housing during emergencies. This may include community centers, schools, churches, recreational facilities, or other public buildings that can accommodate large numbers of people and provide basic amenities such as sleeping quarters, restroom facilities, and clean water.

3. Establish Partnerships:
Establish partnerships with local government agencies, non-profit organizations, faith-based groups, and other community stakeholders to leverage resources, expertise, and support for shelter and housing initiatives. Collaborate with emergency management agencies to integrate shelter planning into broader emergency response and recovery efforts.

4. Secure Resources:
Secure the necessary resources and supplies to support shelter operations, including cots, blankets, sleeping mats, hygiene kits, food, water, medical supplies, and personal protective equipment. Identify sources for funding, donations, and volunteers to support shelter operations and ensure sustainability.

5. Develop Protocols & Procedures:
Develop protocols and procedures for operating shelters and transitional housing facilities during emergencies. Establish guidelines for registration, intake procedures, security protocols, health and safety measures, privacy and confidentiality policies, and referrals to support services.

6. Train Staff & Volunteers:
Provide training and orientation for staff and volunteers who will be involved in shelter operations. Ensure they are familiar with protocols, emergency procedures, conflict resolution techniques, trauma-informed care practices, and cultural competency considerations.

7. Communicate with the Community:
Communicate with the community about the availability of shelter and transitional housing resources during emergencies. Develop public awareness campaigns, distribute informational materials, and use social media and other channels to inform residents about shelter locations, eligibility criteria, operating hours, and available services.

8. Plan for Long-Term Housing Solutions:
Develop strategies for transitioning individuals and families from emergency shelters to more permanent housing solutions. Collaborate with housing agencies, social service providers, and community organizations to connect shelter residents with assistance programs, rental assistance, and supportive services to facilitate their transition.

By taking these steps to make preparations for shelter and transitional housing, mutual aid groups can enhance their capacity to respond effectively to emergencies and provide essential support to people in need.

Evacuation Plans

An **evacuation plan** becomes necessary in circumstances where individuals or communities are faced with imminent threats or hazards that require them to leave their homes or other locations to seek safety. These circumstances may include natural disasters—such as hurricanes, floods, wildfires, earthquakes, tsunamis, or severe storms—where the potential for widespread damage or loss of life poses a significant risk. In such cases, local authorities or emergency management agencies may issue evacuation orders to protect the safety and well-being of residents and facilitate orderly relocation to designated safe zones or shelters.

Similarly, human-made disasters such as industrial accidents, chemical spills, hazardous material releases, or environmental contamination incidents may also necessitate evacuations to protect residents from exposure to toxic substances, pollutants, or other hazardous conditions that pose immediate health risks. Other scenarios that might necessitate an evacuation include building fires, gas leaks, explosions, terrorist attacks, civil unrest, or armed conflicts.

Evacuation plans should be tailored to the needs of vulnerable populations—such as individuals with mobility issues, disabilities, or chronic medical conditions—who may require additional assistance and accommodations. Special considerations must be made to ensure that evacuation routes, transportation options, and shelter facilities are accessible and inclusive to meet the needs of all residents.

Local authorities may issue evacuation orders during emergencies but may not have the capacity to fully assist all members of the community. In such cases, a mutual aid group could provide crucial assistance by offering transportation, shelter, supplies, and support. Here are the steps a group could take to prepare an evacuation plan:

1. Assess Risks & Hazards:
Conduct a comprehensive assessment of potential risks and hazards in the community that could necessitate evacuations, such as natural disasters, industrial accidents, or other emergencies. Identify vulnerable populations, high-risk areas, evacuation routes, and designated safe zones or shelters.

2. Establish Evacuation Zones:
Divide the community into evacuation zones based on geographic location, proximity to hazards, and population density. Determine evacuation zones, assembly points, and primary and secondary evacuation routes for residents to follow in the event of an emergency.

3. Identify Evacuation Resources:
Identify resources and assets available for evacuations, including transportation vehicles, emergency supplies, communication equipment, and trained personnel. Establish partnerships with local agencies, organizations, and volunteers to support evacuation efforts and provide assistance as needed.

4. Develop Communication Protocols:
Establish protocols and procedures for disseminating evacuation orders, alerts, and instructions to residents and stakeholders. Utilize multiple channels—such as emergency alert systems, public announcements, social media, and community networks—to reach residents and provide timely updates during emergencies.

5. Create Evacuation Plans for Vulnerable Populations:
Develop specialized evacuation plans for vulnerable populations, including individuals with disabilities, elderly residents, families with children, and non-English speakers. Provide assistance and accommodations as needed to ensure their safety and well-being during evacuations.

6. Coordinate with Local Authorities:
Collaborate with local emergency management agencies, law enforcement, fire departments, and other relevant authorities to coordinate evacuation planning efforts, share information, and establish mutual aid agreements. Ensure alignment with existing emergency response plans and protocols.

7. Train & Educate Community Members:
Provide training, education, and outreach initiatives to inform residents about evacuation procedures, routes, assembly points, and shelters. Conduct drills, exercises, and simulations to familiarize residents with evacuation protocols and enhance preparedness.

8. Review & Update the Plan Regularly:
Regularly review and update the evacuation plan to reflect changes in the community, population demographics, infrastructure, and emergency response capabilities. Incorporate lessons learned from previous emergencies, feedback from stakeholders, and best practices in emergency management.

By following these steps, mutual aid groups can develop comprehensive evacuation plans that enhance community resilience and readiness to respond effectively to emergencies, protect lives, and minimize the impact of disasters.

Financial Preparedness

Establishing an **emergency fund** is essential for a mutual aid group, providing a dedicated reservoir of resources that can be quickly mobilized in times of crisis. Financial preparedness allows the group to respond effectively to unexpected situations, ensuring that aid can be delivered without delay.

Diversifying funding sources is equally important, as it ensures the sustainability of the fund by minimizing financial risk. By leveraging a mix of donations, grants, fundraising activities, and perhaps even partnerships with local businesses, a mutual aid group can create a robust financial foundation. This diversification not only secures the necessary capital to handle immediate needs during emergencies, but also it contributes to the group's long-term stability.

For mutual aid groups operating with limited financial resources, setting aside funds for emergencies can be a daunting challenge. Balancing immediate community needs with the foresight to prepare for unforeseen crises requires careful financial management and often creative fundraising strategies to ensure they have the necessary reserves when disaster strikes. Here are several steps a mutual aid group might take to set up and manage such a fund:

1. Define the Purpose & Scope:
The group should clearly define what the emergency fund will be used for. This could include specifying the types of emergencies the fund will address, such as natural disasters, economic hardships, or community crises. Clear guidelines will help ensure that the funds are used appropriately and efficiently.

2. Set a Fundraising Goal:
Based on the potential needs assessment, set a realistic fundraising goal that will cover adequate supplies, operational costs, and other emergency-related expenses. This goal can be adjusted as the group grows or as potential threats are reassessed.

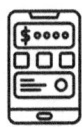

3. Create a Dedicated Account:
It is important to keep emergency funds separate from other finances to ensure they remain earmarked for their intended purpose. This could be a separate bank account or a designated fund within a financial management system that is strictly for emergency response.

4. Fundraising Strategies:
Develop and implement fundraising strategies to build the emergency fund. This could include online crowdfunding, local community events, grants, donations from local businesses, and regular contributions from members of the mutual aid group. Transparency about how funds will be used can help increase community trust and willingness to contribute.

5. Regular Contributions:
Encourage regular contributions to the fund from members and supporters. Even small, consistent donations can grow significantly over time. This could be structured as monthly or annual dues, or through regular fundraising activities.

6. Financial Management Policies:
Establish clear financial management policies, including who has access to funds, how decisions are made about spending money, and how disbursements are tracked. Regular financial audits and reports should be made available to contributors to maintain transparency.

7. Build Partnerships:
Collaborate with local businesses, other non-profit organizations, and government agencies that might contribute to the fund or match donations. Partnerships can also extend the reach and effectiveness of the fund during emergencies.

8. Review & Adapt:
Regularly review the status of the emergency fund, assessing if the current balance meets the group's strategic needs based on potential risks and past emergencies. Adjust fundraising goals and strategies as needed to ensure the fund's readiness.

By carefully planning and maintaining an emergency fund, your mutual aid group will be able to act swiftly and effectively in times of need.

Personal & Family Prepping

Members of a mutual aid group should prioritize emergency preparedness not only within the group but also at their personal residences with their families or roommates. By ensuring that each member is equipped with the necessary supplies and plans for emergencies at home—such as having adequate food, water, medical supplies, and a clear evacuation plan—they fortify their ability to remain resilient in times of crisis.

Individual preparedness is crucial as it enables members to stabilize their immediate circumstances quickly, thereby allowing them to actively participate in the group's broader efforts to assist the community during emergencies. Essentially, when members are not preoccupied with personal emergencies, they can contribute more effectively to the group's collective response efforts.

While personal preparedness is important, members of a mutual aid group should also be reassured that they can rely on the group if they find themselves unprepared in an emergency. Each member's efforts to be ready at a personal level enhance the overall resilience of the group, ensuring that everyone has the basic skills and supplies to manage initial challenges, but the strength of a mutual aid group lies in its collective support system. No one is left to face crises alone.

Recognizing that emergencies can overwhelm even the best-prepared individuals, the group serves as a safety net, providing physical resources, emotional support, and practical assistance when personal preparations might fall short. This dual approach—encouraging personal readiness while reinforcing communal support—enables the group to function effectively and compassionately during crises.

When preparing for an emergency at home, focusing on essentials and readiness can make a significant difference. Here are some critical steps:

1. Stockpile Essentials:
Ensure you have a substantial supply of water (one gallon per person per day for at least three days), non-perishable food items, and a sufficient stock of any necessary medications. These supplies are crucial for maintaining health and hygiene during an emergency.

2. Prepare a "Bug Out" Bag:
Pack a bag with essential items that you can grab quickly if you need to evacuate immediately. Include items like personal documents, extra clothing, emergency contact information, and critical supplies.

3. Secure Backup Power:
Consider options for backup power, such as a generator, solar panels, or portable battery packs. This can be vital for keeping communication devices, medical equipment, and appliances operational if the power goes out.

4. Plan for Personal Safety:
Think about personal safety measures, including ways to defend yourself if needed. This might include weapons or learning basic self-defense techniques, depending on what is legal and appropriate in your area.

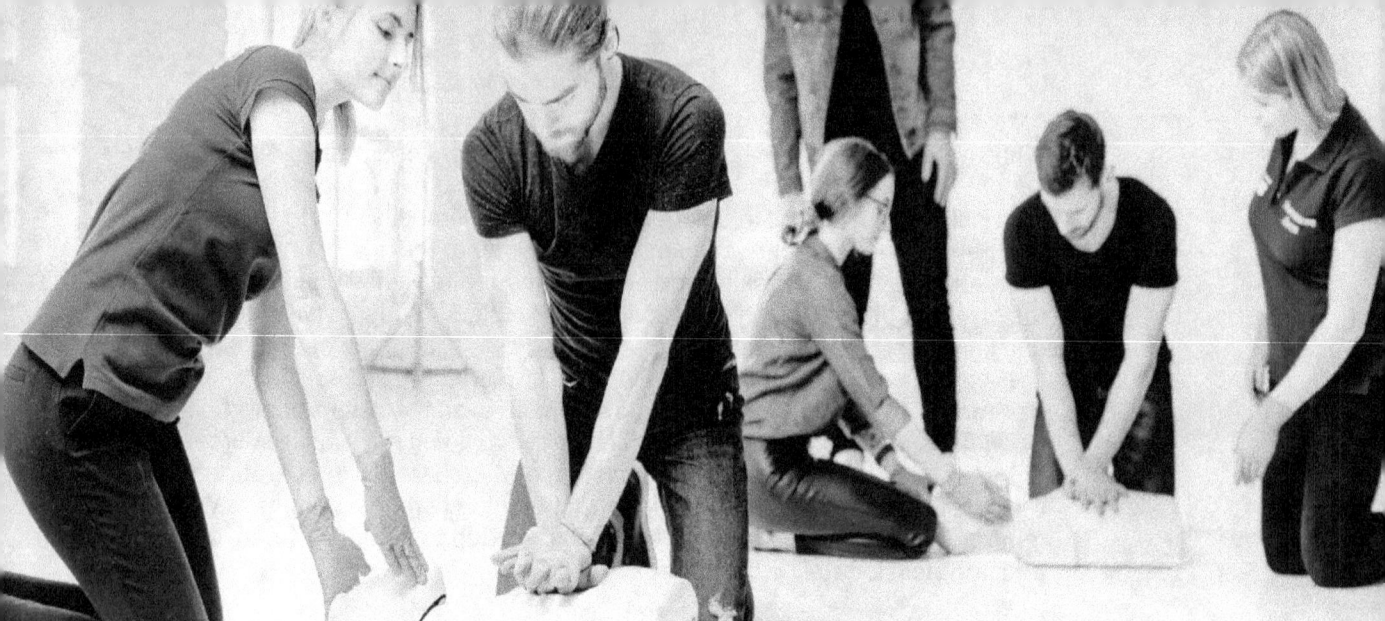

Section 3
Trainings & Simulations

Trainings and simulations are integral components of preparedness for mutual aid groups, offering invaluable opportunities to hone skills, foster teamwork, and enhance readiness for emergencies. By engaging in regular training exercises, members can familiarize themselves with emergency protocols, test response procedures, and identify areas for improvement. Simulations allow groups to experience realistic emergency scenarios, providing a controlled environment to practice decision-making under pressure and evaluate the effectiveness of their strategies.

Data-driven decision-making is an important aspect of emergency training, enabling mutual aid groups to utilize up-to-date information to inform their response efforts. By analyzing data on past emergencies, local risk factors, and community demographics, groups can develop informed strategies and allocate resources effectively. This approach ensures that response efforts are targeted, efficient, and tailored to meet the specific needs of the community.

Legal compliance and ethical decision-making are also important considerations for mutual aid groups during training for emergencies. Understanding relevant laws, regulations, and ethical guidelines ensures that response efforts are conducted in accordance with legal requirements and ethical principles. By adhering to standards of conduct and prioritizing the well-being of all individuals, groups can uphold trust within the community and safeguard their reputation.

Here are some examples of the types of trainings a mutual aid group may want to provide in preparation for emergencies:

 Emergency Response Training:

This training covers essential skills and protocols for responding to different types of emergencies, such as natural disasters or public health crises. Volunteers learn about emergency communication, evacuation procedures, first aid techniques, and how to safely provide assistance in hazardous conditions.

 **De-escalation & Conflict Resolution Workshops:**

These workshops teach volunteers effective communication strategies and de-escalation techniques to defuse tense situations and prevent violence or harm. Volunteers learn how to listen actively, validate feelings, and use non-confrontational approaches to resolve conflicts peacefully.

 **First Aid & CPR Certification:**

Providing volunteers with certification in first aid and CPR equips them with the skills needed to provide immediate medical assistance in emergency situations. Training covers basic life support techniques, wound care, and how to respond to cardiac and respiratory emergencies.

 **Community Outreach & Engagement Training:**

This training focuses on building relationships with community members, identifying needs, and effectively engaging with diverse populations. Volunteers learn how to conduct outreach activities, facilitate community meetings, and collaborate with local organizations to address concerns.

 **Cultural Competency & Diversity Training:**

Cultural competency training helps volunteers understand and respect cultural differences, values, and beliefs within the community. Volunteers learn how to communicate respectfully across cultural boundaries, recognize unconscious biases, and promote inclusivity and diversity in their interactions.

Tabletop Exercises & Simulations:

Tabletop exercises simulate emergency scenarios in a controlled environment, allowing volunteers to practice their response procedures and decision-making skills. These exercises help volunteers assess their readiness and identify areas for improvement.

Legal & Ethical Training:

Volunteers receive training on legal and ethical considerations in their roles, including confidentiality, privacy laws, and informed consent. Training ensures that volunteers understand their responsibilities, uphold professional standards, and protect the rights and dignity of those they help.

De-escalation Techniques

De-escalation is a set of techniques and strategies used to defuse or reduce the intensity of a potentially volatile or confrontational situation. It aims to calm emotions, decrease tension, and prevent the escalation of conflict or aggression. De-escalation techniques prioritize communication, empathy, and non-violent intervention to resolve disputes peacefully and promote safety for all parties involved.

In various contexts—such as law enforcement, mental health settings, or conflict resolution—de-escalation techniques are employed to manage challenging behaviors, diffuse aggression, and promote positive outcomes. These techniques typically involve active listening, empathetic communication, problem-solving, and maintaining a calm and composed demeanor.

The goal of de-escalation is not to impose control or force compliance but to establish rapport, build trust, and foster collaboration between individuals. By addressing underlying emotions, needs, and concerns, de-escalation techniques empower individuals to regain a sense of control and find mutually acceptable resolutions to conflicts.

Training in de-escalation techniques is essential for mutual aid groups to handle potentially volatile situations. By learning effective communication strategies and conflict resolution skills, members can defuse tense situations, minimize the risk of violence, and maintain a safe environment for all involved.

Some common de-escalation techniques include:

DE-ESCALATION TECHNIQUES

Active Listening:
Pay close attention to what the person in distress is saying and demonstrate empathy and understanding. This can help defuse tension and build rapport.

Remain Calm:
Maintain a calm and composed demeanor. This can help relieve tension and reassure others that you are in control.

Use Non-Threatening Body Language:
Avoid aggressive gestures or postures and maintain an open, non-confrontational stance. This can help create a sense of safety and trust.

Respect Personal Space:
Give the individual space and avoid invading their personal boundaries. This can help reduce feelings of threat or aggression.

Validate Feelings:
Acknowledge the person's emotions and validate their feelings. This will help them feel heard and understood, which can defuse anger or frustration.

Offer Choices:
Provide options or alternatives. This can empower the individual and give them a sense of control over the situation, reducing feelings of powerlessness or aggression.

Stay Patient:
De-escalation often takes time, and it's essential to remain patient and persistent in your efforts to calm the situation.

Seek Assistance:
If the situation escalates or becomes unsafe, seek additional support, such as other members of the mutual aid group, trained professionals, or emergency services.

Crisis Intervention

Crisis intervention refers to the immediate and focused psychological assistance given to individuals who are experiencing acute emotional distress or are in crisis situations. It aims to stabilize the individual, provide emotional support, and help them cope with their current situation. This support can be provided by mental health professionals, trained volunteers, or emergency responders in various settings, including hospitals, hotlines, community centers, schools, and yes, mutual aid groups.

Crisis intervention is typically brief and focused on addressing the immediate crisis, with the aim of stabilizing the individual and connecting them with ongoing support services as needed. It is a collaborative process that empowers people to regain a sense of control and autonomy in managing their emotions.

While the specific approach may vary depending on the context and needs of the individual, the following steps are commonly employed in crisis intervention:

1. Assessment:
Begin by assessing the person's safety and immediate needs. Determine the nature and severity of the crisis, any potential risk factors, and their current emotional state.

2. Establish Rapport:
Build rapport and trust by demonstrating empathy and nonjudgmental support. Validate their feelings and reassure them that you are there to help.

3. Active Listening:
Listen attentively to their concerns, allowing them to express their thoughts and emotions freely. Use reflective listening techniques to demonstrate understanding and validate their experiences.

4. Identify Coping Strategies:
Collaboratively explore coping strategies and resources that they can use to manage their distress. Encourage them to draw on their strengths and existing support systems.

5. Problem-Solving:
Help them identify practical solutions to address the immediate crisis and mitigate its impact. Break down the problem into manageable steps and brainstorm possible options together.

6. Provide Emotional Support:
Offer emotional support and validation, acknowledging the individual's feelings and validating their experiences. Reassure them that it is okay to feel overwhelmed and that help is available.

7. Safety Planning:
Develop a safety plan with them to address any immediate safety concerns and prevent future crises. Identify triggers and warning signs, establish coping strategies, and create a plan for accessing support during times of distress.

8. Connect with Resources:
Connect them with appropriate resources and support services, such as crisis hotlines, mental health professionals, support groups, or community organizations. Provide information on how to access these resources and offer assistance in making connections if needed.

9. Follow-Up & Support:
Follow up with them after the crisis intervention to ensure they are safe and okay. Provide ongoing support, encouragement, and assistance as they navigate their recovery process.

First Aid Basics

First aid training equips mutual aid group members and volunteers with essential skills to provide immediate medical assistance in emergency situations. These training programs typically cover a range of topics, including basic life support techniques, wound care, and how to respond to common medical emergencies. By providing first aid training to volunteers, mutual aid groups ensure that they are well-prepared to respond effectively and confidently when faced with injuries or medical emergencies in the community.

First aid training typically begins with instruction on assessing the scene and ensuring personal safety before approaching an injured individual. Volunteers learn how to quickly evaluate the patient's condition, identify any life-threatening injuries or conditions, and prioritize treatment accordingly. This includes techniques such as checking for responsiveness, assessing breathing and circulation, and controlling severe bleeding.

Participants also receive hands-on training in basic life support techniques such as cardiopulmonary resuscitation (CPR) and how to use automated external defibrillators (AEDs) to revive individuals experiencing cardiac arrest. They learn how to recognize the signs of a heart attack, stroke, or choking, and how to respond promptly and effectively to these medical emergencies.

Wound care is another important part of first aid training—teaching participants how to clean and dress wounds, apply bandages and splints, and immobilize injured limbs to prevent further injury. Volunteers also learn how to recognize signs of infection and when to seek professional medical assistance for more serious injuries.

Lastly, first aid training also emphasizes the importance of remaining calm under pressure, communicating effectively with patients and bystanders, and working collaboratively with emergency medical services and other first responders. By providing comprehensive first aid training to its members and volunteers, a mutual aid group ensures that they are well-equipped to provide immediate assistance and support to those in need.

Equipment Training

Mutual aid groups may provide equipment training to volunteers to prepare them for emergencies. The specific training will depend on the types of emergencies the group anticipates responding to and the equipment available to them. Some examples of equipment training for mutual aid volunteers include:

Search & Rescue Equipment Training:

Mutual aid groups involved in search and rescue operations may provide training on using specialized equipment such as ropes, harnesses, pulleys, and personal protective gear. Volunteers may learn techniques for conducting searches, rescuing people from hazardous environments, and providing medical care in remote or difficult-to-access locations.

First Aid & Medical Equipment Training:

Volunteers may receive training on how to use basic first aid supplies such as bandages, splints, and wound dressings, as well as more advanced medical equipment like automated external defibrillators (AEDs), oxygen tanks, and emergency medical kits. Training may cover proper techniques for administering CPR, controlling bleeding, and treating common injuries and medical conditions.

Communication Equipment Training:

Effective communication is critical during emergencies, so volunteers may receive training on how to use two-way radios, cell phones, and other devices used by the group. Training may include proper radio protocols, distress signals, and how to coordinate communications with other emergency responders and agencies.

Firefighting Equipment Training:

Mutual aid groups involved in firefighting and fire suppression efforts may provide training on using equipment such as hoses, nozzles, fire extinguishers, and protective gear. Volunteers may learn techniques for putting out fires, conducting fire assessments, and ensuring their safety in hazardous environments.

Emergency Shelter & Survival Equipment Training:

In preparation for responding to displaced populations, volunteers may receive training on setting up temporary shelters, distributing emergency supplies, and managing logistics. Training may cover how to use equipment such as tents, sleeping bags, portable stoves, and water filtration systems.

Hazardous Materials (HAZMAT) Equipment Training:

Mutual aid groups responding to hazardous materials incidents may provide training on using specialized equipment such as chemical protective suits, respirators, decontamination showers, and detection devices. Volunteers may learn how to safely assess and mitigate hazardous materials spills or releases.

Tabletop Exercises

Tabletop exercises simulate emergency situations in a discussion-based format, allowing participants to explore and refine their response strategies without the need for physical enactment. By gathering members around a table or in an online format, mutual aid groups can walk through various emergency scenarios, assessing their preparedness and identifying potential weaknesses in their plans. These exercises promote critical thinking, enhance communication, and build a cohesive understanding of roles and responsibilities among group members.

During a tabletop exercise, a facilitator presents a scenario based on plausible emergencies the community might face, such as natural disasters, public health crises, or cyberattacks on infrastructure. Participants then discuss their immediate responses, resource allocations, and coordination efforts. This collaborative process helps uncover gaps in knowledge, skills, or resources that might hinder effective emergency response. For example, a group might realize that they lack sufficient medical supplies for a health crisis or identify the need for more robust communication channels during a power outage. By addressing these issues in a low-stakes environment, mutual aid groups can develop more resilient and comprehensive emergency plans.

Here are some examples of tabletop exercises that groups might conduct:

Natural Disaster Scenario:

Participants simulate responding to a natural disaster such as a hurricane, earthquake, or wildfire. The exercise may involve coordinating evacuation procedures, setting up emergency shelters, and providing medical assistance to affected individuals.

Environmental Contamination Incident:

Participants respond to an environmental contamination incident such as a chemical spill, hazardous material release, or pollution event. The exercise may involve assessing environmental risks, implementing cleanup measures, and coordinating with government agencies and stakeholders.

Public Health Emergency:

This scenario focuses on responding to a public health crisis such as a pandemic, infectious disease outbreak, or bioterrorism incident. Participants practice coordinating with local health authorities, implementing disease control measures, and providing public education and outreach.

Mass Casualty Incident:

In this exercise, participants respond to a mass casualty incident, such as a terrorist attack, mass shooting, or large-scale accident. The scenario may involve triaging and treating injured individuals, coordinating with emergency medical services, and managing communications with the media and public.

Community Crisis:

Participants simulate responding to a community crisis such as a neighborhood fire, building collapse, or power outage. The exercise may involve setting up a community command center, coordinating search and rescue efforts, and providing support services to displaced residents.

Cybersecurity Breach:

This scenario focuses on responding to a cybersecurity breach or cyberattack that disrupts critical infrastructure or compromises sensitive data. Participants practice identifying and mitigating security threats, communicating with affected stakeholders, and implementing protocols to prevent future incidents.

Active Shooter Situation:

In this exercise, participants respond to an active shooter situation in a public space such as a school, workplace, or shopping center. The scenario may involve implementing lockdown procedures, evacuating civilians to safety, and providing medical assistance to victims.

Self-Defense Training

Mutual aid groups may choose to offer **self-defense training** that provides community members with the skills and confidence to protect themselves in potentially dangerous situations. In today's world, where people may face a variety of threats, self-defense training equips people with practical techniques to de-escalate conflicts and, if necessary, defend themselves physically. By learning self-defense, participants can feel more secure in their daily lives, knowing they have the knowledge and skills to respond effectively to threats.

Offering self-defense training can serve as a bonding activity for a mutual aid group, strengthening trust and cooperation among members. Additionally, the training can be tailored to address specific needs and concerns of the community, including women, the elderly, and marginalized groups who might face higher risks. By incorporating self-defense training into their programs, mutual aid groups can help build a safer and more confident community.

While the specific approach may vary based on the mutual aid group's resources and priorities, several types of self-defense training may be considered:

Basic Self-Defense Techniques:

Basic self-defense training focuses on teaching people simple yet effective physical techniques to defend themselves against common types of attacks, such as grabs, strikes, or chokes. Participants learn how to use their body's natural strengths and leverage to escape from holds, create distance from an attacker, and incapacitate an assailant using strikes to vulnerable areas.

Situational Awareness & Risk Assessment:

Situational awareness training focuses on paying attention to surroundings, identifying potential threats or danger cues, and assessing the level of risk in different environments. Participants learn how to recognize signs of danger, trust their instincts, and make informed decisions to avoid or mitigate risky situations before they escalate.

Ground Defense & Escaping Techniques:

Ground defense training teaches individuals how to defend themselves and escape from potentially dangerous situations when confronted while on the ground or in a prone position. Participants learn techniques for protecting vital areas, creating space, and executing escapes from various ground positions.

Scenario-Based Training:

Scenario-based training involves simulating realistic self-defense scenarios to provide participants with opportunities to apply their skills and decision-making under pressure. Participants engage in role-playing exercises that replicate common confrontations, allowing them to practice assessing threats, making split-second decisions, and implementing appropriate self-defense strategies.

Chapter Review

Communities face an array of dynamic and unpredictable crises in the 21st century, ranging from natural disasters to public health emergencies and domestic terrorism. The rapidly changing nature of these events demands a flexible and proactive approach to emergency preparedness and response. Mutual aid groups play an important role in this landscape, offering immediate support and resources to those affected.

Emergency planning involves developing detailed emergency plans that outline roles, responsibilities, and procedures for various scenarios. Key elements of these plans include establishing communication protocols and coordinating with local emergency services. Regularly updating and revising these plans is also critical, as it allows the group to adapt to new threats and changing circumstances.

Mutual aid groups may offer regular training sessions for volunteers that cover a range of skills, from basic first aid to more specialized knowledge like search-and-rescue. Tabletop exercises provide practical, hands-on experience, allowing participants to practice their roles in a controlled environment. These activities help identify potential weaknesses in emergency plans and improve overall coordination and response times. By investing in continuous training, groups can ensure that they are well-prepared to support their communities in times of crisis.

Discussion Questions

1 Can you recall a time when you were involved in an emergency situation? How did you respond, and what did you learn from that experience about the importance of being prepared?

2 Think about your community's response to a recent crisis, such as a natural disaster or public health emergency. What were some strengths and weaknesses in the community's preparedness and response efforts?

IN THIS CHAPTER

» Discussing systemic issues &
their root causes

» How to change public policy

» Starting a movement that
inspires collective action &
puts pressure on policymakers

Chapter **11**

Advocating for Systemic Change

As we navigate the complexities of modern society, it becomes increasingly clear that many of the challenges we face are not isolated incidents but symptoms of deeper systemic issues. From wealth inequality and healthcare access to housing instability and climate change, these problems often arise from structures that prioritize profit and power over human well-being. In times like these, we must ask ourselves: Are the systems we rely on truly serving everyone, or are they failing those who need them most?

These systemic issues are not new, and history shows us that top-down solutions often fall short. Government policies and institutional reforms can be slow, bureaucratic, and disconnected from the lived experiences of those most affected. And these efforts often leave gaps that widen inequality rather than close it. When formal systems break down or overlook certain populations, grassroots solutions like mutual aid have emerged to fill the void.

Understanding Systemic Issues

Many of the problems a mutual aid group seeks to address in a community—such as food insecurity, inadequate healthcare, or lack of affordable housing—actually stem from larger systemic issues in society. By understanding the root causes behind these issues, groups can better tailor their efforts to not only provide immediate relief but also to advocate for broader structural changes.

Systemic issues refer to problems or challenges within a system that are deeply ingrained and pervasive. These issues are not isolated incidents or individual shortcomings, but rather they arise from the inherent design, policies, or practices of the system itself. Systemic issues have an impact on governments, organizations, and communities, and they result in inequities, injustices, and disparities that affect large groups of people.

Here are some examples of systemic issues in society:

Systemic Racism:

This refers to the pervasive discrimination and prejudice against certain racial or ethnic groups embedded within societal systems, institutions, and policies. It results in unequal treatment, opportunities, and outcomes for marginalized racial or ethnic communities in education, employment, housing, healthcare, and criminal justice.

Income Inequality:

This refers to the widening gap between the wealthy and the poor, which is driven by inadequate wages for lower-income workers and unequal access to education, job opportunities, and political influence. Income inequality perpetuates cycles of poverty, reduces social mobility, and contributes to broader societal problems.

Systemic Sexism & Genderism:

Systemic sexism and genderism involve the discrimination and marginalization of people based on their sex or gender identity, resulting in unequal treatment, violence, limited opportunities for advancement, and disparities in wages and representation in various sectors and leadership positions.

Systemic Ableism:

Systemic ableism refers to the discrimination and exclusion of people with disabilities, resulting in barriers to access, participation, and full inclusion in society. This includes physical barriers, discriminatory practices, lack of accommodations, and negative stereotypes that perpetuate inequality.

Environmental Degradation:

This refers to environmental destruction, pollution, climate change, and depletion of natural resources. It involves practices such as overconsumption, reliance on fossil fuels, deforestation, industrial pollution, and unsustainable agricultural practices that harm ecosystems and threaten the well-being of present and future generations.

343

Addressing the root causes of systemic issues requires a comprehensive, multi-faceted approach that targets the underlying structures perpetuating inequality and injustice. Here are some key strategies:

Policy Reform:

Effective policy changes at the governmental level can address the foundational aspects of systemic issues. This involves reforming laws and regulations to ensure they promote equity and do not disproportionately disadvantage certain groups. For example, criminal justice reform, housing policies that prevent segregation, and equitable education funding models are essential in tackling systemic racism.

Education & Awareness:

Educating the public about the existence and effects of systemic issues is crucial. This includes integrating social justice education in schools and community initiatives. Education serves as a powerful tool for changing perceptions and motivating collective action.

Economic Redistribution:

Addressing economic disparities involves implementing policies that support wealth redistribution—such as progressive taxation, universal basic income, and social security systems that are designed to eliminate poverty.

Centering Marginalized Voices:

Centering marginalized voices ensures that the perspectives and experiences of those most affected by societal inequities are heard and considered in decision-making processes. This leads to more inclusive and effective solutions.

Legal Accountability:

Strengthening the accountability of institutions and individuals who perpetuate systemic issues is essential. This involves not only legal mechanisms to punish discriminatory practices but also frameworks to monitor and enforce compliance with equity-based laws and regulations.

Collaborative Movements:

Building alliances across different movements and sectors can amplify the impact of efforts to address systemic issues. Solidarity between advocacy groups, non-profits, community organizations, and progressive businesses can lead to more robust and sustainable changes.

By combining these approaches, we can begin to dismantle the deep-seated roots of systemic issues, creating a more just and equitable world. In the rest of this section, we will discuss in greater detail the forces behind some of our most pressing issues so we can better understand our present circumstances.

Capitalism & Neoliberalism

Capitalism and **neoliberalism**—as prevailing economic and political ideologies—significantly shape societal structures and create many systemic issues. Capitalism, characterized by private ownership and the pursuit of profit, inherently prioritizes capital accumulation over social welfare. This economic model leads to significant disparities in wealth and power, concentrating resources in the hands of a few while marginalizing many. Such disparities manifest in limited access to essential services like healthcare, education, and housing for the underprivileged, perpetuating cycles of poverty and social inequality.

Neoliberalism exacerbates these issues by advocating for reduced government intervention in the economy, deregulation, and an increase in privatization. These policies often strip communities of vital public resources and social safety nets, leaving people more vulnerable to the whims of the market. For example, the push towards privatization under neoliberal policies often results in the commodification of basic needs, making them inaccessible to those who cannot afford them. Healthcare becomes a luxury rather than a universal right, and education systems are increasingly driven by profit motives.

Neoliberalism's emphasis on individual responsibility for economic success shifts the blame for poverty and unemployment onto individuals rather than acknowledging structural failings. This ideology supports the stigmatization of those who require public assistance, eroding solidarity and compassion within society. This combination of capitalism and neoliberalism not only creates economic inequalities, but also it weakens the social fabric, making it difficult to address systemic issues comprehensively. Mutual aid groups and other community-driven initiatives often arise in response to these failures, as they strive to provide the support that state mechanisms no longer guarantee.

Addressing the systemic issues spawned by capitalism and neoliberalism is imperative for human survival and the preservation of global stability. The relentless pursuit of profit has led to environmental degradation, economic disparities, and a breakdown in social cohesion, which are unsustainable in the long term. To ensure a sustainable future, it is essential to challenge and reform these systems by advocating for policies that prioritize environmental conservation, equitable distribution of resources, and stronger social safety nets. Advocating for a more inclusive economic model that values human well-being and ecological balance over mere financial gain is not just a moral imperative; it is a practical necessity to mitigate crises that threaten our collective well-being and survival.

Imperialism & Colonialism

Imperialism and **colonialism** have been instrumental in shaping the modern world, leaving behind a legacy of systemic issues that continue to impact societies across the globe. These historical processes involved the domination and exploitation of territories and peoples by powerful nations, leading to the establishment of unequal economic, political, and social structures that persist to this day.

The systemic issues arising from imperialism and colonialism are multifaceted. Economically, colonialism and imperialism facilitated the extraction of resources from colonized territories to enrich the imperial powers. Natural resources, labor, and capital were systematically exploited, often to the detriment of the local populations who received little benefit from the wealth generated. This legacy of exploitation has contributed to persistent poverty and underdevelopment in many former colonies.

Politically, colonialism and imperialism imposed foreign governance structures and legal systems that often ignored or suppressed indigenous forms of governance and sovereignty. This disruption of traditional political institutions and power dynamics has led to enduring conflicts and instability in many regions, as well as a legacy of authoritarianism and weak state institutions. The arbitrary drawing of borders by colonial powers has resulted in ethnic tensions and territorial disputes that continue to fuel conflict in many parts of the world.

Culturally, imperialism and colonialism can lead to the erosion of indigenous cultures and languages as the dominating power imposes its own norms and language. This cultural domination is a form of soft power, helping the imperialist country extend its influence more subtly. The long-term effects include a loss of cultural identity among the dominated populations and a distorted narrative about their historical contributions.

Addressing the systemic issues created by imperialism and colonialism requires acknowledging the enduring legacies of these processes and taking proactive steps towards reconciliation and justice. This includes efforts to redress past injustices, promote decolonization and self-determination for oppressed peoples, and challenge the structural inequalities that perpetuate the marginalization of certain groups. By confronting the systemic issues rooted in colonialism and imperialism, societies can move towards a more equitable and inclusive future.

Patriarchy & Sexism/Genderism

Patriarchy is a system of social organization that prioritizes male dominance and perpetuates gender-based hierarchies. At its core, patriarchy dictates social norms, values, and power structures that uphold the superiority of gender-conforming men while subordinating women and non-binary people. This entrenched system not only perpetuates gender inequalities but also intersects with other forms of oppression—such as racism, classism, and heteronormativity—further exacerbating injustices.

Economically, patriarchy manifests in gendered divisions of labor and unequal access to professional opportunities. Women and non-binary individuals are often relegated to lower-paying jobs, facing systemic barriers to career advancement and financial independence. This economic disenfranchisement perpetuates cycles of poverty and limits the autonomy and agency of marginalized genders.

Politically, patriarchy marginalizes women and non-binary individuals from positions of power and decision-making. Structural barriers—including discriminatory laws, unfair social norms, and institutionalized **sexism** and **genderism**—prevent equal representation in political institutions. As a result, policies often fail to address the diverse needs of marginalized genders, perpetuating systemic inequalities in access to rights and resources.

Socially, patriarchy enforces rigid gender roles and expectations that dictate behavior, appearance, and relationships. These gender norms reinforce harmful stereotypes and contribute to the normalization of gender-based violence, discrimination, and harassment.

Addressing the systemic issues created by patriarchy requires dismantling the structures of power and privilege that perpetuate gender inequalities. This includes challenging gender norms and stereotypes, promoting gender equity in all spheres of society, and amplifying the voices and experiences of marginalized genders.

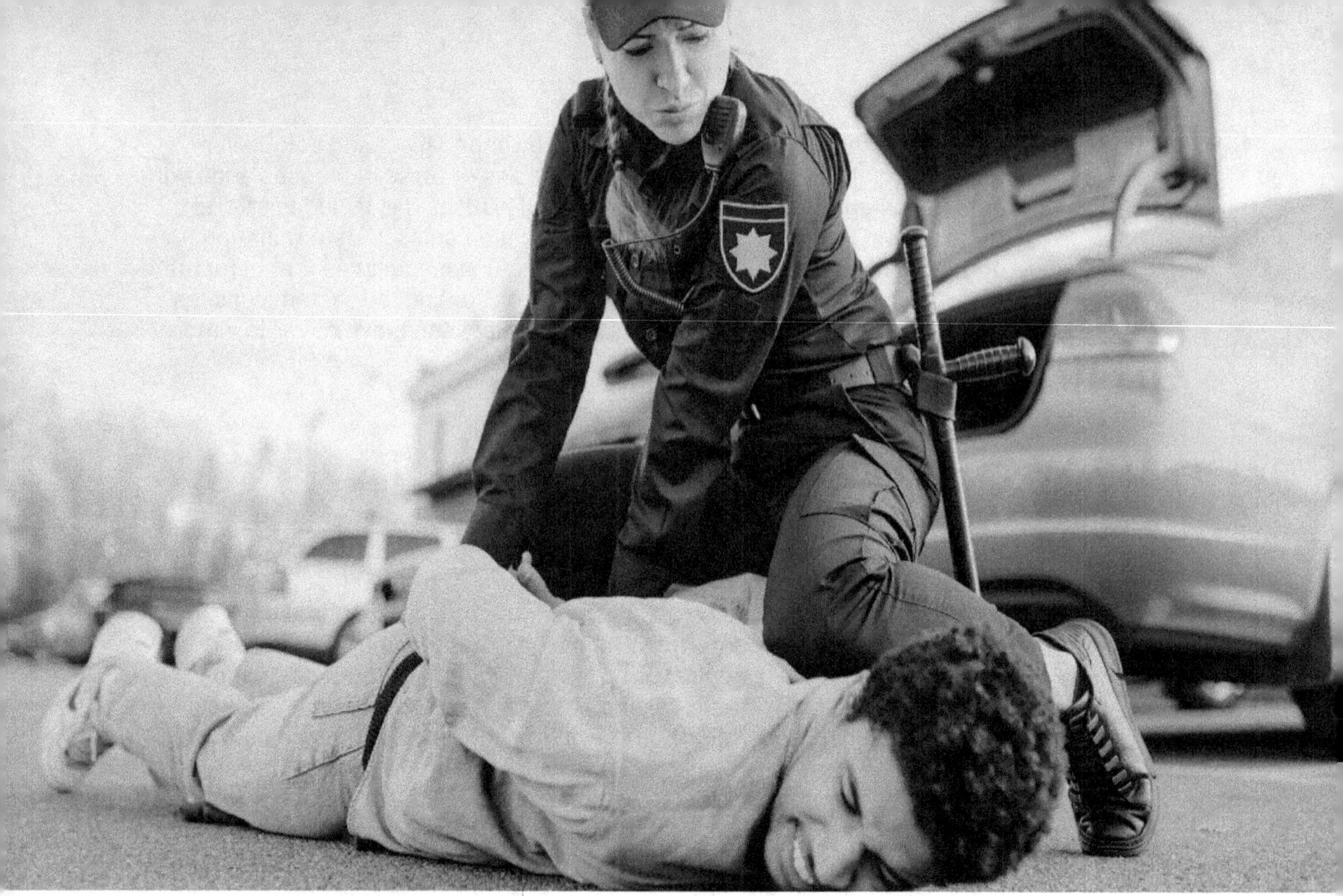

Racism & White Supremacy

Racism and **white supremacy** are deeply ingrained systemic issues that have profound impacts on society, perpetuating inequality and division. These ideologies—rooted in the belief that one race is inherently superior to others—have historically shaped social, political, and economic structures to the disadvantage of racial minorities, particularly Black people, Indigenous people, and other people of color.

The effects of racism and white supremacy are pervasive and manifest in various aspects of life. In the realm of economics, these ideologies contribute to systemic disparities in employment, income, and wealth accumulation. Racial discrimination in hiring practices and workplace biases often hinder career progression for minorities, leading to a racial wealth gap that persists through generations. This economic inequality is compounded by disparities in housing and education, where people of color frequently face segregation and access to lower-quality resources, further limiting their opportunities.

350

In the justice system, racism is evident in the disproportionate incarceration rates of people of color, who are more likely to be stopped, searched, arrested, and sentenced more harshly than their white counterparts. This not only reflects bias in law enforcement but also in the broader legal framework that supports such practices. Health care disparities are another critical issue, with systemic racism affecting the quality of care and health outcomes for racial minorities who experience higher rates of morbidity and mortality.

Addressing these systemic issues requires more than piecemeal reforms; it necessitates a fundamental overhaul of societal structures and attitudes. This includes implementing policies that actively redress racial inequalities—such as affirmative action, fair housing initiatives, and equitable healthcare reforms—as well as educational programs that confront and dismantle racist ideologies. A societal shift towards true inclusivity and equity involves recognizing the historical and ongoing impacts of racism and white supremacy, and committing to sustained action against them. Mutual aid groups, activists, and policymakers must work together to create an environment where the dignity and rights of every individual are upheld, regardless of their race.

Political Corruption

Political corruption—defined as the misuse of public power for private gain—has profound and far-reaching impacts on society, giving rise to systemic issues that undermine democracy, justice, and social cohesion. At its core, political corruption erodes public trust in government institutions and processes, weakening the social contract between citizens and their elected representatives. This erosion of trust can lead to widespread apathy, disillusionment, and disengagement from civic life, ultimately undermining the functioning of societies.

Economically, political corruption distorts markets, impedes growth, and exacerbates income inequality. Through bribery, kickbacks, and embezzlement, corrupt officials divert public resources away from essential services and infrastructure projects, hindering development and perpetuating poverty. Corruption creates barriers to entry for businesses and investors, favoring well-connected elites and stifling competition and innovation. The resulting economic inequality further entrenches social divisions and undermines social mobility.

Political corruption also undermines the rule of law, weakens democratic institutions, and erodes the checks and balances necessary for accountable governance. When public officials prioritize personal gain over the public good, they compromise the integrity of electoral processes, manipulate legislation to serve vested interests, and suppress dissenting voices through censorship and repression. This erosion of democratic norms and institutions threatens the fundamental principles of equality, justice, and human rights, creating fertile ground for authoritarianism.

Socially, political corruption breeds a culture of impunity, where those in positions of power are shielded from accountability for their actions. This undermines the legitimacy of the state and creates a sense of injustice and resentment among marginalized communities. Corruption exacerbates social inequalities by diverting resources away from essential services such as healthcare, education, and social welfare.

Addressing political corruption requires comprehensive reforms aimed at promoting transparency, accountability, and integrity in governance. This includes strengthening anti-corruption laws and enforcement mechanisms, empowering independent oversight bodies, promoting civic engagement and transparency, and fostering a culture of ethical leadership and public service. By combating political corruption at its roots, societies can work towards a more just, equitable, and democratic future.

Corporate Malpractice

Corporate malpractice embodies a range of unethical behaviors and decisions made by corporations for the sake of profit maximization, often at the expense of workers, communities, and the environment. At the heart of corporate malpractice lies a culture that prioritizes short-term financial gains over long-term sustainability, ethical considerations, and social responsibility.

Sociopathic business practices are characterized by a lack of empathy, remorse, and ethical restraint, enabling corporations to prioritize profit at any cost, regardless of the consequences for society or the environment. This mindset often leads to exploitative labor practices, environmental degradation, and disregard for human rights. Sociopathic corporate executives may engage in deceptive marketing tactics and lobbying efforts to advance their interests and evade accountability.

Similarly, **antisocial business practices** reflect a disregard for social norms, ethical standards, and the well-being of stakeholders, focusing solely on maximizing shareholder value and driving revenue. This may manifest in unethical behavior—such as fraud, corruption, tax evasion, and regulatory non-compliance. Antisocial corporate executives may engage in predatory pricing, monopolistic behavior, and anti-competitive practices to maintain market dominance and squash competition.

Addressing corporate malpractice requires reforms aimed at promoting transparency, accountability, and ethical governance within corporations. This includes strengthening governance mechanisms, enhancing regulatory oversight, and holding corporations accountable for their social and environmental impacts. Fostering a culture of responsibility and moral leadership is essential for promoting ethical business practices and ensuring that corporations prioritize the well-being of all stakeholders, not just shareholders.

Environmental Exploitation

 Environmental exploitation is a systemic issue that poses significant threats to ecological integrity, human well-being, and future generations. At its core, environmental exploitation is fueled by a relentless pursuit of profit and economic growth, often at the expense of environmental sustainability and social justice. This exploitation manifests in various forms—including deforestation, overfishing, fossil fuel extraction, and industrial pollution—leading to widespread ecological destruction and imbalance.

Economically, environmental exploitation prioritizes short-term gains over long-term sustainability, perpetuating cycles of resource depletion and environmental degradation. Industries such as mining, logging, and agriculture often prioritize maximizing profits without regard for the ecological consequences—leading to irreversible damage to ecosystems and loss of biodiversity. The externalization of environmental costs—such as pollution and habitat destruction—allows companies to profit while shifting the burden onto communities and future generations.

Politically, environmental exploitation is facilitated by corporate influence in regulatory oversight and weak enforcement of environmental laws. Powerful industries wield significant influence over government policies and decision-making processes, shaping regulations to favor their interests and circumvent environmental protections. This collusion between industry and government perpetuates a cycle of environmental degradation.

Socially, environmental exploitation disproportionately impacts vulnerable populations, including Indigenous and low-income communities, and people of color. These groups often bear the burden of environmental pollution, toxic waste, and ecological destruction—leading to adverse health effects, displacement, and loss of livelihoods. Environmental exploitation exacerbates social inequalities and injustices, perpetuating cycles of poverty and disenfranchisement.

Addressing environmental exploitation requires transformative changes to the way societies produce, consume, and interact with the environment. This includes transitioning to sustainable and regenerative practices, investing in renewable energy and conservation efforts, and promoting environmental justice. By prioritizing the protection of ecosystems and the well-being of communities, societies can work towards a more sustainable and equitable future for all.

Changing Public Policy

Public policy plays a crucial role in shaping the effects of systemic issues by creating the legal and regulatory framework that governs various aspects of society, such as healthcare, education, housing, and labor rights. Policies can either perpetuate inequalities or work towards addressing them, depending on how they are crafted and implemented. Mutual aid groups, through grassroots organizing, can influence public policy by advocating for changes that address the root causes of inequality and injustice.

One way that mutual aid groups and larger social justice movements influence public policy is by raising awareness about marginalized communities' experiences and advocating for their rights and interests. Through protests, media campaigns, and social media activism, these movements amplify marginalized voices, shine a light on systemic injustices, and mobilize public support for policy changes.

Social justice movements can often engage in direct advocacy and lobbying efforts to influence the legislative process and shape public policy. They may work to build coalitions, mobilize grassroots support, and engage with policymakers through meetings, rallies, public hearings, and other advocacy tactics. By leveraging their collective power and engaging in strategic campaigns, social justice movements can push for legislative reforms, regulatory changes, and policy initiatives that advance their goals and promote greater equity, justice, and inclusion.

Moreover, social justice movements can influence policy by shifting public discourse, changing societal norms, and encouraging a culture of activism and civic engagement. By exposing systemic injustices and promoting alternative visions of social change, these movements can reshape public attitudes and build momentum for policy reform. Ultimately, the impact of a social justice movement on public policy depends on its ability to mobilize broad-based support, sustain momentum over time, and effectively translate grassroots activism into tangible policy outcomes.

Political Realities

Public policy advocacy operates within the complex landscape of political realities, where power dynamics, partisan divides, and competing interests shape the policymaking process. Mutual aid groups engaging in advocacy efforts must navigate these political realities strategically to effectively advance their policy goals. One political reality is the influence of partisan politics, where policy decisions are often driven by ideological differences and agendas. In highly polarized environments, mutual aid groups may find it challenging to garner bipartisan support for their proposals, particularly on contentious issues.

The influence of special interest groups and lobbyists can also exert significant sway over policymaking, as they often wield substantial financial resources and political connections to advance their agendas. Mutual aid groups—with limited resources and grassroots support—may struggle to compete with these well-funded interests, facing an uphill battle to ensure that the voices of marginalized communities are heard and represented in the policymaking process.

The role of political leadership and government institutions can also impact the success of advocacy efforts. Changes in political leadership, shifts in legislative priorities, and turnover in key positions can all affect the receptiveness of policymakers to advocacy messages. Mutual aid groups must be adaptable and responsive to these shifting political dynamics, seizing opportunities for advocacy while navigating potential roadblocks and setbacks.

Lastly, the influence of public opinion and media coverage can shape the political landscape and impact the outcomes of advocacy campaigns. Mutual aid groups must engage in strategic messaging and media outreach to effectively communicate their policy goals and mobilize public support for their cause. Building public awareness and grassroots momentum around key issues can help sway public opinion and create pressure on policymakers to take action.

Overall, navigating the political realities of public policy advocacy requires mutual aid groups to employ a multifaceted approach that combines strategic coalition-building, grassroots mobilization, and savvy political maneuvering. By understanding the intricacies of the policymaking process and leveraging their collective power and community support, mutual aid groups can effectively advocate for policy changes that advance social justice and address the needs of marginalized communities.

Challenges in Policy Advocacy

Advocacy is often fraught with challenges that can hinder progress and effectiveness. As discussed in the prior section, a primary obstacle faced by mutual aid groups is limited resources. Unlike well-funded special interest groups, mutual aid groups often operate on shoestring budgets and rely heavily on volunteer labor. This limited capacity can constrain their ability to conduct research, organize advocacy campaigns, and sustain long-term advocacy efforts, making it difficult to compete with more powerful interests.

Additionally, navigating bureaucratic processes and institutional barriers can pose significant challenges for mutual aid groups. Government agencies and legislative bodies are often complex and opaque, with intricate decision-making processes and entrenched bureaucratic structures that can be difficult to navigate. Mutual aid groups may struggle to access decision-makers, understand complex policy issues, and effectively communicate their message within bureaucratic systems designed to accommodate more established and well-connected players.

Mutual aid groups may also encounter political resistance from policymakers and other stakeholders who are reluctant to change or are beholden to powerful vested interests. Political opposition can manifest in various forms, including skepticism, indifference, or outright hostility toward the group's advocacy efforts. Policymakers may resist taking action on controversial issues or challenging the status quo, particularly if it threatens their political careers or alliances with influential donors or interest groups.

Overcoming these challenges requires mutual aid groups to employ strategic advocacy tactics, build coalitions with like-minded allies, and leverage grassroots mobilization. By cultivating relationships with policymakers, building public awareness and support for their cause, and engaging in targeted advocacy campaigns, groups can amplify their voices and increase their influence in shaping policy.

Approaching Policymakers

When a mutual aid group decides to approach a lawmaker about changing public policy, it is crucial to begin with thorough preparation and strategy. The group should research the policymaker's background, including their previous positions, voting record, and key interests. Understanding their priorities and potential areas of alignment is essential for framing the group's advocacy efforts effectively.

Next, the group should clearly define the issue they wish to address and identify specific policy changes they are advocating for. This may involve conducting research, gathering data, and consulting with experts to develop evidence-based recommendations. The group should be ready to articulate how the changes align with their values and mission.

When approaching the policymaker, the group should aim to establish a constructive and collaborative relationship built on mutual respect and shared goals. This may involve requesting a meeting or phone call to discuss the issue in detail, providing relevant information and resources to support the group's position, and actively listening to the policymaker's perspective and concerns.

During the conversation, the group should effectively communicate their message using clear and persuasive language to explain why the proposed policy changes are necessary. This may involve sharing personal stories,

testimonials, and examples from the community to illustrate the real-world impact of the issue and the potential benefits of the proposed solutions.

After the initial meeting, the group should follow up with the policymaker to provide any additional information or answer questions that may arise. It is essential to maintain open lines of communication and continue to build rapport with them over time, as advocacy efforts often require ongoing engagement and relationship-building to achieve meaningful change.

Throughout the advocacy process, the group should also seek to engage and mobilize their community members and supporters to advocate for the proposed policy changes. This may involve organizing letter-writing campaigns, petition drives, or public events to raise awareness and build momentum around the issue.

By approaching lawmakers with a well-researched and strategic plan, mutual aid groups can effectively advocate for changes to public policy that advance their mission. Collaboration, persistence, and community mobilization are key.

Voting & Harm Reduction

Despite the prevalence of corruption in today's political system, it remains crucial for citizens to vote in elections, particularly at the local level. Local elections have a direct impact on communities, influencing policy decisions related to education, public safety, infrastructure, and other essential services. While systemic issues may erode trust in the political process, voting provides an opportunity for citizens to hold elected officials accountable.

In the context of voting for undesirable candidates, **harm reduction** refers to the strategic decision by voters to support a candidate who may not align perfectly with their values or policy preferences but is perceived as "the lesser of two evils" compared to their opponents. This approach recognizes that in some electoral systems, voters may face difficult choices between candidates who do not fully represent their ideals.

Harm reduction typically involves weighing the potential damage associated with each candidate's policies, track record, or character and voting for whomever poses the least harm. This may involve compromising on certain issues or making tactical voting decisions to prevent the election of a candidate deemed more destructive or extreme.

Critics of harm reduction voting argue that it perpetuates a "lesser evil" mentality and fails to hold politicians accountable for their actions or advance progressive agendas. They contend that by settling for incremental change or compromising on fundamental principles, harm reduction voting may perpetuate the status quo and undermine efforts to build more transformative political movements.

However, proponents of harm reduction voting argue that it is a pragmatic and strategic approach to electoral politics, particularly in situations where the stakes are high and the alternatives are perceived as worse. They argue that by prioritizing harm reduction over ideological purity, voters can help prevent or mitigate the worst outcomes and create space for future progress and change.

Ultimately, the decision to engage in harm reduction voting is a deeply personal and context-specific choice—shaped by individual values, priorities, and beliefs about the role of electoral politics in effecting social change. While it may involve difficult compromises and trade-offs, harm reduction voting reflects a practical approach to navigating the complexities of electoral politics and advancing broader goals of justice, equity, and social transformation.

Taking Over Local Government

Mutual aid groups may find it more feasible to influence and engage with government institutions at the local level compared to the state and federal levels. Local governments are smaller in scale, with fewer bureaucratic barriers and a greater degree of accessibility.

Also, local elections typically have low barriers to entry, allowing community members—including mutual aid group members—to run for office and secure positions on city councils, school boards, and other local bodies. This proximity enables groups to more effectively advocate for their priorities, influence decision-making processes, and implement community-driven initiatives.

One approach is for mutual aid groups to organize candidate recruitment and training programs aimed at empowering community members to become effective leaders within local government. These programs can offer guidance on campaign strategy, fundraising, public speaking, and grassroots organizing, equipping aspiring candidates with the skills and knowledge needed to run competitive campaigns.

Mutual aid groups can also leverage their networks and outreach efforts to identify potential candidates who reflect the diverse voices and lived experiences of the community. By actively recruiting candidates from historically underrepresented or marginalized groups, mutual aid initiatives can promote diversity within local government and ensure that a broad range of perspectives are represented in decision-making processes.

Lastly, mutual aid groups can provide logistical support and grassroots organizing efforts to spread the word about endorsed candidates. This may involve canvassing neighborhoods, hosting meet-and-greets, organizing campaign events, and utilizing social media and other channels to build momentum and generate support.

By actively recruiting and supporting candidates who align with their values and priorities, mutual aid groups can play an important role in shaping the composition and direction of local boards and councils. Through strategic recruitment, training, and support, groups can empower community members to become effective advocates for social justice, equity, and community well-being.

Creating a Movement

Mutual aid plays a vital role in social justice movements by providing a grassroots framework for communities to support one another, address systemic inequalities, and advocate for collective liberation. Rooted in principles of solidarity and cooperation, these movements prioritize community-led solutions, direct action, and reciprocal support as essential strategies for challenging injustice and building alternative systems.

Mutual aid serves as a form of resistance against oppressive structures by challenging dominant narratives and redistributing power. By organizing collectively to meet their own needs and assert their rights, communities engage in acts of resistance that challenge the status quo and advocate for systemic transformation.

Creating a social justice movement requires strategic planning, grassroots organizing, and collective action. Here are some steps to consider when embarking on this endeavor:

1. Identify the Issue:
Begin by identifying the issue or cause that you are passionate about addressing. This could be anything from racial injustice and police brutality to environmental degradation or economic inequality. Conduct research to understand the root causes of the issue and the communities most affected by it.

2. Build a Coalition:
A successful social justice movement involves collaboration and coalition-building with diverse individuals, organizations, and communities. Reach out to like-minded activists, advocacy groups, and organizers to build a coalition around your cause. Engage in dialogue, listen to diverse perspectives, and find common ground to unite behind shared goals.

3. Develop a Clear Message & Vision:
Define the mission, goals, and values of your movement, and develop a clear message that resonates with people. Craft compelling narratives that highlight the urgency and importance of your cause, and articulate a vision for the future that inspires hope and mobilizes support. Use storytelling, visuals, and social media to amplify your message.

4. Mobilize Resources:
Funding, volunteers, and educational materials will be needed to support your movement's initiatives. Seek out funding opportunities from philanthropic foundations, grassroots donors, and crowdfunding platforms. Recruit volunteers to help with organizing, outreach, and advocacy efforts.

5. Organize Actions & Campaigns:
Plan a series of actions, campaigns, and events to raise awareness, build momentum, and pressure decision-makers to enact change. This could include protests, rallies, marches, boycotts, petitions, or letter-writing campaigns. Develop strategic actions that leverage media attention, public pressure, and grassroots mobilization to advance your goals.

6. Empower & Amplify Voices:
Center the voices and experiences of those most affected by the issue within your movement. Create opportunities for community members to share their stories, perspectives, and expertise, and empower them to take on leadership roles within the movement. Amplify marginalized voices through media outreach, public speaking opportunities, and storytelling initiatives.

7. Advocate for Policy Change:
Push for policy changes at the local, state, and national levels to address the root causes of the issue you are addressing. Research relevant policies and regulations, and develop targeted campaigns to influence decision-makers. Build relationships with elected officials.

Developing a Clear Message & Vision

A clear message and vision are essential components of successful social justice movements. Here are some examples of movements with compelling messages and visions:

Black Lives Matter (BLM):

The BLM movement emerged in response to systemic racism and police violence against Black communities. Its clear message centers on the affirmation of Black humanity and dignity, and its vision calls for an end to racial injustice and the creation of a world where Black lives truly matter. BLM advocates for police accountability, criminal justice reform, and investments in Black communities.

#MeToo Movement:

The #MeToo movement aims to raise awareness of the prevalence of sexual harassment and assault, particularly in workplaces and other institutional settings. Its message is simple yet powerful: to break the silence and stigma surrounding sexual violence and empower survivors to share their stories. The movement's vision is to create a culture of accountability, consent, and respect where all people can live free from sexual violence.

Sunrise Movement:

The Sunrise Movement is a youth-led movement advocating for bold action on climate change and environmental justice. Its message emphasizes the urgency of the climate crisis and the need for immediate and transformative action to address it. The movement's vision is a Green New Deal—a comprehensive plan to transition to a sustainable and renewable energy economy while creating millions of green jobs.

LGBTQ+ Rights Movement:

The LGBTQ+ rights movement advocates for equality for lesbian, gay, bisexual, transgender, and queer individuals. Its message is one of inclusivity and acceptance of diverse gender identities and sexual orientations. Its vision is a society where LGBTQ+ people are fully protected under the law, free from discrimination and violence.

Land Back Movement:

The Land Back movement's vision is to reclaim and steward Indigenous lands in accordance with Indigenous laws, customs, and traditions. It seeks to restore Indigenous sovereignty, autonomy, and self-determination over ancestral territories and sacred sites. The movement aims to address the legacies of colonialism, extractive industries, and environmental degradation by centering Indigenous land rights, environmental stewardship, and cultural revitalization.

The Power of Inspiration

Inspiration serves as a potent force within social justice movements, fueling momentum, fostering solidarity, and driving transformative change. At its core, inspiration ignites a collective sense of purpose and possibility, compelling people to envision a more just and equitable world and to take action to realize that vision.

One of the most significant ways inspiration manifests within social justice movements is through the stories and experiences of those directly affected by injustice. Personal narratives of resilience, resistance, and triumph in the face of adversity serve as powerful catalysts for empathy, connection, and mobilization. When people share their stories of struggle and survival, they not only humanize complex issues but also inspire others to join the fight for justice.

Inspiration arises from witnessing acts of courage and solidarity within marginalized communities and among allies. Whether it is frontline activists standing up to oppressive systems, grassroots organizers building coalitions, or everyday people engaging in acts of solidarity, these examples of collective action inspire others to join the struggle and amplify their voices in pursuit of change.

Art and culture also play a vital role in inspiring social justice movements. Through music, literature, visual art, film, and other creative expressions, artists and cultural workers capture the spirit of resistance, challenge dominant narratives, and envision alternative futures. Art has the power to evoke emotion, provoke thought, and spark dialogue—inspiring people to engage critically with social issues and imagine new possibilities for liberation and justice.

Direct Actions

Direct actions are purposeful actions taken by individuals or groups to bring attention to a particular issue, challenge unjust systems, or advocate for change. These actions are characterized by their immediacy, visibility, and direct engagement with the target of protest or advocacy. Direct actions can include protests, marches, sit-ins, blockades, strikes, boycotts, and occupations, among others.

One key aspect of direct actions is their focus on disrupting the status quo or challenging power dynamics. By directly confronting institutions, authorities, or policies perceived as oppressive or unjust, participants aim to raise awareness, generate public debate, and pressure decision-makers to address the underlying issues. Direct actions often aim to create a sense of urgency, highlighting the need for immediate action and amplifying the voices of marginalized communities.

Direct actions can also serve as acts of resistance, defiance, and solidarity, particularly in the face of repression or injustice. They provide individuals and communities with a platform to express dissent, assert their rights, and demand accountability from those in positions of authority. Direct actions can build collective power by bringing together diverse groups united by a common cause or shared grievances.

While direct actions can be confrontational and disruptive, they are also strategic tools for social change. By capturing media attention, mobilizing public support, and exerting pressure on decision-makers, direct actions can catalyze broader movements for justice, equality, and liberation. They demonstrate the power of grassroots organizing and collective action in challenging entrenched systems of oppression.

Mutual aid often plays an important role in direct actions by providing logistical support, solidarity, and resources to participants. Here are some examples of how mutual aid is exhibited in direct actions:

Street Medic Collectives:

Volunteer groups of trained medical professionals and first aid responders who provide medical care and assistance to protesters during demonstrations. They offer treatment for injuries, heat exhaustion, tear gas exposure, and other health-related concerns, often operating makeshift clinics or mobile first aid stations at protest sites.

Food & Water Distribution:

Mutual aid networks organize food and water distribution points to ensure that demonstrators have access to nourishment and hydration during prolonged protests. Volunteers distribute snacks, meals, and beverages to protesters, often relying on donations from community members and local businesses.

Legal Support Teams:

Legal support groups offer guidance, resources, and assistance to protesters navigating interactions with law enforcement or facing legal repercussions as a result of their participation in demonstrations. They may provide legal observers to monitor police behavior, offer know-your-rights workshops, and connect protesters with legal representation if they are arrested or detained.

Housing & Accommodation:

Mutual aid networks may coordinate temporary housing and accommodation for out-of-town protesters. They arrange for housing options such as community centers, churches, or private residences—ensuring that protesters have a safe place to rest and recuperate between demonstrations.

Childcare & Family Support:

Some mutual aid groups offer childcare services and family support initiatives to enable parents and caregivers to participate in protests while ensuring the well-being of their children. These efforts may include organizing childcare co-ops, providing family-friendly spaces at protest events, and offering resources for parents navigating the challenges of activism.

Emotional & Mental Health Support:

Mutual aid networks recognize the emotional toll of participating in social justice movements and provide peer support, counseling, and mental health resources to protesters. They create spaces for reflection, healing, and community-building.

Chapter Review

Systemic issues are deeply embedded in our society, often perpetuated by long-standing institutional practices and policies. These issues create persistent barriers for marginalized communities, making it essential for mutual aid groups to not only provide immediate relief but also to challenge and transform the structures that sustain these inequities.

Changing public policy is a key strategy in advocating for systemic change. Mutual aid groups can engage in advocacy by educating the public and policymakers about the impacts of harmful policies and the benefits of proposed reforms. This involves organizing campaigns, lobbying government officials, and collaborating with other advocacy organizations to amplify their message. By influencing legislation, mutual aid groups can work towards creating more equitable and just systems that better serve all members of society.

A social justice movement grounded in mutual aid principles encourages widespread participation and solidarity, creating a sense of shared purpose and community resilience. This involves mobilizing supporters through grassroots organizing, public demonstrations, social media campaigns, and educational events. By highlighting personal stories and shared experiences, the movement can build empathy and a sense of urgency, motivating people to join the cause.

Discussion Questions

1 Have you ever participated in a movement or campaign that sought to address a systemic issue? What was your experience like, and what impact did it have on your understanding of the issue?

2 Have you ever encountered resistance or opposition when advocating for systemic change? How did you address it, and what did you learn from the experience?

Chapter **12**

Interactions with Law Enforcement

The interests of mutual aid groups and law enforcement agencies are sometimes in alignment—and sometimes they are not. For example, during natural disasters or public health emergencies, both parties aim to ensure the safety and well-being of the community. However, when mutual aid groups participate in protests or acts of civil disobedience, this can put them at odds with law enforcement efforts to control or disperse crowds.

Mutual aid groups must navigate this complex relationship carefully. Building bridges where possible can enhance their effectiveness and reach. But they must also remain vigilant and critical of law enforcement practices that undermine their core principles.

A Delicate Relationship

In certain contexts, **law enforcement** agencies may align with the goals or activities of a mutual aid group, particularly when their efforts coincide with maintaining public safety or disaster response. However, in other instances, historical examples illustrate how law enforcement has been a formidable obstacle to mutual aid initiatives—particularly those challenging entrenched power structures or advocating for marginalized communities.

One such example is the case of the Black Panther Party (BPP) in the United States during the 1960s and 1970s. The BPP established initiatives to provide free breakfast programs, healthcare clinics, and other essential services to African American communities marginalized by systemic racism and poverty. These efforts were met with fierce opposition from law enforcement agencies at local, state, and federal levels.

In many instances, police actively disrupted and undermined the Black Panthers' mutual aid initiatives through surveillance, infiltration, and violent raids. Government agencies such as the FBI under its COINTELPRO program targeted the BPP and other civil rights organizations–employing tactics to sow discord, spread misinformation, and discredit their leaders. These actions were part of a broader effort to suppress movements for racial justice and maintain the status quo of racial oppression.

The history of police interference in mutual aid efforts underscores the complex relationship between law enforcement and community organizing. While there may be instances of collaboration or support–particularly in times of crisis–mutual aid groups operating in marginalized communities must remain vigilant of the potential for surveillance, harassment, and violence from law enforcement agencies. This highlights the importance of strategic planning, security protocols, and community solidarity in navigating interactions with law enforcement while upholding the principles of mutual aid and social justice.

Classifying Law Enforcement

Mutual aid groups may interact with a variety of law enforcement agencies and organizations that are responsible for maintaining public order and ensuring the safety and security of communities. Some common types of law enforcement include:

Police Departments:

Police departments are the primary law enforcement agencies in most jurisdictions, and they are responsible for enforcing local, state, and federal laws. They handle a wide range of duties, including patrolling neighborhoods, responding to emergencies, conducting investigations, and making arrests.

Sheriff's Offices:

Sheriff's offices are typically responsible for enforcing law and order in county-level jurisdictions. Sheriffs and their deputies may oversee a variety of functions, including serving warrants, operating county jails, providing courtroom security, and patrolling rural areas.

State Police/Highway Patrol:

State police agencies–also known as highway patrols–have jurisdiction over statewide law enforcement matters, including traffic enforcement, criminal investigations, and providing assistance to local law enforcement agencies. They often focus on patrolling state highways and interstates.

Federal Law Enforcement Agencies:

These agencies operate at the federal level and have jurisdiction over specific areas of law enforcement, such as immigration, drug enforcement, counterterrorism, and financial crimes. Examples include the Federal Bureau of Investigation (FBI), Drug Enforcement Administration (DEA), Bureau of Alcohol, Tobacco, Firearms and Explosives (ATF), and Immigration and Customs Enforcement (ICE).

Tribal Police:

Tribal police departments enforce laws on Native American reservations and tribal lands. They have jurisdictional authority within their respective tribal communities and often collaborate with federal, state, and local law enforcement agencies.

Specialized Units:

Many law enforcement agencies have specialized units dedicated to specific areas of enforcement, such as SWAT teams for handling high-risk situations, K-9 units for tracking suspects and detecting contraband, and cybercrime units for investigating digital crimes.

Motivations & Biases

The motivations behind law enforcement are multifaceted and can vary depending on the specific context, jurisdiction, and historical background. In theory, law enforcement is tasked with upholding laws, maintaining public order, and ensuring the safety and security of communities. However, the underlying motivations driving law enforcement actions are influenced by a combination of institutional objectives, societal norms, and individual beliefs.

One primary motivation behind law enforcement is the preservation of societal stability and the protection of citizens from crime and harm. Police officers can be driven by a sense of duty and commitment to serving and protecting their communities. They may view their role as essential in maintaining law and order, preventing criminal activity, and promoting public safety. This motivation is rooted in the belief that law enforcement agencies play a vital role in safeguarding the well-being of society as a whole.

Law enforcement may also be motivated by a desire for justice and accountability. Officers may be driven by a commitment to upholding the rule of law, ensuring that people are held accountable for their actions, and providing recourse for victims of crime. This motivation reflects a belief in the principles of fairness, equity, and the protection of individual rights within the criminal justice system.

However, it is essential to recognize that law enforcement motivations are not monolithic and can be influenced by various factors, including organizational culture, societal pressures, and individual biases. In some cases, law enforcement agencies may be motivated by political agendas, institutional priorities, or the pursuit of power and control. Systemic issues such as racial bias, discrimination, and corruption can also influence motivations, leading to disparities in policing practices and outcomes.

These systemic problems manifest in racial profiling, disproportionate use of force against marginalized communities, and unequal treatment based on race or ethnicity. Studies have consistently shown that people of color are disproportionately targeted by law enforcement, subjected to harsher treatment, and more likely to experience violence during police encounters. Instances of corruption within law enforcement—such as bribery, abuse of power, and collusion with criminal elements—also undermine public trust and confidence in the justice system.

Ultimately, understanding the motivations behind law enforcement requires a nuanced assessment of the complex interplay between institutional objectives, societal norms, and individual beliefs. While the overarching goal of law enforcement may be to promote public safety and uphold the rule of law, the ways in which these objectives are pursued and prioritized can vary significantly.

Protecting Capitalist Interests

Law enforcement agencies play a key role in protecting capitalist interests by maintaining social order, safeguarding property rights, and enforcing laws that uphold the economic status quo. In capitalist societies, the protection of private property and business interests is a fundamental function of law enforcement, as property rights are central to the functioning of the capitalist economic system. Law enforcement officers are tasked with preventing theft, vandalism, and other property crimes, thereby preserving the stability and integrity of the marketplace.

Law enforcement agencies often prioritize the protection of corporate assets and infrastructure during labor disputes or protests that pose a threat to capitalist interests. In cases where workers engage in strikes or demonstrations to demand better wages, working conditions, or corporate accountability, law enforcement may be deployed to maintain order, suppress dissent, and protect the interests of employers and investors. This often involves the use of tactics such as surveillance, intimidation, and even violence to deter collective action and preserve the profitability of businesses.

Additionally, law enforcement agencies may collaborate closely with corporate entities and industry groups to address perceived threats to business interests, such as intellectual property theft, fraud, or cybercrime. Through partnerships with private sector stakeholders, law enforcement agencies may allocate resources and personnel to investigate and prosecute crimes that jeopardize corporate profitability or undermine consumer confidence in the marketplace.

Overall, law enforcement's role in protecting capitalist interests reflects the broader societal dynamics of power and privilege, where the interests of economic elites and corporate entities are often prioritized over the rights and well-being of marginalized communities. While law enforcement agencies are tasked with upholding the rule of law and maintaining public safety, their close alignment with capitalist interests raises questions about accountability, equity, and the distribution of justice.

Militarization of the Police

The **militarization of police** refers to the process by which law enforcement agencies acquire military-grade equipment, implement military tactics and strategies, and adopt a militaristic mindset in their approach to policing. This trend has been increasingly visible in the United States, where police departments have been equipped with surplus military gear through federal programs, such as armored vehicles, assault rifles, and grenade launchers. Through the 1033 program, eligible law enforcement agencies can request a wide range of military-grade equipment at little to no cost.

One prominent example of police militarization is the use of SWAT (Special Weapons and Tactics) teams for routine law enforcement activities. Initially created to respond to high-risk situations, such as hostage rescues and armed standoffs, SWAT teams are now routinely deployed for low-level drug raids, serving search warrants, and executing arrests. This militarized approach to policing has led to a rise in violent confrontations between law enforcement and civilians, often resulting in unnecessary injury and loss of life.

The use of military tactics and equipment by police has also contributed to the erosion of trust between law enforcement agencies and the communities they serve, particularly in marginalized and minority communities. The deployment of armored vehicles, riot gear, and chemical agents during protests and demonstrations can escalate tensions and further inflame public outrage, undermining efforts to build positive relationships between police and the community.

The militarization of police has subsequently raised concerns about the erosion of civil liberties and the expansion of state power. The use of surveillance technologies–such as drones and facial recognition software–for tracking the movements of citizens has raised significant privacy concerns. Additionally, the use of military tactics and equipment in domestic policing blurs the line between law enforcement and the military, raising questions about the appropriate role of police in a democratic society and the potential for abuse of power.

Overall, the militarization of police represents a troubling trend that threatens to undermine the principles of community-oriented policing, civil liberties, and democratic governance. Addressing this issue requires a reevaluation of policing practices, as well as new policies that prioritize de-escalation, community engagement, and respect for human rights.

Finding Common Ground

While mutual aid groups and law enforcement may seem to operate in disparate spheres, there are instances where their interests can align–particularly in matters related to public safety and disaster response. In emergency situations like natural disasters, accidents, or public health crises, both mutual aid groups and law enforcement share a common goal of ensuring the safety and security of communities. In these scenarios, collaboration between mutual aid groups and law enforcement can enhance coordination efforts, facilitate resource allocation, and optimize response efforts to address immediate needs and mitigate potential risks.

It is important to recognize that law enforcement officers and agents are people with their own beliefs, values, and experiences, and they are not monolithic in their attitudes or behaviors. While the institution of law enforcement is associated with upholding the status quo and protecting the interests of the powerful, individual officers can also be sympathetic to social justice movements and may even choose to defect from oppressive systems.

There have been numerous instances throughout history where law enforcement officers have defected or shown solidarity with social justice movements. For example, during the civil rights movement in the United States, there were police officers who refused to enforce unjust laws or used their positions to support protesters advocating for racial equality. Similarly, during protests against oppressive regimes or authoritarian governments, there have been instances where law enforcement officers have refused orders to use excessive force against demonstrators and instead joined the cause for democracy and human rights.

Additionally, there are law enforcement officers who advocate for reform from within the system. They may push for changes to department policies, training protocols, and community engagement strategies to promote transparency, accountability, and respect for civil liberties. Some officers may even become whistleblowers, exposing corruption or misconduct within their own departments.

In summary, mutual aid groups should keep these factors in mind when interacting with law enforcement. While cooperation can lead to more coordinated and efficient support in emergencies, groups should be aware of potential conflicts in other situations. By balancing collaboration with caution, groups can maximize their impact while safeguarding their independence.

Section 2

Know Your Rights

When interacting with law enforcement, mutual aid groups should understand their rights and responsibilities in order to ensure their personal safety, protect their civil liberties, and promote accountability in policing practices. People have constitutionally protected rights under the Bill of Rights. Being aware of these rights empowers us to assert them effectively during encounters with law enforcement, safeguarding against potential abuses of power.

While people have the right to assert their legal rights, they also have a responsibility to comply with lawful orders and directives from law enforcement officers. Respecting lawful commands, maintaining a calm demeanor, and avoiding confrontational behavior can help to de-escalate tense situations and minimize the use of force by police.

In addition to knowing rights and responsibilities, mutual aid groups should also be informed about the procedures for filing complaints or seeking redress in cases of misconduct or abuse by law enforcement officers. This may involve documenting the details of the encounter, gathering evidence such as witness statements or video recordings, and reporting the incident to the appropriate oversight body, such as a civilian review board or internal affairs division.

If you find yourself confronted by law enforcement in the United States, here are the key rights you should be aware of:

Right to Remain Silent:

You have the right to remain silent. You do not have to answer any questions from the police or other law enforcement officers. You can simply say, "I am exercising my right to remain silent."

Right to an Attorney:

If you are arrested, you have the right to speak to an attorney. You can request an attorney immediately and refuse to answer any questions until your attorney is present. If you cannot afford an attorney, one will be provided for you.

Right to Refuse Searches:

You have the right to refuse consent to a search of yourself, your car, or your home. If law enforcement does not have a warrant or probable cause, they generally cannot search your property without your consent.

Right to Know the Reason for Arrest:

If you are being arrested, you have the right to know why. Ask the officers to tell you the specific reason for your arrest.

Right to a Phone Call:

After being arrested, you generally have the right to make a phone call. This can be used to contact a lawyer, family member, or friend.

Right to be Free from Excessive Force:

Law enforcement officers are prohibited from using excessive force. If you experience excessive force, try to remember as many details as possible and seek legal assistance afterward.

Right to Leave if Not Detained:

If you are not being detained or arrested, you have the right to leave. You can ask the officer, "Am I free to go?" If they say yes, you can calmly walk away.

Right to Record:

In many states, you have the right to record interactions with law enforcement officers as long as you do not interfere with their duties. This includes taking photos, videos, and audio recordings.

Knowing and exercising these rights can help protect you during interactions with law enforcement and ensure that any actions taken against you are lawful and just. If your rights are violated, it is important to seek legal advice as soon as possible.

Freedom of Speech

Freedom of speech—as enshrined in the First Amendment of the United States Constitution—is a fundamental principle that protects peoples' right to express their thoughts, opinions, and beliefs without government censorship or interference. This foundational right is essential for the functioning of a democratic society, as it enables citizens to engage in open dialogue, debate, and criticism of government policies and officials, as well as to advocate for social and political change.

At its core, freedom of speech encompasses a wide range of expressive activities, including verbal speech, written communication, artistic expression, and symbolic gestures. It protects not only popular or socially accepted viewpoints but also unpopular or controversial ideas that may challenge prevailing norms. By safeguarding diverse forms of expression, freedom of speech fosters intellectual diversity and the exchange of ideas, which are vital for a dynamic public discourse.

However, the right to free speech is not absolute and may be subject to limitations in certain circumstances, such as when speech incites violence, poses a clear and present danger to public safety, or constitutes defamation, obscenity, or hate speech. These limitations reflect a delicate balance between protecting individual liberty and safeguarding other important societal interests, such as public order, morality, and the rights of others.

In addition to constitutional protections, freedom of speech is also upheld by legal precedents, legislative safeguards, and societal norms that promote robust debate, tolerance of dissenting viewpoints, and a marketplace of ideas. While controversies and challenges to free speech rights may arise in various contexts—including online platforms, academic institutions, and public spaces—the principle of freedom of speech remains a cornerstone of democratic governance and individual liberty. It is a fundamental right that must be cherished, defended, and upheld to ensure the vitality of democratic societies.

Freedom of Assembly

Freedom of assembly guarantees people the liberty to gather peacefully, associate with others, and express their opinions collectively without interference or repression from the government. It is closely linked to freedom of speech and plays a crucial role in democratic societies by enabling people to engage in political activism, social movements, and public demonstrations.

Freedom of assembly encompasses a wide range of activities, including protests, marches, rallies, meetings, and other forms of collective action. It allows people to come together to express shared concerns, advocate for specific causes, and demand accountability from government authorities. By providing a forum for public discourse and dissent, freedom of assembly fosters civic engagement, political participation, and the expression of diverse viewpoints.

In democratic societies, freedom of assembly is protected by law and upheld as a fundamental human right. Governments have a duty to respect, protect, and facilitate peaceful assemblies, ensuring that people can exercise their right to gather and protest without fear of violence, intimidation, or arbitrary arrest. This includes providing adequate security, traffic control, and logistical support to ensure the safety and orderly conduct of public demonstrations.

However, like freedom of speech, the freedom of assembly is not absolute and may be subject to certain restrictions or limitations in the interest of public safety, national security, or the rights and freedoms of others. Restrictions on the time, place, and manner of assemblies must be reasonable, necessary, and proportionate to the legitimate aims pursued, and should not unduly infringe upon the exercise of this fundamental right.

Overall, freedom of assembly is an essential pillar of democracy that empowers people to engage in collective action, express dissent, and advocate for social change. It is vital for holding governments accountable, advancing human rights and social justice, and promoting a more inclusive and participatory society.

Right to Remain Silent

 The **right to remain silent** is a fundamental legal principle that protects individuals from compelled self-incrimination by ensuring they can refuse to answer questions or provide information to law enforcement or other authorities. This right is rooted in the principle of fair trial and due process—as enshrined in many legal systems around the world—including the United States Constitution's Fifth Amendment and similar provisions in other jurisdictions.

One of the most well-known aspects of the right to remain silent is refusing to answer questions posed by law enforcement during police interrogations. This right ensures that individuals are not coerced into making self-incriminating statements or confessing to crimes against their will. It allows people to protect themselves from potential legal jeopardy and ensures that any statements they do make are voluntary and not obtained through coercion or intimidation.

The right to remain silent also extends beyond interactions with law enforcement to other contexts, such as court proceedings and administrative hearings. In these settings, people have the right to refuse to testify or provide evidence that may incriminate themselves. This right is designed to safeguard against forced confessions, ensure the integrity of legal proceedings, and protect individuals' constitutional rights.

However, it is essential to note that the right to remain silent is not absolute and may be subject to limitations or exceptions in certain circumstances. For example, some jurisdictions have "stop and identify" laws that require individuals to provide their name or other identifying information to law enforcement during a lawful stop or detention. Additionally, failure to invoke the right to remain silent explicitly may be used against an individual in court as evidence of guilt.

Right to Counsel

 The **right to counsel** ensures people have access to legal assistance and representation when facing legal proceedings. This right is enshrined in the Sixth Amendment to the United States Constitution, which guarantees the right to assistance of counsel in criminal prosecutions.

Legal representation plays a important role in safeguarding individuals' rights and ensuring fair and equitable treatment within the criminal justice system. Attorneys provide essential guidance, advocacy, and support to people navigating complex legal processes—helping them understand their rights, options, and potential consequences.

The right to legal representation extends to criminal trials, civil litigation, administrative hearings, and appeals. In criminal cases, the right to counsel ensures that defendants have representation during all stages of the criminal justice process, from arrest and interrogation to trial and sentencing. Attorneys provide critical services such as conducting legal research, investigating the case, preparing defense strategies, negotiating plea deals, and representing clients in court.

Right to Refuse Consent to Searches

The **right to refuse consent to searches** is guaranteed by the Fourth Amendment to the United States Constitution. This right grants individuals the authority to decline consent for law enforcement officers to conduct searches of their person, belongings, or property without a warrant or probable cause. It serves as a critical safeguard against unreasonable searches and seizures and helps uphold the principles of privacy and personal autonomy.

In the United States, the Fourth Amendment requires law enforcement officers to obtain a warrant based on probable cause before conducting a search, except in certain limited circumstances. One of the exceptions to the warrant requirement is when individuals voluntarily consent to a search. However, the right to refuse consent provides people with the power to withhold consent and assert their privacy rights, even when law enforcement officers request permission to search.

Asserting the right to refuse consent to searches empowers people to protect their privacy, dignity, and personal property from unwarranted intrusion by law enforcement. By exercising this right, people can assert control over their interactions with officers and ensure that searches are conducted in accordance with constitutional protections. People should clearly and unequivocally communicate their refusal to consent to a search and avoid engaging in any actions or statements that could be construed as implied consent.

Prioritizing Safety

Mutual aid groups participating in social justice movements must prioritize safety in their interactions with the police, recognizing the significant risks posed by the modern capabilities of law enforcement agencies. In the 21st century, law enforcement entities have access to advanced weapons and surveillance technologies—which can escalate situations quickly and result in harm to both demonstrators and officers.

To prioritize safety, mutual aid groups should encourage de-escalation techniques and conflict resolution strategies. This includes training members on peaceful protest tactics, communication skills, and non-violent protest methods to minimize the likelihood of confrontations and mitigate potential risks. Groups can also establish clear protocols for handling interactions with law enforcement—including designating liaisons who can communicate with authorities and ensure that demonstrations remain peaceful.

It is crucial for mutual aid groups to stay vigilant and adaptive in their approach to safety, recognizing that law enforcement responses can vary widely depending on the context and circumstances. This may involve conducting risk assessments before participating in demonstrations, monitoring developments during protests, and being prepared to adapt tactics and strategies accordingly to ensure the safety of participants.

Mutual aid groups should prioritize the well-being and security of all participants involved in social justice movements, especially marginalized and vulnerable communities disproportionately impacted by police violence and systemic injustice. This requires centering the voices and experiences of these communities in decision-making processes, advocating for their rights and safety, and implementing measures to address their specific needs and concerns during demonstrations and direct actions.

In navigating interactions with law enforcement, mutual aid groups should be mindful of their legal rights and responsibilities (as discussed in the prior section), while also being prepared to assert these rights assertively and responsibly if necessary. By prioritizing safety, groups can contribute to the effectiveness and sustainability of social justice movements while minimizing risks.

Designating a Liaison

Designating a **liaison** to communicate with law enforcement can be a strategic approach for mutual aid groups participating in social justice movements. The liaison serves as a point of contact between the group and the police, facilitating communication, providing information, and helping to maintain a peaceful and productive environment during demonstrations.

The liaison's role involves establishing and maintaining open lines of communication with law enforcement officials before, during, and after events. This includes sharing details about planned demonstrations, routes, and objectives, as well as any concerns or requests for accommodations to ensure the safety and well-being of participants. By fostering a collaborative relationship with law enforcement, the liaison can help build trust, mitigate misunderstandings, and address potential conflicts before they escalate.

In addition to communication, the liaison plays a crucial role in de-escalating tensions and resolving conflicts between demonstrators and law enforcement. They act as a mediator, facilitating dialogue and negotiation to prevent confrontations. This may involve addressing concerns or grievances raised by both parties, advocating for the rights and safety of demonstrators, and seeking mutually agreeable solutions to any issues that arise.

Police Harassment & Violence

In their advocacy efforts as part of a social justice movement, mutual aid groups may incur police harassment and violence. Harassment can include discriminatory profiling, unwarranted surveillance, or intimidation tactics aimed at suppressing dissent and activism. In some cases, this harassment escalates into acts of violence, resulting in physical harm, injury, or even death.

Instances of police violence are fueled by systemic issues, such as racism, bias, and unchecked power dynamics within law enforcement institutions. People of color are disproportionately targeted by police brutality, reflecting deep-seated racial inequalities and historical injustices. Incidents of excessive force, racial profiling, and unjustified arrests perpetuate a cycle of trauma, fear, and mistrust between law enforcement and these communities.

Police harassment and violence pose significant obstacles to social justice movements. These incidents can deter people from participating in demonstrations out of fear of reprisal or retaliation. Police interference and suppression tactics can disrupt the peaceful expression of dissent and hinder the progress of grassroots movements striving for positive social transformation.

Law enforcement might harass or be violent toward participants in a mass demonstration in a variety of ways. Understanding these tactics can help protesters develop strategies to protect themselves and their fellow demonstrators:

Use of Excessive Force:

Police may use batons, rubber bullets, tear gas, pepper spray, and other forms of physical aggression to disperse crowds, often leading to injuries.

Arrests & Detentions:

Law enforcement may conduct mass arrests, sometimes without clear cause, detaining protesters for extended periods without access to food, legal representation, or necessary medical care.

Surveillance & Intimidation:

Authorities might use surveillance tools like drones, facial recognition technology, and undercover officers to monitor and intimidate demonstrators, creating a climate of fear and paranoia.

Kettling:

This tactic involves corralling protesters into a confined area, preventing them from leaving and often resulting in panic, heat exhaustion, or lack of access to basic needs like water and restrooms.

Verbal Harassment & Threats:

Police may use derogatory language, threats of violence, or intimidation tactics to provoke or demoralize protesters, aiming to dissuade them from continuing their demonstration.

Destruction of Property:

Law enforcement might damage or confiscate protest materials, personal belongings, and equipment to disrupt the demonstration.

Targeting Organizers & Leaders:

Authorities may focus on arresting or harassing key organizers and leaders of the protest to undermine the movement and disrupt coordination efforts.

Blocking Access & Communication:

Police might block access to protest sites, cut off communication networks (like cell phone service), or create checkpoints to control the movement of demonstrators and limit their ability to organize effectively.

Protective Gear for Demonstrations

Demonstrators often wear protective gear to mitigate the risks associated with participating in protests, particularly those that may involve confrontations with law enforcement or counter-protesters. Some common types of protective gear include:

Helmets:

Helmets provide protection for the head and are worn to reduce the risk of injuries from projectiles, baton strikes, or falls. Demonstrators may wear helmets made of hard plastic, foam padding, or other durable materials to shield their heads from impact.

Gas Masks:

Gas masks or respirators are worn to protect against the inhalation of tear gas, pepper spray, or other chemical agents deployed by law enforcement. These masks typically feature filters that remove harmful particles and irritants from the air.

Goggles or Safety Glasses:

Goggles or safety glasses protect the eyes from chemical irritants, projectiles, or debris encountered during protests. Clear or tinted lenses provide visibility while shielding the eyes from harmful substances and potential injuries.

Face Shields:

Face shields provide additional protection for the face and eyes against projectiles, baton strikes, or chemical agents. These transparent shields cover the entire face and are often worn in conjunction with helmets for comprehensive protection.

Body Armor:

Some demonstrators wear body armor—such as bulletproof or tactical vests—to safeguard against physical harm from projectiles, baton strikes, or other forms of violence. Body armor may consist of lightweight ballistic materials designed to absorb and dissipate the force of impact.

Knee & Elbow Pads:

Knee and elbow pads offer cushioning and protection for joints during protests, particularly when kneeling, crouching, or engaging in physical activities. These pads help reduce the risk of abrasions, bruises, or fractures in vulnerable areas of the body.

Heavy Clothing:

Demonstrators may wear heavy or layered clothing to provide additional protection against impact injuries, chemical irritants, or exposure to inclement weather conditions. Thick jackets, long sleeves, and durable pants can help minimize the effects of physical and environmental hazards.

Footwear:

Sturdy footwear, such as boots or closed-toe shoes, is essential for navigating uneven terrain, standing for long periods, or evading potential hazards during protests. Demonstrators may choose footwear with non-slip soles and ankle support to enhance stability and mobility.

Before and during protests, mutual aid groups should continually assess their specific needs and risks so that all members remain safe through the entire demonstration.

Getting Arrested

In social justice movements, demonstrations are common methods for raising awareness and pushing for change, but they can also lead to confrontations with law enforcement that result in arrests. Demonstrators might be arrested for a variety of reasons—including civil disobedience, trespassing, failure to disperse, and other charges related to disrupting public order. While many activists participate in protests with the understanding that arrest could be a consequence, such arrests often serve to highlight the urgency of their causes and garner public and media attention.

When someone gets arrested by law enforcement, the process generally follows several standardized steps, though specific details can vary based on jurisdiction and the nature of the offense. Here's an overview of the typical arrest process:

1. Detention & Arrest:
The process begins when law enforcement detains an individual. An officer can only make an arrest if they have probable cause to believe that the person has committed a crime. At the time of arrest, officers are generally required to read the individual their Miranda rights, informing them of their right to remain silent and their right to an attorney.

2. Transportation:
After arrest, the individual is typically transported to a police station or a jail facility. Here, they are booked, a process that includes recording their personal information (like name and date of birth), the details of the alleged offense, and taking fingerprints and photographs.

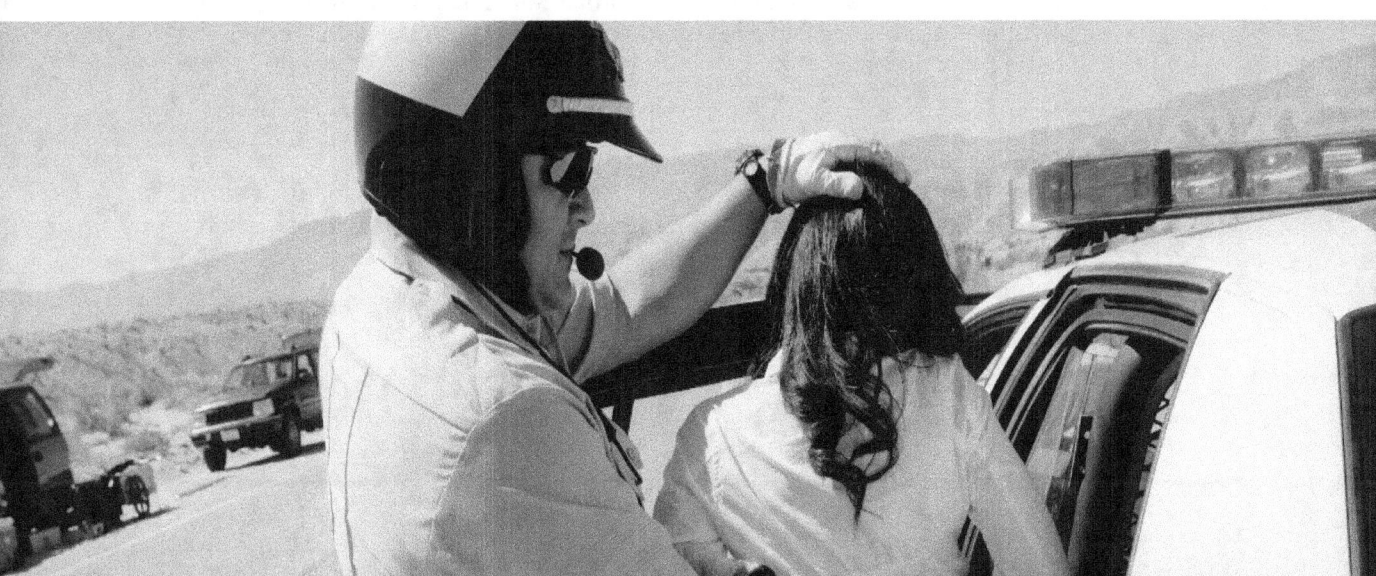

3. Booking:
During booking, the police will also conduct a search of the person to ensure they do not have any weapons or illegal substances. Their personal belongings are collected and stored until they are released.

4. Holding:
After booking, the arrested individual may be held in a jail cell. The length of time they can be held varies by location and the nature of the charges. For most minor offenses, the individual may be eligible for release on bail or bond shortly after booking.

5. Arraignment:
The next step is the arraignment, which must occur within a reasonable time after the arrest, often within 48 hours if the arrest occurs on a weekday. The charges against the individual are formally read in court. The defendant is asked to enter a plea (guilty, not guilty, or no contest). Bail may be set or modified at this time.

6. Bail or Bond:
If bail is granted, the arrested individual can pay the bail amount or post bond through a bail bondsman to be released from custody while awaiting trial. If they cannot afford bail or if bail is denied (typically in more serious cases), they must remain in custody.

7. Preliminary Hearing or Trial:
Depending on the jurisdiction and the nature of the crime, there may be a preliminary hearing before a trial is scheduled. This hearing is where the judge decides whether there is enough evidence to proceed to trial. If the case goes to trial, it will involve a more detailed examination of the evidence, witness testimonies, and legal arguments from both the defense and the prosecution.

8. Resolution:
The process concludes either with a trial, where a jury or a judge determines the guilt or innocence of the defendant, or through a plea bargain, where the defendant agrees to plead guilty in return for a lighter sentence or the dropping of some charges.

Each step in this process is governed by rules designed to protect the rights of the individual, including the right to legal representation and the right to a fair and speedy trial. Understanding these rights is crucial for anyone involved in an arrest situation. For mutual aid groups participating in demonstrations where arrest is a possibility, it is advisable to eat something before being detained. While detention centers do provide meals, it may be many hours before arrested demonstrators can eat again.

Responding to Surveillance

 Law enforcement agencies may conduct surveillance on mutual aid groups involved in social justice advocacy for various reasons, often influenced by perceived threats to public order, national security, or economic interests. Groups may attract the attention of law enforcement due to their activism, potential for civil disobedience, or perceived associations with radicalized groups. Law enforcement agencies might view mutual aid groups as potential sources of civil unrest, dissent, or subversion—prompting surveillance efforts to monitor their activities, communications, and organizational networks.

The rationale for surveillance on mutual aid groups may be influenced by concerns related to political ideology, social movements, or threats to the status quo. Mutual aid groups that advocate for systemic change, challenge authority, and engage in direct action may be seen as disruptive or destabilizing forces by law enforcement agencies seeking to maintain social control and protect established power structures. Mutual aid groups that operate in communities affected by poverty, crime, or social inequality may be subjected to surveillance as part of broader efforts to combat organized crime, terrorism, or other threats to public safety.

The methods used by law enforcement to surveil mutual aid groups can vary widely, ranging from overt monitoring of public activities and social media accounts to covert surveillance techniques such as wiretapping, electronic surveillance, and infiltration by undercover agents or informants. These efforts may be conducted through specialized units or task forces dedicated to monitoring political activism, domestic extremism, or social movements deemed to be potential threats to national security or public order.

Mutual aid groups may respond to surveillance with various strategies aimed at protecting their members, preserving their autonomy, and advocating for their rights. Here are some potential responses:

Transparency & Documentation:

Mutual aid groups can maintain transparency about their activities, organizational structure, and advocacy goals to foster trust within their communities and mitigate misconceptions or misrepresentations by law enforcement. Documenting instances of surveillance can provide evidence of potential civil rights violations and support advocacy efforts.

Security Culture & Digital Privacy:

Mutual aid groups can implement security protocols to protect the privacy and safety of their members, communications, and infrastructure. This may include using encrypted messaging platforms, practicing good digital hygiene, and conducting regular security audits to identify and mitigate vulnerabilities to surveillance or hacking.

Legal Advocacy & Know-Your-Rights Training:

Mutual aid groups can seek legal guidance from civil liberties organizations, legal clinics, or attorneys specializing in constitutional rights to understand their options for responding to the situation. Providing know-your-rights training to members can empower them to assert their rights during interactions with law enforcement.

Community Solidarity & Support Networks:

Mutual aid groups can build alliances with other community organizations, advocacy groups, and grassroots movements to strengthen collective resistance to surveillance and state repression. Building solidarity networks can provide groups with additional resources, support, and strategic guidance to navigate legal challenges, media scrutiny, or harassment.

Direct Action & Resistance:

In some cases, mutual aid groups may choose to engage in direct action or civil disobedience to challenge unjust surveillance practices or assert their rights in the face of government intrusion. This could include organizing protests, demonstrations, or public campaigns to raise awareness, mobilize support, and pressure policymakers to address concerns related to surveillance and state repression.

Documenting Interactions

By documenting interactions with law enforcement, citizens and mutual aid groups can play an active role in their governance, contributing to a more just and accountable system. Documenting interactions serves several important functions:

Transparency:

Video, audio, or written documentation of interactions with law enforcement can help maintain transparency in what might otherwise be he-said-she-said scenarios. It allows third parties—including the media, legal teams, and the general public—to witness the behavior and tactics used by police officers.

Accountability:

Documentation plays a crucial role in holding officers accountable for their actions. In cases where law enforcement actions may exceed their lawful powers or breach the regulations of appropriate conduct, having a clear, unbiased record can be instrumental in pursuing justice.

Legal Protection & Evidence:

In legal contexts, documentation of police interactions can provide critical evidence in both criminal and civil proceedings. Whether it is proving the unlawful behavior of an officer or defending the actions of protestors, video footage, photographs, and detailed notes can significantly impact the outcomes of legal cases.

For effective documentation, members of mutual aid groups engaging in demonstrations should:

1. Record from a safe distance without interfering with police operations.

2. Note the date, time, and location of the incident.

3. Use multiple recording devices if possible to ensure redundancy.

Taking Legal Action

Say a mutual aid group organizes a peaceful protest, but law enforcement officers use excessive force, resulting in injuries to several members. Despite the group having permits and following all legal requirements for the demonstration, the officers deployed tear gas and rubber bullets without provocation. Afterwards, the group might decide that legal action is necessary to hold law enforcement accountable, seek justice for the injured members, and prevent future abuses of power. Taking legal action also serves to highlight systemic issues within law enforcement practices and aims to push for policy changes to protect the rights of peaceful demonstrators.

When a mutual aid group decides to take legal action against law enforcement, securing the assistance of a qualified lawyer is a critical first step. The group should begin by identifying and documenting the specific incidents of harassment, violence, or misconduct experienced during interactions with officers. Collecting evidence—such as videos, photos, witness statements, and medical reports—will be essential for building a strong case. Detailed documentation helps the lawyer understand the extent of the issues and provides a solid foundation for legal action.

Once the evidence is gathered, the mutual aid group should start searching for legal representation. This can be done by reaching out to civil rights organizations, legal aid societies, or law firms that specialize in civil rights, police misconduct, or public interest law. Many of these organizations offer pro bono services or can refer the group to attorneys who have experience in handling cases against law enforcement. It's crucial to select a lawyer who not only has the relevant expertise but also shares the group's commitment to social justice and community advocacy.

The next step involves setting up consultations with potential lawyers to discuss the case. During these meetings, the group should present their evidence, outline their goals for the legal action, and ask questions about the lawyer's experience with similar cases, their approach to handling the case, and any potential costs involved. It's important to clarify whether the lawyer will work on a contingency basis, where fees are only paid if the case is won, or if there will be upfront costs. This clarity helps the group understand their financial commitments and ensures transparency.

Once a lawyer is selected, the group should maintain open and regular communication with their legal representative. This involves keeping the lawyer updated on any new developments, providing additional information or evidence as needed, and working closely to develop a legal strategy. The group might also want to engage in community outreach to garner support and raise awareness about their legal action, as public pressure and media attention can play a pivotal role in the success of such cases. Through careful preparation, strategic selection of legal counsel, and ongoing collaboration, a mutual aid group can effectively pursue justice against law enforcement misconduct.

Chapter Review

The relationship between mutual aid groups and law enforcement can be delicate. While both entities may have overlapping goals, such as maintaining community safety, their methods and broader objectives often diverge. Mutual aid groups typically focus on grassroots support and community empowerment, while law enforcement often operates to protect powerful interests. This fundamental difference can lead to tension and conflict, especially during protests or direct actions. Mutual aid groups need to navigate this relationship carefully, finding common ground when possible but remaining vigilant to the potential for opposition.

Knowing your rights is crucial when interacting with law enforcement. Understanding legal protections—such as the right to remain silent, the right to refuse unwarranted searches, and the right to legal representation—empowers people to protect themselves and their peers during encounters with police. Mutual aid groups should prioritize educating their members about these rights through workshops, informational materials, and regular training sessions.

Prioritizing safety is also important, especially during events that may draw police attention. Developing safety protocols can help mitigate risks. Groups should also have plans in place for de-escalation and conflict resolution to manage potential confrontations. By fostering a culture of vigilance and preparedness, mutual aid groups can protect their members as they advocate for social justice and reform.

Discussion Questions

1. Can you recall an instance where you or someone you know had an interaction with law enforcement? How did it affect your perception of the police and community safety?

2. What strategies do you think are most effective for maintaining safety during events where interactions with law enforcement are likely?

Chapter **13**

Mental Health & Well-Being

Being part of a mutual aid group means we are never alone in our struggles. In times of distress, whether personal or societal, having a network of supportive people can significantly enhance our mental health and well-being. Mutual aid groups operate on principles of solidarity and collective care, ensuring that every member knows they have a community to lean on. This sense of belonging can be a powerful antidote to feelings of isolation and helplessness.

Mutual aid groups often create safe spaces where members can share their experiences, feelings, and challenges without fear of judgment. This open communication helps in normalizing discussions about mental health, reducing stigma, and encouraging people to seek help when needed. Knowing that others genuinely care about our well-being and are ready to offer assistance can be lifesaving in challenging times.

An Emotional Toll

Environmental crises, economic instability, social inequality, and political unrest are just a few of the challenges of the 21st century, and these can have profound emotional repercussions on individuals and communities. These can contribute to heightened stress, anxiety, depression, and feelings of powerlessness. Disasters like wildfires, hurricanes, and droughts not only threaten lives and livelihoods but they also evoke fear, grief, and trauma as people grapple with loss and uncertainty.

Engaging in mutual aid, while deeply fulfilling, can also present challenges that impact mental health and well-being. The nature of this work often involves confronting systemic injustices, witnessing suffering, and advocating for change in the face of significant obstacles. As a result, organizers and participants may experience emotional exhaustion or burnout.

Constant exposure to stories of hardship and injustice can weigh heavily on mutual aid groups, leading to feelings of helplessness and despair. The relentless demands of organizing and providing support can also leave little time for self-care, relaxation, and personal rejuvenation. This can contribute to heightened stress levels and diminished resilience over time.

Acknowledging and addressing mental health within the context of mutual aid is crucial for supporting the well-being of participants and ensuring the sustainability of their collective efforts. Providing space for people to share their struggles, offering practical support, and promoting a culture of compassion can help alleviate their emotional burden.

Despite the challenges, mutual aid work provides opportunities for connection, solidarity, and collective healing. By providing a culture of support and empathy, groups can mitigate the negative effects of stress and promote resilience among members. Prioritizing self-care practices, seeking peer support, and accessing mental health resources can help members navigate the emotional toll of mutual aid work while sustaining their well-being in the long run.

Feelings of Doom & Gloom

In the face of systemic injustices and existential threats, people may experience profound feelings of hopelessness. The enormity of these issues can lead us to feel overwhelmed and paralyzed by the seeming futility of our efforts to effect meaningful change.

This sense of helplessness can be exacerbated by a pervasive narrative of doom and gloom in media discourse, which often emphasizes the scale and severity of global problems without offering tangible solutions or pathways for action. As a result, we may become resigned to the inevitability of societal collapse or ecological catastrophe.

Sometimes we lean into **nihilism,** which is a philosophy that says conditions in the social order are so bad that destruction would be desirable for its own sake, without providing any constructive program or possibility. This can result in apathy and disengagement from personal and collective endeavors. **Cynicism** may also manifest, which is a skepticism or distrust of others' motives and intentions. These attitudes can pose significant barriers to engaging in mutual aid, as we may begin to question the impact of our work and doubt whether our efforts truly make a difference.

At the same time, however, mutual aid offers a powerful antidote to such negative outlooks, as it provides a practical framework for collective action in the face of adversity. By coming together to address shared needs, we can transcend feelings of isolation and powerlessness, finding strength and resilience in community connections.

Mutual aid embodies a rejection of the narrative of inevitability that often accompanies feelings of despair, asserting instead that meaningful change is possible through collective effort. Participating in mutual aid initiatives can allow us to reclaim agency and autonomy—demonstrating that even in the darkest of times, acts of compassion and solidarity have the power to effect positive change.

In this way, mutual aid offers a beacon of hope amidst the challenges of the 21st century, reminding us that in moments of crisis and uncertainty, our greatest source of strength lies in our ability to come together as a community and support one another in the pursuit of a better world.

Fear, Anxiety & Paranoia

Fear and anxiety can significantly impact people participating in mutual aid efforts, particularly in contexts where there is a perceived threat to personal safety or security. In times of crisis or uncertainty—such as during natural disasters, political upheavals, or social unrest—we may experience heightened levels of fear about potential dangers or risks. This can manifest as anxiety or paranoia about our safety, as well as concerns about the stability of our community and future.

Within mutual aid groups, paranoia may arise from various sources—including distrust of external authorities, suspicion of surveillance, or apprehension about potential confrontations with opposing groups. People engaging in mutual aid activities may fear reprisals or retaliation from those who oppose their efforts, leading to heightened vigilance and caution in their interactions.

Fear and anxiety can also intersect with feelings of vulnerability and powerlessness, amplifying our sense of insecurity. This creates barriers to collaboration within mutual aid groups, as we may be hesitant to trust others or share information openly. Fear contributes to a sense of isolation or alienation, as we may withdraw or disengage from collective efforts out of concern for our safety or well-being.

All that being said, it is important for mutual aid groups to acknowledge these feelings of fear and paranoia with empathy and understanding. By encouraging open dialogue and creating supportive spaces for people to express their concerns and anxieties, groups can help alleviate feelings of isolation and promote collective care. By actively working to build trust and cultivate a culture of emotional transparency, groups can mitigate the effects of fear and enable members to participate more fully in collective action.

Grief & Trauma

Members of mutual aid groups may grapple with overwhelming feelings of loss, sadness, and distress in the wake of societal crises or personal tragedies. Whether mourning the loss of loved ones, dealing with the devastation of community infrastructure, or processing the trauma of violence or displacement, grief can profoundly shape our interactions within mutual aid contexts.

Grief and trauma may manifest in various ways, including emotional withdrawal, mood swings, or difficulty concentrating. We may also experience heightened sensitivity to triggers or reminders of past suffering, leading to increased vulnerability and distress. Unresolved grief and trauma exacerbates feelings of isolation, as we may struggle to connect with others and articulate our needs.

However, mutual aid groups can play a vital role in supporting members navigating grief and trauma by providing a compassionate and understanding community of peers. In an environment of empathy, validation, and nonjudgmental support, members can feel safe to express their emotions and share their stories. Mutual aid groups can also offer practical assistance and resources, such as accessing mental health services, securing housing, or rebuilding networks.

Mutual aid groups serve as catalysts for collective healing and resilience, harnessing the power of community solidarity to navigate through grief and trauma together. By mourning losses, honoring memories, and commemorating shared experiences, groups can create a sense of kinship and connection that helps extinguish individual suffering.

Guilt & Shame

In the context of mutual aid, we may experience guilt when we feel that we have not contributed enough or when we perceive ourselves as failing to meet the needs of others adequately. This guilt may arise from a sense of responsibility to support our community, coupled with feelings of inadequacy or self-doubt. Similarly, shame can emerge when we internalize negative judgments about our perceived failures or shortcomings. This leads to feelings of worthlessness or unworthiness, hindering our ability to fully engage in mutual aid activities.

Guilt and shame can be exacerbated by comparisons to others within the mutual aid group, especially if we perceive our contributions as falling short. Societal attitudes and expectations around self-sufficiency and individual responsibility may also contribute to feelings of guilt and shame, particularly for those who rely on mutual aid support themselves.

However, it is important to recognize that guilt and shame are natural human emotions that can serve as signals of our values and moral compass. Rather than allowing these feelings to paralyze or discourage us, mutual aid groups can create supportive and compassionate environments where we feel empowered to acknowledge and process our emotions.

By encouraging open communication and empathy, mutual aid groups can help alleviate feelings of guilt and shame, allowing us to channel our energy into collective action and meaningful contributions to our communities. Ultimately, by addressing these emotions with care and understanding, groups can cultivate a sense of belonging and purpose among members.

Signs & Symptoms

In these increasingly complex and uncertain times, experiencing mental health challenges is more common than ever. It's important we recognize that struggling with mental health is not a sign of weakness or personal failure. The stigma surrounding mental illness can often exacerbate feelings of shame and prevent people from seeking the help they need. But the truth is that mental health issues can affect anyone—no matter our age, gender, ethnicity, or socioeconomic status.

Experiencing mental health issues is a normal and natural response to the complex and often overwhelming circumstances of modern life. Just as we would seek medical treatment for a physical ailment, it is equally important to prioritize our mental well-being and seek professional help when needed. By destigmatizing mental illness and encouraging open and supportive conversations about mental health, we can create a more compassionate and understanding society where we feel empowered to seek help without fear of judgment.

Signs of Depression

Depression is a pervasive mental health condition that affects millions of people worldwide. Its prevalence is staggering, with estimates suggesting that over 280 million individuals of all ages suffer from depression globally. The condition can manifest in a variety of mild and severe forms, and it can significantly impair one's ability to function in daily life.

Signs of depression can vary from person to person, and individuals may experience a combination of emotional, behavioral, and physical symptoms. Some common signs of depression include:

Persistent sadness or feelings of emptiness:

People may experience prolonged periods of sadness, hopelessness, or despair, even when there is no apparent reason for their mood.

Loss of interest or pleasure in activities:

People with depression may lose interest in activities they once enjoyed, such as hobbies, socializing, or spending time with loved ones.

Changes in appetite or weight:

Depression can affect appetite, leading to significant changes in weight, either through increased or decreased eating habits.

Sleep disturbances:

Individuals may experience changes in sleep patterns, such as insomnia (difficulty falling or staying asleep) or hypersomnia (excessive sleeping).

Fatigue or loss of energy:

Depression can cause persistent feelings of fatigue, low energy levels, and difficulty having motivation to do anything.

Irritability or agitation:

Some people with depression may exhibit irritability, restlessness, or agitation, especially if their depression manifests as a result of anxiety.

Feelings of worthlessness or guilt:

People may experience intense feelings of worthlessness, guilt, or self-blame, even when there is no rational basis for these emotions.

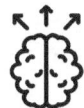

Difficulty concentrating or making decisions:

Depression can impair cognitive function, making it challenging to concentrate, remember details, or make decisions.

Physical symptoms:

In addition to emotional and cognitive symptoms, depression can also manifest with physical symptoms, such as headaches, digestive issues, or chronic pain without a clear medical cause.

Suicidal thoughts or behaviors:

In severe cases of depression, people may experience thoughts of death or suicide, or they may engage in self-harming behaviors as a way to cope with their emotional pain.

Experiencing one or more of these symptoms does not necessarily mean someone has depression, as many factors can contribute to changes in mood and behavior. However, if these symptoms persist for an extended period of time and significantly interfere with daily functioning and quality of life, it may indicate the presence of clinical depression. If you or someone you know is experiencing symptoms of depression, it's important to seek support from a mental health professional for evaluation, diagnosis, and treatment.

Social Media & Doom Scrolling

 Social media platforms have become integral parts of modern life, offering avenues for connection, information sharing, and community building. However, the pervasive use of social media has also brought about concerns about its impact on mental health, particularly through doom scrolling. **Doom scrolling** refers to the habit of continuously scrolling through distressing or negative news feeds, often resulting in feelings of anxiety and despair.

The constant barrage of alarming headlines, divisive content, and sensationalized stories on social media can contribute to a sense of emotional fatigue. Doom scrolling tends to amplify stress, as we become absorbed in a cycle of consuming negative information without reprieve. The curated nature of social media feeds can create unrealistic comparisons and foster feelings of inadequacy or FOMO (fear of missing out), further exacerbating mental health challenges.

Research has linked excessive social media use and doom scrolling to various mental health issues—including heightened levels of anxiety, depression, and feelings of isolation. The constant exposure to distressing content can disrupt sleep patterns, increase stress levels, and negatively impact overall well-being. Doom scrolling reinforces a sense of powerlessness about the state of the world, further fueling negative emotions.

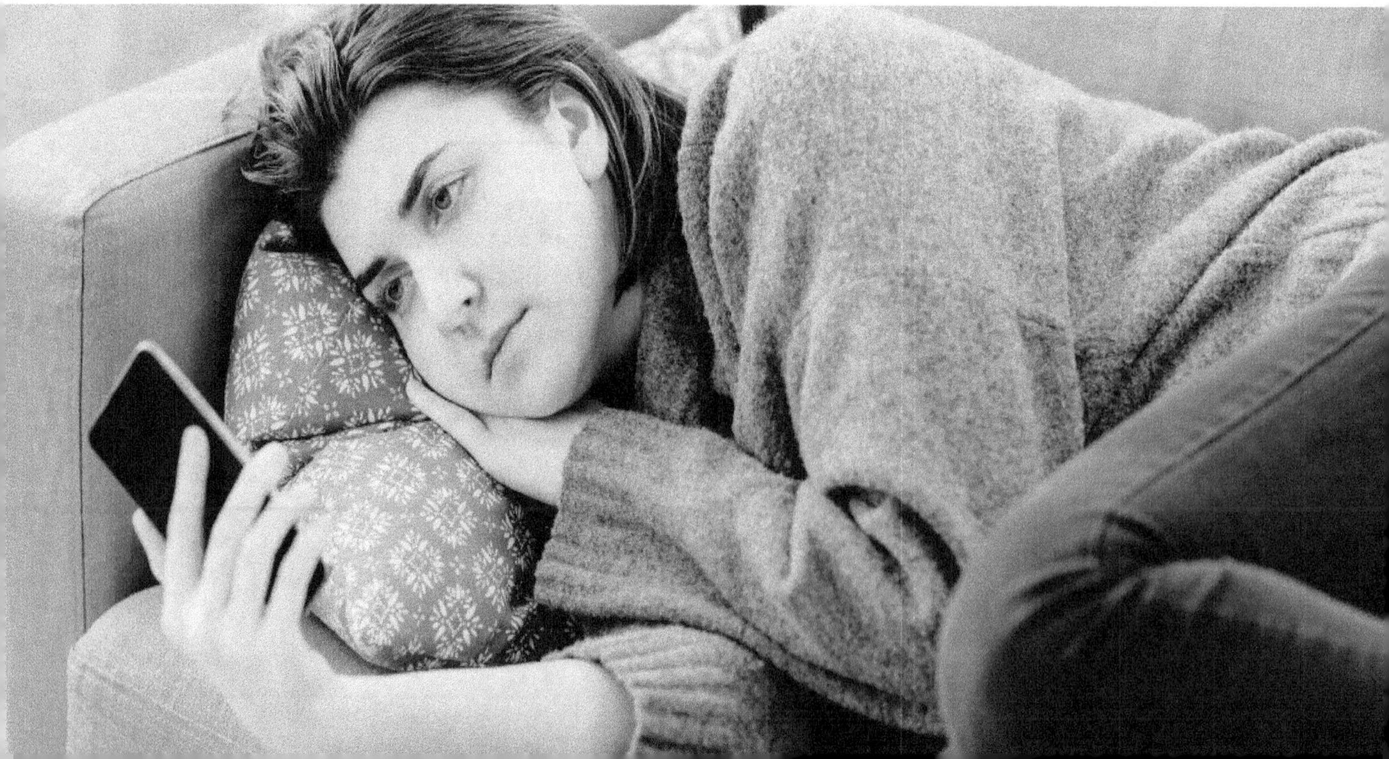

The good news is that we can take proactive steps to cultivate healthier digital habits. This may include setting boundaries around social media usage, limiting exposure to triggering content, or practicing mindfulness techniques to stay grounded. Engaging in activities that promote relaxation—such as exercise, hobbies, or spending time in nature –can also help. Ultimately, we should try to remain aware of our time online and back away when necessary.

Substance Abuse

Substance abuse can be caused by a variety of factors, including genetic predispositions, environmental influences, trauma, mental health disorders, and socioeconomic stressors. People may turn to substances as a way to cope with difficult emotions, alleviate pain, or seek temporary relief from stress. Societal norms and cultural attitudes towards substance use can also play a role in shaping someone's behaviors and perceptions. In mutual aid groups, it's important to recognize the signs of substance abuse in ourselves and others to ensure the well-being of all members.

Some common indicators of substance abuse include changes in behavior or mood, social withdrawal, neglect of responsibilities, financial problems, and physical symptoms, such as bloodshot eyes or slurred speech. Mutual aid groups should approach these situations with empathy, compassion, and non-judgment, as substance abuse is often a complex and deeply personal issue.

Creating a supportive and non-stigmatizing environment within mutual aid groups can encourage members to seek help when struggling with substance abuse. Providing resources, education, and access to professional support services can empower people to address their substance use issues and work towards recovery. Encouraging open communication and destigmatizing discussions around substance abuse can help break down barriers and facilitate honest dialogue.

In recognizing substance abuse in ourselves, it's important to reflect on our own behaviors, patterns, and motivations for using. Seeking feedback from trusted peers or professionals and being open to self-reflection can help us see problematic behaviors and take steps towards positive change. Practicing self-care, stress management techniques, and healthy coping strategies can support overall well-being and reduce the risk of substance abuse. Ultimately, by fostering a culture of care and understanding within mutual aid groups, we can create spaces where everyone feels empowered to address substance abuse and work towards healing and recovery.

Burnout & Fatigue

People engaged in community organizing often find themselves grappling with burnout and fatigue. The demands of addressing urgent needs—coupled with the emotional toll of confronting systemic injustices—can weigh heavily on our mental and physical well-being. As we invest our time, energy, and resources into supporting others, we may neglect our own self-care and neglect to replenish our reserves.

Burnout—characterized by feelings of exhaustion, apathy, and a reduced sense of efficacy—can undermine the sustainability of mutual aid initiatives. The persistent nature of systemic issues and the often slow pace of progress can contribute to a sense of disillusionment and frustration.

Mutual aid groups must therefore prioritize the well-being of their members and implement strategies to mitigate burnout and fatigue. This may involve creating a culture of self-care and mutual support within the group, encouraging members to prioritize their own well-being and seek support when needed. Groups should set clear boundaries and realistic expectations for involvement in activities to help prevent people from becoming overwhelmed.

Examples of burnout in mutual aid may include:

Physical Exhaustion:

People may experience physical fatigue and exhaustion from long hours of volunteering, organizing events, or providing direct assistance to community members in need. This can manifest as sleep disturbances, chronic fatigue, or other physical health issues.

Emotional Drain:

Constant exposure to the struggles and suffering of others, coupled with the inability to alleviate all the challenges faced by the community, can lead to emotional exhaustion. Volunteers may feel overwhelmed, despondent, or emotionally drained by the constant demands placed on them.

Reduced Motivation:

Burnout can lead to a loss of motivation and passion for the work, causing people to feel apathetic about their ability to effect meaningful change. This can result in decreased engagement in mutual aid activities and a sense of disconnection from the cause.

Cynicism & Disillusionment:

Over time, people may develop a sense of cynicism or disillusionment about the efficacy of their efforts or the possibility of achieving meaningful social change. This pessimistic outlook can erode morale and lead to feelings of hopelessness.

Decreased Resilience:

Burnout can compromise peoples' resilience in the face of adversity, making it harder for them to cope with stressors and setbacks. This may manifest as increased irritability, mood swings, or difficulty managing emotions.

Withdrawal & Isolation:

Some people experiencing burnout may withdraw from social interactions and disengage from mutual aid activities. They may feel isolated or disconnected from their peers and struggle to seek support or communicate their needs.

Physical Symptoms:

Burnout can also manifest in physical symptoms, such as headaches, gastrointestinal issues, or muscle tension. These physical manifestations may further exacerbate peoples' sense of distress and discomfort.

These examples illustrate the multifaceted nature of burnout in mutual aid settings and underscore the importance of addressing it proactively to safeguard the well-being of members and sustain the effectiveness of the group's initiatives.

Mutual aid groups can employ the following strategies to overcome burnout among their members:

Self-Care Practices:

Encourage members to prioritize self-care by engaging in activities that promote physical and mental well-being, such as exercise, meditation, hobbies, and spending time with loved ones. Providing resources and support for self-care can help members recharge and replenish their energy.

Establish Boundaries:

Encourage members to set boundaries around their involvement in mutual aid activities to prevent overcommitment and burnout. Emphasize the importance of balancing personal and volunteer responsibilities and respecting individual limits.

Rotate Responsibilities:

Distribute tasks and responsibilities among group members to prevent them from feeling overwhelmed or overburdened. Rotating roles and sharing the workload can create a sense of collective ownership and prevent burnout among specific individuals.

Offer Training & Skill Development:

Provide opportunities for members to enhance their skills, knowledge, and capacity to effectively contribute to mutual aid efforts. Offering training sessions, workshops, and resources can empower members and boost their confidence in their ability to make a meaningful impact.

Create Safe Spaces:

Cultivate a supportive and empathetic community within the mutual aid group where members can openly discuss their challenges, seek guidance, and receive validation and encouragement from their peers. Creating safe spaces for mutual support and solidarity can help alleviate feelings of isolation and burnout.

Regular Check-Ins:

Conduct regular check-ins with group members to assess their well-being, identify signs of burnout, and offer support as needed. Encourage open communication and provide opportunities for members to express their concerns, seek assistance, and access resources.

Promote Flexibility & Adaptability:

Remain flexible and adaptable in response to changing circumstances and member needs. Allow for adjustments to schedules, roles, and strategies as necessary to accommodate members' evolving needs and minimize stressors.

Encourage Time Off:

Encourage members to take breaks and prioritize time off to rest, recharge, and engage in activities unrelated to mutual aid. Acknowledge the importance of downtime in preventing burnout and maintaining long-term sustainability.

Seek External Support:

Encourage members to seek professional support from mental health professionals or counselors if they are struggling with burnout or mental health challenges. Provide resources and referrals for mental health services and destigmatize seeking help for mental well-being.

Achieving Balance

Being a part of a mutual aid group can significantly benefit members' mental health because it creates a feeling of belonging and community. We can connect with others who share similar values and goals, reducing our isolation and loneliness. The act of helping others and receiving support in return can enhance our self-esteem and provide a sense of purpose. Mutual aid groups often create safe spaces for open communication, where we can share their experiences and challenges without judgment. This supportive environment alleviates stress, builds resilience, and promotes a positive outlook on life.

Emotional balance is important for ensuring that mutual aid group members can sustain their involvement over the long term. This involves developing self-awareness and coping strategies to manage stress, anxiety, and other difficult emotions that may come with community organizing.

Asking for Help

Asking for help is a courageous and important step in taking care of our mental health and well-being. But it can also be one of the most challenging things to do, as it involves acknowledging vulnerabilities and reaching out to others for support. Whether it's seeking professional therapy, confiding in a trusted friend or family member, or sharing with a support group, asking for help is a sign of strength, not weakness.

It's essential to recognize that we all face struggles and challenges in life, and there's no shame in needing assistance to navigate difficult times. Asking for help is an act of self-compassion and self-care, demonstrating a commitment to our own well-being and growth. By seeking support from others, we can gain valuable insights, perspectives, and coping strategies that can help us overcome obstacles and move forward in a positive direction.

When asking for help, we should just be honest and transparent about our feelings and needs. Communication is key, and expressing ourselves openly and authentically can create deeper connections with those who care about us. It's also essential to remember that asking for help is not a burden to others but an opportunity to strengthen relationships and build a supportive community around us.

Ultimately, asking for help is a powerful act of self-advocacy and resilience. It's a recognition of our own worth and value, and it's a willingness to take proactive steps towards healing. By reaching out for support when we need it, we not only honor our own journey but also inspire others to do the same, creating a culture of empathy, compassion, and mutual support.

Coping with Stress

Emotional stress can have profound effects on the body, impacting physiological systems and contributing to both short-term discomfort and long-term health problems. When the body perceives a threat or experiences intense emotions, it triggers the release of stress hormones like cortisol and adrenaline, which prepare the body for a "fight or flight" response.

Chronic stress can lead to persistent activation of these stress pathways, resulting in elevated blood pressure, increased heart rate, weakened immune function, disrupted sleep patterns, and digestive issues. Over time, prolonged exposure to stress can increase the risk of developing serious health conditions such as cardiovascular disease, immune disorders, and mental health disorders like anxiety or depression.

Managing stress is essential—especially for those engaged in activism and community organizing—where people often face high levels of pressure and emotional intensity. Here are some effective strategies for managing stress in this context (also see "Burnout & Fatigue" earlier in this chapter):

Self-Care Practices:

Activists and mutual aid groups should prioritize self-care practices to replenish their physical, emotional, and mental well-being. This may include regular exercise, meditation, journaling, or engaging in hobbies that bring joy and relaxation. Taking breaks and setting boundaries are also crucial for preventing burnout.

Mindfulness & Relaxation Techniques:

Practicing mindfulness techniques such as deep breathing, progressive muscle relaxation, or guided imagery can help calm the mind and reduce stress levels. Engaging in activities that promote relaxation, such as listening to music, reading, or spending time with loved ones, can also be beneficial.

Healthy Lifestyle Habits:

Adopting healthy lifestyle habits—such as maintaining a balanced diet, getting adequate sleep, and avoiding excessive alcohol and caffeine consumption—supports overall well-being and resilience to stress. Regular physical activity can also help alleviate stress and improve mood.

Community Support:

Building a supportive network can provide valuable emotional support and solidarity. Connecting with like-minded people and sharing experiences helps alleviate stress and combat feelings of isolation.

Effective Time Management:

Activists and mutual aid groups often juggle multiple responsibilities and commitments, which can be overwhelming. Implementing effective time management strategies—such as prioritizing tasks, setting realistic goals, and delegating responsibilities when possible—can help people stay organized and reduce stress levels.

Maintaining Perspective:

It's essential for mutual aid group members to maintain perspective and recognize that they cannot single-handedly solve every social justice issue. Celebrating small victories, acknowledging progress, and focusing on long-term goals can help prevent feelings of hopelessness and burnout.

Seeking Support:

It's okay to seek help from mental health professionals or support groups when needed. Therapy, counseling, or peer support can provide a safe space to process emotions, develop coping strategies, and gain perspective on challenging situations.

Anger Management

Anger—or even rage—can serve as a powerful catalyst for people to engage in social justice movements or mutual aid groups. When we witness or experience injustice, oppression, or systemic inequalities, it can evoke intense feelings of frustration, indignation, and outrage. These emotions may fuel a deep sense of moral conviction and compel people to take action in pursuit of change.

While anger can serve as a powerful motivator, unchecked anger can also lead to conflict, hostility, and alienation within a mutual aid group. Learning how to recognize, understand, and channel anger constructively is essential for promoting positive interactions and achieving collective goals.

One effective strategy for managing anger in a mutual aid group is to cultivate emotional intelligence and self-awareness. By developing an understanding of the underlying causes and triggers of anger, members can better regulate emotions and respond more skillfully in challenging situations. This may involve practicing mindfulness techniques, such as deep breathing, meditation, or progressive muscle relaxation to calm the mind and body and gain perspective on the situation.

Also, encouraging open communication and conflict resolution skills within the group can help address issues of anger and prevent escalation into more significant conflicts. Creating a safe space for members to express feelings, concerns, and grievances can facilitate constructive dialogue and promote understanding and empathy. Establishing ground rules for respectful communication can also help prevent misunderstandings.

Grief Circles

A **grief circle** is a supportive gathering where people come together to share their experiences, emotions, and memories related to loss and grief. These circles provide a safe and compassionate environment for participants to express their feelings openly, without fear of judgment. Facilitated by a trained leader or an experienced peer, grief circles often follow a structured format that includes opening remarks, sharing rounds, and closing reflections. The goal is to create a space of mutual support and understanding, where each person's grief is acknowledged and respected.

Mutual aid groups can effectively incorporate grief circles into their activities to support members dealing with loss, whether it's the death of a loved one, the end of a significant relationship, or other forms of personal and collective grief. These circles align with the core principles of mutual aid by emphasizing solidarity and empathy. By organizing grief circles, groups can help members feel less isolated in their sorrow and provide them with tools to cope and heal. These circles strengthen the bonds within the group, as members come to understand each other's vulnerabilities and offer mutual support.

Grief circles can also be tailored to address specific needs within the community. For example, a mutual aid group might hold circles for those grieving due to community violence, environmental disasters, or social injustices. By addressing these unique contexts of grief, the group can offer more relevant support and advocacy. These compassionate gatherings can help members navigate the grieving process and emerge stronger together.

Joy Is an Antidote

 In today's world, it's often challenging to find space for joy amidst the overwhelming presence of systemic issues. Our collective anxiety can easily overshadow our daily lives, making it seem almost impossible to carve out moments of happiness and contentment. However, it's precisely during these tough times that making room for joy becomes not only important, but also essential for our mental health and well-being.

Joy is a powerful antidote to despair. It provides a respite from relentless stress and allows us to recharge. Finding joy in small moments, whether it's through a hobby, spending time with loved ones, or simply appreciating nature, can offer a sense of normalcy and stability. These joyful experiences remind us of what we are fighting for and help maintain our hope and motivation. They are not a distraction from the issues at hand but a necessary component of the strength required to address them.

When we share joyful experiences with others, we create bonds and a sense of solidarity that can make our mutual aid efforts more effective. Celebrations, communal meals, and moments of laughter and creativity can strengthen relationships within the community, making it easier to collaborate and support each other in challenging times. By intentionally creating space for joy, we acknowledge that life is multifaceted and that nurturing our spirits is just as important as addressing systemic issues.

Ultimately, making room for joy is an act of resistance in itself. It asserts that we refuse to let oppressive systems dictate every aspect of our lives. Embracing joy amidst adversity is a way to affirm our humanity and our right to a fulfilling life. It's a reminder that while we work towards a better future, we must also cherish and create moments of happiness in the present.

Chapter Review

Mutual aid work, while deeply fulfilling, can take an emotional toll on those involved. The constant engagement with community needs, systemic injustices, and traumatic crises can lead to feelings of burnout and exhaustion. Mutual aid participants often witness firsthand the struggles and suffering within their communities, which can be distressing and overwhelming. This emotional burden, if not properly managed, can impact mental health, leading to a decline in overall well-being and effectiveness.

Recognizing the signs and symptoms of mental health problems is crucial for mutual aid groups to support their members effectively. Symptoms like persistent sadness, anxiety, irritability, or changes in sleep patterns can indicate that someone is struggling. Other signs include difficulty concentrating, feeling detached from others, and a loss of interest in activities. By being aware of these indicators, mutual aid groups can intervene early and provide help, whether through professional counseling, peer support, or creating a more supportive environment.

Achieving balance is essential for maintaining mental health and well-being within mutual aid groups. Encouraging members to set boundaries, take regular breaks, and engage in self-care activities can help mitigate the emotional toll of the work. Creating a culture where taking time for oneself is not only accepted but encouraged, helps sustain long-term engagement. Also, providing a supportive community where members can share their experiences and feelings openly will create a sense of solidarity and mutual understanding. Balancing the demands of mutual aid work with personal well-being ensures that members remain healthy, resilient, and capable of contributing effectively over time.

Discussion Questions

1 Have you ever experienced burnout or emotional exhaustion in a volunteer or work role? How did you recognize these feelings, and what steps did you take to address them?

2 How do you incorporate self-care into your daily routine, especially when you are involved in emotionally demanding work? What activities or practices do you find most effective?

Chapter **14**

Future Trends in Mutual Aid

Imagine a society where mutual aid is the norm and communities are characterized by a strong sense of solidarity. People are more connected and invested in each other's well-being, leading to a decrease in social isolation and an increase in resilience and sustainability.

In this chapter, we lean more heavily on the power of artificial intelligence to forecast what a world would like if most of humanity practiced mutual aid. These sections are a series of edited dialogues with ChatGPT that present a vision of the future where we humans live more in balance—as well as the path to get there.

Our Present Circumstances

As humanity faces increasingly complex challenges—such as climate change, resource depletion, and social inequality—our collective survival will depend on how we adapt as a species. In this context, the principles of mutual aid are poised to become more important and necessary than ever before. Mutual aid encourages collaborative problem-solving and offers a powerful framework for addressing the interconnected crises of the 21st century.

It is becoming clear that we must shift from a paradigm of competition and individualism to one of cooperation and mutual support. As resources become scarcer and environmental pressures intensify, the idea of "every person for themselves" becomes untenable. Communities must work together, share resources, and support each other through difficult times. There is simply no other way. This shift requires a reorientation of values towards empathy and collective responsibility.

As the impacts of global challenges become more acute, traditional systems of governance may prove insufficient. In times of crisis, mutual aid networks fill gaps left by formal institutions—providing essential services, distributing resources, and offering emotional support to those in need. These networks operate on the principle of solidarity, recognizing that the well-being of each individual is interconnected with that of the entire community.

The rise of technological advancements and globalization has also made it easier than ever to connect with others and coordinate collective action. Mutual aid groups can leverage these tools to amplify their impact, mobilize resources, and build support across geographic and cultural boundaries. From crowdfunding platforms to online organizing tools, technology offers new avenues for mutual aid initiatives to flourish and adapt to evolving challenges.

In essence, the future of humanity hinges on our ability to recognize our interdependence and work together towards common goals. Mutual aid provides a roadmap for this collective endeavor, offering a path towards resilience, equity, and sustainability in an increasingly unstable world. As we confront the challenges ahead, embracing the principles of mutual aid is undeniably our best hope.

Societal Changes

Societal changes are occurring at a rapid pace, driven by a confluence of technological advancements, cultural shifts, and global challenges. One of the most notable changes is the increasing digitization and connectivity of everyday life. The proliferation of smartphones, social media platforms, and digital services has fundamentally transformed how people communicate, work, and interact with the world around us. This digital revolution has both empowered us and exposed us to new vulnerabilities, raising important questions about privacy, security, and the ethics of technology.

Another significant societal change is the growing awareness and activism around social justice issues. Movements advocating for racial justice, gender equality, LGBTQ+ rights, and environmental sustainability have gained momentum worldwide—challenging entrenched power structures. These movements have sparked important conversations about privilege, oppression, and the need for greater inclusivity and representation in all sectors of society.

Demographic shifts are also reshaping the fabric of communities and institutions. Aging populations, urbanization, and migration patterns are altering the makeup of cities and countries, leading to increased diversity and cultural exchange. These demographic changes pose both opportunities and challenges, requiring societies to adapt and create inclusive spaces that accommodate people from diverse backgrounds and experiences.

Additionally, the ongoing climate crisis is driving urgent calls for action to address environmental degradation and promote sustainable practices. Extreme weather events, biodiversity loss, and resource scarcity are threatening ecosystems and livelihoods around the world, underscoring the need for collective efforts to mitigate climate change and build resilience to its impacts. This existential threat has galvanized movements for environmental justice and sparked innovation in renewable energy, conservation, and sustainable development.

In summary, contemporary society is undergoing profound transformations driven by technological innovation, social activism, demographic shifts, and environmental challenges. These changes present both opportunities and obstacles as we navigate complex issues, such as inequality, injustice, and sustainability. Adapting to these changes requires a collective commitment to dialogue, collaboration, and innovation as we work towards a more equitable and ecologically balanced future.

Emerging Artificial Intelligence

Artificial intelligence (AI) is poised to have a transformative impact on humanity, with far-reaching implications across many aspects of society. As AI technologies continue to advance, they are expected to revolutionize industries, reshape economies, and redefine the way we live and work.

One of the most significant impacts of AI is its potential to revolutionize labor markets and employment patterns. AI-powered automation is expected to streamline and optimize various tasks and processes, leading to increased productivity and efficiency in industries ranging from manufacturing and logistics to healthcare and finance. However, the widespread adoption of AI-driven automation also raises concerns about job displacement and the future of work, as some roles become obsolete and others emerge in AI-related fields.

In addition to its economic impacts, AI is also expected to profoundly influence societal dynamics and human interactions. Algorithms already play a significant role in shaping our online experiences, from personalized recommendations on social media platforms to predictive analytics in healthcare and finance. As AI technologies become more advanced and pervasive, they have the potential to augment human capabilities, enhance decision-making processes, and revolutionize many aspects of everyday life.

However, the widespread adoption of AI also raises important ethical, legal, and social implications that must be addressed. Concerns about algorithmic bias, privacy violations, and the concentration of power in the hands of AI developers and tech giants have prompted calls for greater transparency, accountability, and ethical oversight in the development and deployment of AI technologies.

AI also has the potential to spread misinformation, amplify harmful content, and manipulate public opinion. Malicious actors can exploit AI-driven tools and platforms to disseminate propaganda, sow discord, and undermine democratic processes—leading to social polarization, distrust in institutions, and erosion of democratic norms. AI technologies can be weaponized for cyberattacks, surveillance, and autonomous warfare—posing serious threats to cybersecurity, privacy, and global peace.

Overall, the impact of AI on humanity will depend on how these technologies are developed, regulated, and integrated into society. While AI has the potential to drive innovation, improve efficiency, and enhance quality of life, it also poses significant challenges and risks that must be carefully managed to ensure a positive and equitable future. As we navigate the opportunities and challenges of the AI revolution, it will be essential to promote transparency and accountability so that AI serves the collective interests and well-being of humanity.

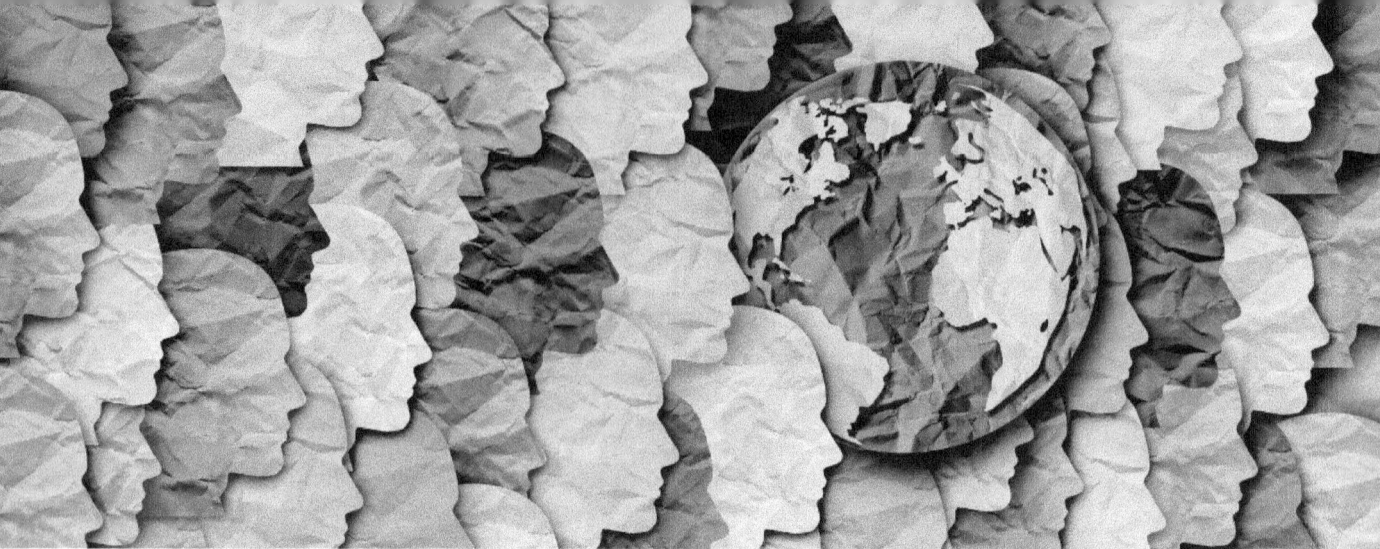

A Vision of the Future

If humanity were to fully embrace the principles and practices of mutual aid, the world would likely undergo a massive transformation characterized by increased empathy, cooperation, and solidarity. People would prioritize the well-being of others alongside their own—recognizing that collective flourishing is essential for individual happiness.

At the societal level, mutual aid would manifest in the form of robust social safety nets and support systems designed to uplift and empower marginalized and vulnerable populations. Access to healthcare, education, housing, and other basic necessities would be considered universal rights rather than privileges—ensuring that no one is left behind or excluded from essential services.

Economically, mutual aid principles would challenge the dominance of profit-driven models and prioritize the well-being of all members of society. Wealth and resources would be distributed more equitably, ensuring that everyone has access to the essentials for a dignified life. Cooperative enterprises and community-owned initiatives would flourish, providing opportunities for economic empowerment and shared prosperity.

In terms of social dynamics, mutual aid would strengthen community bonds and foster a culture of reciprocity. People would feel a greater sense of belonging and responsibility towards one another, leading to increased levels of trust and social cohesion. Communities would become more resilient in the face of challenges, as people come together to address shared concerns and build collective solutions.

In such a world, mutual aid would not be limited to formal organizations but it would permeate everyday interactions and relationships. People would naturally celebrate each other's successes and support one another during times of crisis.

Environmental stewardship would also be a cornerstone of a society guided by mutual aid principles. Communities would work collaboratively to protect and preserve the natural world, recognizing the interconnectedness of all living beings and the importance of sustainability for future generations.

Overall, a society grounded in mutual aid would be characterized by compassion, resilience, and collective well-being. By embracing the ethos of mutual aid, humanity would move closer to realizing its full potential—creating a more just, equitable, and compassionate world for everyone.

A New World Economy

The world economy would undergo a significant overhaul if humanity were to adopt the principles of mutual aid. Mutual aid prioritizes cooperation and the equitable distribution of resources—challenging the current economic paradigm that is often driven by competition, exploitation, and inequality. Here's how a new world economy might function:

Cooperative Enterprises:

Mutual aid would result in the proliferation of cooperative enterprises where workers collectively own and manage businesses. These cooperatives would prioritize the well-being of their members and the community over maximizing profits. Workers would have a say in decision-making processes, leading to more democratic workplaces and equitable distribution of wealth.

Resource Sharing:

Mutual aid encourages sharing resources based on need rather than hoarding or exploiting them for individual gain. In this economy, resources would be distributed among communities and regions to ensure everyone's basic needs are met. This could involve sharing food, shelter, healthcare, and other essentials through mutual aid networks and community initiatives.

Localized Economies:

Mutual aid emphasizes local self-reliance and resilience. Communities would prioritize producing goods and services locally, reducing dependence on long-distance trade and global supply chains. This localization of economies would promote sustainability, reduce carbon emissions, and strengthen community bonds.

Solidarity Economics:

Mutual aid principles would underpin a shift towards solidarity economics, where business activities are guided by social and environmental justice. This would involve supporting marginalized communities, empowering small-scale producers, and promoting fair trade practices that prioritize workers' rights and environmental sustainability.

Redistribution of Wealth:

Mutual aid challenges the concentration of wealth and power in the hands of a few. In this economy, wealth would be redistributed more equitably through progressive taxation, redistribution programs, and initiatives to address systemic inequalities. This would ensure that everyone has access to resources and opportunities for a dignified life.

Community-led Development:

Mutual aid encourages bottom-up approaches to development, where communities have agency and control over their own destinies. Instead of top-down policies dictated by governments or corporations, communities would identify their needs and collectively work towards solutions that benefit everyone.

Social Safety Nets:

Mutual aid prioritizes the well-being of all members of society, especially the most vulnerable. As such, there would be robust social safety nets in place to ensure that no one falls through the cracks. This could include universal healthcare, education, housing, and income support programs to guarantee a basic standard of living for all.

The widespread adoption of mutual aid could also lead to a reevaluation of the concept of work itself. In addition to recognizing the importance of paid labor, our society might place greater value on unpaid labor—such as caregiving, volunteer work, and community service. This recognition could translate into policies and practices that support and compensate these forms of work, contributing to a more holistic understanding of labor and its contributions to society.

Overall, a world economy based on mutual aid principles would be more equitable, sustainable, and humane. It would prioritize people and the planet over profits.

Environmental Sustainability

If humanity were to fully adopt the principles of mutual aid, it would have a profound and positive effect on environmental sustainability. Here's how:

Local Self-Reliance:

Mutual aid encourages communities to prioritize local self-reliance, reducing dependence on long-distance trade and global supply chains. This localization of economies would lead to fewer carbon emissions associated with transportation and logistics.

Resource Conservation:

Mutual aid promotes the responsible and equitable use of resources based on need rather than greed. Communities would prioritize conservation and sustainable management of natural resources, such as water, land, and forests to ensure their long-term viability for future generations.

Renewable Energy Transition:

Mutual aid initiatives would support the transition towards renewable energy sources, such as solar, wind, and hydroelectric power. Communities would invest in decentralized renewable energy systems, reducing reliance on fossil fuels and mitigating the impacts of climate change.

Regenerative Agriculture:

Mutual aid principles promote regenerative agriculture practices that prioritize soil health, biodiversity, and carbon sequestration. Communities would adopt organic farming methods, agroforestry, and permaculture techniques to restore ecosystems and improve food security.

Eco-friendly Infrastructure:

Mutual aid initiatives would prioritize the development of eco-friendly infrastructure, such as green buildings, sustainable transportation systems, and waste reduction programs. Communities would invest in energy-efficient buildings, public transit, and recycling facilities.

Environmental Justice:

Mutual aid recognizes the interconnectedness of social and environmental justice. Communities would address environmental injustices, such as pollution, habitat destruction, and climate change impacts that disproportionately affect marginalized people. There would be a focus on addressing the root causes of environmental degradation and ensuring equitable access to clean air, water, and natural resources.

Habitat Restoration:

Mutual aid efforts would prioritize projects to protect and restore ecosystems, biodiversity, and natural habitats. Communities would engage in reforestation, wetland restoration, and conservation initiatives to preserve ecological integrity.

Overall, adopting the principles of mutual aid would create a deep connection to the environment and promote practices that prioritize the well-being of both people and the planet. By working together with a common purpose, humanity can create a more sustainable and balanced relationship with Earth that will last for generations to come.

Sanity & Peace

Mutual aid encourages the dismantling of oppressive systems and structures that perpetuate violence and injustice, paving the way for a more balanced and equitable world. If humanity were to adopt the principles of mutual aid, it would likely lead to significant improvements in terms of sanity and peace. Here's how:

Conflict Resolution:

Mutual aid promotes cooperation, empathy, and communication, which are essential for resolving conflicts peacefully. Communities that practice mutual aid are more likely to prioritize dialogue and reconciliation over violence and aggression, leading to greater harmony and social cohesion.

Social Support Networks:

Mutual aid encourages communities to support one another during times of need. This sense of solidarity and belonging can have a positive impact on mental health, reducing feelings of isolation and loneliness that contribute to anxiety and depression.

Reduced Inequality:

Mutual aid initiatives aim to address systemic injustices and inequalities that contribute to social unrest and conflict. By promoting equity, mutual aid can help reduce the socioeconomic disparities that often fuel tensions, violence, and crime.

Empathy & Compassion:

Mutual aid encourages people to consider the needs and experiences of others. This shift towards a more compassionate worldview can lead to greater understanding, tolerance, and acceptance—ultimately promoting peaceful coexistence.

Community Resilience:

Mutual aid builds resilience within communities, enabling them to respond effectively to crises and emergencies. When people feel supported and empowered to help one another, they are better able to navigate challenges and adversities, reducing stress and anxiety levels.

———————————

Adopting the principles of mutual aid requires a cultural shift towards cooperation, solidarity, and collective well-being. As people embrace these values, they are less likely to engage in behaviors that harm others or perpetuate cycles of violence, leading to greater sanity and peace.

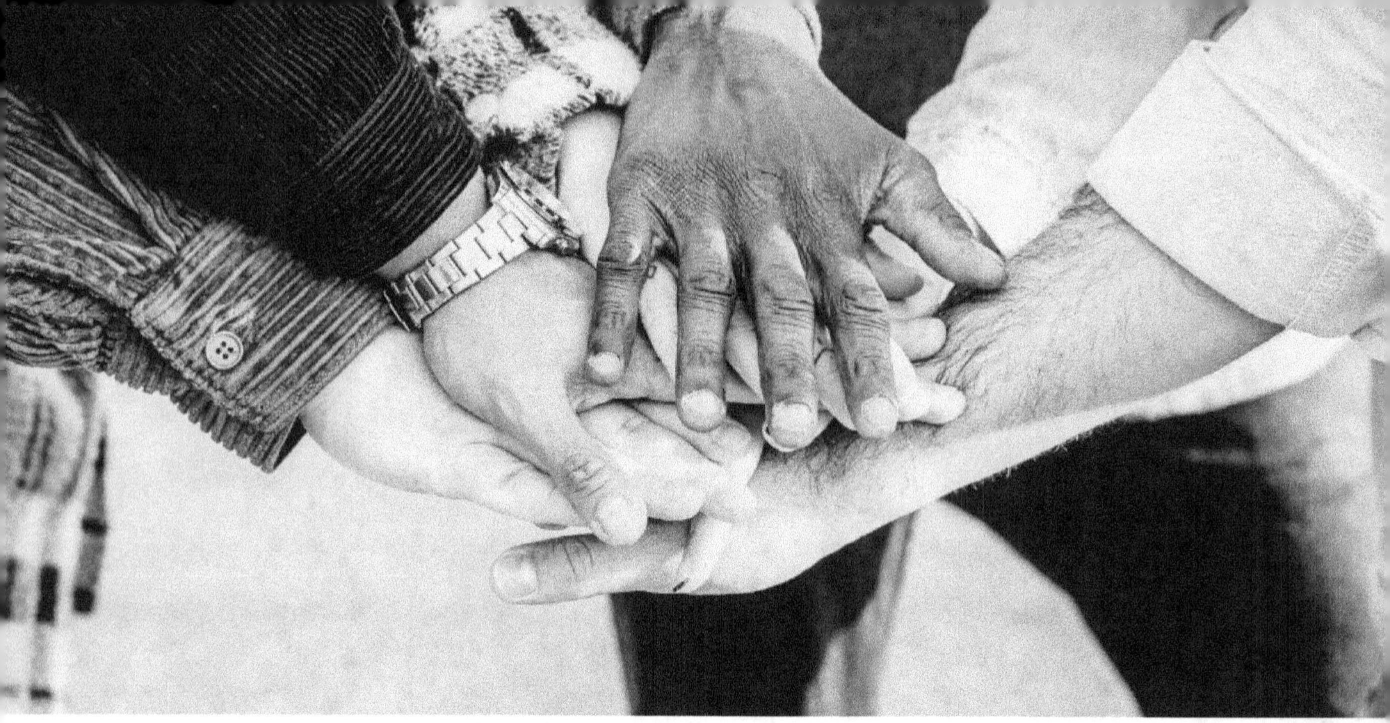

How We Get There

Achieving a society where the principles of mutual aid are universally embraced requires a collective effort that spans across communities, institutions, and systems. Here are some ways we can move towards this vision:

Education & Awareness:

Raising awareness about the principles and benefits of mutual aid is essential for creating a societal shift towards these values. This includes incorporating education on mutual aid into school curricula, promoting public discussions and forums, and sharing stories of successful mutual aid initiatives.

Community Organizing & Grassroots Activism:

Grassroots organizing plays a crucial role in promoting mutual aid at the local level. By mobilizing communities, creating mutual aid groups, and addressing specific needs, we can demonstrate the power of collective action.

Policy Advocacy & Structural Change:

Advocating for policies and structural changes that support mutual aid and address systemic inequalities is essential for creating a legal environment for mutual aid to thrive. This may include advocating for policies that prioritize social welfare, equity, and community resilience, as well as challenging systems of oppression and exploitation.

Building Inclusive & Accessible Spaces:

Creating inclusive and accessible spaces for participation in mutual aid is critical for ensuring that everyone can contribute and benefit from collective action. This involves actively engaging marginalized groups, prioritizing accessibility and diversity, and addressing barriers to participation.

Technology & Innovation:

Technology can enhance the reach, efficiency, and impact of mutual aid efforts. By harnessing digital platforms, data analytics, and other tools, we can amplify our initiatives, connect with broader networks, and overcome logistical challenges.

Crisis Response & Resilience Building:

In times of crisis or emergency, mutual aid often emerges as a spontaneous response to address immediate needs and challenges. Building resilience and preparedness at the community level can help us respond effectively to crises and demonstrate the power of collective action.

Ultimately, achieving a society based on mutual aid requires cultural and normative shifts that prioritize cooperation, solidarity, and collective well-being over individualism and competition. This involves challenging ideologies that perpetuate inequality and promoting alternative visions of society grounded in social justice.

By embracing these principles and taking concrete actions at individual, community, and societal levels, we can work towards creating a world where mutual aid is not only valued but deeply ingrained in the fabric of our social, economic, and political systems.

Data-Driven Decision-Making

In a world marked by uncertainty and volatility, embracing data-driven decision-making offers a beacon of clarity and direction amidst the chaos. Basing decisions on science and data is crucial for several reasons, especially as we navigate the complexities of the future:

Accuracy & Reliability:

Science provides a foundation of empirical evidence and rigorous analysis, enabling us to rely on accurate and reliable information. By grounding decisions in evidence-based practices, we can minimize uncertainties and make more informed choices with greater confidence.

Predictive Power:

Science leverages predictive analytics and modeling techniques to anticipate future trends, behaviors, and outcomes. By harnessing historical data and statistical models, we can forecast potential scenarios, identify risks, and devise proactive strategies to mitigate challenges and act on opportunities.

Complex Problem-Solving:

Many of the challenges we face are multifaceted and interconnected. Science offers powerful tools for understanding complex systems, analyzing root causes, and devising effective solutions that address underlying dynamics and interdependencies.

Ethical Considerations:

Incorporating scientific evidence and data analysis into decision-making processes helps mitigate biases, prejudices, and subjective judgments. By adopting a systematic and objective approach, we can uphold ethical principles, promote fairness and equity, and safeguard against unintended consequences or harmful outcomes.

Accountability & Transparency:

Basing decisions on science promotes accountability in governance, policymaking, and organizational management. By adhering to evidence-based practices and transparent decision-making processes, leaders can build and maintain public trust.

Innovation & Progress:

Science drives innovation by fostering curiosity, exploration, and experimentation. Data-driven insights fuel technological advancements, scientific discoveries, and creative problem-solving—driving progress across domains and shaping the trajectory of human development.

In an increasingly interconnected and interdependent world, addressing global challenges requires collaborative and evidence-based approaches. Science serves as a universal language that transcends borders, ideologies, and cultural differences, enabling cooperation and collective action to tackle shared threats and promote sustainable development. Overall, basing decisions on data empowers us to navigate the complexities of the future with greater clarity, foresight, and resilience.

Restructuring Government

If humanity were to adopt the principles of mutual aid, it would necessitate significant shifts in how governments function. Here are some key considerations for organizing governments in a mutual aid-oriented society:

Decentralization & Local Empowerment:

Governments would need to decentralize power and decision-making authority, empowering local communities to address their own needs and priorities through participatory processes. This could involve devolving authority to local councils, organizations, and cooperatives—enabling communities to take ownership of their development and well-being.

Participatory Democracy:

Governments would need to embrace participatory democracy models that engage citizens in decision-making processes, prioritize community input and feedback, and promote transparency and accountability in governance. This could include mechanisms like citizen assemblies, participatory budgeting, and deliberative forums to ensure that diverse voices are heard and represented in policy-making.

Social Welfare & Safety Nets:

Governments would need to prioritize social welfare programs and safety nets to ensure that all members of society have access to essential services, healthcare, education, housing, and income support. This could involve implementing universal basic income, universal healthcare systems, and robust social assistance programs to address poverty, inequality, and social exclusion.

Collaborative Governance:

Governments would need to adopt collaborative approaches that facilitate partnerships between government agencies, civil society organizations, businesses, and communities to address complex challenges and achieve shared goals. This could involve establishing multi-stakeholder platforms and collaborative decision-making processes.

Emphasis on Human Rights & Social Justice:

Governments would need to prioritize human rights protection, social justice, and equity in all aspects of governance, policymaking, and service delivery. This could include enacting anti-discrimination laws, advancing gender equality, and addressing systemic injustices to ensure that all people have equal opportunities and access to resources.

Environmental Stewardship:

Governments would need to prioritize environmental stewardship and sustainability in policy-making and governance practices. This could involve implementing climate action plans, promoting renewable energy sources, and adopting sustainable land-use practices to mitigate climate change, protect ecosystems, and ensure a healthy planet for future generations.

Conflict Resolution & Peacebuilding:

Governments would need to prioritize peaceful resolution of conflicts, invest in diplomacy and dialogue, and support grassroots peacebuilding initiatives to address root causes of conflicts and promote social cohesion. This could involve investing in mediation, reconciliation, and peace education programs to build trust and foster understanding among diverse communities.

———

Overall, organizing governments in a mutual aid-oriented society would require a fundamental reimagining of governance structures and practices to prioritize community empowerment, participatory democracy, social justice, environmental sustainability, and peacebuilding. By embracing these principles and working collaboratively to address shared challenges, we can create governments that better serve our communities.

Staying Resilient & Adaptable

To navigate the turbulent waters that potentially lie ahead, we must cultivate resilience and adaptability as our guiding principles. Resilience allows us to weather the storms of adversity, bouncing back from setbacks and forging ahead in the face of uncertainty. Adaptability empowers us to embrace change, to pivot when circumstances demand, and to evolve in response to shifting landscapes. Remaining resilient and adaptive in the face of future challenges requires a multifaceted approach, including:

Anticipate & Prepare:

Resilience begins with proactive planning and preparedness. By anticipating potential risks, disruptions, and uncertainties, we can develop robust contingency plans, diversify resources, and enhance adaptive capacities to respond effectively to changing circumstances.

Invest in Education & Skills Development:

Education and skills development are critical components of resilience-building efforts. By investing in lifelong learning and skill development, we can acquire the knowledge, competencies, and expertise needed to thrive in dynamic environments and navigate transitions with confidence.

Strengthen Social Connections:

Social connections and support networks play a vital role in bolstering resilience. By creating strong social ties, building community cohesion, and promoting solidarity, we can draw upon collective resources, share knowledge and expertise, and provide mutual assistance during times of adversity.

Promote Mental Health & Well-being:

Prioritizing mental health and well-being is essential for maintaining resilience in the face of stress, trauma, and uncertainty. This involves cultivating self-awareness, practicing self-care strategies, and accessing mental health support services to cope with challenges, manage stressors, and build emotional resilience.

Embrace Innovation:

By harnessing technology, encouraging creativity, and embracing innovative solutions, we can identify new opportunities, overcome barriers, and pivot in response to changing circumstances—driving continuous improvement.

Cultivate Environmental Sustainability:

By adopting sustainable practices, mitigating climate risks, and protecting natural resources, we can safeguard ecosystems, enhance resilience to environmental threats, and ensure a sustainable future for generations to come.

Having Hope

There are many reasons to be hopeful about the future, despite the challenges we face. Here are some points of optimism:

Advancements in Science & Technology:

Ongoing innovations in science and technology hold the potential to address pressing global issues, from climate change and renewable energy to healthcare and food security. Breakthroughs in fields like biotechnology and artificial intelligence offer promising solutions to complex problems.

Global Cooperation:

Increasing recognition of the interconnectedness of our world has led to greater international cooperation on issues such as environmental conservation, public health, and human rights. Collaborative efforts between governments, NGOs, and grassroots organizations are paving the way for more effective solutions to global challenges.

Social Movements & Activism:

The rise of social movements and grassroots activism around the world demonstrates the power of collective action to drive meaningful change. Movements advocating for racial justice, gender equality, LGBTQ+ rights, and environmental sustainability are challenging entrenched systems of power and creating greater awareness.

Youth Leadership:

Young people are playing an increasingly influential role in shaping the future, with youth-led movements mobilizing for action on issues ranging from climate change to gun violence. Their energy, passion, and commitment to social justice inspire hope.

Resilience & Adaptability:

Throughout history, humanity has demonstrated remarkable resilience and adaptability in the face of adversity. Despite facing unprecedented challenges, communities around the world continue to innovate, collaborate, and support one another.

Cultural & Artistic Expression:

Art, culture, and creativity have long served as sources of inspiration, healing, and resistance in times of uncertainty. Artists, writers, musicians, and cultural creators play a vital role in imagining alternative futures, demonstrating empathy, and promoting social change through their work.

Individual & Collective Agency:

Each person possesses the capacity to make a difference in their own lives and communities, and collective action amplifies our impact. By exercising agency, empathy, and solidarity, we can contribute to positive change and shape a more equitable and sustainable future.

445

Remaining hopeful about the future is essential for maintaining resilience and motivation, especially in the face of uncertainty and challenges. Here are some ways we can cultivate and sustain hope:

Focus on Collective Action:

Recognize the power of collective action and solidarity in effecting positive change. By coming together with others who share similar values and aspirations, we can amplify our impact and create meaningful progress towards a better future.

Celebrate Small Victories:

Acknowledge and celebrate small achievements, no matter how incremental they may seem. Each step forward contributes to a larger trajectory of progress and transformation.

Seek Inspiration & Role Models:

Look for sources of inspiration and role models who embody resilience, perseverance, and courage in the face of adversity. Learning from the experiences of others can provide valuable insights and encouragement.

Focus on Solutions:

Instead of dwelling solely on problems and challenges, we should our focus towards solutions and possibilities. Adopting a solution-oriented mindset can help generate creative ideas for addressing complex issues.

Practice Self-Care:

Prioritize self-care and well-being to maintain a healthy balance and perspective. Engage in activities that bring joy, relaxation, and fulfillment, and be mindful of physical and emotional needs.

Stay Informed, but Set Boundaries:

We should stay informed about current events and issues, but we must also be aware of how much distressing news and information we consume. Set boundaries around media consumption and prioritize sources of information that are credible and constructive.

Engage in Meaningful Action:

We should take meaningful action towards the causes and issues we care about. Whether it's volunteering with a local organization, participating in advocacy campaigns, or supporting mutual aid efforts, engaging in tangible action can instill a sense of purpose and agency.

Cultivate Gratitude:

We should cultivate a practice of gratitude by reflecting on the positive aspects of our lives and expressing appreciation for the people, experiences, and opportunities that enrich our journey.

———————

While the challenges ahead may seem daunting, it is important to acknowledge the seeds of hope and possibility that exist within our world. By nurturing these seeds and working together with compassion, determination, and vision, we can create a future that is brighter, more inclusive, and more sustainable for all of us here on planet Earth.

Chapter Review

Our society faces numerous challenges, including economic inequality, social injustice, and the climate crisis. Traditional institutions and systems often fall short, leaving many communities vulnerable and underserved. This has led to a growing recognition of the need for alternative forms of support and solidarity. Mutual aid, with its emphasis on community-driven collective action, is increasingly seen as a viable solution to address these systemic issues.

Mutual aid presents a hopeful vision of the future where communities are empowered to support themselves and each other. This future is characterized by interconnected networks, where resources and skills are shared freely and equitably. The principles of mutual aid—solidarity, reciprocity, and self-determination—offer a blueprint for a more inclusive and sustainable society. By prioritizing collective well-being over individual profit, mutual aid can help to dismantle oppressive systems and create spaces where everyone has the opportunity to thrive. This vision is not just about survival but about flourishing together as interconnected communities.

Making this vision a reality requires concerted effort and commitment. To advance mutual aid, we must invest in community education, build robust networks of support, and advocate for systemic change. This involves creating and sustaining mutual aid groups, forming partnerships with like-minded organizations, and developing strategies to mobilize resources effectively. It is essential to engage in continuous reflection and adaptation to ensure that mutual aid practices remain relevant and responsive to evolving needs. By embracing mutual aid, we can lay the groundwork for a more just, equitable, and sustainable society.

Discussion Questions

1 How do you envision mutual aid evolving in the next decade to address future societal challenges?

2 What does a more sustainable society look like to you, and how do you see mutual aid contributing to that vision?

Glossary

accountability: taking responsibility for one's actions, decisions, and commitments, and being answerable to others for their outcomes

active listening: the act of fully concentrating, understanding, responding, and remembering what is being said by someone who is speaking, demonstrating empathy and interest without interruption

anti-discrimination policy: a set of guidelines and rules implemented by an organization to prevent discrimination based on characteristics such as race, gender, age, or disability

antisocial business practices: behaviors by companies that disregard social norms, ethical considerations, or community well-being, often focusing solely on profit maximization at the expense of societal interests or values

articles of association: a legal document detailing an organization's objectives, rules for governance, and operational procedures

babysitting co-op: a community organization where parents trade babysitting services with one another without exchanging money, allowing each member to take turns caring for each other's children

board of directors: a group of individuals elected to represent shareholders or members of a company or organization, responsible for making decisions on policies, finances, and strategic direction

book club: a group of people who meet regularly to discuss books they have read and share their thoughts and insights

brand identity: the collection of elements—such as a company's name, logo, design, and messaging—that conveys the unique personality and values of a brand to its audience and distinguishes it from others in the field

burnout: a state of emotional, physical, and mental exhaustion caused by prolonged stress or overwork, often leading to a diminished sense of accomplishment and detachment from activities that were once enjoyable

buy-nothing group: a community-based organization where members share goods and services without monetary exchange

bylaws: rules and regulations adopted by an organization to govern its internal operations and management, outlining procedures for decision-making, membership, and other organizational matters

capitalism: an economic system characterized by private ownership of the means of production, where goods and services are produced for profit in competitive markets, driven by supply and demand

centralized volunteer management system: a structured and organized approach to overseeing and coordinating volunteers within an organization from a single, central platform

collective action: the effort by a group of people to achieve a common goal or address a shared issue, often involving coordinated activities and strategies

colonialism: the establishment, maintenance, and exploitation of colonies in one territory by people from another territory

communications hub: a central point or system within an organization or community that coordinates communications, ensuring efficient information dissemination and response during emergencies or operations

community assessment: a systematic process of gathering and analyzing information to understand the strengths, needs, assets, and challenges of a community

conflict of interest: a situation that occurs when an individual or organization is involved in multiple interests, financial or personal, that could potentially compromise their impartiality, objectivity, or decision-making integrity

conflict-of-interest policy: a formal document or set of guidelines that outlines how an organization or group handles situations where individuals may have competing interests that could potentially influence their decision-making or actions

conflict resolution: the process of addressing and resolving disputes or disagreements between individuals or groups through negotiation, mediation, or other methods to reach a mutually satisfactory outcome

consensus: a general agreement reached by a group as a whole, where all members support the decision even if it is not their first choice

cooperation: the process of individuals or groups working together towards a common goal, often involving mutual support, collaboration, and shared efforts

cooperative (co-op): a business or organization owned and operated by its members, who share profits and decision-making authority, typically to meet common economic, social, or cultural needs

coordination mechanism: a structured approach or system used to facilitate and manage communication, collaboration, and the allocation of resources among individuals or groups working towards a common goal or objective

core team: a small group of key individuals who are responsible for leading, organizing, and making strategic decisions for a project or organization

corporate malpractice: unethical or illegal actions by corporations that violate laws, regulations, or ethical standards, potentially harming stakeholders or the broader public interest

crisis intervention: immediate and targeted efforts to address and mitigate the impact of a crisis on individuals or communities, often involving mental health professionals, social workers, or trained volunteers

crisis management: the process of anticipating, preparing for, responding to, and recovering from events or situations that pose a significant threat to an organization, community, or individual

crowdfunding: a method of raising money for a project or venture by collecting small contributions from a large number of people, typically through online platforms

cultural competence: the ability to effectively interact with individuals from diverse cultural backgrounds, encompassing understanding, respecting, and valuing their beliefs, customs, languages, practices, and needs

cynicism: a general distrust or skepticism towards the motives of others, often accompanied by a belief that people are motivated purely by self-interest

data protection & privacy policy: an organization's procedures and practices for handling personal data to ensure compliance with privacy laws and protect individuals' information

de-escalation: techniques and strategies aimed at reducing tension, aggression, or conflict in a situation, typically involving active listening, empathy, and non-confrontational communication

depression: a mental health disorder characterized by persistent feelings of sadness, loss of interest or pleasure in activities once enjoyed, changes in appetite or sleep patterns, low energy, and difficulty concentrating or making decisions

direct actions: the proactive and often confrontational methods used by individuals or groups to achieve social or political goals outside of conventional institutional channels

disciplinary policy: the rules, procedures, and consequences for addressing misconduct or breaches of conduct within an organization, aiming to maintain discipline and uphold standards of behavior among members or employees

diversity: the presence of a variety of identities, perspectives, backgrounds, and experiences within a group or community

doom scrolling: the act of obsessively consuming negative news and information online, which can contribute to feelings of anxiety and hopelessness

emergency fund: financial reserves set aside specifically to cover unexpected expenses or financial emergencies, providing a safety net for individuals or organizations during times of crisis

empathy: the ability to understand and share the feelings and perspectives of another person

environmental exploitation: the unsustainable use of natural resources, often leading to degradation of ecosystems, pollution, and depletion of biodiversity

equity: the fair and just distribution of resources, opportunities, and outcomes for all individuals, regardless of their background or circumstances

evacuation plan: a structured and coordinated strategy outlining procedures and protocols for safely relocating individuals or groups from a potentially dangerous or threatened area to a designated safe location during emergencies or disasters

facilitator: a person who helps guide discussions, meetings, or processes to ensure they run smoothly and achieve their objectives

first aid: initial medical assistance and treatment provided to people who are injured or suddenly taken ill, typically administered before professional medical help arrives

flexible learning format: an educational approach that allows learners to access and engage with learning materials and activities at their own pace, location, and preferred time, often utilizing digital tools and resources for customization and adaptation

freedom of assembly: the constitutional right to gather peacefully and protest

freedom of speech: the right to express one's opinions and ideas without censorship, interference, or retaliation from the government or other authorities

free store: a community-based initiative where goods and services are provided to people without any monetary exchange

friendly society: an organization popular in the 19th and early 20th centuries that was formed by people who join together to provide mutual financial support, social benefits, and assistance in times of need

genderism: attitudes, beliefs, or practices that uphold traditional gender roles and reinforce the idea that one gender identity is superior to others

goods exchange: the process of transferring goods from one party to another in return for compensation, typically involving a transaction where items of value are exchanged based on mutual agreement and benefit

grief circle: a structured gathering where people come together to share their experiences of loss, express emotions, and support one another in processing grief and mourning

harm reduction: an electoral strategy where voters choose a candidate who may not align perfectly with their ideals but is perceived as less harmful or problematic compared to other candidates in the race

haters: individuals who express strong negative opinions or criticism towards a person, group, or idea, often without constructive feedback or valid reasoning

horizontal leadership: a leadership style where power and decision-making are distributed among all members of a group or organization rather than being concentrated in a single individual or hierarchical structure

imperialism: the policy or practice of extending a nation's authority over other countries, often through military force or economic domination

inclusion: creating an environment where all people are welcomed, respected, supported, and valued, and where diverse perspectives and contributions are actively sought and integrated

inclusive language: using words and phrases that avoid excluding particular groups of people based on gender, race, ethnicity, disability, sexual orientation, socioeconomic status, or other characteristics

intersectionality: the interconnected nature of social categorizations such as race, class, gender, and other forms of identity as they relate to systems of oppression and discrimination, creating overlapping systems of disadvantage or advantage

individualism: a social and political philosophy that favors freedom of action for individuals over collective or state control

intrinsic motivation: engaging in an activity for the inherent satisfaction or enjoyment derived from the activity itself, rather than for any external rewards or incentives

key performance indicators (KPIs): quantifiable metrics used to evaluate the success or effectiveness of an organization, project, or individual in achieving specific objectives

key stakeholder: an individual, group, or organization that has an interest or concern in a particular community or issue, and who can significantly impact or be impacted by the outcomes of decisions or actions related to that issue

labor union: an organization of workers formed to protect and advance their rights and interests through collective bargaining and other means

law enforcement: the agencies and personnel responsible for enforcing laws, maintaining public order, and ensuring compliance with legal standards within a jurisdiction

learning space: a physical or virtual environment intentionally designed to facilitate learning through interaction, collaboration, and engagement among participants

liability: legal responsibility for one's actions or debts, especially within the context of business or organizational operations

liaison: a person who acts as a link or intermediary between different groups, organizations, or individuals to facilitate communication and cooperation

logistics: the detailed coordination of complex operations involving the procurement, transportation, and distribution of goods or services to achieve specific objectives efficiently

marginalized group: people within society that experience exclusion, discrimination, or limited access to resources, opportunities, and rights due to factors such as race, ethnicity, gender, sexual orientation, socioeconomic status, or disability

material resources: physical assets and supplies that are used or distributed by organizations, businesses, or groups for various purposes such as production, operations, or support activities

menu of opportunities: a curated selection of roles, tasks, or engagement options offered to participants or members within an organization, providing a variety of ways to contribute based on interests and capabilities

meeting minutes: a written record of the discussions, decisions, and actions taken during a meeting

militarization of police: the process by which law enforcement agencies acquire military equipment, adopt military tactics, and increase cooperation with military forces

mission statement: a brief, formal summary of a mutual aid group's core purpose, goals, and values

mutual aid: a form of voluntary and reciprocal exchange of resources, support, and assistance among people within a community

mutual benefit proposition: an arrangement where all parties involved derive advantages or gains from the exchange or collaboration, ensuring that each participant receives value or benefits that meet their specific needs or objectives

neoliberalism: a political and economic ideology emphasizing free-market capitalism, deregulation, privatization, and reduced government intervention in the economy

nihilism: a philosophy that says conditions in the social order are so bad that destruction would be desirable for its own sake

organizer: someone who coordinates and mobilizes individuals or groups to achieve a common goal, often within social or political movements

outreach campaign: a strategic initiative aimed at reaching and engaging a specific audience or community through various communication channels to achieve specific goals, such as raising awareness, promoting a cause, or driving action

partner: an individual who collaborates with an organizer to establish a mutual aid group

patriarchy: a social system in which men hold primary power and dominate in roles of political leadership, moral authority, social privilege, and control of property

political corruption: the misuse of public power or resources by government officials or individuals in positions of authority for personal gain or to maintain power, often involving bribery, fraud, or other unethical conduct

polycrisis: a situation characterized by the occurrence of multiple simultaneous or successive crises, often requiring coordinated responses across different sectors

power structures: systems or hierarchies within societies or organizations that determine who holds authority, influence, and control over resources, decisions, and outcomes

press release: a written communication that provides information to the media about a newsworthy event, announcement, or development related to an organization, product, service, or issue

print-on-demand: a production method where products are made individually in response to customer orders, rather than in large batches or runs

privilege: unearned advantages or benefits granted to certain individuals or groups based on characteristics such as race, gender, socioeconomic status, or other factors, often resulting in systemic advantages over others

project management: the process of planning, organizing, and overseeing the completion of a specific project, ensuring it meets its goals, timelines, and budget

racism: prejudice, discrimination, or antagonism directed against someone of a different race based on the belief that one's own race is superior

reciprocal altruism: a theory in evolutionary biology and social psychology where individuals behave altruistically towards others, expecting that such behavior will be reciprocated in the future

reciprocity: the practice or principle of exchanging things with others for mutual benefit, where actions are returned in kind

reliability: the quality of being trustworthy and consistent in performance or behavior over time

resource inventory: a detailed list or database that catalogs all available resources within an organization or community that are essential for effective planning and allocation during crises or operations

right to refuse consent to searches: the legal right of individuals to decline or withhold permission for law enforcement or other authorities to search their person, belongings, or property without a warrant or probable cause

right to remain silent: the legal right of a person to refuse to answer questions or provide information to law enforcement or other authorities

risk management: identifying, assessing, and prioritizing risks followed by coordinated efforts to minimize, monitor, and control the probability or impact of unfortunate events or to maximize the realization of opportunities

scarcity mentality: a belief or mindset where people perceive resources, opportunities, or wealth as limited, leading to fear of not having enough and competition rather than cooperation

self-defense training: instruction and practice aimed at equipping people with physical and mental skills to protect themselves from harm

self-determination: the right and ability of individuals or groups to make their own decisions, pursue their own interests, and govern themselves without external influence or coercion

service gaps: areas or needs within a community where existing services or resources are insufficient or unavailable, leaving individuals or groups underserved

sexism: prejudice, stereotyping, or discrimination based on a person's sex or gender, typically against women and girls, but also affecting people of other genders

skill matching: the process of pairing individuals' skills, expertise, or interests with specific tasks, roles, or projects that require those particular abilities within a group or organization

skill-sharing: the process of people exchanging knowledge, expertise, or abilities with others, typically in an informal or collaborative setting, to promote mutual learning and development

solicitation laws: regulations that govern the process of seeking donations or funds from individuals or entities, ensuring transparency and compliance with legal standards

solidarity: the unity and mutual support among individuals or groups, often based on shared interests, objectives, or values

systemic issues: fundamental problems or challenges within a system that affect multiple aspects of society

tabletop exercises: simulated scenarios designed to practice emergency responses and decision-making processes in a controlled environment

transparency: openness and clarity in actions, decisions, and communication, ensuring that information is easily accessible and understandable to all stakeholders involved

tokenism: the practice of making only a symbolic effort to be inclusive to members of minority groups, often to give the appearance of equality

unconscious bias: refers to attitudes or stereotypes that affect our understanding, actions, and decisions in an unconscious manner, often leading to unfair treatment or assumptions about certain groups of people

unincorporated association: a group of individuals who come together for a common purpose without formal registration or legal status as a separate entity

virtual event: an organized gathering that takes place online rather than in a physical location, allowing participants to interact, engage in activities, and attend presentations remotely using digital platforms and tools

vulnerable populations: groups at higher risk of adverse health outcomes or social disadvantages due to factors like socioeconomic status, age, disability, ethnicity, or geographic location, necessitating targeted support and attention

white supremacy: a belief system that asserts the superiority of white people over people of other racial backgrounds and often seeks to maintain or establish white dominance through social, political, and economic means

zero-sum mindset: the belief that any gain for one party must result in an equivalent loss for another, based on a fixed amount of resources or opportunities

501(c)(3) organization: a nonprofit organization in the United States that is exempt from federal income tax under Section 501(c)(3) of the Internal Revenue Code because it is organized and operated exclusively for charitable, educational, religious, scientific, or literary purposes

501(c)(4) organization: a nonprofit in the U.S. exempt from federal income tax under IRS Section 501(c)(4), primarily dedicated to promoting social welfare and advocacy, with more flexibility in lobbying and political activities compared to 501(c)(3) organizations

Sources

Chapter 1: What is Mutual Aid?

Aberg-Riger, Ariel. "'Solidarity, Not Charity': A Visual History of Mutual Aid." Bloomberg, Dec. 22, 2020, https://www.bloomberg.com/news/features/2020-12-22/a-visual-history-of-mutual-aid.

Belblidia, Miriam and Chenier Kliebert. "Mutual Aid: A grassroots model for justice and equity in emergency management." Imaginewaterworks.org, Jan. 27, 2022, https://www.imagine-waterworks.org/mutual-aid-a-grassroots-model-for-justice-and-equity-in-emergency-management/.

Blakemore, Erin. "How the HIV/AIDS Crisis Redefined the Concept of Family." *The Washington Post*, Jul. 29, 2017, https://www.washingtonpost.com/national/health-science/how-the-hivaids-crisis-redefined-the-concept-of-family/2017/07/28/faaf574c-7099-11e7-8839-ec48ec4cae25_story.html.

Cartwright, Mark. "Medieval Guilds." Worldhistory.org, Nov. 14, 2018, https://www.worldhistory.org/Medieval_Guilds/.

Conde, Kantuta. "Reciprocity: An Indigenous Teaching for a Better 2021." Voicesofyouth.org, Dec. 29, 2020, https://www.voicesofyouth.org/blog/reciprocity-indigenous-teaching-better-2021.

CUNY staff. "Mutual Aid 101: History, Politics, and Organizational Structures of Community Care." Cunyurbanfoodpolicy.org, Aug, 23, 2023, https://cunyurbanfoodpolicy.org/news/2023/08/22/mutual-aid-101-history-politics-and-organizational-structures-of-community-care/.

Doerr, Elizabeth. "The Babysitting Co-op that Reshaped My Family Life." Romper.com, Jan. 29, 2024, https://www.romper.com/parenting/babysitting-co-op-swap-childcare-neighbors.

Dubb, Steve. "Edgar Cahn's Second Act: Time Banking and the Return of Mutual Aid." Nonprofitquarterly.org, Feb. 9, 2022, https://nonprofitquarterly.org/edgar-cahns-second-act-time-banking-and-the-return-of-mutual-aid/.

Evelly, Jeanmarie. "Months into Pandemic, City's Mutual Aid Networks Evolve to Meet New Need." Citylimits.org, Nov. 2, 2020, https://citylimits.org/2020/11/02/months-into-pandemic-citys-mutual-aid-networks-evolve-to-meet-new-need/.

Fareground staff. Fareground.org, August 28, 2024, https://www.fareground.org/.

Fassler, Ella. "Free Stores Offer an Alternative to the Exploitative Capitalist Economy." Truthout.org, Oct. 2, 2022, https://truthout.org/articles/free-stores-offer-an-alternative-to-the-exploitative-capitalist-economy/.

Gran, Michele. "Ayni: Honoring the Humanity in All." Globalvolunteers.org, Mar. 20, 2020, https://globalvolunteers.org/ayni-honoring-the-humanity-in-all/.

Jones, Sophie. "Mutual Aid in Queens Amidst COVID-19." Counterpunch.org, May 22, 2020, https://www.counterpunch.org/2020/05/22/mutual-aid-in-queens-amidst-covid-19/.

Kinna, R. "Kropotkin's Theory of Mutual Aid in Historical Context." *International Review of Social History*, 40(2), 259-283.

Kropotkin, Peter. *Mutual Aid: A Factor in Evolution*. New York, NY: McClure Phillips & Co, 1902.

Maldonado, Samantha. "Ten Years Ago, Occupy Sandy Didn't Just Help New Yorkers, It Redefined Disaster Response." Thecity.nyc, Oct. 28, 2022, https://www.thecity.nyc/2022/10/28/ten-years-occupy-sandy-disaster-response/.

Martinez, Marissa. "Texans Used Mutual Aid to Help Their Communities Through a Devastating Winter Storm." *The Texas Tribune*, Feb. 23, 2021, https://www.texastribune.org/2021/02/23/mutual-aid-texas-storm/.

McElroy, Isle. "Where Does Mutual Aid Go From Here?" Bonappetit.com, Dec. 17, 2021, https://www.bonappetit.com/story/nyc-mutual-aid.

Oldridge, Jennifer. "Growing Together: Lawrence Touts Strong Crop of Community Gardens." Ljworld.com, Jun. 1, 2006, https://www2.ljworld.com/news/2006/jun/01/growing_together/.

Rodriguez, Alexandria. "Harvey 2017: Waze Carpool Offers Free Ride-sharing." Caller.com, Sep. 6, 2017, https://www.caller.com/story/weather/hurricanes/2017/09/06/harvey-2017-waze-carpool-offers-free-ride-sharing/639687001/.

Root, Cate. "What is Mutual Aid (and How Can It Build Power)?" Currentaffairs.org, Oct. 7, 2020, https://www.currentaffairs.org/news/2020/10/what-is-mutual-aid-and-how-can-it-build-power.

Sheperds Friendly staff. "The History of Friendly Societies." Sheperdsfriendly.co.uk, Oct. 24, 2017, https://www.shepherdsfriendly.co.uk/resources/the-history-of-friendly-societies/

Spade, Dean. "Mutual Aid: Building Solidarity During this Crisis (and the Next)." London: Verso, 2020.

Takahama, Elise."AIDS Crisis from 1980s to Today: How Seattle Responded with Hope, Healing." *The Seattle Times*, Jun 27, 2024. https://www.seattletimes.com/seattle-news/health/aids-crisis-from-1980s-to-today-how-seattle-responded-with-hope-healing/.

Waxman, Olivia. "With Free Medical Clinics and Patient Advocacy, the Black Panthers Created a Legacy in Community Health That Still Exists Amid Covid-19." Time, Feb. 25, 2021, https://time.com/5937647/black-panther-medical-clinics-history-school-covid-19/.

Chapter 2: The Principles of Mutual Aid

Byanyima, Winnie, et al. "Community Pandemic Response: The Importance of Action Led by Communities and the Public Sector." The Lancet, vol. 401, Is. 10373, Jan. 28, 2023, https://www.thelancet.com/journals/lancet/article/PIIS0140-6736(22)02575-2/fulltext.

Garrova, Robert. "SAG-AFTRA Reaches Tentative Agreement with Studios to End Strike." LAist.com, No. 9, 2023, https://laist.com/news/arts-and-entertainment/sag-aftra-reaches-tentative-agreement-with-studios-to-end-strike.

Levine, Martin. "Community-based Mutual Aid: Reciprocity Rather than Charity in Chicago." Nonporfitquarterly.org, Oct. 9, 2020, https://nonprofitquarterly.org/community-based-mutual-al-aid-reciprocity-rather-than-charity-in-chicago/.

Mendez, Victoria. "What is Mutual Aid and How Can it Transform our World?" Globalgiving.org, Feb. 3, 2022, https://www.globalgiving.org/learn/what-is-mutual-aid.

Pearlman, Savannah L. "Mutual Aid and a Pluralistic Account of Solidarity." *The Philosopher*, vol. 110, no. 4, (Autumn 2022), https://www.thephilosopher1923.org/post/mutual-aid-and-a-pluralistic-account-of-solidarity.

Schneirov, Richard. "To the Ragged Edge of Anarchy: The 1894 Pullman Boycott." *OAH Magazine of History*, Vol. 13, No. 3, The Progressive Era (Spring 1999), pp. 26-30, https://www.jstor.org/stable/25163289.

Sharples, Carinya. "Think Global, Act Local: How Ebola Taught the World that Change Begins in the Community." Whatsonafrica.org, Mar. 18, 2016, https://whatsonafrica.org/think-global-act-local-how-ebola-taught-the-world-that-change-begins-in-the-community/.

Taylor, Derrick Bryson. "Who Were the Freedom Riders?" New York Times, Jul. 18, 2020, https://www.nytimes.com/2020/07/18/us/politics/freedom-riders-john-lewis-work.html.

Chapter 3: Understanding Community Needs

Community Tool Box staff. "Developing a Plan for Assessing Local Needs and Resources." Community Tool Box, The University of Kansas. ctb.ku.edu, https://ctb.ku.edu/en/table-of-contents/assessment/assessing-community-needs-and-resources/develop-a-plan/.

Global Citizen staff. "Why It's Important to Think About Privilege and Why It's Hard." Globalcitizen.org, Feb. 27, 2015, https://www.globalcitizen.org/en/content/why-its-important-to-think-about-privilege-and-why/.

Oregon Heritage staff. "Researching Historically Marginalized Communities." Oregon Heritage Bulletin, Is. 34, Apr. 2018, https://www.oregon.gov/oprd/OH/Documents/HB34_Researching_Historically_Marganized_Communities.pdf.

Spacey, John. "44 Examples of Power Structures." Simplicable.com, Sept. 9, 2023, https://simplicable.com/new/power-structures.

Taylor, Bridie. "Intersectionality 101: What it is and why is it important?" Womankind.org.uk, Nov. 24, 2019, https://www.womankind.org.uk/intersectionality-101-what-is-it-and-why-is-it-important/.

Waisel, DB. "Vulnerable Populations in Healthcare." Curr Opin Anaesthesiol: 26(2):186-92, Apr. 2013, https://pubmed.ncbi.nlm.nih.gov/23385323/.

Chapter 4: Building Trust & Relationships

Gallo, Amy. "What Is Active Listening?" *Harvard Business Review*, Jan. 2, 2024, https://hbr.org/2024/01/what-is-active-listening.

Kitch, Brian, "10 Ways to Build Trust in a Team." Mural.co, Dec. 13, 2022, https://www.mural.co/blog/build-team-trust.

Krockett, Emily. "Safe Spaces, Explained." Vox.com, Aug. 25, 2016, https://www.vox.com/2016/7/5/11949258/safe-spaces-explained.

McKinsey and Company staff. "What Is Diversity, Equity, and Inclusion?" McKinsey.com, Apr. 17, 2022, https://www.mckinsey.com/featured-insights/mckinsey-explainers/what-is-diversity-equity-and-inclusion.

Scaglione, Jenna. "What Is Horizontal Leadership?" Superhuman.com, July 19, 2022, https://blog.superhuman.com/horizontal-leadership/.

Team Asana. "19 Unconscious Biases to Overcome and Help Promote Inclusivity." Asana.com, Jan. 4, 2024, https://asana.com/resources/unconscious-bias-examples.

Chapter 5: Organizing a Mutual Aid Group

Eduardo, Angel. "What is a Mutual Aid Network?" Idealist.com, Apr. 22, 2020, https://www.idealist.org/en/days/what-is-a-mutual-aid-network.

MRSC staff. "Parliamentary Procedure: A Brief Guide to Roberts' Rules of Order." Municipal Research and Services Center, https://mrsc.org/explore-topics/public-meetings/procedures/parliamentary-procedure.

Peek, Sean. "The Art of Words: How to Write the Perfect Mission Statement." Business.com, Mar. 22, 2023, https://www.business.com/articles/the-art-of-words-how-to-write-the-perfect-mission-statement/.

SELC staff. "Mutual Aid Legal Toolkit." Sustainable Economies Law Center, https://www.the-selc.org/mutual_aid_toolkit.

Zerkel, Mary. "How to Create a Mutual Aid Network." American Friends Service Committee, Jan. 7, 2022, https://afsc.org/news/how-create-mutual-aid-network.

Chapter 6: Legal & Ethical Considerations

CharityFirst staff. "What Your Nonprofit Clients Need to Know about the Volunteer Protection Act." Charityfirst.com, Oct. 14, 2022, https://www.charityfirst.com/blog/what-your-nonprofit-clients-need-to-know-about-the-volunteer-protection-act/.

Community Tool Box staff. "Writing Bylaws." Community Tool Box, The University of Kansas. ctb.ku.edu

Fermin, Jeffrey. "What to Include in Your Company's Code of Ethics." Allvoices.co, Feb. 23, 2023, https://www.allvoices.co/blog/what-is-code-of-ethics.

Fishman, Stephan. "What is an Unincorporated Nonprofit Association?" Nolo.com. https://www.nolo.com/legal-encyclopedia/what-an-unincorporated-nonprofit-association.

Freedman, Max. "Articles of Association: What new business owners should know." Business News Daily, February 2, 2024, https://www.businessnewsdaily.com/4038-articles-of-incorpo-ration.

Rudder, Alana and Kelly Maine. "501(c)(3) Vs. 501(c)(4): Differences, Pros & Cons." Forbes Advisor, June 8, 2024, https://www.forbes.com/advisor/business/501c3-vs-501c4/.

NCBA staff. "What is a Cooperative?" National Cooperative Business Association, https://ncbaclusa.coop/resources/what-is-a-co-op/.

Leonard, Kimberlee, Jane Haskins, and Cassie Bottorff. "501(c)(3) Application: How to Obtain Nonprofit Status." Forbes Advisor, Feb. 11,2024, https://www.forbes.com/advisor/busi-ness/501c3-application-online/.

Chapter 7: Fundamentals of Resource Mobilization

Community Tool Box staff. "Developing Volunteer Orientation Programs." Community Tool Box, The University of Kansas, https://ctb.ku.edu/en/table-of-contents/structure/volunteers/orientation-programs.

Instrumentl staff. "Grant Application Guidelines: A comprehensive guide for 2024." Instrumentl, Sept. 2023, https://www.instrumentl.com/blog/grant-application-guidelines.

Smith, Tim. "Crowdfunding: What it is, how it works, and popular websites." Investopedia, May 2024, https://www.investopedia.com/terms/c/crowdfunding.asp.

Winerman, Lea. "Helping Others, Helping Ourselves: Psychologists are studying why people volunteer, and how organizations can hold onto volunteers in the long term." *Monitor*, vol. 37, no. 11, 2006, pp. 37, https://www.apa.org/monitor/dec06/helping.

Chapter 8: Communicating with the Public

Carson, Nick and David Airey. "How to Design a Logo: 15 Pro Tips." Creativebloq.com, Apr. 11, 2024, https://www.creativebloq.com/graphic-design/pro-guide-logo-design-21221.

Dragilev, Dmitry. "How to Write a Press Release in 2023 that Gets Results (Expert Tips)." Justreachout.io, July 5, 2023, https://blog.justreachout.io/how-to-write-press-release/.

Forbes Agency Council. "13 Golden Rules of PR Crisis Management." Forbes.com, Apr. 14, 2022, https://www.forbes.com/sites/forbesagencycouncil/2017/06/20/13-golden-rules-of-pr-crisis-management/.

Morand, Tatiana. "The Ultimate Guide to Nonprofit Branding." Wildapricot.com, Jan. 28, 2020. https://www.harpersbazaar.com/culture/features/a35232889/mutual-aid-groups-covid-19-pandemic/.

Zhang, Jenny. "Mutual Aid Groups Supported Communities When the Government Wouldn't." Harpersbazaar.com, Mar. 9, 2021, https://www.harpersbazaar.com/culture/features/a35232889/mutual-aid-groups-covid-19-pandemic/.

Chapter 9: Education & Skill-Sharing Programs

Donahue, Jack. "How to Plan a Workshop: A Quick and Easy Guide." Makeiterate.com, Dec. 21, 2022, https://makeiterate.com/how-to-plan-a-workshop-a-quick-and-easy-guide/.

Evans, Katie Wills. "When Teachers Practice Mutual Aid, the Whole School Thrives." The Progressive, June, 24, 2021, https://progressive.org/public-schools-advocate/teachers-mutual-aid-willsevans-210624/.

Kim, Nicole. "How to Start a Scholarship Fund in 5 Steps." Bold.org, July 18, 2024, https://bold.org/blog/irs-guidelines-for-starting-a-scholarship-fund/.

Learning Space Solutions staff. "7 Steps to Creating a Successful Modern Learning Space." Learningspacesolutions.com, 2022, https://www.learningspacesolutions.com/modern-learning-spaces/.

Chapter 10: Emergency Preparedness & Response

Homer-Dixon, Thomas. "Why So Much Is Going Wrong at the Same Time: Lots of things are going wrong. Does that make it a polycrisis?" Vox, Oct. 18, 2023, https://www.vox.com/future-perfect/23920997/polycrisis-climate-pandemic-population-connectivity.

Fernando, Christine. "Mutual Aid Networks Find Roots in Communities of Color." Associated Press, Jan. 21, 2021, https://apnews.com/article/immigration-coronavirus-pandemic-7b1d-14f25ab717c2a29ceafd40364b6e.

Greenfield, Nicole. "Mutual Aid and Disaster Justice: 'We Keep Us Safe.'" NRDC.org, Oct. 6, 2022, https://www.nrdc.org/stories/mutual-aid-and-disaster-justice-we-keep-us-safe.

GAO staff. "The Rising Threat of Domestic Terrorism in the U.S. and Federal Efforts to Combat It." U.S. Government Accountability Office, Mar. 2, 2023, https://www.gao.gov/blog/rising-threat-domestic-terrorism-u.s.-and-federal-efforts-combat-it.

Cal OES News Staff. "Mutual Aid Resources Are Pivotal to Disaster Response." California Governor's Office of Emergency Services, May 30, 2023, https://news.caloes.ca.gov/mutual-aid-resources-are-pivotal-to-disaster-response/.

Chapter 11: Advocating for Systemic Change

Belblidia, M. and Kliebert, C. (2022), "Mutual Aid: A Grassroots Model for Justice and Equity in Emergency Management", Jerolleman, A. and Waugh, W.L. (Ed.) Justice, Equity, and Emergency Management (Community, Environment and Disaster Risk Management, Vol. 25), Emerald Publishing Limited, Bingley, pp. 11-30, https://www.imaginewaterworks.org/mutual-aid-a-grassroots-model-for-justice-and-equity-in-emergency-management/.

Braveman, Paula et al."Systemic and Structural Racism: Definitions, Examples, Health Damages, and Approaches to Dismantling." Health Affairs, Vol. 41, No. 2, Feb. 2022, https://www.healthaffairs.org/doi/10.1377/hlthaff.2021.01394.

Eisenmenger, Ashley. "Ableism: What Is It, What It Looks Like, and How to Become a Better Ally." Accessliving.org, Dec. 12, 2019, https://www.accessliving.org/newsroom/blog/ableism-101/.

Hayes, Kelly and Mariame Kaba. "Let This Radicalize You: Organizing and the Revolution of Reciprocal Care." Chicago, IL: Haymarket Books, 2023.

Menand, Louis. "The Rise and Fall of Neoliberalism." The New Yorker, Jul. 17, 2023, https://www.newyorker.com/magazine/2023/07/24/the-rise-and-fall-of-neoliberalism.

Ochoa, Melissa Kumari. "Systemic Sexism in Our Everyday Lives." Doctoral dissertation, Texas A&M University, 2019, https://oaktrust.library.tamu.edu/handle/1969.1/187932.

Osman, Jamila. "What is Colonialism? A History of Violence, Control and Exploitation." Teen Vogue, Oct. 11, 2020, https://www.teenvogue.com/story/colonialism-explained.

Peluso, Cody. "The Origins of Patriarchy." Populationmedia.org, Nov. 8, 2023, https://www.populationmedia.org/the-latest/unmasking-the-patriarchy-its-origins-impact-and-the-path-to-equality.

Pepperdine University staff. "Driving Change: The Dynamics of Public Policy." Publicpolicy.pepperdine.edu, Oct. 25, 2023, https://publicpolicy.pepperdine.edu/blog/posts/driving-change-tthe-dynamics-of-public-policy.htm.

Chapter 12: Interactions with Law Enforcement

Adachi, Jeff. "Police Militarization and the War on Citizens." Americanbar.org, July 20, 2024, https://www.americanbar.org/groups/crsj/publications/human_rights_magazine_home/2016-17-vol-42/vol-42-no-1/police-militarization-and-the-war-on-citizens/.

Davis, James. "Your Rights to Refuse a Search at a Traffic Stop." HG.org, July 20, 2024, https://www.hg.org/legal-articles/your-rights-to-refuse-a-search-at-a-traffic-stop-26261.

Lindwall, Courtney. "How to Protest Safely." Nrdc.org, Oct. 26, 2022, https://www.nrdc.org/stories/how-protest-safely.

Okuda, Soraya et al. "Keeping Each Other Safe When Virtually Organizing Mutual Aid." Eff.org, Mar. 30, 2020, https://www.eff.org/deeplinks/2020/03/keeping-each-other-safe-when-virtually-organizing-mutual-aid.

Rojas, Nikki. "Why Police Resist Reforms to Militarization." The Harvard Gazette, Mar. 3, 2023. https://news.harvard.edu/gazette/story/2023/03/expert-looks-at-how-and-why-police-resist-reforms-to-militarization/.

Smithsonian Institute staff. "The Black Panther Party: Challenging Police and Promoting Social Change." Nmaahc.si.edu, July 19, 2024, https://nmaahc.si.edu/explore/stories/black-panther-party-challenging-police-and-promoting-social-change.

Chapter 13: Mental Health & Well-Being

Barber, Nigel. "Generosity and Guilt Are Connected." Psychologytoday.com, Dec. 14, 2022, https://www.psychologytoday.com/us/blog/the-human-beast/202212/generosity-and-guilt-are-connected.

Cleveland Clinic Staff. "What is Burnout?: Here's how to deal with feeling physically and emotionally tired." Clevelandclinic.org, Feb. 1, 2022, https://health.clevelandclinic.org/signs-of-burnout.

Gertz, Nolen. "What Nihilism Is Not." MIT Press Reader, Jan. 16, 2020, https://thereader.mitpress.mit.edu/what-nihilism-is-not/.

Mayo Clinic Staff. "Drug Addiction (Substance Use Disorder)." Mayoclinic.org, Oct. 4, 2022, https://www.mayoclinic.org/diseases-conditions/drug-addiction/symptoms-causes/syc-20365112.

Mayo Clinic Staff. "What Is Depression? A Mayo Clinic Doctor Explains." Mayoclinic.org, Dec. 14, 2022, https://www.mayoclinic.org/diseases-conditions/depression/symptoms-causes/syc-20356007.

McClean Hospital Staff. "The Social Dilemma: Social Media and Your Mental Health." Mcleanhospital.org, Mar. 29, 2024, https://www.mcleanhospital.org/essential/it-or-not-social-medias-affecting-your-mental-health.

Morris et al. "Fuck Capitalism: Mutual Aid Participants' Experience of Burnout During the Early Months of the Covid-19 Pandemic." Abolitionist Perspectives in Social Work: Vol. 1, No. 1, 2023, https://apsw-ojs-uh.tdl.org/apsw/article/view/13.

Chapter 14: Future Trends in Mutual Aid

Gutierrez et al. "Mutual Aid Sustains Human Rights Movements Around the World." Openglobalrights.org, Jun. 19, 2023, https://www.openglobalrights.org/mutual-aid-sustains-human-rights-movements-around-world/.

Thomas, Mike. "The Future of AI: How Artificial Intelligence Will Change the World." Builtin.com, Mar. 13, 2024, https://builtin.com/artificial-intelligence/artificial-intelligence-future.

Solidarity Economy Principles Project staff. "What Do We Mean by Solidarity Economy?" Solidarityeconomyprinciples.org, 2023, https://solidarityeconomyprinciples.org/what-do-we-mean-by-solidarity-economy/.

Recommended Reading

Spade, Dean. "Mutual Aid: Building Solidarity During this Crisis (and the Next)." London: Verso, 2020.

Hayes, Kelly and Mariame Kaba. "Let This Radicalize You: Organizing and the Revolution of Reciprocal Care." Chicago, IL: Haymarket Books, 2023.

Appendix: How to Start a Union

Organizing a **union** in a workplace is a powerful form of mutual aid, as it brings employees together to collectively support and advocate for one another's rights and well-being. By forming a union, workers pool their resources, knowledge, and efforts to negotiate better wages, benefits, and working conditions, which ultimately benefit the entire workforce. This collaborative effort not only addresses individual grievances, but it also creates a sense of solidarity and community among employees. Through mutual aid, workers can create a more equitable and just workplace where their voices are heard and their needs are met.

Here are the general steps you would take to form a union at your workplace:

1. Assess Interest & Gather Information
Start by informally discussing the idea of forming a union with your colleagues to gauge their interest and support. Research the benefits of unionizing and understand the legal framework in your country or region. Look into the specific labor laws and workers' rights that apply.

2. Form an Organizing Committee
Identify a diverse group of employees who are committed to the idea of unionizing. This organizing committee should represent different departments, job roles, and shifts. Provide the members with information about union benefits, the unionization process, and potential challenges.

3. Conduct Research & Develop a Strategy
Conduct surveys, hold informal meetings, and have one-on-one discussions to identify the key issues and concerns of the workforce. Develop a clear plan for how you will communicate with employees, gather support, and address potential objections from management.

4. Build Support
Hold meetings, distribute literature, and use social media to inform employees about the benefits of unionizing and the unionization process. Collect signatures on authorization cards or petitions to demonstrate that a majority of employees support the union. Most regions require at least 30% of employees to sign cards to trigger a union election, but aiming for a higher percentage can strengthen your position.

5. File for a Union Election
Once you have a significant number of signed authorization cards, submit them to the relevant labor relations board or agency. Request that the board hold an election to determine whether employees wish to be represented by the union.

6. Campaign for the Election
Continue to communicate with employees, addressing any concerns or misinformation that may arise. Use meetings, flyers, and one-on-one conversations to maintain support. Be prepared for potential anti-union tactics from management, such as mandatory meetings or the distribution of anti-union literature.

7. Vote in the Election
Ensure that all employees understand the importance of voting and know the details of when and where the election will take place. If possible, have observers present to ensure the election is conducted fairly and legally.

8. Establish Union Leadership
Hold elections for union officers and establish a leadership structure that will represent employees and manage union activities. Start programs for grievance handling, member education, and ongoing communication to keep the union strong and effective.

9. Negotiate a Contract
The next step is to negotiate a contract with the employer. This contract should address the key issues and concerns identified during the organizing process. Continue to keep employees informed and involved in the negotiation process to ensure that the final contract reflects their needs and priorities.

10. Ongoing Engagement & Advocacy
Continue to engage with union members, address their concerns, and advocate for their rights and interests. Foster a strong sense of community and solidarity among members to ensure long-term success and resilience.

About the Author

J.R. Mortimer is a writer, editor, and social media content creator who has worked with National Geographic, Scholastic, and other educational publishers. Originally from rural Kentucky, he attended Boston University and then moved to New York City to work in book publishing. His passion for mutual aid began when he started volunteering weekly with the Rutgers Thursday Meal program, which has been serving food-insecure residents on the Upper West Side for over 35 years. In 2023, J.R. cofounded RevolutionTV, a mutual aid group of content creators who make videos about community organizing and other revolutionary subjects. Follow J.R. on TikTok @jrmortimer.

Acknowledgements

Thank you to the team at RevolutionTV for all of your support through the writing and editing process. David, Reo, Heather, Nik, Natalie, James, Tricia, and Mika – your feedback was invaluable. Thank you also to my friends Dan and Adam for feedback on Chapter 11, and to Stephanie for providing direction on the design. And lastly, thank you to my husband Michael for supporting me in my creative pursuits for all of these years.

Notes

Notes

www.ingramcontent.com/pod-product-compliance
Lightning Source LLC
Chambersburg PA
CBHW081527120626
46550CB00009B/2639